ALL TOO FAMILIAR

Sexual Abuse of Women in U.S. State Prisons

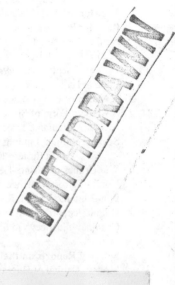

PREVIOUSLY PUBLISHED HUMAN RIGHTS WATCH REPORTS ON WOMEN'S HUMAN RIGHTS, THE U.S., AND PRISONS

Selected Reports on Women's Human Rights

Shattered Lives: Sexual Violence during the Rwandan Genocide and its Aftermath, September 1996

No Guarantees: Sex Discrimination in Mexico's Maquiladora Sector, August 1996

Violence Against Women in South Africa: State Response to Domestic Violence and Rape, November 1995

The Human Rights Watch Global Report on Women's Human Rights, August 1995

Rape for Profit: Trafficking of Nepali Girls and Women to India's Brothels, June 1995

Neither Jobs Nor Justice: Discrimination Against Women, March 1995

Second Class Citizens: Discrimination Against Women Under Botswana's Citizenship Act, September 1994

Rape in Haiti: A Weapon of Terror, July 1994

A Matter of Power: State Control of Women's Virginity in Turkey, June 1994

A Modern Form of Slavery: Trafficking of Burmese Women and Girls into Brothels in Thailand, December 1993

Seeking Refuge, Finding Terror: The Widespread Rape of Somali Women Refugees in North Eastern Kenya, October 1993

War Crimes in Bosnia-Hercegovina: Volume II, April 1993

Untold Terror: Violence Against Women in Peru's Armed Conflict, December 1992

Punishing the Victim: Rape and Mistreatment of Asian Maids in Kuwait, July 1992

Double Jeopardy: Police Abuse of Women in Pakistan, May 1992

Criminal Injustice: Violence Against Women in Brazil, October 1991

Selected Reports on the United States

Modern Capital of Human Rights?: Abuses in the State of Georgia, June 1996

Children in Confinement in Louisiana, October 1995

Crossing the Line: Human Rights Abuses Along the U.S. Border with Mexico Persist Amid Climate of Impunity, April 1995

United States: A World Leader in Executing Juveniles, March 1995

Breach of Trust: Physician Participation in Executions in the U.S., February 1994

Human Rights Violations in the United States, January 1994

Frontier Injustice: Human Rights Abuses Along the U.S. Border with Mexico Persist Amid Climate of Impunity, May 1993

Brutality Unchecked: Human Rights Abuses Along the U.S. Border with Mexico, June 1992

Police Brutality in the United States, July 1991

Detained, Denied, Deported: Asylum Seekers in the U.S., June 1986

Mother of Exiles: Refugees Imprisoned in America, June 1986

Selected Reports on Prison Conditions

Our findings on many of the countries listed below can be found in *The Human Rights Watch Global Report on Prisons*, June 1993. We have reported on conditions in Algeria, Brazil, China, Cuba, Former Czechoslovakia, Egypt, India, Indonesia, Israel and Israeli-Occupied West Bank and Gaza Strip, Jamaica, Japan, Mexico, Poland, Puerto Rico, Romania, South Africa, Former Soviet Union, Somalia, Spain, Sudan, Syria, Tibet, Turkey, United Kingdom, United States, Venezuela, Vietnam, and Zaire.

ALL TOO FAMILIAR

Sexual Abuse of Women in U.S. State Prisons

Human Rights Watch Women's Rights Project

Human Rights Watch
New York · Washington · London · Brussels

ISBN 1-56432-153-3
Library of Congress Catalogue Card Number: 96-79706

Human Rights Watch Women's Rights Project
The Human Rights Watch Women's Rights Project was established in 1990 to monitor violence against women and gender discrimination throughout the world. Dorothy Q. Thomas is the director; Regan E. Ralph is the Washington director; Samya Burney and LaShawn R. Jefferson are research associates; Robin Levi is the staff attorney; Sinsi Hernandez-Cancio is the Sophie Silberberg Fellow; Jane Kim is the Women's Law and Public Policy Fellow; and Evelyn Miah and Kerry McArthur are the associates. Kathleen Peratis is chair of the advisory committee and Nahid Toubia is the vice chair.

Addresses for Human Rights Watch
485 Fifth Avenue, New York, NY 10017-6104
Tel: (212) 972-8400, Fax: (212) 972-0905, E-mail: hrwnyc@hrw.org

1522 K Street, N.W., #910, Washington, DC 20005-1202
Tel: (202) 371-6592, Fax: (202) 371-0124, E-mail: hrwdc@hrw.org

33 Islington High Street, N1 9LH London, UK
Tel: (171) 713-1995, Fax: (171) 713-1800, E-mail: hrwatchuk@gn.apc.org

15 Rue Van Campenhout, 1000 Brussels, Belgium
Tel: (2) 732-2009, Fax: (2) 732-0471, E-mail: hrwatcheu@gn.apc.org

Website Address: http://www.hrw.org
Gopher Address://gopher.humanrights.org:5000
Listserv address: To subscribe to the list, send an e-mail message to majordomo@igc.apc.org with "subscribe hrw-news" in the body of the message (leave the subject line blank).

HUMAN RIGHTS WATCH

Human Rights Watch conducts regular, systematic investigations of human rights abuses in some seventy countries around the world. Our reputation for timely, reliable disclosures has made us an essential source of information for those concerned with human rights. We address the human rights practices of governments of all political stripes, of all geopolitical alignments, and of all ethnic and religious persuasions. Human Rights Watch defends freedom of thought and expression, due process and equal protection of the law, and a vigorous civil society; we document and denounce murders, disappearances, torture, arbitrary imprisonment, discrimination, and other abuses of internationally recognized human rights. Our goal is to hold governments accountable if they transgress the rights of their people.

Human Rights Watch began in 1978 with the founding of its Helsinki division. Today, it includes five divisions covering Africa, the Americas, Asia, the Middle East, as well as the signatories of the Helsinki accords. It also includes three collaborative projects on arms transfers, children's rights, and women's rights. It maintains offices in New York, Washington, Los Angeles, London, Brussels, Moscow, Dushanbe, Rio de Janeiro, and Hong Kong. Human Rights Watch is an independent, nongovernmental organization, supported by contributions from private individuals and foundations worldwide. It accepts no government funds, directly or indirectly.

The staff includes Kenneth Roth, executive director; Michele Alexander, development director; Cynthia Brown, program director; Holly J. Burkhalter, advocacy director; Barbara Guglielmo, finance and administration director; Robert Kimzey, publications director; Jeri Laber, special advisor; Lotte Leicht, Brussels office director; Susan Osnos, communications director; Dinah PoKempner, acting general counsel; Jemera Rone, counsel; and Joanna Weschler, United Nations representative.

The regional directors of Human Rights Watch are Peter Takirambudde, Africa; José Miguel Vivanco, Americas; Sidney Jones, Asia; Holly Cartner, Helsinki; and Eric Goldstein, Middle East (acting). The project directors are Joost R. Hiltermann, Arms Project; Lois Whitman, Children's Rights Project; and Dorothy Q. Thomas, Women's Rights Project.

The members of the board of directors are Robert L. Bernstein, chair; Adrian W. DeWind, vice chair; Roland Algrant, Lisa Anderson, William Carmichael, Dorothy Cullman, Gina Despres, Irene Diamond, Edith Everett, Jonathan Fanton, James C. Goodale, Jack Greenberg, Vartan Gregorian, Alice H. Henkin, Stephen L. Kass, Marina Pinto Kaufman, Bruce Klatsky, Harold Hongju Koh, Alexander MacGregor, Josh Mailman, Samuel K. Murumba, Andrew Nathan, Jane Olson, Peter Osnos, Kathleen Peratis, Bruce Rabb, Sigrid Rausing, Anita Roddick, Orville Schell, Sid Sheinberg, Gary G. Sick, Malcolm Smith, Domna Stanton, Nahid Toubia, Maureen White, Rosalind C. Whitehead, and Maya Wiley.

CONTENTS

ABBREVIATIONS

ACLU	American Civil Liberties Union
BOFQ	Bona Fide Occupational Qualification
BOJS	Bureau of Justice Statistics
CCWF	Central California Women's Facility
CDC	California Department of Corrections
CIW	California Institution for Women
CLAIM	Chicago Legal Aid to Incarcerated Mothers
CRC	California Rehabilitation Center
CORC	Central Office Review Committee (New York)
CRIPA	Civil Rights of Institutionalized Persons Act
CEDAW	Convention on the Elimination of All Forms of Discrimination Against Women
CTF	Correctional Treatment Facility (District of Columbia)
DCDC	District of Columbia Department of Corrections
DOCS	Department of Correctional Services (New York)
DOJ	Department of Justice
DR	Disciplinary Report
GBI	Georgia Bureau of Investigations
GDC	Georgia Department of Corrections
GWCI	Georgia Women's Correctional Institution
HVM	Huron Valley Men's Prison (Michigan)
IAD	Internal Affairs Division
ICCPR	International Covenant on Civil and Political Rights
IDOC	Illinois Department of Corrections
IG	Inspector General
LSPC	Legal Services for Prisoners with Children
MHU	Mental Health Unit
MDOC	Michigan Department of Corrections
MPC	Model Penal Code
NCCD	National Council on Crime and Delinquency
NIC	National Institute of Corrections
NWLC	National Women's Law Center
NCWF	Northern California Women's Facility
PAC	Prison Action Committee (Illinois)
PLRA	Prison Litigation Reform Act
PLS	Prisoners Legal Services (New York)
RUO	Resident Unit Officer
SHU	Segregated Housing Unit
VSPW	Valley State Prison for Women (California)
YACA	Youth and Adult Correctional Agency (California)

ACKNOWLEDGMENTS

This report was researched and written by Dorothy Q. Thomas, director of the Women's Rights Project; Deborah Blatt, former fellow of the Women's Rights Project; Robin S. Levi, staff attorney of the Women's Rights Project; Sarah Lai, former research associate of the Women's Rights Project; Joanne Mariner, associate counsel of Human Rights Watch; and Regan E. Ralph, Washington director of the Women's Rights Project. In addition, Joanna Weschler, United Nations representative of Human Rights Watch, conducted interviews for this report, and Allyson Collins, senior researcher with Human Rights Watch, helped to frame all its recommendations. Research assistance was provided by Jane Kim, fellow of the Women's Rights Project, and Mona Papillon, former intern of the Women's Rights Project. The report was edited by Dorothy Q. Thomas, Sarah Lai, Joanna Weschler, Joanne Mariner, and Regan E. Ralph, with invaluable editorial oversight from Cynthia Brown, program director of Human Rights Watch. Juan Méndez, former general counsel of Human Rights Watch, and Kenneth Roth, executive director of Human Rights Watch, provided legal review. The report was formatted and proofread by Robert Kimzey, publications director of Human Rights Watch. Special thanks to Evelyn Miah and Kerry McArthur, associates of the Women's Rights Project, and Sonja Lichtenstein, former intern of the Women's Rights Project, for their assistance in the production of this report.

This report would not have been possible without the leadership, guidance, assistance, and on-going work of the organizations and individuals endeavoring to combat sexual misconduct in U.S. state prisons. In particular, we would like to thank Leslie Acoca, Ellen Barry (Legal Services for Prisoners with Children), Karen Bower (American Civil Liberties Union-National Prison Project), Lisa Boardman Burnette, Margaret Byrne, Robert Cullen, Ruth Cassell (Prisoners Legal Services), Barbara Echols (Prison Action Committee), Betsy Fuller (Prisoners' Legal Services), Gail Grieger, Carrie Hempel (University of Southern California Law Center), Christina Jose-Kampfner, Rebecca Jurado (Western State School of Law), Deborah LaBelle, Rhea Mallett, Millard Murphy (University of California/Davis Law School), Brenda Smith (National Women's Law Center), and Gail Smith (Chicago Legal Aid to Incarcerated Mothers). We also wish to thank the Department of Justice staff and state departments of corrections officials and employees who agreed to speak with us.

Most of all, we would like to acknowledge with gratitude and respect the many women prisoners who agreed to speak with us, despite fear of retaliation, for this report. It would not have been possible without them.

The Human Rights Watch Women's Rights Project would also like to thank Herbert and Marion Sandler, the Ford Foundation, the MacArthur Foundation, the Moriah Fund, the Shaler Adams Foundation, and the Sister Fund for their support of its work. This report also was made possible in part by funds granted to Robin S. Levi and Jane Kim through a fellowship program sponsored by the Charles H. Revson Foundation and funds granted to Deborah Blatt through the New York University Law School Public Service Fellowship Fund. The statements and views expressed in the text of this report are solely the responsibility of Human Rights Watch.

I. SUMMARY AND RECOMMENDATIONS

This report examines the sexual abuse of female prisoners largely at the hands of male correctional employees at eleven state prisons located in the north, south, east, and west of the United States. It reflects research conducted over a two-and-a-half-year period from March 1994 to November 1996 and is based on interviews conducted by the Human Rights Watch Women's Rights Project and other Human Rights Watch staff with the U.S. federal government, state departments of corrections and district attorneys, correctional officers, civil and women's rights lawyers, prisoner aid organizations, and over sixty prisoners formerly or currently incarcerated in women's prisons in California, Georgia, Illinois, Michigan, New York, and the District of Columbia, which is the nation's capital.

Our findings indicate that being a woman prisoner in U.S. state prisons can be a terrifying experience. If you are sexually abused, you cannot escape from your abuser. Grievance or investigatory procedures, where they exist, are often ineffectual, and correctional employees continue to engage in abuse because they believe they will rarely be held accountable, administratively or criminally. Few people outside the prison walls know what is going on or care if they do know. Fewer still do anything to address the problem.

The United States has the dubious distinction of incarcerating the largest known number of prisoners in the world, of which a steadily increasing number are women. Since 1980, the number of women entering U.S. prisons has risen by almost 400 percent, roughly double the incarceration rate increase of males. Fifty-two percent of these prisoners are African-American women, who constitute 14 percent of the total U.S. population. According to current estimates, at least half of all female prisoners have experienced some form of sexual abuse prior to incarceration. Many women are incarcerated in the 170 state prison facilities for women across the United States and, more often than not, they are guarded by men.

The custodial sexual misconduct documented in this report takes many forms. We found that male correctional employees have vaginally, anally, and orally raped female prisoners and sexually assaulted and abused them. We found that in the course of committing such gross misconduct, male officers have not only used actual or threatened physical force, but have also used their near total authority to provide or deny goods and privileges to female prisoners to compel them to have sex or, in other cases, to reward them for having done so. In other cases, male officers have violated their most basic professional duty and engaged in sexual contact with female prisoners absent the use or threat of force or any material exchange. In addition to engaging in sexual relations with prisoners, male

1

officers have used mandatory pat-frisks or room searches to grope women's breasts, buttocks, and vaginal areas and to view them inappropriately while in a state of undress in the housing or bathroom areas. Male correctional officers and staff have also engaged in regular verbal degradation and harassment of female prisoners, thus contributing to a custodial environment in the state prisons for women which is often highly sexualized and excessively hostile.

No one group of prisoners appears to suffer sexual misconduct more than any other, although those in prison for the first time and young or mentally ill prisoners are particularly vulnerable to abuse. Lesbian and transgendered prisoners have also been singled out for sexual misconduct by officers, as have prisoners who have in some way challenged an officer, either by informing on him for inappropriate conduct or for refusing to submit to demands for sexual relations. In some instances, women have been impregnated as a result of sexual misconduct, and some of these prisoners have faced additional abuse in the form of inappropriate segregation, denial of adequate health care, and/or pressure to seek an abortion.

One of the clear contributing factors to sexual misconduct in U.S. prisons for women is that the United States, despite authoritative international rules to the contrary, allows male correctional employees to hold contact positions over prisoners, that is, positions in which they serve in constant physical proximity to the prisoners of the opposite sex. Under the United Nations Standard Minimum Rules for the Treatment of Prisoners (Standard Minimum Rules), which constitute an authoritative guide to international law regarding the treatment of prisoners and are appended to this report, male officers are precluded from holding such contact posts. However, since the passage of the Civil Rights Act of 1964, U.S. employers have been prohibited from denying a person a job solely on the basis of gender unless the person's gender was reasonably necessary to the performance of the specific job. In the absence of unusual circumstances, U.S. federal courts have been unwilling to recognize a person's gender as meeting this standard with respect to correctional employment. As a result, most restrictions on male officers working in women's prisons that predated the Civil Rights Act have been removed and, by some estimates, male officers working in women's prisons now outnumber their female counterparts by two and in some facilities, three to one.

As a matter of policy, Human Rights Watch supports U.S. anti-discrimination laws and has no objection *per se* to male officers guarding female prisoners. Nor do we believe that all male officers abuse female prisoners. However, we are concerned that the states' adherence to U.S. anti-discrimination laws, in the absence of strong safeguards against custodial sexual misconduct, has often come at the expense of the fundamental rights of prisoners. Our investigation revealed that where state departments of correction have employed male staff or officers to guard female prisoners, they have often done so absent clear prohibitions on all forms of custodial sexual misconduct and without either training officers or educating prisoners about such prohibitions. Female officers have also sexually abused female prisoners and should, without exception, receive such training. However, in the state prisons for women that we investigated, instances of same-sex sexual misconduct were relatively rare.

Under both international and national law, states are clearly required to prevent and punish custodial sexual misconduct. The International Covenant on Civil and Political Rights (ICCPR) and the International Convention Against Torture and Other Cruel, Inhuman and Degrading Treatment or Punishment (Torture Convention), both of which the United States has ratified, require state parties to prohibit torture and other cruel, inhuman, or degrading treatment or punishment and to ensure that such abuse is investigated and punished. The ICCPR further guarantees prisoners a basic right to privacy, which has been interpreted to preclude strip searches by officers of the opposite sex. These rights are further enumerated in the Standard Minimum Rules, which call on governments to prohibit custodial sexual abuse, provide prisoners with an effective right to complain of such misconduct, ensure appropriate punishment, and guarantee that these obligations are met in part through the proper training of correctional officers. In addition, the United States Constitution expressly protects prisoners from cruel and inhuman punishments and has been interpreted to accord prisoners limited privacy rights as well as to guarantee them access to the courts.

The United States is thus clearly bound under its own constitution to prevent and punish custodial sexual misconduct. It is equally bound by international human rights law to take these steps, although in ratifying the ICCPR and the Torture Convention, the United States attempted to limit its treaty obligations in ways that were particularly adverse to the elimination of custodial sexual misconduct. In Human Rights Watch's view, these efforts by the United States to shirk its full international human rights obligations are both bad policy and legally indefensible. Accordingly, we hold the United States to the full scope of the relevant obligations in each treaty.

Neither the nation's capital nor any of the five states investigated for this report are adequately upholding these international and national obligations. All five states and the District of Columbia do have prison rules concerning sexual misconduct, but they are often so vague as to be of little effective use. Rape and sexual assault or abuse, which should clearly be covered by these rules, often are not explicitly mentioned and must usually be read into vague prohibitions on "overfamiliarity" or "fraternization." Few prisons have express policies protecting the privacy rights of prisoners, and fewer still deal expressly with the impropriety of verbal harassment and degradation. While state departments of corrections will usually investigate employees suspected of the most egregious violations of prison rules that govern sexual misconduct, the officers frequently are not punished in accordance with the seriousness of these crimes, and lesser offenses may not be investigated or punished at all.

The District of Columbia and all of the states investigated in this report, with the exception of Illinois, do expressly criminalize sexual misconduct that takes the form of actual sexual contact between officers and prisoners. In some states and the District of Columbia, a first offense of this sort is classified as a felony. In others, it is classified merely as a misdemeanor. But no matter how the offense is classified, state laws are rarely enforced, and when they are, they often carry very light penalties. States' failure to uphold their own laws regarding custodial sexual misconduct reflects their reluctance to prosecute such crimes, largely because of an ingrained belief, except in the most egregious cases, that the prisoner was complicit in the sexual abuse committed against her. In this sense, state officials still widely view criminal sexual misconduct as a victimless crime.

In Human Rights Watch's view, any correctional employee who engages in sexual intercourse or sexual touching with a prisoner is guilty of a crime and should be prosecuted to the fullest extent of the law. As discussed in the legal section of this report, the exact nature of the crime depends on the circumstances under which it is committed and, in particular, on the type and level of pressure the correctional employee exerts on the prisoner. Given the inherently unequal nature of the custodial relationship, however, some type of pressure on the prisoner should be presumed.

In many instances, the use of force by correctional employees to secure sexual relations from a prisoner takes the form of an offer of privileges or goods. Because prisoners are completely dependent on officers for the most basic necessities, the offer or, by implication, threat to withhold privileges or goods is a very powerful inducement. Even when the officer promises or supplies goods or benefits to the prisoner without any implied or perceived threat to her, it is still a more serious offense than if he bestows no goods or benefits at all. This stiffer penalty reflects the fact that prisoners, by definition, have limited resources and privileges, and thus the promise of such rewards always carries special weight.

Even in those cases where an officer engages in sexual relations with a prisoner absent any form of pressure or exchange, he should still be liable for a serious criminal offense. In prison, correctional employees have nearly absolute power over the well-being of prisoners and a corresponding obligation to ensure that this power is never abused. When an officer has sexual contact with a person in his custody, even without any overt pressure or exchange, he commits a gross violation of his professional duty. An inquiry into the victim's alleged consent to such conduct should be unnecessary to establish this professional breach or any other crime of custodial sexual abuse. Rather, the focus should be on the degree of pressure exerted by the guard or employee.

One of the biggest obstacles to the eradication of custodial sexual misconduct is its invisibility at the state and national level. In the Georgia and District of Columbia correctional systems, for example, it took class actions suits in 1992 and 1994, respectively, to make the problem of sexual misconduct visible outside the confines of the correctional system itself. Only after being sued did the departments of corrections admit that the problem of custodial sexual misconduct existed in their facilities for women and that reforms were needed. Sexual misconduct is often so entrenched that, in those correctional systems where class action suits have not yet occurred or have only recently been initiated, such abuse is still largely an invisible problem or one that the respective correctional systems flatly deny.

The invisibility of custodial sexual misconduct, and hence its deniability, are further fueled by the failure of the states we investigated and the District of Columbia to establish credible internal grievance and investigatory procedures that do not expose complainants to retaliation or punishment. In virtually every prison that we investigated, we found grievance procedures that required the prisoner to confront informally the implicated officer before filing a formal grievance or that informed the officer of a complaint lodged against him while he was still in a contact position with the complainant. Both of these procedures exposed prisoners to retaliation by officers and routinely deterred them from filing sexual misconduct complaints.

Even if a prisoner succeeded in pursuing a complaint of sexual misconduct, we found that internal investigatory procedures, while they exist in all five states and the District of Columbia, were often fraught with conflicts of interest and a bias against prisoner testimony. At times, officers accused of sexual misconduct were assigned to investigate themselves. We also found that in almost every case of custodial sexual misconduct, correctional officials assumed that the prisoner lied and thus refused, absent medical reports or witnesses who were not prisoners, to credit prisoner testimony. Given the closed nature of the prison environment, and the reluctance of officers to testify against their peers, such evidence is often very hard to obtain. Thus, complaints of sexual misconduct can be extremely difficult to substantiate. In Georgia, which took steps to credit prisoner testimony more fairly, the investigation and punishment of sexual misconduct markedly improved.

Virtually every prisoner we interviewed who had lodged a complaint of sexual misconduct faced retaliation by the accused officer, his colleagues, or even other prisoners. In some cases, they also faced punishment by correctional officials. These punishments took the form of write-ups for sexual misconduct, the loss of "good time" accrued toward an early parole, or prolonged periods of disciplinary segregation. In other cases, officials did not overtly discipline prisoners but made use of administrative segregation, ostensibly a protective mechanism, effectively to punish them. Thus, prisoners who had committed no disciplinary infraction whatsoever were subjected to the same treatment as prisoners serving disciplinary sentences. In our view, no justification exists for punishing prisoners for sexual misconduct by officers or staff. Whatever penological benefit that may flow from such measures is far outweighed by their deterrent effect on prisoners who might seek to report such abuse.

As noted above, unless outside organizations or individuals are made aware of incidents of custodial sexual misconduct, complaints of such abuse are likely to be handled almost entirely from within the departments of corrections or even from within the given prison. While most correctional systems that we investigated did sometimes refer suspected criminal sexual misconduct to the state police, these referrals did not always occur, nor were they necessarily carried out promptly, with the result that crucial medical evidence may have been compromised. Moreover, once correctional officials referred such charges to the state police, this often had the unconscionable side effect of ending the departments' own internal investigations into the alleged misconduct. It is at this point in the investigatory process that serious allegations of sexual misconduct can escape the grasp of the prison administration. Often, prison administrators fail to deal appropriately with cases that are returned to them because the allegations do not meet prosecution standards. An employee who may not have been found to commit a crime, but who may nonetheless have violated prison rules, can thus escape punishment altogether.

Meanwhile, in cases of suspected sexual misconduct that authorities consider less than criminal, it is likely that no investigation outside of the prison facility will occur, whether by departmental investigators or the state police. Moreover, any investigation into custodial sexual misconduct at whatever level that does occur may not be recorded or monitored by any central authority. In fact, in no correctional system that we investigated, with the exception of Georgia's, did any such reliable centralized database of sexual misconduct, whether criminal or otherwise, exist. The absence of such a database makes it all the more difficult to monitor the incidence of sexual misconduct, to record the steps taken to remedy it, and to keep track of allegedly abusive employees or those who have been found to have violated prison rules and/or criminal law.

One obvious way to address the clear conflict of interest that exists when a department of corrections investigates itself is to establish independent monitors to oversee correctional facilities. However, in the correctional systems that we investigated, such independent oversight was virtually nonexistent. The District of Columbia, for example, pursuant to a judicial order resulting from the 1994 class action suit, was required to appoint a special monitor who would independently investigate and make recommendations to remedy sexual misconduct within the district's correctional system. But under an August 1996 circuit court decision, the special monitor's position was eliminated pending appeal. The state of Michigan does have a legislative corrections ombudsman who is mandated by the state legislature to oversee conditions in the state's correctional institutions. The ombudsman's investigatory and oversight powers are fairly limited, however, and under 1995 legislation, have been even further curtailed. To our knowledge, none of the other states that we investigated have any kind of effective mechanism for securing the independent monitoring of conditions within their correctional facilities.

Given the lack of independent mechanisms legally authorized to oversee the departments of corrections, nongovernmental monitors and private attorneys have become crucial players in the effort to expose and remedy custodial sexual misconduct. Unfortunately, few national or local organizations or private attorneys that focus on prisoners' rights consistently focus on the problem of sexual misconduct in women's prisons. Those that do face enormous obstacles. These independent nongovernmental monitors, including attorneys, who investigate sexual misconduct often have unduly limited access to prisoners, are shut out of complaint or investigatory processes, are publicly attacked by correctional and even state officials, and find that their work with respect to other custodial issues can be compromised by their attempts to address this one. In addition, these groups and individuals uniformly face severe resource constraints which limit their ability to monitor departments of corrections and which have recently been exacerbated by the passage of the Prison Litigation Reform Act (PLRA), discussed below.

The PLRA, which was signed into law by President Bill Clinton in April 1996, has seriously compromised the ability of any entity, private or public, to combat sexual misconduct in custody. Among other measures, the PLRA dramatically limits the ability of individuals and nongovernmental organizations to challenge abusive prison conditions through litigation. The PLRA invalidates any settlement by parties to such a litigation that does not include a finding or statement that the prison conditions being challenged violate a federal statute or the

U.S. Constitution. Because prison authorities never want to admit such violations in the consent decrees that frequently settle prison litigation without trial, such findings are extremely rare. The PLRA further arbitrarily terminates any court order regarding unlawful conditions or practices in a given prison after two years, regardless of the degree of compliance; this is often an unreasonably short time to achieve any meaningful change in the way a prison is operated. Thus, a new trial will usually have to be held in order to make a new finding that problems persist. Finally, the PLRA also restricts court-awarded attorneys' fees, which are the main income for prisoner rights attorneys, and severely limits the authority of federal courts to assign judicial officers to oversee prison reform, a key tool for implementing remedial court orders.

The passage of the PLRA removes the one effective external check on serious abuses—such as those described in this report—and increases the urgency of the need for states themselves to ensure that female prisoners in their custody are not being sexually abused or harassed by male staff in their employ. Where they fail to do so, the United States Department of Justice has the power to prosecute correctional officials who violate federal civil rights statues. These prosecutions are difficult, in part due to stringent intent requirements, and are quite rare. In addition, the DOJ has the statutory right to investigate and institute civil actions under the Civil Rights of Institutionalized Persons Act (CRIPA) whenever it finds that a state facility engages in a pattern or practice of subjecting prisoners to "egregious or flagrant conditions" in violation of the constitution. Unfortunately, the PLRA is likely to have a chilling effect on the DOJ's oversight efforts, as well as those of private groups, and has already prompted the department to engage in an ill-advised review of all outstanding consent decrees to establish whether they should be terminated under the PLRA, regardless of whether a state department of corrections has yet filed such a request.

Even prior to the passage of the PLRA, the DOJ fell far short of its international and national obligations to protect against custodial sexual misconduct and to ensure that such abuse was appropriately investigated and prosecuted. Currently the DOJ has no guidelines that stipulate when and how to launch CRIPA investigations into conditions at state prisons and has conducted few such inquiries. The only state that we investigated for this report in which the DOJ has launched a formal investigation under CRIPA is the state of Michigan. Unfortunately, the Justice Department has yet to file suit against the state—despite its clear finding of sexual abuse of women prisoners by guards in Michigan's prisons and the fact that the forty-nine day period that the DOJ must legally wait after issuing findings before it can file such a suit lapsed well over a year ago.

Moreover, although the DOJ regularly receives complaints of custodial sexual misconduct, the department maintains no system for recording such complaints, nor does it systematically monitor the number of complaints concerning any particular institution or type of abuse. Absent such information, it is virtually impossible for the DOJ to ensure that it is fully aware of all the sexual misconduct problems that fall within its jurisdiction. Unfortunately, even if the DOJ were to take much-needed steps to monitor the problem of custodial sexual misconduct more effectively, it would still have to contend with serious budgetary constraints.

The tendency of the U.S. government to neglect the problem of custodial sexual misconduct in state prisons for women is perhaps best exemplified by its first report to the U.N. Human Rights Committee, which monitors compliance with the ICCPR. In the entire 213-page report, the problem of custodial sexual misconduct in U.S. state prisons for women is mentioned only once and then only to state that it is "addressed through staff training and through criminal statutes prohibiting such activity." This statement is at best disingenuous. At worst, it makes clear to the international community, to the people of the United States, to the state departments of corrections and the women they incarcerate, and to us, that the United States has almost completely abdicated its responsibility to guarantee in any meaningful way that the women held in its state prisons are not being sexually abused by those in authority over them.

Human Rights Watch calls on the United States to demonstrate its clear commitment to its international and national obligations to prevent, investigate, and punish custodial sexual abuse in U.S. state prisons for women and makes the following recommendations to the federal government and its constituent states, urging them to step up their efforts to acknowledge and eliminate this pressing problem. Recommendations specific to the District of Columbia and the five states investigated for this report appear at the close of each relevant chapter.

RECOMMENDATIONS TO THE FEDERAL GOVERNMENT

I.   U.S. Congress

1.   The U.S. Congress should pass legislation that requires states, as a precondition to receiving federal funding for the construction and maintenance of state prisons and holding cells, to criminalize all sexual contact between correctional staff and prisoners and, as discussed below, to report annually to the DOJ regarding conditions of incarceration in their respective facilities.

2.   The U.S. Congress should pass legislation that requires states to prohibit departments of corrections from hiring staff who have been convicted on criminal charges, or found liable in civil suits, for custodial sexual misconduct. The names and identifying information of such individuals should be maintained by each department of corrections, in a database that must be checked prior to hiring any correctional staff. This information should be collected by the DOJ data collection office, discussed below, for use by all states.

3.   The U.S. Congress should appropriate the funds necessary to enable the DOJ to conduct increased and thorough investigations of custodial sexual misconduct and to enjoin prohibited conduct pursuant to CRIPA. These funds should also be used by the DOJ to create an office of data collection, mandated to keep track of complaints of sexual abuse on a state-by-state basis, to issue semi-annual reports regarding such complaints, to provide complainants with information about the mechanisms available to remedy such abuse, and to follow up with the relevant state departments of corrections or federal prisons regarding any issues of concern. The DOJ should be mandated to do outreach about this office to federal and state correctional facilities, prisoners, and other relevant actors, including through the publication of materials about the data collection office that could be posted within correctional facilities. The state-level independent review boards or other oversight mechanisms, discussed below, should also supply information on a regular basis to this office.

4.   The U.S. Congress should revise certain provisions of the Prisoner Litigation Reform Act that severely limit the ability of prisoners, nongovernmental organizations, and the Department of Justice to challenge unconstitutional conditions in state correctional facilities. Those revisions, at a minimum, should include:
    •   repealing 18 United States Code Section 3626(a)(1), which requires that judicially enforceable consent decrees contain findings of federal law violations;
    •   repealing 18 United States Code Section 3626(b), which requires all judicial orders to terminate two years after they are issued; and

- restoring funding for special masters' and attorneys' fees to the levels that prevailed before the passage of the Prison Litigation Reform Act.

5.   The U.S. Congress should engage in a review of the CRIPA procedures for certifying the grievance procedures of U.S. correctional systems to ensure that certified procedures will function effectively for complaints of custodial abuse.

6.   The U.S. should withdraw the restrictive reservations, declarations, and understandings that the it has attached to the ICCPR and the Torture Convention.

7.   The U.S. Congress should introduce implementing legislation for the ICCPR and the Torture Convention such that persons in the United States could legally enforce the protections of these treaties in U.S. courts; or it should formally declare that both treaties are self-executing and thus capable of sustaining claims in U.S. courts without further legislation.

II.   U.S. Department of Justice

Civil Rights Division

1.   The U.S. Department of Justice, as a necessary step toward improving its responsiveness to sexual misconduct and the quality of its information about same, should establish a secure, toll-free telephone hotline to receive complaints of sexual misconduct by correctional staff and should publicize the existence of this service. The hotline should

- provide prisoners information about their rights and about nongovernmental organizations that they may contact for assistance;
- forward complaints to both the state officials and the Special Litigation Section and Criminal Section of the DOJ's Civil Rights Division;
- ensure confidentiality;
- be accessible under all circumstances, including times when prisoners are in segregation;
- be viewed as exercising the constitutional right to legal representation, and therefore be free from monitoring by prison officials; and

- extend its confidentiality to any written correspondence emerging from a prisoner's contact with the hotline.

2. The information collected through the hotline should be used to help compile the semi-annual reports of the office of data collection, suggested above.

3. The DOJ should formulate and issue specific, public procedures that detail its investigative process under CRIPA.

4. The DOJ should use the information contained in this report and information from other reliable sources to consider initiating additional criminal investigations under 18 U.S.C. Sections 241 and 242.

5. The DOJ should exercise its full authority under CRIPA to initiate, with the participation of its Office of Violence Against Women, investigations in the states examined in this report.

6. The DOJ should require states, as a condition of continued federal assistance, to report annually to the Civil Rights Division regarding conditions of incarceration in their respective correctional facilities. Such reports should include, among other things, patterns of rape, sexual abuse, and other forms of violence against women. The DOJ should publish an annual report based upon this information.

7. The DOJ should appoint an attorney within its Special Litigation section responsible for overseeing all complaints of sexual misconduct lodged with the section.

National Institute of Corrections
The National Institute of Corrections (NIC) should develop standards akin to the U.N.'s Standard Minimum Rules, in order to provide national guidelines for the treatment of prisoners to ensure that state corrections procedure and practice comport with international and constitutional protections. One valuable contribution from the NIC would be the development of model grievance, investigatory, and training mechanisms to address in particular many of the concerns raised in this report. These procedures should be developed in close consultation with all relevant parties, including those nongovernmental

organizations familiar with prisoner work, including with work on sexual misconduct in women's facilities.

III.   Executive Branch

1.   The U.S. should reinvigorate its efforts to secure ratification of the Convention on the Elimination of All Forms of Discrimination Against Women (CEDAW) to the U.S. Senate for ratification, and after ratification, to include in its periodic compliance reports to the CEDAW Committee information regarding federal measures to eradicate the problem of custodial sexual misconduct in U.S. state, as well as federal, prisons.

2.   The U.S. should include information on custodial sexual misconduct against women prisoners in its next report to the United Nations Human Rights Committee and in its first compliance report to the Committee Against Torture.

ISSUES FOR CONSIDERATION BY ALL STATE GOVERNMENTS

Most of the recommendations in this report are tailored to address the specific circumstances surrounding the problem of custodial sexual misconduct in each state. Nonetheless, based on our observations in these five states and in the District of Columbia, there are a number of critical cross-cutting concerns that merit urgent consideration by all states. Moreover, based on information that we gathered in the preparation of this report but did not investigate independently, Human Rights Watch is concerned that the problem of custodial sexual misconduct in state prisons, jails, and other custodial facilities for women exists in many states beyond the scope of this report. Accordingly, we call on all U.S. states to consider:

•   the need to prohibit expressly sexual misconduct in custody in both the administrative codes for departments of corrections and, where appropriate, in criminal law, in fulfillment of international human rights prohibitions on cruel, inhuman, or degrading treatment and punishment;

•   the need, in every state, to set forth and enforce policies that secure privacy protections and protections against verbal degradation that are consistent with U.S. obligations under international human rights law, such as policies that limit strip searches, pat-frisks, and inappropriate visual surveillance of prisoners by employees of the opposite sex;

- the need for thorough training for all current and future correctional employees regarding sexual misconduct and cross-gender guarding issues and regarding the implications of international human rights treaties and federal and state laws for the conduct of each prison system and its staff;

- the need to reward correctional employees, and in particular deputy wardens and wardens, for taking clear action to prevent and punish custodial sexual misconduct and to sanction those who do not;

- the need to ensure that prisoners who are impregnated by corrections staff are not automatically subject to administrative segregation and that they receive timely and adequate medical care, including psychiatric counseling when requested;

- the need to ensure that prisoners who become pregnant as a result of custodial sexual abuse are not pressured in any way to undergo abortions;

- the need to prevent the hiring or rehiring of employees who have previously been fired or resigned from a job as a corrections employee pursuant to allegations of sexual misconduct;

- the need to establish accessible and effective grievance and investigatory procedures consistent with the right under the ICCPR, the Torture Convention, and the Standard Minimum Rules to file complaints of official misconduct without fear of retribution or punishment;

- the need to guarantee that such procedures would ensure, *inter alia*, confidentiality of the complainant during the period of time in which the officer is still potentially in contact with her, ensure that her name is not made available to the general population, and impartial investigations are conducted by persons other than the implicated officials, and include meaningful appeal mechanisms;

- the need to protect prisoners from retaliation by implicated officers;

- the need to refrain from directly or indirectly punishing prisoners for sexual misconduct and, in particular, to examine the inappropriate and *de facto* punitive use of administrative segregation to punish and/or intimidate prisoners involved in investigations of sexual misconduct;

- the need, consistent with the U.S.'s international human rights obligations, to ensure that those employees who engage in the sexual abuse of prisoners under their protection are punished to fullest extent of the law;

- the need to ensure that independent monitoring groups, like many of those mentioned in this report, are able to investigate and evaluate the compliance of the state governments and the U.S. federal government with international human rights and domestic civil rights obligations; and

- the need to establish independent review boards or the equivalent of a legislative corrections ombudsman mandated to receive and investigate complaints of sexual misconduct, including from prisoners, and to provide information on the complaints by these independent entities received to the DOJ office of data collection suggested above.

II. HISTORICAL AND LEGAL BACKGROUND

HISTORICAL BACKGROUND

Sexual misconduct by prison guards[1] in U.S. women's prisons is occurring in the context of a steadily increasing population of female prisoners—many of whom are first offenders—in state (and federal) prisons. Female prisoners historically have experienced disparate treatment compared to their male counterparts. Many of these female prisoners have personal histories of sexual abuse and are now being guarded more often than not by male officers. Moreover, this misconduct is occurring in a context where prison rules and state law do not adequately address the problem, federal law either does not apply or is sporadically enforced, and international human rights law, which provides clear protections against and remedies for such abuse, is largely ignored. This section describes this historical and legal context.

The Characteristics of the Female Prison Population

Women constitute only a tiny minority of the prison population in the United States,[2] representing just over 6 percent of all prisoners at the end of 1995.[3]

---

[1] Not all sexual misconduct is committed by prison guards. Non-security correctional employees also have been found to engage in such abuse. Throughout this report, we use the terms guard, officer, employee, and staff interchangeably, except in describing specific acts of sexual misconduct. In this case, we give the exact professional status of the officer or non-security employee involved.

[2] The U.S. has the largest known prison population in the world at 1.6 million. China has the next largest known figure at 1.2 million. However, estimates from the U.S. General Accounting Office from July 1990 places the number of Chinese prisoners between one and twenty million, with most believing that the actual population is much higher than official estimates.

[3] According to the Bureau of Justice Statistics, women represented 6.3 percent of all U.S. prisoners in 1995. Leslie Acoca and James Austin, *The Crisis: Women in Prison* (San Francisco: National Council on Crime and Delinquency, 1996), p. 1. The *Women in Prison* study, while including an analysis of national data, concentrated primarily on three states—California, Connecticut and Florida—during an eighteen-month period between May 1994 and December 1995. The study included face-to-face interviews with 151 randomly selected women in state prisons in these three states.

16

However, their relatively small presence should not obscure a dramatic increase in their numbers over the last fifteen years. According to the Department of Justice's Bureau of Justice Statistics (BOJS), the number of women entering U.S. state and federal prisons between 1980 and 1994 has increased by 386 percent.[4] This increase is significantly higher than that of men, whose population rose 214 percent in the same period.[5] The growth in the number of female prisoners, according to observers, results less from a shift in the nature of the crimes women commit than it does from the so-called war on drugs and related changes in legislation, law enforcement practices, and judicial decision-making.[6] In fact, drug-related offenses accounted for 55 percent of the increase in the female prison population between 1986 and 1991.[7] African American women, who make up 14.5 percent of the general U.S. population,[8] constitute 52.2 percent of the prison population[9] and have been hardest hit by this increase.[10] Moreover, BOJS figures indicate that almost 70 percent of women in U.S. prisons are incarcerated for drug, property, or public order offenses. Just over 30 percent are incarcerated for violent crimes, such as

---

[4] Ibid.

[5] Ibid.

[6] Russ Immarigeon and Meda Chesney-Lind, *Women's Prisons: Overcrowded and Overused* (San Francisco: National Council on Crime and Delinquency, 1992), p. 3.

[7] Tracy L. Snell and Danielle C. Morton, Bureau of Justice Statistics Special Report, "Women in Prison: Survey of State Prison Inmates 1991," March 1994.

[8] See http://www.census.gov/population/socdemo/race/black/tab1.dat.

[9] Telephone interview, Tracy Snell, statistician, Bureau of Justice Statistics, Nov. 6, 1996.

[10] Between 1986 and 1991, the number of black non-Hispanic women in state prisons for drug offenses nationwide increased more than eightfold, from 667 to 6,193. The increase was almost double that for black non-Hispanic males and more than triple that for white non-Hispanic females. Marc Mauer and Tracy Huling, *Young Black Americans and the Criminal Justice System: Five Years Later* (Washington, D.C.: The Sentencing Project, 1995).

murder, robbery, or assault.[11] Many are incarcerated in the 170 state confinement facilities across the United States that house women.[12]

The increasing incarceration of women has had a tremendous impact on their families and children. Eighty percent of incarcerated women have at least one child, and the majority of these are single mothers.[13] In New York, for example, more than 75 percent of all women in prison have children, and two-thirds of the women have children under the age of eighteen.[14] While many women maintain contact with their children during incarceration, 54 percent are never visited by their children.[15] Several factors contribute to this small percentage of visits, including the distance of the prison from the children's home, the travel time, and the lack of resources to finance such trips. Research indicates that the children of incarcerated mothers suffer from immediate and enduring adverse effects on their relationships with peers and irreparable harm to the mother-child relationship.[16]

---

[11] Snell and Morton, "Women in Prison: Survey."

[12] Telephone interview, Tracy Snell, statistician, Bureau of Justice Statistics, Nov. 6, 1996.

[13] Acoca and Austin, *The Crisis*, p. 8.

[14] The Correctional Association of New York, "Women in Prison Fact Sheet" (November 1994).

[15] Barbara Bloom and David Steinhart, *Why Punish the Children? A Reappraisal of the Children of Incarcerated Mothers in America* (San Francisco: National Council on Crime and Delinquency (NCCD), 1993), Table 2-9. The NCCD's figures are based on a survey of mothers in jail and prisons in eight states and the District of Columbia.

[16] Barbara Bloom, "Incarcerated Mothers and Their Children: Maintaining Family Ties," in *American Correctional Association: Female Offenders: Meeting the Needs of a Neglected Population* (1993). According to Ellen Barry, Director, Legal Services for Prisoners with Children in San Francisco, children who enter the foster care system when their mother is incarcerated are at serious risk of never being reunified with her. Barry attributes this problem to the lack of programs and services within the prisons to prepare the women for reunification after release. Without such programs, Barry argues, it is "virtually impossible for her . . . to reunify with the child." Ellen Barry, "Reunification Difficult for Incarcerated Parents and Their Children," *Youth Law News*, July-August 1985, p. 16.

More disturbing, these children may be at a greater risk of future incarceration themselves.[17]

Statistics indicate that anywhere from 40 to 88 percent of incarcerated women have been victims of domestic violence and sexual or physical abuse prior to incarceration, either as children or adults.[18] According to Christine Kampfner, a clinical psychologist who has worked with women who kill their batterers, "sexual abuse is an important consideration when you look at incarcerated women."[19] She studied seventy women around the country who had killed their batterers and found that 85 percent had been sexually abused at some point prior to their incarceration.[20] The abuse had an enormous impact on how the women responded to incarceration, particularly their relationships with male guards. Kampfner asserted that the women often relive the trauma and suffer flashbacks, particularly when the corrections officers search them and conduct pat-frisks. Many women with a prior history of sexual abuse are particularly vulnerable to sexual abuse in prison. According to Kampfner, women prisoners respond to abusive authority figures in prison much as they have prior to incarceration. She continued, "The women are so needy and in need of love, they are set up for

---

[17] Bloom, "Incarcerated Mothers and Their Children...," citing an unpublished doctoral study conducted at Brandeis University which estimated that the children of inmates were five to six times more likely than their peers to be incarcerated.

[18] BOJS studies repeatedly find that four in ten women in prison were either physically or sexually abused at some time prior to incarceration. Snell and Morton, "Women in Prison: Survey," p. 5; Lawrence A. Greenfield and Stephanie Minor-Harper, *Special Report: Women in Prison* (Virginia: Bureau of Justice Statistics, 1991), p. 6. These figures, however, may be conservative, as state-specific studies have generally yielded a higher percentage of women reporting prior sexual or physical abuse. A 1988 study found that 88 percent of the incarcerated women sampled had experienced at least one major form of prior abuse: childhood physical abuse, childhood sexual abuse, adult rape or adult battering. Immarigeon and Chesney-Lind, *Women's Prisons: Overcrowded and Overused*, p. 6. The NCCD study found that 67.5 percent of women reported physical or sexual abuse as children, and 71.5 percent reported such abuse as adults. Acoca and Austin, *The Crisis*, p. 58.

[19] Interview, Christina Kampfner, psychologist, Ann Arbor, Michigan, May 17, 1994.

[20] Ibid.

oppression. The only way they know is to exchange their bodies [to meet this need]."[21]

This history of sexual abuse among many women prisoners has prompted two federal appellate courts to uphold or impose restrictions on the role of male corrections officers within two particular women's prisons. In one case, the U.S. Court of Appeals for the Seventh Circuit held that, considering the women's history of sexual and physical abuse, sex could be used as a *bona fide* occupational qualification (BFOQ) to restrict male officers from working on the housing units.[22] In the second case, the female prisoners' histories of sexual and physical abuse led the Ninth Circuit to rule that cross-gender pat-frisks constitute cruel and unusual punishment under the Eighth Amendment of the U.S. Constitution.[23]

Male Guards in Women's Prisons

Men have historically worked in U.S. women's prisons as corrections officers, although, in deference to the potential for sexual misconduct, their role has at times been restricted to noncontact positions.[24] However, with the passage of Title VII of the Civil Rights Act of 1964 and the introduction of equal employment rights for women, many of the restrictions on male corrections officers working in women's prisons were eliminated to make way for female corrections officers working in men's prisons.[25] According to a 1992 survey in *Corrections*

---

[21] Ibid.

[22] *Torres v. Wisconsin Department of Health and Human Services*, 859 F.2d 1523 (7th Cir. 1988), *cert. denied*, 489 U.S. 1017 (1989).

[23] *Jordan v. Gardner*, 986 F.2d 1521 (9th Cir. 1993).

[24] For example, in New York, prior to 1976, only women could serve as corrections officers at the women's prison at Bedford Hills, while men were allowed to work on the grounds and in the schools and library. See also Clarice Feinman, *Women in the Criminal Justice System* (Connecticut: Praeger Books, 1994), pp. 159-177.

[25] Under Title VII, an employer may not discriminate on the basis of sex unless an employee's sex is a bona fide occupational qualification (BFOQ), i.e. a qualification that is "reasonably necessary" to perform the specific job. In the absence of unusual circumstances, U.S. federal courts have been unwilling to characterize a person's sex as a BFOQ. *Dothard v. Rawlinson*, 433 U.S. 321 (1977); *Forts v. Ward*, 621 F.2d 1210 (2d Cir. 1980); *Griffin v. Michigan Department of Corrections*, 654 F. Supp. 690 (E.D. Mich. 1982); *Gunther v. Iowa State Men's Reformatory*, 462 F. Supp. 952 (N.D. Iowa 1979), *affirmed*, 612 F.2d

Compendium, a monthly newsletter for corrections professionals, men now constitute the majority of corrections officers working in women's prisons, outnumbering their female counterparts at times by two or three to one.[26]

The introduction into U.S. prisons of cross-gender guarding was met with a flurry of lawsuits, filed primarily by male prisoners contesting the invasion of their privacy by female officers. Female prisoners, traditionally less litigious and outspoken, have contested the role of male officers to a lesser extent. Corrections officers of both sexes also have sued in several cases with some success to contest sexually discriminatory hiring practices and restrictions imposed by prison administrators. In *Torres v. Wisconsin Department of Health and Social Services,* the Seventh Circuit permitted the superintendent of a women's prison in Wisconsin to restrict male correctional officers from working in the housing units, because, considering the women's histories of physical and sexual abuse, rehabilitation could not be achieved with male officers in the units. The Seventh Circuit found that, "given the very special responsibilities of these [male correctional officers] and the obvious lack of guideposts for them to follow," a certain measure of discretion in restricting their employment was permissible.[27]

In addition, in a suit in Georgia alleging sexual misconduct in women's prisons, lawyers negotiated a consent decree that prohibited male officers from working in the housing units. However, rather than adhering to this limited restriction, in March 1996 the Georgia Department of Corrections commissioner, Wayne Garner, began transferring male officers out of one women's prison altogether. He planned to continue transferring staff—and to implement similar transfers at Georgia's other two women's prisons—until no male staff was in a contact position with women prisoners. The new policy was challenged immediately by the Georgia State Employees Union on anti-discrimination grounds. In late August 1996, after the Georgia Equal Employment Opportunity Commission initiated an investigation into the transfers, the Georgia Department of Corrections ended the policy and returned all the transferred guards back to their original facilities.

While, as noted below, Human Rights Watch does not as a matter of policy oppose the presence of male officers in female prisons *per se,* we agree in

---

1079 (6th Cir. 1980), *cert. denied,* 446 U.S. 966 (1980).

[26] In Illinois, for example, 29 percent of male corrections officers, or around 1,700, worked in women's facilities while the state employed only 793 women as corrections officers.

[27] *Torres,* 859 F.2d, p. 1523.

principle with the notion that some restrictions should be placed on the role of the male officers within women's prisons, particularly in light of evidence that incarcerated women in the United States and elsewhere have been raped and sexually assaulted by male employees.[28] While we recognize that incarceration brings with it necessary and legitimate limitations on certain rights of the prisoner, in no way does it justify the complete abrogation of her rights to bodily integrity and to some degree of privacy.

Male vs. Female Prisoners: Disparate Treatment

Historically, incarcerated women have been treated less well than men while their gender-specific needs have been ignored.[29] Until recently, most states maintained only one prison facility for women, often located a significant distance from a major urban center. As a result, many female prisoners were, and remain, geographically isolated from their children, as well as from legal and community resources.[30] Statistics reveal that more than 60 percent of all women are incarcerated more than one hundred miles from their child's place of residence, while under 9 percent are incarcerated within twenty miles.[31] As the female prison population has grown, a number of states have opened additional facilities to hold women prisoners, although these facilities have not necessarily eased their

---

[28]   See Asia Watch (now Human Rights Watch/Asia) and Women's Rights Project, *A Modern Form of Slavery: Trafficking of Burmese Women and Girls into Brothels in Thailand*, (New York: Human Rights Watch, 1993), pp. 89-94; Asia Watch (now Human Rights Watch/Asia) and Women's Rights Project, *Double Jeopardy: Police Abuse of Women in Pakistan*, (New York: Human Rights Watch, 1992); Americas Watch (now Human Rights Watch/Americas) and Women's Rights Project, *Untold Terror: Violence Against Women in Peru's Armed Conflict* (New York: Human Rights Watch, 1992).

[29]   For a historical overview of incarcerated women since the nineteenth century, see Nicole Hahn Rafter, *Partial Justice: Women, Prisons and Social Control* (London: Transaction Publishers, 1990). According to Rafter, women historically have received inferior care, including less attention and fewer resources. Their care has also been marked by gender stereotyping, with vocational training and opportunities targeted at jobs traditionally viewed as appropriate for women. These disparities, she found, remain entrenched in the treatment of women in prison today. Ibid., p. xxx.

[30]   Rafter found that women's reformatories were intentionally built in rural communities to "shield inmates from the corrupting influence of the city." Ibid., p. xxvii.

[31]   Bloom and Steinhart, *Why Punish the Children*, Table 2-10.

geographic isolation.[32]   California, for example, opened three new prisons for women in the last ten years, all located in rural communities. Similarly, Illinois converted two of its men's prisons to co-correctional facilities. Both facilities are located even further from Cook County, which is home to almost 60 percent of the female prison population in the state, than Dwight, the original women's prison.

Because of their small numbers, women are more likely to be incarcerated in a maximum security facility, where women of all security levels are either commingled or separated by internal housing classifications. Men, in contrast, generally are assigned to prisons based on a variety of factors, including their criminal offense, prior criminal history, and psychological profile. Also, because of the greater number of male institutions, men stand a much better chance of being housed near their place of residence, thus making it easier for family, friends, and attorneys to visit.[33]

In comparison to prisons for men, rules within women's prisons tend to be greater in number and pettier in nature. Women prisoners are commonly cited for disciplinary offenses that are typically ignored within male institutions, and, while they are less violent than their male counterparts, they appear to receive a greater number of disciplinary citations for less serious infractions.[34] A study of Texas prisons conducted by Dorothy McClellan, an associate professor of criminal justice at Corpus Christi State University, found that female prisoners in the course of one year received almost five times as many citations as male prisoners.[35] McClellan found that the women were cited most commonly for offenses such as

---

[32] While this problem is not unique to women prisoners, it is more extreme because there are relatively fewer women's prisons.

[33] For example, in Connecticut all incarcerated women were designated as "Placement in facility nearest to community of residence not necessary," while 58 percent of male inmates received priority placement in the facility nearest their community of residence, significant others/family members or community resources. Considering the large number of single mothers who are incarcerated in Connecticut, this assessment was based upon the availability of women's facilities rather than on the women's or their families' needs. Acoca and Austin, *The Crisis*, p. 30.

[34] Dorothy Spektorov McClellan, "Disparity in the Discipline of Male and Female Inmates in Texas Prisons," *Women & Criminal Justice*, Volume 5, Number 2, 1994.

[35] According to McClellan's study, 245 incarcerated women received 3,698 citations in the course of a year while 271 male prisoners received only 786. Ibid., p. 76.

disobeying a direct order or violating a written or posted rule.[36] In fact, more than one in three citations for women over a one-year period were for violating written or posted rules.[37]

In addition, women in prison often do not receive comparable educational and vocational programs to those made available to men, and they also have fewer opportunities for job-training and work-release, less access to social services, fewer visitors, and "they are more likely to be treated like children."[38] Beginning in the late 1970s, incarcerated women began to sue state departments of corrections all over the United States to challenge such disparate treatment as a violation of the equal protection clause of the U.S. Constitution.[39] Over the years, incarcerated women have successfully challenged certain conditions of incarceration—in particular, the denial of minimum security facilities and their related privileges,[40] harsher parole standards,[41] and the transfer of women to other states to serve their

---

[36] Ibid.

[37] Of the 3,698 citations received by women, 1,322 were for disobeying a written or posted rule and 841 for refusing to obey orders. Ibid.

[38] Ibid., p. xxxi.

[39] In 1983 twenty-seven states were involved in litigation involving the women's prisons, but only three of those faced discrimination suits. By 1988 one author found that at least fifteen states were involved in equal protection suits. Rafter, *Partial Justice*, p. 198. Relying on the Equal Protection Clause in the Fourteenth Amendment of the U.S. Constitution, the U.S. Supreme Court has held that no state may discriminate on the basis of sex unless such discrimination serves an important government objective and is substantially related to the achievement of that objective. *United States v. Virginia*, 116 S.Ct. 2264 (1996). For further discussion of the application of the Equal Protection Clause to sex discrimination, see Susan Deller Ross and Ann Barcher, *The Rights of Women: Basic ACLU Guide to a Woman's Rights* (New York: Bantam, 1983), pp. 1-15. The Fourteenth Amendment provides in its relevant part "No State shall make or enforce any law which shall . . . deny to any person within its jurisdiction the equal protection of the law."

[40] *Molar v. Gates*, 98 Cal. App. 3d 1 (1979).

[41] *Cosgrove v. Smith*, 697 F.2d 1125 (D.C. Cir. 1983).

sentences because their home state lacked a long-term prison facility for women.[42] On these issues, courts generally have ruled in the women's favor.

However, challenges to disparate educational and vocational programming have met with more mixed success. In contrast to the above issues, which tend to focus on a particular state, the absence of equal education and programming opportunities in women's prisons is an issue that cuts across state lines. When suits have been settled out of court, states have generally agreed to augment and improve prison programming for women.[43] But, when a department of corrections declines to settle a suit and the case goes to trial, incarcerated women have fared less well. Many courts reviewing such suits have permitted states a degree of discretion to develop programming for women, limited by the requirement that states provide women with "parity of treatment" rather than equal treatment to that of male prisoners. This test requires prison officials "to provide women inmates with treatment facilities that are substantially equivalent to those provided for men—i.e., equivalent in substance, if not in form—unless their actions . . . nonetheless bear a fair and substantial relationship to achievement of the State's correctional objectives."[44]

In 1994, in *Klinger v. Department of Corrections*,[45] the Eighth Circuit Court of Appeals reversed a district court decision directing the state of Nebraska to provide programs and services "substantially equivalent" to those offered men. In that case, the circuit court determined that inferior programming could be justified because women prisoners in the state were not "similarly situated" to incarcerated men. Similarly, in 1996 the U.S. Court of Appeals for the District of Columbia reversed a district court decision mandating additional programming for women prisoners because the appellate court found that the lower number of

---

[42] *Park v. Thompson*, 356 F. Supp. 783 (D. Haw. 1973).

[43] Lawsuits filed in Illinois and California, for example, were settled out of court. In both cases, the respective department of corrections introduced improvements in the programming they provided for incarcerated women.

[44] *Glover v. Johnson*, 478 F. Supp. 1075, p. 1079 (E.D. Mich. 1979). The reforms won by incarcerated women in Michigan were ultimately undermined by departmental noncompliance. See Rafter, *Partial Justice*, pp. 199-201.

[45] 31 F.3d 727 (8th Cir. 1994), *certiorari denied*, 115 S.Ct. 1177 (1995).

female prisoners made it reasonable that fewer programs were offered.[46] The circuit court's decision in *Klinger* and its doctrine of "parity of treatment" leave women prisoners with fewer resources and opportunities for personal improvement than male prisoners.

PERTINENT NATIONAL AND INTERNATIONAL LAW

U.S. Law

U.S. law clearly obligates both the federal and state governments to prohibit sexual misconduct. The U.S. Constitution prohibits cruel and unusual punishment—including official sexual misconduct—and guarantees a right to privacy. In addition, federal statutory law expressly criminalizes custodial sexual contact between prisoners and corrections staff. Unfortunately, however, these constitutional protections have rarely been applied for the benefit of women prisoners, and the Department of Justice (DOJ), which is authorized to protect prisoners' constitutional rights, has pursued cases of custodial sexual misconduct only to a very limited extent.[47] Moreover, federal statutory provisions barring custodial sexual contact between prisoners and corrections staff apply only to federal facilities, not state facilities, where the majority of prisoners in the United States are held.[48] Finally, while just over half of the states have enacted criminal provisions barring custodial sexual contact, these state laws have been, at best, erratically enforced and in some twenty-three states, simply do not exist.

The result is that even though there are, in theory, a variety of laws designed to protect female prisoners in the United States against custodial sexual misconduct, relatively few instances exist in which these protections have

---

[46] *Women Prisoners of the District of Columbia Department of Corrections v. District of Columbia,* 93 F.3d 910 (D.C. Circuit, 1996). The appellate court compared the programming difference between female and male prisoners to that between Smith College, a small, private women's college, and Harvard University, a large, co-educational university. Ibid., pp. 26-27.

[47] Telephone interview, Karen Bower, staff attorney, National Prison Project, American Civil Liberties Union, November 1, 1996.

[48] Each of the fifty states operates and maintains its own prison system. These systems are separate and distinct from the federal prison system, which is overseen by the Federal Bureau of Prisons. Most crimes are prosecuted in state courts, under state criminal law, and prisoners are sentenced to terms in state institutions.

functioned successfully. This section describes such protections in detail and illustrates how inadequacies in the laws and limits to their enforcement contribute to the problem of sexual misconduct in U.S. women's prisons. This section also demonstrates that, although international human rights law offers additional protection against criminal sexual misconduct, the U.S. government is bound by but has not fully complied with these international norms as they relate to this abuse.

The U.S. Constitution

States are bound to uphold a prisoner's rights under the U.S. Constitution. If a state neglects that duty, the main method of enforcement is through litigation, primarily through lawsuits filed by prisoners alleging personal harm. Such a lawsuit may seek injunctive relief; that is, it may request the court to stop the state from engaging in the unconstitutional conduct. In addition, prisoners may seek financial compensation from government authorities for a violation of his or her constitutional rights. The two constitutional amendments most relevant to custodial sexual misconduct are the eighth, which bars cruel and unusual punishments, and the fourth, which prohibits unreasonable searches and seizures.

The Eighth Amendment

The Eighth Amendment to the U.S. Constitution bars cruel and unusual punishments. The Supreme Court has ruled that the provision prohibits "only the unnecessary and wanton infliction of pain."[49] This prohibition has been given content through judicial interpretation. To prove an Eighth Amendment violation, plaintiffs must prove not only an objective injury, either physical or otherwise, but also subjective intent on the part of authorities to cause that injury. In terms of objective injury, the pain must be sufficiently serious such that it violates contemporary standards of decency.[50] In addition, the responsible prison official must have had a "sufficiently culpable state of mind."[51] The standard for "sufficiently culpable" differs depending on whether the suit alleges excessive physical force or abusive conditions of incarceration. To receive redress under the Eighth Amendment for excessive physical force, a prisoner must prove that a

---

[49] *Whitley v. Albers*, 475 U.S. 312, p. 319 (1986).

[50] *Hudson v. McMillian*, 503 U.S. 1, p. 14 (1992)

[51] *Wilson v. Seiter*, 501 U.S. 294, p. 298 (1991)

prison official or officials acted "maliciously and sadistically."[52] To challenge abusive conditions of incarceration, a prisoner must demonstrate that prison officials acted with "deliberate indifference" in subjecting her to such conditions.[53]

A number of federal courts have examined the protections provided by the Eighth Amendment in the context of sexual abuse. In *Farmer v. Brennan*, the Supreme Court ruled that a prison official violates the Eighth Amendment if, acting with deliberate indifference, he exposes a prisoner to substantial risk of sexual assault.[54] The court found in *Farmer* that sexual abuse "serves no legitimate penological objective." In 1993 in *Jordan v. Gardner*, the Ninth Circuit found that in light of the fact that 85 percent of the women prisoners in the Washington Corrections Center for Women had experienced sexual or physical abuse, pat searches conducted by male officers violated the Eighth Amendment's prohibition on cruel and unusual punishment.[55] In addition, two recent cases in the District of Columbia have ruled that sexual contact between prison officials and prisoners violates the Eighth Amendment.[56]

The Fourth Amendment

In addition to providing protection against custodial sexual abuse, the U.S. Constitution also provides a right to privacy through the Fourth Amendment. The Fourth Amendment states in relevant part, "the right of the people to be secure in their persons . . . against unreasonable searches and seizures, shall not be violated."[57] While the Supreme Court has stated that prisoners should be accorded those rights that are not inconsistent with the legitimate objectives of incarceration,

---

[52] *Hudson*, p. 10; and *Whitley*, pp. 320-321.

[53] *Wilson*, p. 303. The Supreme Court did not define "deliberate indifference" in *Wilson*. In a 1994 decision, however, it ruled that prison officials must know of the risk and fail to take reasonable measures. *Farmer v. Brennan*, 114 S. Ct. 1970 (1994).

[54] *Farmer*, pp. 1976-1984.

[55] *Jordan v. Gardner*, 986 F.2d 1521 (9th Cir. 1993)

[56] *Women Prisoners of the District of Columbia Department of Corrections v. District of Columbia*, 877 F. Supp. 634 (D.D.C. 1994), *reversed on other grounds*, No. 95-7041 (D.C. Cir. August 30, 1996); *Thomas v. District of Columbia*, 887 F. Supp. 1 (D.D.C. 1995).

[57] Fourth Amendment, U.S. Constitution.

the actual scope of prisoners' right to privacy has not yet been established by the Supreme Court. Two Supreme Court cases have examined the right to privacy for incarcerated persons. The first, *Bell v. Wolfish*,[58] found that body cavity searches after contact visits were reasonable because of security concerns but also stated that convicted prisoners do not forfeit all constitutional protections by reason of confinement.[59] The second relevant case, *Hudson v. Palmer*,[60] held that prisoners do not have a reasonable expectation of privacy in their cells but did not address whether prisoners retain a right to bodily privacy.

In fact, many lower federal courts have recognized this limited right to bodily privacy. Courts have upheld limitations on cross-gender frisks[61] and almost uniformly prohibited cross-gender strip searches.[62] Several courts have held that occasional or infrequent viewing of prisoners naked during showers or during body searches is acceptable when it occurs respectfully and in the least intrusive manner possible.[63] But the regular viewing of prisoners of the opposite sex who are

---

[58] 441 U.S. 520 (1979).

[59] The Supreme Court stated that "courts must consider the scope of the particular intrusion, the manner in which it is conducted, the justification for initiating it and the place in which it is conducted." *Bell*, p. 559.

[60] 468 U.S. 517 (1983).

[61] See, for example, *Jordan v. Gardner*, 986 F.2d 1521 (9th Cir. 1993); *Smith v. Fairman*, 678 F.2d 52 (7th Cir. 1982). In addition, the Seventh Circuit in *Madyun v. Franzen*, 704 F.2d 954 (7th Cir. 1983), *cert. denied*, 464 U.S. 996 (1983), upheld an Illinois policy prohibiting male guards from pat-frisking female prisoners while permitting female guards to pat-frisk male prisoners. The Seventh Circuit examined the policy difference from the perspective of employment rights rather than privacy. It found that a restriction on the role of female guards in male prisons would negatively impact their equal employment opportunities, while there was no indication that men suffered from a lack of opportunity because they were precluded from pat-frisking female prisoners. *Madyun*, p. 962.

[62] See, for example, *Hardin v. Stynchcomb*, 691 F.2d 1364 (11th Cir. 1982), *rehearing denied*, 696 F.2d 1007 (11th Cir. 1983) and *Canedy v. Boardman*, 16 F.3d 183 (7th Cir. 1994).

[63] See, for example, *Cookish v. Powell*, 945 F.2d 441, p. 447 (1st Cir. 1991); *Grummett v. Rushen*, 779 F.2d 491, p. 495 (9th Cir. 1985); *Miles v. Bell*, 621 F. Supp. 51, p. 67 (D. Conn. 1985)

engaged in personal activities, such as undressing, using the toilet facilities or showering, when not reasonably necessary, has been found to constitute a violation of the prisoners' right to bodily privacy.[64] Only rarely have courts refused to recognize a right to privacy at all.[65]

Despite court rulings upholding prisoners' limited right to bodily privacy, prison authorities in the states we visited have largely neglected to establish clear guidelines and procedures to protect this right. At the same time, male guards constitute a significant percentage of the officers in the women's prisons we investigated, and their presence in women's prisons without such guidelines often has limited prisoners' ability to maintain their privacy rights. Moreover, even in those states where policies upholding prisoners' right to bodily privacy do exist, they are routinely violated. As a result, female prisoners also suffer inappropriate searches and visual surveillance by guards, frequently accompanied by lewd remarks and gestures.

U.S. Department of Justice

The U.S. Constitution may be enforced by the U.S. Department of Justice (DOJ) acting under statutory authority. The DOJ may criminally prosecute a person "acting under the color of state law"[66] for violating a prisoner's

---

[64] See, for example, *Fortner v. Thomas*, 983 F. 2d 1024, p. 1030 (11th Cir. 1993); *Cookish v. Powell*, 945 F.2d 441, p. 447 (1st Cir. 1991); *Cumbey v. Meachum*, 684 F.2d 712 (10th Cir. 1982); *Lee v. Downs*, 641 F.2d 1117, p.1119 (4th Cir. 1981); *Forts v. Ward*, 471 F. Supp. 1095, p. 1099 (S.D.N.Y. 1979).

[65] *Johnson v. Phelan*, 69 F.3d 144 (7th Cir. 1995), *petition for certiorari filed* 64 U.S.L.W. 3823, Civil Action No. 95-1951 (May 28, 1996); *Griffin v. Michigan Department of Corrections*, 654 F. Supp. 690, p. 703 (E.D. Mich. 1982)("inmates do not possess any protected right under the Constitution against being viewed while naked by corrections officers of the opposite sex") ; *Bagley v. Watson*, 579 F. Supp. 1099 (D. Or. 1983) ("male prisoners . . . have no federal constitutional rights to freedom from clothed 'pat-down' frisk searches and/or visual observations in states of undress performed by female correctional officer guards").

[66] "Under color of state law" means that a state official must be using her authority as a state official when the violation occurs. A state official may still be acting under color of law even if her conduct violates state law. *Screws v. United States*, 325 U.S. 91, p. 109 (1945). The "misuse of power" must be made possible by the actor's authority under state law. Ibid.

constitutional rights, under Title 18, United States Code, Sections 241 and 242.[67] The DOJ also may investigate allegations of constitutional rights violations in a state's prisons under the Civil Rights of Institutionalized Persons Act (CRIPA) and sue a state civilly. In addition, the Violent Crime Control and Law Enforcement Act of 1994 (1994 Crime Bill) added Title 42, United States Code, Section 14141, under which the DOJ also may enforce the constitutional rights of prisoners through a civil suit. These statutes, however, are subject to prosecutorial discretion, and the DOJ has no affirmative obligation to act.

Criminal Enforcement: Title 18, U.S. Code, Sections 241 and 242

The evidentiary burden under Title 18, United States Code, Sections 241 and 242 makes it extremely difficult to convict someone under criminal law for violating a prisoner's constitutional rights. To convict a public official, the DOJ must not only prove beyond a reasonable doubt that a constitutional right has been violated, but also that the public official had the "specific intent" to deprive a prisoner of a constitutional right.[68] The specific intent requirement creates a

---

[67] Sections 241 and 242 are both general civil rights provisions, and their application is not limited exclusively to abuses within prisons. Title 18, United States Code, Section 241 provides, in relevant part: "[i]f two or more persons conspire to injure, oppress, threaten, or intimidate any person in any State . . . in the free exercise or enjoyment of any right or privilege secured to him [or her] by the Constitution or laws of the United States, or because of his [or her] having so exercise of the same . . . [t]hey shall be fined or imprisoned not more than ten years, . . . or both."

Section 242 provides, in relevant part: "Whoever, under color of law, statute, ordinance, regulation, or custom, willfully subjects any person in any State . . . to the deprivation of any rights, privileges, or immunities secured or protected by the Constitution or laws of the United States . . . shall be fined under this title or imprisoned not more than one year, or both; and if bodily injury results from the acts committed in violation of this section or if such acts include the use, the attempted use, or threatened use of a dangerous weapon, explosives, or fire, shall be fined under this title or imprisoned not more than ten years, or both; and if death results from the acts committed in violation of this section or if such acts include . . . aggravated sexual abuse, or an attempt to commit aggravated sexual abuse, . . . shall be fined under this title, or imprisoned for any term of years or for life, or both, or may be sentenced to death."

[68] Screws, p. 103 (regarding 18 U.S.C. Section 242); United States v. Guest, 383 U.S. 745, p. 760 (1966) (regarding 18 U.S.C. Section 241).

substantial burden for the DOJ to meet because it must show that an official knowingly and willfully participated in violating a prisoner's constitutional right.[69]

One commentator has noted that the U.S. government has provided only limited resources for the prosecution of such suits.[70] During the Reagan and Bush administrations, the number of personnel and amount of money dedicated to investigating and prosecuting civil rights violations by law enforcement remained constant, as did the number of investigations, indictments, and convictions. Yet, at the same time, money allocated to law enforcement increased. According to Justice Department data, of approximately 11,000 complaints reviewed under these statutes, only sixty-five cases were filed for prosecution in 1994—half of 1 percent.[71] To our knowledge, no corrections officials in the states that we investigated are being criminally prosecuted for violating a woman prisoner's civil rights through sexual misconduct.

Civil Enforcement: CRIPA

The DOJ may also institute civil suits for abuses in state and local prisons which violate the civil rights of prisoners under the Civil Rights of Institutionalized Persons Act (CRIPA).[72] Congress passed CRIPA in 1980 to enable the federal government to investigate and pursue civil suits against state institutions that the U.S. attorney general suspects of violating constitutional rights. Prior to the enactment of CRIPA, the U.S. government had only limited authority to intervene in private lawsuits alleging a violation of constitutional rights inside state institutions.[73] Prior to suing a state under CRIPA, the DOJ must have "reasonable cause to believe" that a state institution engages in a pattern or practice of

---

[69] *Screws,* pp. 101-103.

[70] Paul Hoffman, "The Feds, Lies and Videotape: The Need for an Effective Federal Role in Controlling Police Abuse in Urban America," *Southern California Law Review,* Volume 66, p. 1522 (1993).

[71] 1995 Department of Justice Congressional Authorization and Budget Submission, Volume 1, Civil Rights Division.

[72] 42 U.S.C. Section 1997 *et seq.*

[73] See, for example, *Canterino v. Wilson,* 538 F. Supp. 62 (W.D. Ky. 1982); Senate Reports Number 96-416, 96th Congress, Second Session (1980), *reprinted in* 1980 United States Code Congressional and Administrative News, pp. 787, 797.

subjecting prisoners to "egregious or flagrant conditions" that violate the U.S. Constitution. Reasonable cause may be obtained through an investigation of a prison. According to the DOJ, it decides to investigate when it acquires a "sufficient body of information" to indicate the existence of abuses that may rise to the level of a constitutional violation.[74] The DOJ receives information from a variety of sources, including individual prisoners, public interest and defense attorneys, corrections staff, and politicians. The DOJ receives very few complaints about sexual misconduct directly from women prisoners; rather, private attorneys relay the majority of such complaints.[75] Although the DOJ regularly receives prisoner complaints, it maintains no system for recording individual complaints, nor does it monitor the number of complaints concerning any particular institution or type of problem.

Once the DOJ decides to investigate, it must first file a letter with the state and the prison's director stating its intention to investigate and giving state officials seven days notice. In practice, we were told, the time between giving notice and visiting a facility often exceeds seven days for logistical reasons.[76] During an investigation, DOJ investigators—attorneys with the DOJ and consultants—conduct personal interviews with prisoners, tour the facilities, and review documentation and institutional records to determine whether unconstitutional conditions exist. The DOJ takes the position that it has the authority under CRIPA to determine whether unconstitutional conditions exist, including the right to enter state prisons to examine such conditions.[77] In 1994, one federal court in Michigan refused to issue a court order giving the DOJ access to

---

[74] The investigation itself must be triggered by a published report or information from a source with personal knowledge about allegations that constitutional rights are being violated.

[75] It is important to note that the special litigation section of the DOJ (which enforces CRIPA) does not accept collect telephone calls—the only means by which prisoners can make long-distance telephone calls.

[76] Telephone interview, Department of Justice, Washington D.C., May 8, 1995.

[77] Ibid.

investigate.[78] This decision, however, appears to be the exception rather than the rule.[79]

Once the on-site investigation is complete, the DOJ must issue a letter to the state which summarizes its findings and sets forth the minimum steps necessary to rectify any unconstitutional conditions found. Under CRIPA, forty-nine days after this letter is received by the state, the DOJ may sue the state to remedy the constitutional violations. The U.S. attorney general must personally sign the complaint and, according to DOJ representatives, all possibility of a settlement must be exhausted. As a result, suits are generally filed well after this forty-nine-day period has passed. The DOJ told us that CRIPA contemplates that the state and the DOJ will attempt an amicable resolution of the problem and that many cases are, in fact, resolved through negotiated settlements and consent decrees.[80]

The DOJ is currently exercising its authority under CRIPA to examine conditions in Michigan's women prisons.[81] In June 1994, the DOJ notified Michigan Governor John Engler of its intent to investigate allegations of sexual abuse and other constitutional violations in Michigan's two women's prisons, Scott

---

[78] *United States v. Michigan*, 868 F. Supp. 890 (W.D. Mich. 1994).

[79] Courts prior to the Michigan decision repeatedly upheld DOJ requests to enter institutions and conduct investigations. See *U.S. v. County of Los Angeles*, 635 F. Supp. 588 (C.D. Cal. 1986); *U.S. v. County of Crittenden*, Civil Action No. JC89-141, 1990 WESTLAW 257949 (E.D. Ark. December 26, 1990).

[80] Telephone interview, Department of Justice, May 8, 1995.

[81] The DOJ also has investigated conditions in women's prisons in Alabama and Arizona. It issued findings letters regarding both states. In Alabama, the DOJ found violations involving health care, discipline, and the physical plant. In addition, it found "credible reports" of sexual contact between corrections staff and prisoners. The DOJ denounced such contact as "reprehensible and intolerable" and stated that, given the custodial environment, "the sexual relationships are not appropriate or truly 'voluntary.'" Letter from Deval Patrick, assistant attorney general, Civil Rights Division, U.S. Department of Justice, to Fob James, governor, Alabama, March 27, 1995. The DOJ's investigation in Arizona identified "an unconstitutional pattern or practice of sexual misconduct and constitutionally unacceptable invasions of privacy rights." Such misconduct included, but was not limited to, rape, sexual touching, and degrading language. The privacy violations consisted of officers viewing women prisoners while they used showers and toilets. Letter from Deval Patrick, assistant attorney general, Civil Rights Division, U.S. Department of Justice, to J. Fife Symington, governor, Arizona, August 8, 1996. Both investigations remain open.

Correctional Facility and Florence Crane Correctional Facility. As stated above, Michigan declined to give the DOJ investigators access to the prison. When the DOJ filed suit to compel access, a district court judge refused to issue a temporary restraining order requiring that access be granted.[82] The state subsequently permitted DOJ attorneys to interview prisoners during regular visiting hours and in a nonconfidential setting, but denied the DOJ permission to tour the prisons.[83]

Following these interviews the assistant U.S. attorney general, Deval Patrick, sent a letter to Governor Engler setting forth the DOJ's findings.[84] The DOJ found:

> [T]he sexual abuse of women inmates by guards, including rapes, the lack of adequate medical care, including mental health services, grossly deficient sanitation, crowding, and other threats to the physical safety and well-being of inmates violates their constitutional rights.[85]

The letter recommended remedies to resolve these constitutional violations.[86] To our knowledge, the Michigan Department of Corrections has taken no steps to adopt the recommended measures. Although the mandatory forty-nine-day waiting period has long since elapsed, no suit has been filed, and the DOJ maintains that Michigan is still "under investigation."[87]

---

[82] *United States v. Michigan*, pp. 902-903.

[83] Letter from Deval Patrick, assistant attorney general, Civil Rights Division, U.S. Department of Justice, to John Engler, governor, Michigan, March 27, 1995.

[84] Ibid. This letter is required under CRIPA prior to actually filing suit against the state.

[85] Ibid.

[86] Suggested remedies included developing policies and procedures requiring the reporting of any suspected sexual abuse; not disciplining prisoners for reporting alleged sexual abuse; requiring pat-down searches to be conducted in a professional manner and not to be more intrusive than necessary; and mandating that guards, individual maintenance workers, and other visitors not be permitted to observe prisoners while naked, showering, or using toilet facilities. Ibid.

[87] Interview, Department of Justice, October 1, 1996.

Civil Enforcement: Title 42, U.S. Code, Section 14141

The Violent Crime Control and Law Enforcement Act of 1994 (1994 Crime Bill) added another statute under which the DOJ may enforce the constitutional rights of prisoners. This statute, codified as Title 42, United States Code, Section 14141, states that it is unlawful for any governmental authority or person acting on behalf of any governmental authority

> to engage in a pattern or practice of conduct by law enforcement officers . . . that deprives persons of rights, privileges, or immunities secured or protected by the Constitution or laws of the United States.[88]

The DOJ may sue for declaratory and equitable relief if there is reasonable cause to believe that such a pattern or practice exists. Because the law was enacted recently, its exact scope remains unclear. However, some indications as to its potential application to custodial sexual misconduct are available. The DOJ cited the statute in its findings letter to Michigan Gov. John Engler and stated that, in addition to CRIPA, "the pattern or practice of sexual abuse of women inmates by guards violates [Section 14141]."[89]

The law appears to require a lower burden of proof to challenge abusive treatment by law enforcement officials than CRIPA. CRIPA requires showing a pattern or practice of "egregious or flagrant conditions" causing grievous harm before the DOJ may file suit. By contrast, the new statute does not require that the "pattern or practice of conduct" be "flagrant and egregious," only that it deprive a person of her constitutional rights or rights secured under federal law. In addition, the DOJ may sue under Section 14141 without extensive prior consultation with the relevant department of corrections, as required under CRIPA.

---

[88] 42 U.S.C. Section 14141(a).

[89] Letter from Deval Patrick, assistant attorney general, Civil Rights Division, U.S. Department of Justice, to John Engler, governor, Michigan, March 27, 1995.

Prison Litigation Reform Act

In April 1996 President Clinton signed the Prison Litigation Reform Act (PLRA) into law as part of the Balanced Budget Down Payment Act II of 1996.[90] PLRA dramatically limits the ability of individuals, nongovernmental organizations, and even the Department of Justice to challenge abusive prison conditions through litigation. PLRA invalidates any settlement by the parties to such litigation that does not include an explicit finding or statement that the conditions challenged in the lawsuit violate a federal statute or the constitution. Because prison authorities never want to admit such violations in the consent decrees which frequently settle litigation without trial, such findings are extremely rare. Requiring such findings will make it difficult for parties to reach a settlement in any future prison reform suits, particularly because they would render correctional officials vulnerable to private civil suits. Consequently, most cases are likely to be pursued through a costly and time-consuming trial stage. Further, PLRA arbitrarily terminates any court order against unlawful prison conditions or practices after two years, regardless of the degree of compliance; this is often an unreasonably short time in which to achieve any meaningful change in the way a prison is operated. Thus, a new trial will usually have to be held in order to make a new finding that the old problems persist. The PLRA also restricts court-granted attorneys' fees, the main income for prisoners' rights attorneys. Such restrictions are clearly likely to curtail prison reform litigation. Finally, PLRA severely limits the authority of federal courts to assign judicial officers to oversee prison reform, a key tool for implementing remedial court orders.

PLRA has already begun to affect prison reform efforts. According to Associate Attorney General John Schmidt, the DOJ is engaging in an ill-advised review of all outstanding consent decrees to establish whether they should be terminated under PLRA, regardless of whether the state department of corrections has yet filed any such request.[91] Several municipalities have filed to have their

---

[90] This discussion is drawn from a memorandum by Mark Kappelhoff, legislative counsel, American Civil Liberties Union, on Prison Litigation Reform Act-Impact on Children and Women, June 14, 1996.

[91] Written Testimony of John Schmidt, associate attorney general, U.S. Department of Justice, before the Committee on the Judiciary U.S. Senate concerning Implementation of the Prison Litigation Reform Act, September 25, 1996.

consent decrees overturned,[92] and consent decrees in New York City (governing jails) and in South Carolina were terminated under PLRA,[93] pending appeal. In addition, in the District of Columbia the U.S. Court of Appeals recently remanded the issue of general living conditions and fire safety for female prisoners to the district court to be decided in light of PLRA.[94]

Sexual Contact in Custody: Federal and State Law

The federal government and a fair number of states have criminalized sexual intercourse or sexual contact with a prisoner by a prison employee. Under Title 18, United States Code, Section 2241, it is a felony offense, classified as aggravated sexual abuse, to knowingly cause a person in a federal prison to engage in sexual intercourse by using or threatening the use of force. This offense carries a sentence of imprisonment for any term of years or life. Under Title 18, United States Code, Section 2243 it is also a criminal offense, classified as sexual abuse of a minor or ward, for a person with "custodial, supervisory, or disciplinary" authority to engage in sexual intercourse with or to touch sexually a prisoner in a federal prison.[95] The possible term of imprisonment for this offense is up to one

---

[92] As of June 1996, those included New York City, California, Texas, Iowa, South Carolina and the District of Columbia.

[93] Summary of Prison Litigation Reform Act, National Prison Project, American Civil Liberties Union, August 29, 1996.

[94] *Women Prisoners of the District of Columbia Department of Corrections v. District of Columbia*, 93 F.3d 910 (D.C. Cir. 1996).

[95] 18 United States Code Section 2243 "Sexual abuse of a minor or ward." In its relevant part, Section 2243 (b) reads: "Whoever, . . . in a federal prison, knowingly engages in a sexual act with another person who is (1) in official detention; and (2) under the custodial, supervisory, or disciplinary authority of the person so engaging; or attempts to do so, shall be fined under this title, imprisoned not more than one year, or both."

A "sexual act" is defined under 18 United States Code Section 2246(2) as: "(A) contact between the penis and the vulva or the penis and the anus and . . . contact involving the penis occurs upon penetration, however, slight; (B) contact between the mouth and penis, the mouth and vulva, or the mouth and the anus; or (C)the penetration, however slight, of the anal or genital opening of another by a hand or finger or by any object, with an intent to abuse, humiliate, harass, degrade, or arouse or gratify the sexual desire of any person."

Sexual contact is defined as "the intentional touching, either directly or through

year for sexual intercourse and six months for sexual touching. The only defense specified for this crime is for the defendant to prove that he is married to the victim. These provisions apply only to federal prisons and cannot be applied against corrections officers in state prisons.

The Model Penal Code (MPC),[96] a suggested framework for state penal laws, includes a provision criminalizing both sexual intercourse with and sexual touching of a prisoner by prison staff. Although the MPC is in many respects outdated and in need of amendment, it does classify sexual intercourse with a prisoner as sexual abuse[97] and classifies sexual contact[98] as a form of sexual assault. However, both constitute only misdemeanor offenses under the MPC. The majority of states follow neither the federal law's nor the MPC's framework.

To our knowledge, twenty-seven states and the District of Columbia expressly criminalize sexual intercourse with or sexual touching of a prisoner by

---

clothing, of the genitalia, anus, groin, breast, inner thigh, or buttocks of any person with an intent to abuse, humiliate, harass, degrade or arouse or gratify the sexual desire of any person." 18 United States Code Section 2246(3).

[96] The Model Penal Code was drafted by the American Law Institute in 1962 as a model for state and federal penal codes. To our knowledge, no state has adopted the Model Penal Code in its entirety.

[97] Model Penal Code Section 213.3(1)(c). Sexual intercourse with a prisoner falls under the Section entitled "Corruption of Minors and Seduction," which addresses statutory rape and abuse by those in a guardian or supervisory position. The provision reads in its relevant part: "A male who has sexual intercourse with a female not his wife, or any person who engages in deviate sexual intercourse or causes another to engage in deviate sexual intercourse, is guilty of an offense if: . . . the other person is in custody of the law or detained in a hospital or other institution and the actor has supervisory or disciplinary authority over [her]." Deviate sexual intercourse is defined in Model Penal Code Section 213.0 as "sexual intercourse per os or per anum between human beings who are not husband and wife...."

[98] Sexual contact is defined as "any touching of the sexual or other intimate parts of the person for the purpose of arousing or gratifying sexual desire." Ibid., Section 213.4(8). Section 213.4 further provides: "A person who has sexual contact with another not his spouse, or causes such other to have sexual conduct with him, is guilty of sexual assault, a misdemeanor, if . . . the other person is in custody of law or detained in a hospital or other institution and the actor has supervisory authority over [her]."

prison staff.[99] Five other states have laws that could be read to prohibit sexual contact with a prisoner but which do not refer specifically to incarceration or prison.[100] There are significant differences in the scope of these laws, the way they are categorized, the defenses allowed under them, and their accompanying penalties.[101] In some states, the crime of custodial sexual abuse is limited to sexual activity involving actual penetration; other states define it to include a broad range of sexual acts. In addition, the classification of the offense of custodial sexual

---

[99] In analyzing state laws prohibiting sexual contact between women prisoners and correctional staff we relied on extensive research done by the National Women's Law Center. For a full text of the report, see National Women's Law Center, Fifty-State Survey on State Criminal Laws Prohibiting the Sexual Abuse of Women Prisoners, November 1996. The states that criminalize sex in custody are Alaska, Arizona, Arkansas, California, Colorado, Connecticut, Delaware, Florida, Georgia, Hawaii, Idaho, Indiana, Iowa, Kansas, Louisiana, Maine, Michigan, Missouri, Nevada, New Jersey, New Mexico, New York, North Dakota, Rhode Island, Wisconsin, and South Dakota. See Ariz. Rev. Stat. Ann. §13-1419; Ark. Code Ann. §5-14-109; Cal. Penal Code §289.6; Colo. Rev. Stat. Ann. §18-3-404; Conn. Gen. Stat. §§53a-71 and 53a-73a; Del. Code Ann. title 11, §1259; Fla. Stat. Ann. §944.35; Ga. Code Ann. §16-6-5.1; Haw. Rev. Stat. §§707-731 and 707-732; Idaho Code §18-6110; Iowa Code §709.16; La. Rev. Stat. Ann. title 14, §134.1; Me. Rev. Stat. Ann. title 17-a, §253; Mich. Comp. Laws Ann. §750-520e(d); Nev. Rev. Stat. Ann. §212.187; N.J. Stat. Ann. title 2C, Chapter 14 §2; N.M. Stat. Ann. §30-9-11; N.Y. Penal §130.05(3)(e); N.D. Cent. Code §12.1-20-06; R.I. Gen. Laws § 11-25-24; S.D. Codified Laws Ann. §24-1-26.1.

There has been a fair amount of recent legislative action on this issue. A few of the above states—Arizona, California, Delaware, Florida, New York, Rhode Island and the District of Columbia—enacted their laws within the past two years.

[100] North Carolina has a provision that bars someone with supervisory or disciplinary power over someone or "having custody over someone in an institution, whether such institution be private, charitable or governmental," from having sexual intercourse or contact with that person. N.C. Gen. Stat. §14-27.7. Ohio and Oklahoma have similar prohibitions. Ohio Rev. Code Ann. §2907.03 and Okla. Stat. Ann. title 21, §114. Wyoming's statute is the broadest of this type—it bars anyone in a "position of authority" from using that authority to "cause the victim to submit" to sex. Wyo. Stat. §6-2-303. The Texas statute bars a public servant from coercing another person "to submit or participate" in sexual conduct. Tex. Code Ann. §22.011.

[101] The criminal sanctions for engaging in custodial sexual contact vary from state to state. In most states, the crime is classified as a felony, but a few states classify it as a misdemeanor. There is a fair degree of variation in the possible prison sentences that may be imposed, although most states' penalties stay within the one to five year range.

contact varies greatly from state to state. Oklahoma, for example, classifies it as a form of rape, while many other states describe it as a form of sexual assault or sexual abuse. Significantly, some states, such as Georgia, Arkansas, and Florida, explicitly provide in their criminal statutes that consent is not a defense. By contrast, in a small number of other states, coercion is specifically required. Further, in three states—Arizona, Nevada, and Delaware—the prisoner is also guilty of a crime if the two are found to have engaged in sexual activity.[102] In the view of Human Rights Watch, whatever penological interests may be served by laws that penalize the prisoner for sexual contact with a corrections employee are outweighed by the deterrent effect such punishments will have on the reporting of custodial sexual abuse by prisoners. In addition, while Human Rights Watch does not oppose punishment for prisoners who knowingly submit false allegations of sexual misconduct, such punishment should be used sparingly and only in those instances in which the false report was malicious or manifestly in bad faith.

When we began this investigation, only two of the states that we visited, Michigan and Georgia, had provisions in their penal codes criminalizing sexual contact with a prisoner, and those two states categorize the crime quite differently. While Michigan classifies all sexual contact with a prisoner as a high misdemeanor offense under its rape law, in Georgia the prohibition against sexual contact with prisoners is not contained in the state's rape law but is defined as the distinct felony of sexual assault. Georgia's law does not differentiate between touching and intercourse. The District of Columbia enacted a provision in December 1994 making both sexual intercourse and sexual contact with a prisoner a form of "sexual abuse." Both are felonies.[103] In New York, a bill passed by the New York

---

[102] Nevada law punishes prisoners for sexual conduct with prison staff only when the conduct is voluntary. By contrast, the Arizona statute punishes prisoners who have sexual contact with custodial staff without reference to whether such contact was voluntary; and the Delaware statute specifies that prisoners are criminally responsible for sexual relations with corrections employees and that consent is no defense to the crime. When a guard rapes a prisoner, state statutes criminalizing rape can be used to prosecute the guard. In such instances, prisoners clearly should not be prosecuted for sexual misconduct. However, given the unwillingness of states to recognize the different forms of coercion used by guards to secure sexual contact with prisoners, the real possibility exists under these statutes that a victim of rape could have the crime against her go unrecognized and instead be prosecuted for unlawful sexual relations.

[103] A person found guilty of sexual intercourse with a prisoner, or first degree sexual abuse of a ward, may be imprisoned up to ten years and fined; and, a person found guilty of sexual contact with a prisoner, second degree sexual abuse of a ward, may be imprisoned up to five

state legislature and signed by Gov. George Pataki on July 2, 1996 criminalized all sexual contact between a corrections employee and a prisoner.[104] California passed a bill in 1994 that prohibits all sexual intercourse in custody between corrections staff and prisoners—the first violation of this prohibition is a misdemeanor; any subsequent violation is a felony. Illinois has no such law.

As the above summary suggests, existing federal and state laws regarding sexual contact in custody—both intercourse and touching—provide a hodgepodge of often inadequate and inconsistent protections against sexual intercourse or sexual touching between an officer and a prisoner. The absence of appropriate, clear and consistent federal and state legal prohibitions on sexual intercourse and other forms of sexual contact only contributes to the prevalence of such abuse in women's prisons across the United States and the failure adequately to prosecute it. Legal reform is therefore of utmost importance if custodial sexual abuse in U.S. prisons is to be successfully eliminated.

Accordingly, Human Rights Watch supports legislative changes in state rape and sexual assault laws to recognize that a correctional officer who engages in sexual relations with a prisoner is committing a serious crime. Where sexual intercourse or touching is accompanied by the overt use or threat of force, retribution, or coercion, it constitutes rape or sexual assault and should be considered a felony offense.

In many instances, the use of force by correctional staff to secure sexual relations with prisoners can take the form of the promise or provision of goods or other non-material benefits. Because of the restricted nature of the prison environment, promises of privileges or goods which the corrections officers are authorized to withhold or supply can carry with them actual or implied threats of deprivation. When correctional employees abuse their authority in this way, it should be understood as a form of pressuring the prisoner to engage in sexual relations and should be prosecuted as rape or sexual assault.

In other cases, correctional officers may offer goods or privileges but without any actual or perceived threat to the prisoner. This conduct should still be punished more severely than in those cases in which no rewards are offered or bestowed at all. This stiffer penalty reflects a recognition that prisoners have limited resources and privileges, and thus the promise of benefits always carries special weight. These cases, in which the provision or promise of benefits or goods

---

years and fined. It appears that the District of Columbia uses the term "sexual abuse" for all forms of sexual assault, including rape. D.C. Code 1981 Section 22-4100 et seq.

[104] N.Y. Penal §130.05(3)(e).

in exchange for sexual relations was not overtly or, by implication, coercive, nor was it understood by the prisoner as such, should be prosecuted as felonious sexual abuse.

In still other cases, guards engage in sexual intercourse or touching with prisoners absent force, coercion or the exchange of material goods or privileges. Despite the lack of overt or implied force or coercion or of any type of exchange, this conduct should still be considered a criminal sexual act. Any person with custodial power over another has enormous authority; within the confines of a prison, that authority is nearly absolute. Officers have the power to influence everything from a prisoner's parole date, to her work assignment, to her access to essential goods and amenities, and they have a corresponding obligation to ensure that this power is never abused. Thus even in the absence of the implied or actual use of force or any exchange of privileges or goods, for an officer to step across the line and have sexual relations with a person in his custody is a gross violation of professional duty. This act may not constitute rape, sexual assault, or sexual abuse but should, at a minimum, be recognized as criminal sexual contact and be punishable as a felony. An inquiry into the victim's alleged consent to such conduct should be unnecessary to establish this breach of professional duty or any other crime of custodial sexual abuse. Rather, the focus should be on the degree of pressure exerted by the officer or other correctional employee to determine the seriousness of the offense.

Access to the Courts and Grievance Mechanisms

Under the U.S. Constitution, prisoners are guaranteed access to the courts to challenge their incarceration, prison conditions, or other abuses. The U.S. Supreme Court has held that the constitution requires that prisoners have access to either adequate law libraries or legal services to exercise their right of access to the courts.[105] However, the Supreme Court recently limited the right to legal assistance. The court held in *Lewis v. Casey* that a prisoner must prove that shortcomings in the law library or legal assistance program actually hindered her efforts to pursue a "nonfrivolous" legal claim.[106] The court also stated that delays of up to sixteen days in providing legal assistance or materials to prisoners segregated from the general population for disciplinary or security reasons, which were the product of regulations reasonably related to legitimate penological interests, were constitutional, even if such delays caused the prisoner actual

---

[105] *Bounds v. Smith*, 430 U.S. 817 (1977).

[106] *Lewis v. Casey*, 116 S.Ct. 2174 (1996).

injury.[107] Although *Casey* stated that such prisoners are usually the most dangerous and violent prisoners,[108] we found that women prisoners were often placed in administrative segregation for reporting custodial sexual misconduct. Thus, the holding in *Casey* could allow prison officials to prevent these women from pursuing legitimate legal claims based on this misconduct.

Lower federal courts, interpreting the constitutional right of access to the courts, have rejected as unconstitutional practices or procedures instituted by prison administrators that hinder or restrict open access.[109] Nor may prisoners be punished for allegations made in their court papers.[110] In addition, legal correspondence and legal papers are protected from censorship by prison administrators. While the Supreme Court has upheld rules that allow prison administrators to open and inspect correspondence to or from attorneys, such inspection must occur in the prisoner's presence.[111] Lower federal courts have interpreted the Supreme Court's ruling to mean that prison administrators should not read a prisoner's legal mail and that legal mail may not be withheld from a prisoner on the basis of its content.[112] The states we visited have incorporated such provisions into their administrative codes, policies, or directives governing legal correspondence but do not always respect such protections in practice.[113]

While access to the courts is a constitutionally guaranteed right, federal law permits and encourages state departments of corrections to enact grievance mechanisms to handle prisoner complaints outside the context of a lawsuit. These mechanisms are intended to respond to a broad array of complaints within the prison, ranging from problems receiving mail, to inaccuracies in a prisoner's

---

[107] Ibid., p. 2185.

[108] Ibid.

[109] Sheldon Krantz, *Corrections & Prisoners Rights* (Minnesota: West Publishing, 1988), p. 252.

[110] *Hilliard v. Scully*, 537 F. Supp. 1084 (S.D.N.Y. 1982).

[111] *Wolff v. McDonnell*, 418 U.S. 539 (1974).

[112] Krantz, *Corrections & Prisoners Rights*, p. 252, citing *Thornley v. Edwards*, 671 F. Supp. 339 (M.D. Pa. 1987) and *Goodwin v. Oswald*, 462 F.2d 1237 (2d Cir. 1972.)

[113] See Illinois chapter.

account of a particular incident, to staff misconduct and abuse. States may, at their option, request to have their grievance procedure certified under CRIPA.[114]

Notwithstanding women prisoners' formally recognized right to complain of abuses, in every women's prison discussed in this report, we found routine violations of these basic due process protections with respect to complaints of sexual misconduct. No state we visited adequately ensures that female prisoners can speedily and effectively complain of such abuse with confidence that it will be impartially investigated and remedied and without fear that they will face retaliation or even punishment. International human rights law sets forth additional protections against and potential remedies for such problems, but unfortunately, as the next section details, U.S. noncompliance with these norms effectively denies women prisoners their full array of rights.

International Human Rights Law

As the above section suggests, U.S. state and federal laws do provide some important protection from custodial sexual misconduct. However, international human rights laws, by which the U.S. is also bound, provide some protections currently denied to prisoners under U.S. law. Unfortunately, in both law and practice, the U.S. often falls short of meeting its obligations to ensure that these protections are available to those who suffer such abuse. The United States has ratified the two principal international treaties that protect the human rights of prisoners: the International Covenant on Civil and Political Rights (ICCPR) in 1993 and the Convention Against Torture and Other Cruel, Inhuman, or Degrading Treatment and Punishment (Torture Convention) in 1994. The U.S. is also bound by the principles set forth in the Universal Declaration of Human Rights on torture

---

[114] CRIPA sets forth a limited number of conditions for certification of a grievance procedure. Under the statute, prisoners must have an opportunity to participate in the "formulation, implementation and operation of the system." 42 U.S.C. Section 1997e(b)(2)(A)-(E). In addition, there must be maximum time limits for each level of review, within which each state must provide a written disposition of the complaint and the reasons for the disposition. Third, the plan must include a mechanism for rapid processing of emergency grievances. Next, there must be safeguards in place to protect prisoners against reprisals. Finally, the plan must provide a mechanism for independent review by a person or entity not under the direct supervision or control of the institution. Guidelines promulgated by the U.S. Attorney General pursuant to CRIPA also mandate that the grievance system apply to a broad range of complaints, including "actions by employees and [prisoners], and incidents occurring within the institution that affect them personally," and that it provide meaningful remedies to prisoners using the system. 28 C.F.R. Section 40 (1984).

and cruel, inhuman or degrading treatment or punishment, which have the weight of customary law.[115] In addition, the United Nations Standard Minimum Rules for the Treatment of Prisoners,[116] the Basic Principles for the Treatment of Prisoners,[117] and the Body of Principles for the Protection of All Persons under Any Form of Detention or Imprisonment[118] provide authoritative guidance under international law for interpreting the more general rules of the ICCPR and Torture Convention.[119]

These international laws contain protections that clearly apply to custodial sexual abuse. Under the ICCPR and the Torture Convention, for example, state parties are obligated to ensure that no one is subjected to torture or to cruel, inhuman or degrading punishment and treatment.[120] These treaties and the

---

[115] Montreal Statement of the Assembly for Human Rights, *Journal of the International Commission of Jurists*, volume 9, p. 94 (1968).

[116] Standard Minimum Rules for the Treatment of Prisoners, adopted by the First United Nations Congress on the Prevention of Crime and the Treatment of Offenders, reprinted in United Nations, *A Compilation of International Instruments:* Volume 1 (first part) Universal Instruments (New York: United Nations, 1993), E.93.XIV.I, pp. 243-62.

[117] Adopted and proclaimed by General Assembly resolution 45/111 of December 14, 1990, reprinted in *A Compilation of International Instruments*, pp. 263-264.

[118] Adopted by General Assembly resolution 43/173 of December 9, 1988, reprinted in *A Compilation of International Instruments*, pp. 265-274.

[119] Nigel Rodley, *The Treatment of Prisoners Under International Law* (New York: Oxford University Press, 1987), p. 222. In *Lareau v. Manson*, 507 F. Supp. 1177 (D. Conn. 1980), affirmed in part, remanded in part on other grounds, 651 F.2d 96 (2d Cir. 1981), the court described the Standard Minimum Rules for the Treatment of Prisoners as ". . . establishing standards for decent and humane conduct by all nations" or as "[c]onstituting an authoritative international statement of basic norms of human dignity and of certain practices that are repugnant to the conscience of mankind." *Lareau*, pp. 1192-93, 1188.

[120] International Covenant on Civil and Political Rights, adopted and opened for signature, ratification and accession by General Assembly resolution 2200 A (XXI) of 16 December 1966, reprinted in United Nations, *A Compilation of International Instruments:* Volume 1 (first part) Universal Instruments (New York: United Nations, 1993), E.93.XIV.I, art. 7, p. 23; Convention against Torture and Other Cruel, Inhuman or Degrading Treatment or Punishment, adopted and opened for signature, ratification and accession by General Assembly resolution 39/46 of 10 December 1984, reprinted in United Nations, *A*

Standard Minimum Rules for the Treatment of Prisoners further require states to ensure that those who engage in such abuse are appropriately punished and that individuals seeking to complain about such ill-treatment are provided with an effective remedy. Finally, Article 17 of the ICCPR protects all individuals against arbitrary interference with their privacy, and the Standard Minimum Rules specify that the privacy of female prisoners should be respected by male corrections staff.

The remainder of this section details the full scope of the U.S. obligations under international human rights law, the manner in which the U.S. is wrongfully attempting to limit these obligations or is failing to apply them, and the specific acts of custodial sexual misconduct to which the U.S. should ensure that the full scope of its international obligations are applied.

The United States' Non-Compliance

The U.S. government has ratified the ICCPR and the Torture Convention and thus is bound by the instruments. At the same ti me, however, the U.S. attempted to limits obligations under these treaties by attaching reservations, declarations, and understandings to both.[121] Several of these reservations, declarations, and understandings were designed to limit U.S. accountability under the treaties in ways that are extremely adverse, among other things, to the elimination of custodial sexual misconduct. In Human Rights Watch's view, as discussed below, the U.S. reservations and declarations in this regard are both politically ill-conceived and legally indefensible. Accordingly, we hold the U.S. to the full scope of the relevant international obligations.

Human Rights Watch takes particular issue with the fact that in ratifying the ICCPR and Torture Convention, the United States declared the provisions of

---

Compilation of International Instruments: Volume 1 (first part) Universal Instruments (New York: United Nations, 1993), E.93.XIV.I, pp. 293-307.

[121] The United States government attached three reservations, five understandings, and two declarations to its ratification of the Torture Convention. Five reservations, five understandings, and four declarations accompanied the ICCPR.

In addition, the United States has not ratified the First Optional Protocol to the ICCPR and did not declare itself bound by Article 22 of the Torture Convention. The protocol and Article 22 allow the committees responsible for monitoring compliance with the treaties to receive complaints from individuals and organizations, in addition to complaints from other governments. The effect of these positions, combined with the lack of adequate enforcement at the state level of prohibitions on torture and cruel, inhuman, and degrading treatment, is to deny U.S. citizens and others who allege that rights contained in those treaties have been violated any means of having their grievances heard or resolved.

both treaties to be "non-self-executing;" that is, without enabling legislation, they could not be relied upon to bring suit in U.S. courts. The United States then failed to adopt any enabling legislation to remedy this shortcoming. If the U.S. retains the non-self-executing declarations and fails to adopt legislation, it effectively denies individuals the right to sue the government for noncompliance with these treaties.[122]

The U.S. government justifies the lack of such legislation by asserting that existing state and federal law adequately protect against violations of the treaty. Thus far, the U.S. has not enacted legislation to implement the provisions of the ICCPR, and the only legislation enacted to implement the Torture Convention allows individuals who claim that they were tortured outside the United States to file suit in U.S. courts.[123] According to an internal State Department memorandum, the U.S. government believes that no further implementing legislation is necessary to allow individuals tortured within the U.S. to file suit under the Torture Convention because all fifty U.S. states already prohibit torture under their criminal statutes.   But this rationale is inadequate to meet U.S. obligations under international human rights law. The State Department view presupposes that state legal systems are enforcing prohibitions on torture and other cruel, inhuman, or degrading treatment or punishment, when, as this report demonstrates, some states are not. In such circumstances, the federal government has a duty to enforce the prohibition against these acts both by pressuring state prosecutorial authorities to pursue such cases and by creating a separate federal crime to ensure that the failure of states to enforce these protections does not leave victims of such abuse without any federal recourse.

Moreover, to the extent that state or federal law defines torture, for example, more narrowly than does international law, individuals should be able to invoke the broader definition of torture available under international law to attack actions not prohibited by the narrower definition of torture under the state or federal law. For example, the existing U.S. implementing legislation regarding the Torture Convention defines torture much more restrictively than does international law. The Torture Convention defines one element of torture as causing "severe

---

[122] Restatement of the Law Third: The Foreign Relations Law of the United States, volume 1 (Minnesota: American Law Institute, 1987), Section 111(3).

[123] The U.S. government did enact limited provisions under the Torture Convention to broaden its jurisdiction over acts that were committed outside its territory but where the alleged abuser was located in the United States. 18 U.S.C. Section 2340 et. seq., Chapter 113B, "Torture."

mental pain or suffering." The U.S. legislation, however, recognizes only mental suffering that is prolonged and that results from one of four things—intentional or threatened harm, administration of "mind-altering substances," threat of imminent death, or threat that another person will be killed or physically harmed.[124] The U.S. legislation thus recognizes as torture only those acts that meet additional requirements not found in the international standard. This definition of torture limits the applicability of the Torture Convention and denies the treaty's broader protections to individuals who have suffered acts that, under the internationally recognized definition, would constitute torture.

Human Rights Watch is equally concerned that in ratifying the ICCPR, the U.S. government attempted, through its reservation to Article 7 prohibiting torture or cruel, inhuman, or degrading treatment, to limit the treaty's applicability to only the eight amendment, which addresses exclusively cruel and unusual punishments. As a consequence, individuals that suffer acts that Article 7 of the ICCPR prohibits but that have not been recognized as violations of the U.S. Constitution, cannot claim the broader protection of the treaty and may thus be left with no recourse whatsoever. Although much of the sexual misconduct discussed in this report is arguably prohibited by the U.S. Constitution as cruel and unusual punishments, not all of it is encompassed by this protection. Thus, acts of torture or cruel and inhuman punishment that do not meet the eighth amendment's stringent intent requirements—whereby, as discussed above in greater detail, prison officials are culpable only if they acted maliciously and sadistically—may not be covered. Moreover, the U.S. government itself has stated that degrading treatment—clearly prohibited by the ICCPR and the Torture Convention—is "probably not . . . prohibited by the U.S. Constitution."[125]

While international law does permit governments to make reservations to international treaties, such reservations cannot be incompatible with the object and purpose of the treaty.[126] The view of Human Rights Watch that the U.S. reservations and declarations discussed above are in fact incompatible, is supported by comments of the U.N. Human Rights Committee, which has responsibility for

---

[124] Ibid.

[125] Message from the President of the United States Transmitting the Convention Against Torture and Other Cruel, Inhuman or Degrading Treatment or Punishment, May 23, 1988, p. 15.

[126] Article 19(3) of the Vienna Convention on the Law of Treaties stipulates that a State may make a reservation provided it is not incompatible with the object and purpose of the treaty.

interpreting and monitoring compliance with the ICCPR. In a General Comment, the committee stated that countries must not ratify a treaty with exceptions "designed to remove [guarantees to provide the necessary framework for securing the rights in the ICCPR]."[127] The U.S. reservations have also been challenged by several other states parties to the treaties.

The U.S. reservation to Article 7—limiting its scope to acts already prohibited by U.S. law—has been cited as incompatible with the object and purpose of the ICCPR by several governments, including Denmark, Finland, France, Germany, Italy, the Netherlands, Norway, Portugal, Spain, and Sweden.[128] Since treaties have to be interpreted in good faith and in accordance with their plain meaning, the effect is not that the ratification of the treaty is invalid, but that the reservation is invalid. Therefore, Human Rights Watch holds the U.S. to be bound by the full scope of the right.

The Human Rights Committee has further asserted that reservations that effectively deprive individuals of the means to secure their rights are not acceptable.[129] The fact that the United States has declared the ICCPR and the Torture Convention to be non-self-executing and thus has denied individuals federal recourse to remedy human rights violations prohibited by these treaties that are not being remedied in state courts, effectively denies individuals the ability to challenge these violations in any court. Arguably then, the U.S. declaration effectively denies individuals access to the means by which they might secure the

---

[127] Human Rights Committee, General Comment 24, Adopted by Human Rights Committee Under Article 40, Paragraph 4 of the International Covenant of Civil and Political Rights, CCPR/C/21/ Rev.1/Add.6, November 2, 1994, p. 4. Consistent with the Vienna Convention, the Human Rights Committee, the U.N. body of experts created to interpret the provisions of the ICCPR, stated "reservations that offend preemptory norms would not be compatible with the object and purpose of the Covenant." Ibid., p. 3.

[128] Multilateral Treaties Deposited with the Secretary General, ST/LEG/Ser.E/13., December 31, 1994, pp. 127-130.

[129] Human Rights Committee, General Comment 24, para.11.

rights protected by the ICCPR.[130] As such, the declaration that the treaty is non-self-executing is incompatible with the object and purpose of the treaty.[131]

However, regardless of whether a treaty is self-executing, the president or executive branch is obligated to ensure that it is executed faithfully, because under the constitution international treaties are part of the supreme law of the land. Therefore, at a minimum, if the U.S. government is to live up to its international obligation to prevent and remedy custodial sexual misconduct, it should revise existing federal laws to comply with its international obligations under both the ICCPR and the Torture Convention, instruct law enforcement and other government bodies to act in conformity with the ratified treaties, monitor federal and state bodies for compliance with the treaty obligations, and sue state authorities for noncompliance. The U.S. Supreme Court has stated that U.S. domestic law should be construed by courts to avoid violations of the U.S. government's obligations under international law, including customary law.[132]

Moreover, the fifty states, although not themselves parties to international treaties, are obliged to obey federal law, which includes customary international law and all international treaties ratified by the U.S. Senate.[133] Where state practices or laws are inconsistent with international treaties acceded to by the U.S., the state must change such practices or laws, or the federal government must

---

[130] Although the U.S. position on the self-executing nature of the ICCPR is laid out in a declaration and not in a reservation, the standard of compatibility with the object and purpose of the treaty still applies. According to the committee, "Regard will be had to the intention of the State, rather than the form of the instrument. If a statement, irrespective of its name or title, purports to exclude or modify the legal effect of a treaty in its application to the State, it constitutes a reservation." Human Rights Committee, General Comment 24, para. 3.

[131] In regard to the Convention on the Elimination of Racial Discrimination recently ratified by the U.S. government, Human Rights Watch also believes the U.S. has an obligation to "ensure that the guarantees of the treaty are available to all persons within the U.S., whether through provision of independent federal remedies or through appropriate action to ensure that state and local laws are in compliance with the obligations of the treaty." Letter from Human Rights Watch, International Human Rights Law Group, and NAACP Legal Defense and Education Fund to Warren Christopher, U.S. Secretary of State, October 27, 1995.

[132] *Murray v. The Schooner Charming Betsy*, 6 U.S. 64, p. 118 (1804).

[133] Restatement of the Law Third, Section 111(1).

compel the state to comply with the international treaties.[134] The U.S. government itself acknowledged in an understanding to the ICCPR that the federal government would implement the ICCPR to "the extent that it exercises legislative and judicial jurisdiction over the matters," and that it would ensure that state and local authorities fulfill their obligations under the ICCPR in the areas over which they have jurisdiction.[135]

The Use of International Law as an Interpretative Guide
Custodial Sexual Misconduct as Torture and Cruel, Inhuman, and Degrading Treatment

Most of the custodial sexual misconduct in this report constitutes either torture or cruel, inhuman, or degrading treatment as defined by international law. A number of instances of sexual intercourse between officers and prisoners in custody documented in this report involve prison staff members who use force, the threat of force, or other means of coercion to compel a prisoner to engage in sexual intercourse. These cases constitute rape and therefore, torture.[136] Prison staff have also used force or coercion to engage in sexual touching of prisoners, including aggressively squeezing, groping, or prodding women's genitals or breasts. As the testimonies in this report demonstrate, these acts often involve a violent assault that causes severe physical and mental suffering. As such, they, too, amount to torture.

Other instances of sexual intercourse that we documented which do not amount to rape but constitute sexual abuse as defined above, may also constitute torture or cruel or inhuman treatment, depending on the level of physical or mental suffering involved. This is also true of sexual touching that amounts to sexual assault. Other forms of sexual misconduct that do not constitute rape or sexual assault or abuse, rise to neither the level of torture nor of cruel or inhuman treatment, but may be condemned as degrading treatment, that is, treatment that

---

[134] Ibid., Section 111, comment d.

[135] Understanding 5, U.S. Reservations, Understandings, and Declarations to the ICCPR, October 5, 1992.

[136] Rape has been recognized as a form of torture. The U.N. Special Rapporteur on Torture, for example, has documented the use of rape in custody as a method of torture. Report by the Special Rapporteur, P. Koojimans, appointed pursuant to Commission on Human Rights resolution 1985/33, U.N. Doc. E/CN.4/1986/15 (February 19, 1986), p. 29.

causes or is intended to cause gross humiliation or an insult to a person's dignity.[137] This includes inappropriate pat or strip searches and verbal harassment.

The manner in which strip searches and pat searches are conducted, while clearly infringing upon the privacy rights of prisoners, can also constitute a form of degrading treatment. The mere performance of a strip search or a pat search by a correctional officer for the purpose of controlling contraband is not, in and of itself, degrading treatment. For example, the use of close body searches for a valid purpose has been upheld under international law.[138] However, the fondling and groping of women in the course of a strip search or a pat search serves no penological purpose; it is extraneous to the search for contraband and unnecessarily invades a prisoner's physical integrity and humiliates her. Furthermore, the use of pat searches as a means of retaliation, and the targeting of specific women for such searches without due cause, also violates these principles and constitutes degrading treatment.

The prohibition on degrading treatment also extends to the use of demeaning language, where the employment of such language is intended to dehumanize and weaken an incarcerated person.[139] In the *Greek* case, the European Commission found that "psychological pressure designed to break the will" of prisoners, including verbal harassment and humiliation, was prohibited under Article 3 of the European Convention on Human Rights. It specifically relied on examples in which officials told prisoners, "you have excrement in your soul. . . . Your daughters are prostitutes."[140] While isolated name calling may not rise to the

---

[137] The European Commission on Human Rights has done the most to clarify a definition of degrading treatment. In the *Greek Case*, the commission defined degrading treatment as that which "grossly humiliates one before others or drives him to act against his will or conscience." *Greek Case*, 1969 Y.B. Eur. Conv. on H.R. (Eur. Comm'n on H.R.) 186. The Commission elaborated in the *East Asian Africans Case*: degrading treatment must "lower the victim in rank, position, reputation or character whether in his own eyes or in the eyes of other people," as well as cause serious humiliation. *East Asian Africans v. United Kingdom*, App. No. 4403/70, 3 Eur. H.R. Rep. 76, 80 (1981) (Commission report).

[138] The European Commission upheld the use of close body searches where there was a history of concealed objects. *McFeeley v. United Kingdom*, App. No. 8317/78, 3 European Human Rights Reporter, p. 201 (1980) (Commission Report).

[139] *The Greek Case*, 1969 Yearbook of European Convention on Human Rights, pp. 462-3 (1969).

[140] Ibid., p. 463.

level of degrading treatment, a pattern of such language or the use of such language in combination with obscene gestures and physical advances may create an environment of pressure or harassment that leads to humiliation sufficient to constitute degrading treatment.

Custodial Sexual Misconduct: A Violation of the International Right to Privacy

In the same way that the U.S. government is accountable under international law for preventing torture and ill-treatment, it is also required to uphold prisoners' privacy rights as codified in the ICCPR and the Standard Minimum Rules. In fact, unlike the articles governing torture and ill-treatment, the U.S. government did not enter a reservation to Article 17 of the ICCPR with respect to the right to privacy other than the non-self-executing declaration that applied to all the substantive articles of the treaty. The U.S. government's decision not to enter any reservations with respect to this right in particular, suggests that the U.S. intends to comply fully with the ICCPR standard or, at least, that such standard is not understood to impose any obligation greater than that under current U.S. law.

The Human Rights Committee, which interprets the ICCPR, has spoken directly to the use of personal and body searches. In its General Comment 16 to Article 17, the committee stated:

> So far as personal and body searches are concerned, effective measures should ensure that such searches are carried out in a manner consistent with the dignity of the person who is being searched. Persons being subjected to body searches by State officials, or medical personnel acting at the request of the State, should only be examined by persons of the same sex.[141]

In hearings before the U.N. Human Rights Committee, the U.S. government has taken the position that it is substantially in compliance with the right to privacy as established by the ICCPR. The U.S. government told the Human Rights Committee that:

---

[141] General Comment 16 to Article 17, "Compilation of General Comments and General Recommendations Adopted by Human Rights Treaty Bodies," U.N. Document HRI/GEN/Rev.1, July 29, 1994.

> In order to protect the privacy of female inmates, only female officers are permitted to conduct strip searches or body cavity searches, except in cases of emergency situation. Male officers work in the women's housing units, but they are admonished to respect the inmates' privacy by not intentionally observing them in a state of undress.[142]

However, our investigation revealed that such protections quite often are not in place in the state prisons, and that in practice, norms regulating the role of male officers are not followed for both body searches and housing areas. With respect to the use of male guards to conduct strip searches, in particular, we find that the U.S. falls far short of ensuring the protections provided under international law. We found that strip searches often occur in the presence of male officers and that pat-frisks are conducted in an abusive manner by male guards. Moreover, Michigan and California explicitly permit all corrections officers to make random and unannounced searches of housing areas.

We affirm the Human Rights Committee's general comment opposing cross-gender strip searches as a necessary measure to protect the privacy of incarcerated women as well as their individual dignity and bodily integrity. Strip searches, except in extreme and limited cases of emergency, should only be conducted by corrections officers of the same sex as the prisoner and in a location where individuals of the opposite sex are not in a position to observe the search. To the extent possible, we also believe that pat searches should be carried out by corrections officers of the same sex. We recognize that pat searches are less invasive than strip searches, but evidence indicates that corrections officers have used such searches to grope women and violate their personal dignity and bodily integrity. Corrections officers of both sexes must be fully trained to conduct pat searches in a respectful and professional manner.

Custodial Sexual Misconduct and International Rights to an Effective Remedy

International law also obliges the United States to ensure that prisoners may raise complaints of ill-treatment, that such complaints are investigated promptly and impartially that abusers are punished, and that complainants are protected from retaliation or punishment. As with respect to the right of privacy, the U.S. did not reserve on any of these articles under either the ICCPR or the

---

[142] Press Release, General Assembly, "Human Rights Committee Concludes Consideration of Initial Report of the United States," HR/CT/405, March 31, 1995, p. 4.

Torture Convention. Thus, the U.S. has indicated its willingness to comply fully with these protections. Unfortunately, U.S. practice with respect to guaranteeing an effective remedy in cases of custodial misconduct again falls far short of the international standards set forth in detail below.

Article 13 of the Torture Convention requires the United States to ensure that a person alleging she was tortured or ill-treated has the right to complain,[143] as does Article 3 of the ICCPR, which requires an effective remedy for all rights contained in the convention. As noted above, the authoritative Standard Minimum Rules provide a more detailed structure to protect this right and to ensure that prisoners are able to gain access to a complaint mechanism. Rule 35 mandates that prisoners receive written information about the "authorized methods of seeking information and making complaints, and all such other matters as are necessary to enable [her] to understand [her] rights and [her] obligations." Rule 36 stresses the right of prisoners to raise a complaint to one of several individuals, including the director of a prison, a prison inspector or the central administration.[144] The Rule also provides that unless these complaints are "evidently frivolous or groundless," prison administrators must respond promptly and "without undue delay." The authoritative Body of Principles for the Protection of All Persons under Any Form of Detention or Imprisonment provides that prisoners "have the right to make a request or complaint regarding [their] treatment . . . to the authorities responsible

---

[143] Article 13 of the Torture Convention must be read together with Article 16 regarding allegations of cruel, inhuman or degrading treatment or punishment.

[144] Rule 36 provides:

> (1) Every prisoner shall have the opportunity . . . of making requests or complaints to the director of the institution or the officer authorized to represent [her].

> (2) It shall be possible to make requests or complaints to the inspector of prisons during his [or her] inspection. The prisoner shall have the opportunity to talk to the inspector or to any other inspecting officer without the director or other members of the staff being present.

> (3) Every prisoner shall be allowed to make a request or complaint, without censorship as to substance but in proper form, to the central prison administration, the judicial authority or other proper authorities through approved channels. . . .

for the administration of the place of detention and to higher authorities, and, when necessary, to appropriate authorities vested with reviewing or remedial powers."[145]

The ICCPR and Torture Convention, furthermore, obligate the U.S. to provide and ensure that certain remedies are available to those prisoners alleging acts of torture or cruel, inhuman or degrading treatment or punishment. The Human Rights Committee, the body officially charged with interpreting the ICCPR, has ruled that the prohibition on torture and cruel, inhuman, or degrading treatment or punishment in Article 7 carries with it a positive obligation for state parties to investigate complaints of ill-treatment effectively, punish those found guilty, and provide remedies to the victim, including compensation.[146] The Torture Convention explicitly sets forth these requirements in Article 12.[147] The Body of Principles also underscores the importance of these protections by imposing in Principle 7 an obligation on government agents to report allegations of misconduct and by directing governments to conduct impartial investigations when they receive such complaints.[148]

Each of the states we visited provides a grievance mechanism to prisoners. However, we found that obstacles often hinder the ability of prisoners to file complaints or to see them fully pursued. Prisoners do not always receive information about the grievance mechanism, and some women we interviewed were entirely unfamiliar with the grievance process. In addition, an informal stage included in the grievance process in several states we visited often discourages women from filing complaints and prevents their complaints from reaching appropriate higher authorities. The informal level is particularly problematic in cases of sexual misconduct because it requires the woman to confront her abuser, and in essence, request him to acknowledge that he has abused her and violated her rights before she can file a formal complaint. Women prisoners who understandably fear taking this step are thus effectively shut out of the grievance system and denied the right to raise their charge through the complaints procedure.

---

[145] Body of Principles, Principle 33 (1).

[146] General Comment 7 to Article 7, "Compilation of General Comments and General Recommendations Adopted by Human Rights Treaty Bodies," U.N. Document HRI/GEN/Rev.1, July 29, 1994.

[147] Article 16 of the Torture Convention provides that the obligations under Articles 10, 11, 12, and 13 apply to acts of cruel, inhuman or degrading treatment or punishment.

[148] Body of Principles, Principle 7.

We also found that official investigations of staff misconduct often were fraught with many of the same irregularities as the grievance process.

Provisions governing the right of prisoners to complain of misconduct and the duty of state officials to investigate such allegations frequently are accompanied by an obligation to protect complainants from retaliation and mistreatment. Article 13 of the Torture Convention provides that steps must be taken to protect the complainant and her witnesses from all ill-treatment or intimidation in retaliation for filing a complaint or providing information. Such protections are reiterated in the Body of Principles; Principle 33 emphasizes a prisoner's right to complain of mistreatment and explicitly requires that a complainant not "suffer prejudice" for making a complaint. Yet, in the U.S. women's prisons that we investigated, such retaliation—and in some cases, official punishment—was commonplace.

We found that many prisoners who raised allegations of staff sexual misconduct were placed in administrative segregation or protective custody. There is nothing in either U.N. resolutions or any international human rights convention providing for the physical separation of either the prisoner who raises a complaint of staff misconduct or her witnesses. Rather, international law recognizes that such segregation is often punitive.[149] Within the Standard Minimum Rules, segregation is addressed solely in terms of the punishment of prisoners and is viewed as a punitive measure.[150] International law also mandates that efforts be made to limit the application of solitary confinement, for whatever purpose.[151]

This does not mean, however, that segregation or solitary confinement *per se*, constitutes a violation of a prisoner's rights, in particular, since a state has a positive obligation to protect the bodily integrity of the prisoner. In the U.S. this protective, rather than punitive, practice is often termed "administrative segregation" or "protective custody." Unfortunately, in the women's prisons that

---

[149] Human Rights Watch does not oppose the use of disciplinary punishment as a valid measure to discipline prisoners who violate prison rules. Both the Standard Minimum Rules and Body of Principles recognize its use and set forth rules governing its exercise. Standard Minimum Rules, Rule 29, and Body of Principles, Principle 30.

[150] The Standard Minimum Rules refer to segregation as "close confinement."

[151] Principle 7 of the 1990 Basic Principles states, "Efforts addressed to the abolition of solitary confinement as a punishment, or to the restriction on its use, should be undertaken and encouraged." Moreover, in its General Comment 20, the U.N. Human Rights Committee noted that "prolonged solitary confinement of the detained or imprisoned person may amount to acts prohibited by Article 7 [of the ICCPR]." U.N. Human Rights Committee General Comment 20 (Forty-fourth session, 1992).

we visited, we found that administrative segregation or protective custody is not only viewed as punitive by many prisoners, but, in fact, often is punitive. Such protective custody has in some cases amounted to solitary confinement. (Prisoners placed in administrative segregation or protective custody, who have committed no disciplinary offense, are subjected to the same treatment as prisoners serving disciplinary sentences.) To make matters worse, they are denied the basic protections that are available to those prisoners placed in segregation on disciplinary grounds.

Therefore, in our view, administrative segregation or protective custody is inherently punitive for prisoners who have filed a complaint of staff misconduct because it results in the physical separation of the prisoner from the general population and correspondingly results in a certain loss of freedom within the confines of the prison when the prisoner herself has done nothing wrong. Its use, therefore, should be restricted to circumstances when the prison administration has reasonable cause to believe that the prisoner's safety is in jeopardy, consistent with the international legal obligation to protect a prisoner's bodily integrity, or when a prisoner explicitly requests protective custody within prison, particularly since segregated custody on nondisciplinary grounds may be perceived as a repercussion for raising a complaint of staff mistreatment. The use of such segregated custody must be accompanied by procedural regulations that are at least as protective as those required for prisoners sentenced to segregation for disciplinary offenses since the prisoner has committed no offense. And, as much as possible, ordinary treatment and privileges should be maintained for prisoners in segregation for non-punitive purposes.

Training

One important method for preventing sexual misconduct is to provide appropriate training for guards. The Standard Minimum Rules mandate training for officers on how to carry out their professional duties. Rule 47(2) requires that all corrections personnel "be given training in their general and specific duties and be required to pass theoretical and practical tests." Rule 47(3) further specifies that prison staff maintain and improve their knowledge and professional capacity by attending training during their employment in prisons. Standard Minimum Rule 35(1) also calls for prisoners to be provided with written information about the regulations governing the treatment of prisoners, authorized methods of seeking such information and making complaints, and whatever else is necessary to enable her to understand her rights and obligations. If the prisoner is illiterate, such information must be provided orally.

Yet, in the prisons we investigated we found little voluntary effort by the departments of corrections to train corrections officials charged with guarding women in custody. For example, little, if any, information was provided concerning the impact of previous sexual abuse on incarcerated women. Security techniques, prisoner profiles, and other training materials are often based upon the model of a male prisoner. States inadequately train corrections officers working in women's prisons on the obligation to refrain from sexual contact, verbal degradation or privacy violations. The departments of corrections that did conduct training for guards with which we are familiar, Georgia and the District of Columbia, were both compelled to do so pursuant to court orders. The state of Michigan did initiate a training program that would include cross-gender guarding situations, but to our knowledge, it has yet to address the specific issue of custodial sexual contact.

In addition, according to our interviews, most women in prison were not informed of what constituted proper conduct by guards or staff and were unaware of the procedures for filing grievances and complaints. In our investigation, we found that the only women well-informed about these standards and procedures were those who had been in prison for a long time or who had received instruction from outside nongovernmental organizations—instruction provided when departments of corrections took the positive step of facilitating training for prisoners. Most notably, Brenda Smith of the National Women's Law Center conducts a voluntary training for women incarcerated in the District of Columbia. This four-month class occurs three times a year and provides information on issues from child custody, medical care, and reproductive health to sexual misconduct, dispute resolution, and plans for post-incarceration life. This series, according to Smith, has made the women more sophisticated about these issues and better able to resolve problems without external intervention. Nongovernmental organizations in the other states we visited also conducted training, but most were unable to get the access necessary for such a complete program.

CONCLUSION

Given the grave nature of custodial sexual misconduct described in this report, there is simply no excuse for the U.S. government to deny women in prison the full scope of protections against this abuse available to them under international law. Nor is it defensible in any way for the United States to argue, as it did in its first report to the U.N. committee responsible for overseeing compliance with the ICCPR that the problem of custodial sexual misconduct is addressed under U.S.

law, "through staff training and through criminal statutes prohibiting such activity."[152]

Nothing could be further from the truth. In fact, the problem of sexual misconduct is not being adequately addressed under state administrative or criminal laws, and protections available at the federal level, while they cover much of the abuse discussed in this report, do not protect against it all. Human Rights Watch calls on the federal government, as a matter of some urgency, to recognize this fact and to take immediate steps to guarantee to women and all other persons incarcerated in the U.S. the full scope of rights available to them under international law.

> Most U.S. department of corrections' regulations do not incorporate the United Nations standard that no male staff shall enter a women's institution unless accompanied by a woman. *Nonetheless, the important underlying issue of sexual abuse is addressed*

---

[152] Consideration of Reports Submitted by State Parties Under Article 40 of the Covenant, United States of America, CCPR/C/81/Add.4, August 24, 1994, para. 260. Emphasis added.

III. CALIFORNIA

California has the largest number of incarcerated women in the United States and the world's two largest women's prisons, the Central California Women's Facility and the recently opened Valley State Prison for Women, both in Chowchilla. Two lawsuits filed in 1995 alleging constitutional violations in California's prisons for women, one of which concerned sexual assault[1] and the other alleging inadequate medical care,[2] have led the California Department of Corrections (CDC) to take some action against individual employees when directly confronted with evidence of their misconduct. Overall, however, the CDC has failed to prevent sexual misconduct in its women's facilities, and such abuse is commonplace, in some instances amounting to sexual abuse, assault, or rape.

Our investigation, based on interviews with female prisoners, their attorneys, attorneys active on two civil suits, and sociologists familiar with the California prison system and the CDC, revealed serious flaws in the system's current pattern of response to sexual misconduct in its facilities. California has few administrative or, where appropriate, criminal protections against custodial sexual misconduct and fails to train male officers adequately concerning appropriate conduct or to counsel female prisoners about this issue. Moreover, the CDC procedures for reporting and investigating complaints of such abuse are inadequate, biased in favor of officers and often expose female prisoners to retaliation. Not until 1994 did California take the welcome step of criminalizing all sexual contact in custody.

Given California's steadily growing female prison population, it behooves the state to engage in substantial prison reform before the problem of sexual misconduct escalates. We strongly urge California to adopt substantive reforms in its prison rules and general practice relating to sexual misconduct that will ensure the reporting, effective investigation and, ultimately, punishment of custodial sexual misconduct. We also call on the CDC to make significant improvements in officer training and prisoner counseling with respect to this problem.

---

[1] *Patterson v. Deshores*, Civil Action File No. ECDV-95-397, filed October 31, 1995, in United States District Court for the Central District of California.

[2] *Shumate v. Wilson,* filed April 4, 1995, in the District Court for the Eastern District of California. *Shumate* is significant because it gives attorneys increased access to prisoners whereby they have begun to hear additional allegations of sexual misconduct.

CONTEXT

Custodial Environment

At present, slightly over 50 percent of corrections officers within California's women's prisons are men.[3] This means that, day to day, female prisoners in California are supervised by male officers more often than by female officers. Yet, California has few effective guidelines for male guards working with female prisoners in women's prisons.

As noted above in the legal background section, Human Rights Watch does not oppose the presence of male guards in contact and supervisory positions in women's prisons *per se*. However, we are concerned that California has taken few steps to protect against the potential for sexual misconduct that arises out of this cross-gender guarding situation. In fact, we found that training for California corrections officers regarding security and contact with prisoners concentrates primarily on male prisoners. According to a 1995 report described in greater detail below, the only training provided for corrections officers of either sex assigned to work with women addresses the proper procedure for pat-searching women.[4]

---

[3] *Corrections Compendium* (Nebraska), October 1992. According to information we received from the CDC, the overwhelming majority of corrections officers in three of its women's prisons are men. As of June 5, 1996, men constituted nearly 74 percent of all officers at Central California Women's Facility, 73 percent at Valley State Prison for Women, 60 percent at Northern California Women's Facility, and 51 percent at California Institute of Women. Women we interviewed at Central California Women's Facility reported that the overwhelming majority of officers on the housing units are men. Letter from William B. Anderson, Chief, Institutions Services Unit, California Department of Corrections, to Human Rights Watch, June 5, 1996.

[4] In some facilities, such as at Avenal, which no longer houses women, prison administrators have concocted their own "training" for corrections officers. A review of staff depositions related to Avenal litigation revealed that one program administrator held an oral briefing for her officers wherein she relayed her personal views about female prisoners. Deposition of Steven Garcia, June 10, 1993. Until December 1988, when female prisoners began to be housed in Avenal, the majority of these officers had worked exclusively with male prisoners. No written materials were provided to train for guarding the new female prisoners. The program administrator told her officers that incarcerated women were "manipulative" and should be treated no differently from male prisoners. She encouraged, rather than directed, them to use the back of the hand when conducting pat-frisks. Incarcerated women were required to submit to pat-frisks, and officers were instructed to assume a woman was carrying contraband if she refused a search or pulled away. In such circumstances, a strip search was deemed justified.

Correctional authorities also fail to inform female prisoners about the risk of custodial sexual misconduct or the availability of mechanisms to report such misconduct should it occur. Yet most women enter prison ill-equipped to deal with the potential problem. A 1995 study found that an overwhelming percentage of women incarcerated in California experienced physical, sexual and emotional abuse prior to incarceration.[5] According to the study, 71 percent experienced physical abuse on an ongoing basis before the age of eighteen, while 62 percent reported ongoing physical abuse after the age of eighteen. Forty-one percent of incarcerated women reported being sexually abused before they turned eighteen, while 41 percent reported such abuse after the age of eighteen. This is a population largely unaccustomed to having recourse against abuse; all the more necessary, then, for the state to present the available means of recourse clearly and in an accessible fashion.

The potential for custodial sexual abuse in California is exacerbated by the rising female prison population and resultant overcrowding. California's female prison population increased by 450 percent between 1980 and 1993, a rate that significantly outpaced that of men.[6] By 1995, the women's population in California had risen to over 9,000 prisoners, compared to 1,316 in 1980,[7] and women now account for nearly 6.5 percent of the total California prison population. As of November 30, 1995, approximately 40 percent of women incarcerated in California state facilities were African American, and approximately 30 percent were Latina.[8] Nearly 55 percent were serving their first prison sentence. The majority of women within the California prison system are committed for nonviolent offenses; in fact, since 1982, the proportion of women

---

[5] Barbara Owen & Barbara Bloom, "Profiling the Needs of California's Female Prisoners," February 1995 (this report was prepared with a grant from the National Institute of Corrections, a division of the U.S. Department of Justice), p. 30.

[6] In roughly the same time period, the overall prison population in California, including men and women, grew at 346 percent. Senate Concurrent Resolution 33, Commission Report on Female Inmates and Parolee Issues, June 1994, p. A-1 [hereinafter *Commission Report*]. The Commission Report, while dated June 1994, was withheld for seven months and not released until March 1995.

[7] By June 5, 1996, there were 9,239 women incarcerated in the California system. Letter from William B. Anderson to Human Rights Watch, June 5, 1996.

[8] California Department of Corrections, "Institution: Ethnic Group by Population," December 1995.

imprisoned for violent offenses has decreased.[9] The war on drugs, in particular, has contributed to the rapid growth of the female prison population: one-third of all women in the California prisons are serving sentences for nonviolent drug offenses. Of these, most were convicted for offenses such as "possession" or "possession for sale."[10]

This burgeoning female prison population has led to serious overcrowding in the California Institution for Women (CIW), Central California Women's Facility (CCWF), and Northern California Women's Facility (NCWF), all three of which, as well as the California Rehabilitation Center (CRC), a drug treatment and rehabilitation facility, were operating at between 60 to almost 100 percent over capacity as of April 9, 1995.[11] The recently opened Valley State Prison for Women (VSPW) has reduced the pressure on the other prisons somewhat, but they continue to operate over capacity. Attorneys and volunteers told us that this overcrowding places a severe strain on prison resources and has reduced the correctional system's

---

[9] Barbara Bloom, Meda Chesney Lind and Barbara Owen, "Women in California Prisons: Hidden Victims of the War on Drugs," (Center for Juvenile and Criminal Justice (CJCJ): California, 1994).

[10] Ibid.

[11] *Commission Report*, p. A-5. As of June 5, 1996, CCWF's population exceeded 3,000 (a decrease from over 4,000 as of April 1995) prisoners while NCWF housed 2,174 incarcerated women. CDC Analysis Unit, Estimates and Statistical Analysis Section, "Weekly Report of Population," April 9, 1995. Before California built NCWF and CCWF, women housed at CIW were double- then triple-bunked. All available spaces, including ice-rooms, classrooms and the auditorium were converted to dormitories and cells. Some of these spaces continue to be used for housing prisoners. The overcrowded conditions, which limit women's access to health care, education and vocational training and basic necessities such as showers and toilets, have led to a number of lawsuits. In 1986 the American Civil Liberties Union of Southern California sued the state's department of corrections in an unsuccessful effort to stop the conversion of the prison's auditorium and other indoor recreation facilities into dormitories. *Jenny v. Alexander,* San Bernadino Superior Court (1986). Then in 1988, according to reports in the *Orange County Register*, women at CIW sued the CDC alleging that there was a shortage of toilets and showers; prisoners, as a result, were often forced to urinate in stairwells and shower in stalls overflowing with "ankle-deep slimy water." "Prison: Drugs, Sex, Overcrowding and Violence makes Frontera a 'horrible environment for guards and prisoners alike,'" *Orange County Register*, July 29, 1990.

capacity to supervise the conduct of male officers with respect to female prisoners.[12]

Close to 80 percent of all women incarcerated in California are mothers who have at least two dependent children.[13] Nonetheless, most California women's prisons are located far from the major urban areas where most of the prisoners' children and families live. For instance, CIW is approximately five hours by bus from Los Angeles, the nearest city, and Chowchilla is similarly inaccessible. Further, the CDC has taken action specifically to limit visitation; it is considering requiring children to visit their incarcerated parents unsupervised. The accompanying adult already is refused admittance to a state prison in many cases, requiring the child to undergo a body search alone.[14] Moreover, California has recently decided to reduce attorneys' and volunteers' access to women prisoners for interviews and telephone contact.[15] We ourselves received cooperation from the CDC only after repeated requests for information.[16]

---

[12] When VSPW opened in May 1995, women prisoners who were transferred there were subjected to extremely chaotic conditions, because adequate custodial and medical staff were not in place, construction had not been completed and records were not transferred to the new facility in a timely fashion.

[13] *Commission Report.*

[14] Telephone interview, Rebecca Jurado, professor of law, Western State University, March 4, 1996.

[15] The CDC has reduced visiting hours, reduced access to the telephone, and in the case of the California Institution for Women, did not inform the prisoners about scheduled trips by the National Association of Social Workers. Ibid.

[16] We contacted Gregory W. Harding, CDC deputy director for evaluation and compliance, on March 14, 1995 to request an interview. Harding was one of two representatives from the CDC who served on a Commission on Female Inmates and Parolee Issues that examined various issues affecting incarcerated women in California. Harding referred us to Teena Farmon, warden at CCWF. Farmon also served on the commission. After we wrote to Farmon, as she requested, setting forth the purpose of our interview, her staff notified us that we should again contact Harding. After repeated calls to Harding's office, he informed us, on April 24, 1995, that Farmon declined to be interviewed and he would try to locate another person within the CDC whom we could interview. On April 25, 1995, we were contacted by a representative of the CDC's communications department and told that we needed to put our request in writing and submit it to David Tristan, deputy director of the Institution Services Unit. We wrote to Mr. Tristan on May 3, 1995, but received no

State Legal and Regulatory Framework

The state of California prohibits all sexual intercourse between corrections staff and prisoners. The first violation of this prohibition is a misdemeanor; any subsequent violation is a felony. Beyond this criminal prohibition, Title 15 of California's administrative code (also known as the Director's Rules), which governs the CDC and the treatment of prisoners, contains only a general and vague provision prohibiting corrections staff from engaging in "personal transactions" with prisoners, parolees or their relatives.[17] The administrative code does prohibit prisoners from engaging in sex,[18] but we were unable to learn from the CDC whether prisoners sexually involved with corrections staff, rather than with other prisoners, may be punished under this provision.

The CDC's operations manual, which reflects the Director's Rules for the CDC, states that employees should be suspended, or placed on administrative leave, "in most cases [where they are] subject to dismissal because they . . . have shown unacceptable familiarity with inmates."[19] But, exactly what constitutes "unacceptable familiarity" is nowhere explained. Thus, California's prison rules

---

response. We also requested and received some documentation from the CDC. We then wrote to William Anderson, chief of the CDC Institution Services Unit, on May 20, 1996. Anderson contacted us by telephone and requested that we contact either Harding, Tristan or Eddie Meyers. After we sent a letter to Meyers, Anderson telephoned us on May 31, 1996, and agreed to respond to our requests for information.

[17] 15 California Administrative Code, Section 3399, titled "Transactions," merely states: "Employees shall not directly or indirectly trade, barter, lend or otherwise engage in any other personal transactions with any inmate, parolee or person known by the employee to be a relative of an inmate or parolee. Employees shall not, directly or indirectly, give to or receive from any inmate, parolee or person known by the employee to be a relative of an inmate or parolee, anything in the nature of a tip, gift or promise of a gift."

[18] "[I]nmates may not participate in illegal sex acts. Inmates are specifically excluded in laws which remove legal restraints from acts between consenting adults," 15 California Administrative Code, Section 3007. According to the CDC, certain sexual acts, such as sodomy, have been decriminalized in California over the last twenty years. Section 3007 was included in Title 15 to make clear that while these acts are not criminal outside prisons, they remain criminal offenses within prisons. Telephone interview, John Winn, staff counsel, Legal Affairs Division, California Department of Corrections, May 3, 1995.

[19] California Department of Corrections, Operations Manual, February 16, 1990, p. 33030-21.

contain no clear definition of nor prohibitions on sexual misconduct, nor do they set forth the appropriate disciplinary sanctions for such conduct should it occur.

Despite the vagueness of the operations manual, at least one warden of a California women's prison has interpreted Title 15 clearly to prohibit any personal involvement by guards with prisoners. Teena Farmon, warden of CCWF, wrote in a memorandum to staff dated July 24, 1995, that the Director's Rules "are clear regarding expectations of staff. . .Anything other than authorized physical contact, authorized verbal or written communications, or involvement with any inmate/parolee or their family, is a violation of policies and procedures and in some cases can be a violation of the law."[20] In her memorandum, Farmon explicitly asserted that officers must not establish a personal relationship with a prisoner or provide personal favors or preferential treatment to any prisoner. In addition, Farmon required guards to inform supervisors if any of their colleagues were violating the rules. Farmon also stated that since CCWF opened in October 1990, eighteen employees have been fired because of "overfamiliarity" with prisoners and parolees. However, no independent prisoner advocates were able to confirm this figure.

California does expressly mandate that prisoners be treated humanely by prison staff. Title 15, Section 3004, of the state's administrative code establishes that "inmates have the right to be treated respectfully, impartially and fairly by all employees." With respect to verbal abuse in particular, the code goes on to provide, in Section 3391, that:

> Employees shall be alert, courteous, and professional in their dealings with inmates . . . Inmates shall be addressed by their proper names and never by derogatory or slang reference . . . Employees shall not use indecent, abusive, profane, or otherwise improper language while on duty.

This express protection of prisoners' right not to be subjected to verbal degradation by officers is welcome and might serve as a model for other states that we visited, most of which do not possess such prohibitions. Unfortunately, it is rarely honored in practice within the California correctional system.

National and International Law Protections

As discussed in the legal background chapter of this report, sexual misconduct is clearly prohibited under both U.S. constitutional law and

---

[20] Teena Farmon, Memorandum on Staff/Inmate Over-Familiarity, July 24, 1995.

international treaty and customary law that is binding on the U.S. federal government as well as its constituent states.[21] The eighth amendment to the constitution, which bars cruel and unusual punishments, has been interpreted by U.S. courts to protect prisoners against rape and sexual assault. This constitutional shield is augmented by the Fourth Amendment's guarantee of the right to privacy and personal integrity, which, in a series of lower court cases, has been interpreted to prohibit male guards from inappropriately viewing or strip searching female prisoners or conducting intrusive pat-frisks on female prisoners.

Constitutional protections for prisoners' rights are enforceable via lawsuits filed by or on behalf of prisoners, or by the U.S. Department of Justice (DOJ). Historically, U.S. prisoners have achieved most of their landmark victories through private litigation, particularly suits litigated by prisoners' rights such as the National Prison Project of the American Civil Liberties Union (ACLU). However, if certain stringent requirements are met, the DOJ may criminally prosecute abusive prison officials under federal civil rights provisions. In addition, the DOJ has the statutory right to investigate and institute civil actions under the Civil Rights of Institutionalized Persons Act (CRIPA) whenever it finds that a state facility engages in a pattern or practice of subjecting prisoners to "egregious or flagrant conditions" in violation of the Constitution.

In addition to constitutional protections, prisoners' rights are protected under international human rights treaties that are legally binding on the United States. The primary international legal instruments protecting the rights of U.S. prisoners are the International Covenant on Civil and Political Rights (ICCPR), ratified by the United States in 1993, and the Convention Against Torture and Other Cruel, Inhuman or Degrading Treatment or Punishment, ratified in 1994. The ICCPR guarantees prisoners' right to privacy, except when limitations on this right are demonstrably necessary to maintain prison security. Both treaties bar torture and cruel, inhuman or degrading treatment or punishment, which authoritative international bodies have interpreted as including sexual abuse. To constitute torture, an act must cause severe physical or mental suffering and must be committed for a particular purpose, such as obtaining information from a victim, punishing her, intimidating or coercing her, or for any reason based on discrimination of any kind. Cruel, inhuman or degrading treatment or punishment includes acts causing a lesser degree of suffering that need not be committed for any particular purpose.

---

[21] For a detailed discussion of United States obligations under U.S. constitutional law and international law pertaining to the treatment of prisoners, see the legal background chapter of this report.

When prison staff members use force, the threat of force, or other means of coercion to compel a prisoner to engage in sexual intercourse, their acts constitute rape and, therefore, torture. Torture also occurs when prison staff use force or coercion to engage in sexual touching of prisoners where such acts cause serious physical or mental suffering. Instances of sexual touching or of sexual intercourse that does not amount to rape may constitute torture or cruel or inhuman treatment, depending on the level of physical or mental suffering involved. Other forms of sexual misconduct, such as inappropriate pat or strip searches or verbal harassment, that do not rise to the level of torture or of cruel or inhuman treatment, may be condemned as degrading treatment.[22]

ABUSES[23]

The abuses discussed in this section occurred from 1990 through 1996. Our own investigation took place between July 1994 and November 1996. We found that custodial sexual misconduct in California includes rape, sexual assault, and criminal sexual contact. In addition, we found pervasive and constant violations of women's privacy and degrading language and treatment.

Unless indicated by the use of a full name, the names of the prisoners have been changed to protect their anonymity. In some cases, the location and exact date of prisoner interviews have also been withheld.

---

[22] For a detailed discussion of the prohibition against torture, and other cruel, inhuman or degrading treatment or punishment under international law and its applicability to custodial sexual misconduct, see the legal background chapter of this report.

[23] By rape, we mean sexual intercourse between a prison employee and a prisoner that is accompanied by the use or threat of force or coercion which, under certain circumstances, can take the form of the provision or denial of privileges, money, or goods. Sexual assault is sexual touching, short of intercourse, involving the same coercive influences. Sexual abuse is sexual intercourse or touching involving the offer of goods or privileges absent any actual or perceived threat to the prisoner. Criminal sexual contact refers to sexual intercourse or sexual touching that cannot be shown to involve any of the above elements but which nonetheless constitutes a gross breach of official duty. Rape, sexual assault or abuse, and criminal sexual contact should all be prosecuted as felonies. For a more detailed discussion, see the legal background chapter.

Rape, Sexual Assault or Abuse, and Criminal Sexual Contact

Prisoners in California are subjected to sexual misconduct in many different forms. It can involve sexual intercourse or inappropriate sexual touching between corrections staff[24] and prisoners, constant and highly sexualized verbal degradation of the prisoners, and unwarranted invasions of their privacy.

California has a history of inappropriate sexual contact between male officers and female prisoners in its women's prisons. In July 1990 the *Orange County Register* ran a series of investigative articles on CIW alleging rape, corruption, and negligent medical care and documenting retaliation against women and correctional employees who spoke out about such practices. According to the *Register*, Harold Delon Anderson, the son of the former CIW warden, Kathleen Anderson, was dismissed in October 1987 amid allegations that he had forced ten incarcerated women to submit to sexual relations with him.[25] Internal investigations and other documentation obtained by the *Register* indicated that Anderson forced some of the women into sexual relations repeatedly, over a period of months or years. Corrections staff reportedly discovered him on three separate instances in "compromising positions" with prisoners before any disciplinary action was taken. One female corrections officer who exposed Anderson's actions was allegedly threatened and harassed by coworkers.[26] At the time the article ran in the *Register*, the CDC had treated Anderson's behavior as a personnel matter and had not referred the case to the county prosecutor for a criminal investigation.[27]

Three years after the *Register* story, the state Commission on Female Inmate and Parolee Issues also raised concerns relevant to sexual misconduct in custody.[28] A report issued by the commission in 1995 found that the CDC had no

---

[24] By use of the term "corrections staff" or "prison employees" we mean to include not only corrections officers but all levels of security personnel and nonsecurity personnel. We attempted to use a particular staff person's title where available.

[25] "Abuse: guard not prosecuted for sexual attacks," *Orange County Register*, July 29, 1990.

[26] "Speaking out: guard says she was terrorized," *Orange County Register*, July 29, 1990.

[27] Ibid.

[28] The commission was formed to examine and identify situations in which gender differences influence a need for different treatment, care and services for male and female prisoners. Members of the commission were appointed by California state senators and Assembly members, the governor and the chief justice of the California Supreme Court. The commission included judges, academics, leaders of organizations working with prisons,

policy for respecting the privacy rights of incarcerated women and that the only training the CDC provided for male correctional staff working with incarcerated women was procedural training on how to conduct appropriate body searches.[29] The commission recommended that several changes be instituted, among other things to protect prisoner privacy rights and train correctional staff about characteristics specific to incarcerated women. With respect to sexual misconduct in particular, the commission recommended:

> The CDC should continue to aggressively conduct training regarding inappropriate sexual conduct toward female inmates. The CDC should maintain its policy of treating as a matter of utmost seriousness, any inmate grievance alleging a breach of these rules by its employees, and should respond through disciplinary channels and, where appropriate, through criminal sanctions.[30]

Our own investigation, conducted from April 1994 to November 1996, indicates that rape, sexual assault and abuse, and criminal sexual contact persist in California's women's prisons. Two women we interviewed alleged that male corrections officers raped or attempted to rape them. Uma M. told us that she first experienced a long period of harassment in late 1993 by a male corrections officer, including being observed by him while in the shower, being "cornered" by him in the prison laundry room, and having him hit her on her buttocks or grab her breasts as she walked by. On one occasion the guard, Officer G, left her a note under her pillow with his phone number and address on it. He also once went to her family's home and started asking questions about her personal life.

The situation with Officer G escalated until one day he entered Uma M.'s cell while her cellmates were at breakfast and raped her. She told us:

> I felt fear real quick. I knew something was wrong and I didn't want to look. [Officer G] pulled the blanket. I sat up and tugged

---

the warden from CCWF and a member of the CDC administrative staff. Commission members examined family-related issues, substance abuse, sentencing, classification, programming, community sentencing and management policies.

[29] Commission Report, p. 37.

[30] Ibid., p. 39.

at the blanket. The other guard had the garbage can in the door and then the whole blanket came off. . . . He just tore my whole shirt. That's when he assaulted me sexually. [Officer H] yelled at [Officer G] to calm down and left. I was screaming, yelling and crying. Martha across the hall was banging on her window. While he was still in the room, I went into the shower. I felt dirty.[31]

According to Quintin N., another prisoner we interviewed, a young Hispanic woman approached her in the fall of 1994 to complain about Officer G.[32] Officer G allegedly told the young woman that he would "take care of her" and asked her whether "she likes a big *chorizo* [sausage]."

Rose S. told us that she was sexually assaulted by a corrections officer on her work assignment.[33] According to Rose S., Officer R began pressuring her for sex and making sexually explicit comments in early 1994 shortly after she arrived at the prison. Officer R would approach her on "the yard" [prison grounds] and ask her when she was going to lay out because "he wanted me to show him some skin." Then, when she was on the yard, she said, "He and two other officers would say things like, 'Let's go in and have a threesome.'" One day Rose S. arrived at her work assignment early and discovered Officer R alone. When she noticed that the supervising officer was not there, Officer R replied that he had arranged time for them to be alone. Rose S. wrote in a statement that Officer R:

got up off [the] couch. [He] went to the front door and locked it. Came back, turned the lights out and walked up to me, put his hand on my shoulders, and said, "Are you going to break me off some of that?" I told him, "No, I have only eleven [months] left, and I don't need any trouble." Then he unzipped his pants pulled out his penis, started playing with it, then he started [fondling] my breast. Then he said, "You are at least going to give me some head." I shoved him and told him no, got up off the desk and turned the lights on. By this time, there were other workers outside the door. One of the workers had seen me

[31] Interview, California, July 1994.

[32] Interview, California, July 1994.

[33] Interview, California, July 1994.

locked inside. [Officer R] told me, "Sit down in the chair and
don't say anything," because he was not going to let any of them
in, so I did as I was ordered but one of the workers, pushed her
way in and . . . came straight back and saw me sitting in the
chair.[34]

Rose S. told us that she later learned that another woman allegedly was
raped by Officer R a year earlier. Officer R reportedly picked the other woman up
in a prison vehicle and took her to a supply area where he forced her to perform
oral sex on him.

In addition to the cases of rape and attempted rape, we also learned of
cases involving sexual assault of prisoners by corrections staff. Staff of Legal
Services for Prisoners with Children (LSPC), a San Francisco-based organization,
told us that several women at CCWF have been sexually assaulted by a prison
doctor.[35] This attorney told us that one prisoner had described being assaulted
during a medical visit regarding a lump on her neck in August 1994. The doctor
conducted a vaginal examination and, according to the prisoner, made remarks
about how tight she was and how long it had been since she had sexual intercourse.
A medical assistant was present during the exam, but she reportedly moved behind
a screen and did nothing to stop the doctor. The prisoner stated that the doctor then
"played with her" and touched her in a sexual way. He never examined the lump
on her neck.

The same doctor reportedly forced another female prisoner, who had
complained of stomach cramps, to get on all fours on the examining table and then
gave her a prolonged and painful rectal examination.[36] In addition, LSPC also has
received complaints about a male nurse on the CCWF prison medical staff. One
woman, who has a disabling medical condition that leaves her physically unable
to resist sexual assault, reported that the male nurse repeatedly entered her cell and

---

[34] Statement prepared by Rose S. for a prisoner who assists other prisoners in filing
complaints about officer misconduct.

[35] Telephone interview, Ellen Barry, attorney, Legal Services for Prisoners with Children,
California, March 9, 1996.

[36] Memorandum from Ellen Barry and Cassandra Shaylor, Legal Services for Prisoners with
Children, to Human Rights Watch, March 15, 1996.

at times, groped and fondled her.[37]   Other times, he would make sexual and degrading comments.   Such actions made the prisoner vividly recall her experiences of childhood sexual abuse.   In 1996 another prisoner also complained to the prison officials that this same nurse was sexually assaulting her. She wore a hidden microphone that led to prison officials catching the nurse attempting to assault her. The nurse was reportedly removed from the premises immediately and is reportedly on administrative leave without pay while CDC investigates the situation.[38]

In 1995 the Post-Conviction Justice Project at the University of Southern California filed a lawsuit against the Protestant chaplain and his supervisors at the California Institute for Women.[39] The suit alleges that the chaplain sexually assaulted female prisoners, thus violating the eighth amendment's prohibition against cruel and unusual punishment. In addition, the suit asserts that women prisoners were afraid to worship with the chaplain and thus, their freedom of religion was infringed. Although some prisoners reported the sexual assaults to prison staff in October 1994, no action was taken against the chaplain until February 1996. At that time, subsequent to the filing of the lawsuit in October 1995, the chaplain was barred from the prison, but only after he reportedly assaulted another women.[40]

We found that, at times, sexual relations between officers and prisoners do not involve the officers' overt use or threat of force, punishment or retaliation. Instead, officers abuse their authority by offering prisoners otherwise unavailable goods and services if they submit to sexual demands. Women we interviewed told us that male corrections officers often use the promise of such favorable treatment to draw female prisoners into sexual relations. According to Rebecca Jurado, a law professor and attorney who has worked for many years with female prisoners in California, the women may see nothing out of the ordinary or abusive about this exchange. Given that a number of women prisoners' personal histories include

---

[37] Ibid.

[38] Letter from Cassandra Shaylor, Legal Services for Prisoners with Children, to Human Rights Watch, June 3, 1996.

[39] *Patterson v. Deshores*, Civil Action File No. EDCV-95-397, First Amended Complaint,, October 31, 1995.

[40] Telephone interview, Carrie Hempel, professor of law, University of Southern California Law School, March 6, 1996.

sexual abuse, she told us many women often simply accept such practices as a condition or element of incarceration.[41]

Uma M. told us of a pattern on her hall, where one officer would "pop" [release] certain prisoners' doors while other prisoners were at breakfast. The prisoners would then meet the officer at his station or another location. She told us:

> He would shut the lights down low and pop certain women's doors. One girl Jeanne F. used to go to the officer's room and get stuff. Or, she would go to the laundry room. Other days, he would pop another girl.[42]

Uma M.'s observations were supported by Ximena L., another prisoner, who reported similar conduct by other officers. She told us that the relationships often start in a familiar pattern: "They start calling them into the office or come on very nice. They give you ice [cubes], pop you out after hours. They give you an extra phone call."[43] In exchange for such favorable treatment, the prisoners provide sex.

According to women whom we interviewed, male officers in California target "like radar" younger female prisoners who are new to the prison system or unfamiliar with the prison environment. Nancy C. told us that the male officers often "pick on the first timers, it seems. They mess with newcomers." While in the receiving area[44] at CCWF, Nancy C. said she observed one male officer who "went through" three women on her unit over a period of approximately six months. According to Nancy C., who worked with one of these women, the officer:

> would have things for her [the other prisoner] to do where she would have to go to a vacant room or the supply closet. It happened several times . . . The one girl was a little disoriented.

---

[41] Telephone interview, Rebecca Jurado, Western State University, March 21, 1995.

[42] Interview, California, July 1994.

[43] Interview, California, July 1994.

[44] The receiving area is a separate place in the prison where prisoners are held for a period of time when they first arrive and before they are transferred to the general population or to other facilities.

> The police was just being an opportunist and taking advantage of it.[45]

She believes the officer was subsequently transferred to a men's facility.

In some instances, prisoners engage in sexual contact with officers absent any overt coercion or exchange. Ximena L., who has been serving a long prison term, told us, "There are relationships going on. Some are consensual and some not. There have always been sexual relationships. The majority are not consensual. They are doing it for drugs and can't say no. Some are initiated by the girls."[46]

Susan R. has been incarcerated for several years. She told us that beginning in 1990, she became sexually involved with a corrections officer, primarily out of loneliness. She said:

> I have no visits. No outside contacts whatsoever. So when a male figure shows you a little attention it made me feel special, worthy of something, someone . . . When he showed me attention, I jumped at it. I built this up in my mind. When I first saw him, I was attracted to him. He's no prize but for some reason I was attracted. He started joking, making catty remarks . . . I jumped at it. I wanted the attention.[47]

Susan R. said that she often stayed at her work assignment during dinner to be with him. Later, she said, when he was assigned to her housing unit, she had sexual relations with him in the laundry room, ice room, storage closet or the showers.

Patty T. told us that she became involved with an officer for many of the same reasons that motivated Susan R.—she was alone, separated from her family, and seeking care and attention. Patty T. described her situation. "I wasn't really close with others in prison. I worked and went to school and kept myself busy. I was just interested in getting out of prison."[48] She was drawn to an officer who supervised her work assignment and had a relationship with him that lasted over

---

[45] Telephone interview, California, July 1994.

[46] Interview, California, August 1994.

[47] Interview, California, July 1994.

[48] Telephone interview, July 1994.

a year and a half. According to Patty T., "I totally initiated it. I went after him for a while. I worked the guard and finally he decided he would deal with me." The relationship ended when she became pregnant by the officer and he received a transfer to another facility.[49]

Unfortunately, prisoners who considered themselves to be equal partners in sexual relations with officers often later found that it was difficult to extricate themselves from the officers' control. Nancy C., a former prisoner who has served in both CIW and CCWF, told us that she was sexually involved with a corrections officer at CIW in the mid-1980s. She said the officer "was always bringing me stuff, cologne, money." She told us she had sexual intercourse with the corrections officer on two occasions, but met him several times, in her words, "to mess around." Ultimately, Nancy C. had difficulty getting away from the officer. After she refused to continue sexual relations, he persisted in his pattern of appearing outside her door. He reportedly wanted to meet her at the airport upon her release from prison.

Mistreatment of Prisoners Impregnated by Guards

Over the years, incarcerated women have become pregnant by California's corrections employees. These women, or those with knowledge about the pregnancy or about efforts to terminate the pregnancy, often are harassed and punished by prison officials. In early 1994 we learned that a prisoner at CIW was impregnated by a civilian employee and tried to terminate the pregnancy herself. The prisoner's attempt to abort came to the attention of prison officials and, in March 1994, three other women who reportedly had knowledge about the pregnancy and abortion attempt were sent to administrative segregation for extended periods. They were eventually released without charges.

Patty T., mentioned above, became pregnant as a result of a sexual relationship with a corrections officer in the mid-1980s. After learning she was pregnant, she indicated to the prison doctor that she wanted an abortion. Prison officials reportedly used Patty T.'s desire to have an abortion as a tool in their investigation to press her to reveal the identity of the man who impregnated her. The authorities waited approximately two months after she came forward before sending her out for the abortion. During the investigation, Patty T. was repeatedly questioned by high-ranking officers at the prison. She told us, describing their questioning:

---

[49] Patty T.'s pregnancy is discussed more fully below.

> They'd bring me into the office and ask how, when and who—even to the point of saying things about my son who was eleven or twelve years old. I had family visits and he could stay over. They were insinuating this was the only male I had come into contact with.[50]

She, however, was not willing to provide the officer's name to prison officials. She was placed in administrative segregation for two weeks after the abortion. After a hearing was held, she was released, and no charges were filed against her.

The following year, prison officials reportedly attempted to use Patty T.'s hopes of entering the Community Prisoner Mother Infant Care program again to pressure her to reveal the identity of the officer who had impregnated her. The Mother Infant Care program is an alternative sentencing program that allows a limited number of women who are mothers to serve their sentence in a residential community setting with their children.[51] A few days before a court hearing regarding the program, Patty T. was called into the administration offices and, she told us, "They went through it all over again. They said they wouldn't let me go . . . until I told them who the father was."[52]

Abusive and Degrading Language

We found that some male corrections officers disregard the California Administrative Code's provisions on humane treatment, described above, and employ sexually abusive and obscene language when speaking with or referring to prisoners. At times, such language is used as a prelude to groping and making physical advances toward the prisoners. Such language and conduct pervade the prison environment in California and reinforce among many women prisoners the belief that there are no regulations on how the corrections staff behaves toward them.

Patty T. told us that another officer who supervised her work assignment harassed and badgered her and other prisoners.[53] According to Patty T., "The police [corrections officer] who used to work there used to harass the women and

---

[50] Telephone interview, July 1994.

[51] See 15 California Administrative Code, Section 3410 *et seq.*

[52] Patty T. was eventually admitted to the Mother Infant Care Program.

[53] Telephone interview, California, July 21, 1994.

say real nasty things. Like if they were ugly, he would tell them." The officer was also assigned to her housing unit for a time, during which he reportedly tried to watch her undress and made "little remarks." According to Patty T., women were permitted to hang towels over the windows in their cell doors when changing to allow for a certain amount of privacy. One day, the officer repeatedly pulled the towel down each time she hung it up. She told us, "Because I would not give him attention, he did things to upset me."

Women we interviewed said that female prisoners are often referred to as, and directly called, bitches, whores, sluts and prostitutes. Corrections officers at CCWF have reportedly announced over the loudspeaker, "If you want to get your dinner, you better get your asses over here" or, "All you bitches and whores get into your rooms."[54] Some male corrections officers perceive the women as prostitutes and persistently label them as such. Vanessa B. told us that corrections officers said things to her when she had family visits such as, "Have you visited your tricks?" or "One of your johns?"[55]

At times, degrading language and sexual innuendo are accompanied by offensive groping of women's bodies. Tammy P., a former prisoner, told us she was groped by an officer while incarcerated at Avenal State Prison (which no longer holds women).[56] Once, she was changing her tampon when she noticed that Officer A had followed her into the bathroom and was watching her. As Tammy P. turned to leave, Officer A reportedly grabbed her vagina and asked, "Do you think I could have a piece of that?" Officer A was also the corrections officer assigned to her work detail, where he propositioned women and commented on their bodies. According to Tammy P., "He'd come into the kitchen, at breakfast or lunch, and say things like. 'How big do you like 'em?' or, 'Is it big enough for you?' He did this all the time." At other times, he would come into the kitchen and grab his genitals, or tell the women, "You shouldn't bend over like that in front of me." As Tammy P. told us, "It was the way he looked at you, like he was undressing you." Other women on her shift reportedly filed grievances regarding his conduct, but no action apparently was taken to reprimand Officer A and his conduct continued unabated.

---

[54] Interview, California, July 1994.

[55] Interview, California, July 1994.

[56] Interview, California, July 20, 1994. Avenal is a male correctional facility that housed women on a temporary basis in the early 1990s, before CCWF opened.

Degrading language is also prevalent at Valley State Prison for Women's (VSPW) Special Housing Unit.[57] One woman housed at VSPW wrote, "Because I am twenty pounds overweight, I am constantly harassed by certain male guards and called names. . . . I feel we should be treated with the same respect we must show the guards. We definitely are not shown that."[58] Guards there also specifically abuse those prisoners identified as lesbians.

Many of the prisoners are deeply disturbed by such degrading, sexual language and behavior. According to Vanessa B., "Nothing that you do that's positive and right is taken that way . . . If you look nice, they will try to humiliate you and make you feel less than human." Vanessa B. considers herself a positive role model for other prisoners and has served on the Warden's Advisory Committee[59] but finds it difficult to endure the badgering from correctional staff.

At CCWF, women's sanitary supplies often are rationed or distributed in ways that seem designed to humiliate women prisoners. Women in some units at CCWF are provided a limited ration of sanitary napkins, tampons and toilet paper bimonthly, regardless of need.[60] Under the policy, prisoners told us, additional supplies are not provided either when women run out or if they are locked out of their cells when they begin menstruating. Some corrections officers use the requests for sanitary supplies as an opportunity to denigrate women. According to Vanessa B., "They will throw it [the sanitary napkin] to you and say, 'Here's your surfboard,' or they will say, 'Use toilet paper.'" Male corrections officers have also reportedly told women who request additional supplies to "stuff toilet paper in your pants," "turn it over," or "recycle it." Women who requested toilet paper have been told to "use your muumuu"[61] or "use your shirt." Women in

---

[57] "Torturas at Chowchilla: The Pelican Bay for Women," *Pelican Bay Prison Express* (California) Chowchilla, November 1995, p. 3.

[58] "Women Prisoners Speak Out at 'Pelican Bay for Women,' Chowchilla, CA," *Pelican Bay Prison Express,* April 1996, p. 18.

[59] The Warden's Advisory Committee is a group of women prisoners who meets periodically with the prison warden to raise concerns.

[60] On July 6, 1994, officials issued a memorandum allocating prisoners in Facility "B" only seven sanitary napkins, three tampons and two rolls of toilet paper bimonthly. The allocation is based on supplies provided to the unit and not according to the needs or requirements of individual women.

[61] A muumuu is a state-issued sack dress.

administrative segregation in VSPW who need extra sanitary napkins must request them, one at a time, from the mostly male guards. One woman reported that she had to wait until she had menstrual blood running down her leg before she could get a sanitary napkin.[62] In another reported case, male guards threw a packet of sanitary napkins onto the floor, in response to a request for sanitary napkins, and the prisoner had to "fish" for the packet by using a string, with which she was supposed to catch the packet and drag it along the floor into her cell. While she tried to get the napkin, the guards shouted encouragement and bet on whether she would be successful.[63]

Privacy Violations

As discussed in more detail in the legal background section of this report, prisoners retain an internationally protected right to privacy except when limitations on this right are demonstrably required by the nature of the prison environment. In addition, several U.S. courts, including the Ninth Circuit Court of Appeal, which has jurisdiction over California, have concluded that prisoners retain some right to bodily privacy. In particular courts in the Ninth Circuit have recognized that prisoners have a right not to be strip searched by officers of the opposite sex, except in cases of emergency, to be protected from routine inappropriate visual surveillance by officers of the opposite sex and, in case of female prisoners, not to be subjected to pat-frisks by male officers.

In 1981, in *Bowling v. Enomoto,* a male prisoner sued the CDC alleging his right to privacy was violated by the presence of female officers who often saw him undressing, showering, and using the toilet.[64] The court in *Bowling* directed the CDC to develop a procedure for protecting prisoner privacy similar to that employed in New York's women's prisons pursuant to *Forts v. Ward.*[65] In a suit

---

[62] "Torturas at Chowchilla . . ." *Pelican Bay Prison Express.*

[63] Millard Murphy, "Inhuman and Degrading Treatment and Punishment of Women Segregated Prisoners in the California State Prisons at Chowchilla," October 23, 1995 (based on research conducted by Pelican Bay Information Project, a prisoners' rights advocacy group based in San Francisco, California).

[64] 514 F. Supp. 201 (N.D. Calif. 1981)

[65] Ibid., p. 204. *Forts v. Ward,* 621 F.2d. 1210 (2d Cir. 1980).

with similar allegations filed a few years later, *Grummett v. Rushen*,[66] the Ninth Circuit Court of Appeals, while recognizing that the prisoners had a constitutional right to privacy, rejected the male prisoners' claims because the CDC already had in place definitions of the duties of female corrections officers designed to minimize viewing of male prisoners in a state of undress.[67] The court also rejected the prisoners' claim that pat-searches conducted by female officers violated their constitutional right to privacy under the Fourth Amendment.

However, the Ninth Circuit Court of Appeals later determined that the use of male corrections officers to pat-search female prisoners violates the eighth amendment to the U.S. Constitution. In *Jordan v. Gardner*,[68] women incarcerated in Washington State challenged the introduction of a policy that would have permitted male corrections officers to conduct pat-searches on female prisoners. The Ninth Circuit determined that in light of the women's history of abuse, pat-searches carried out by male officers violated the eighth amendment's prohibition on cruel and unusual punishment. Materials sent to us by the CDC indicate pat-searches are still governed by a provision in the Operations Manual drafted in 1989, which does not mandate same-sex pat-searches.[69]

Despite these rulings and clear international standards upholding prisoners' privacy rights, the 1995 Report of the California Commission on Female Inmates and Parolee Issues, mentioned at the start of this chapter, found that in California "in the case of issues such as female inmate privacy, the CDC has developed no policy at all."[70] Under California's administrative code, male corrections officers may not perform strip searches but are otherwise granted broad authority to enter prisoners' cells and living areas.[71] Corrections officers, in general, may conduct clothed searches of prisoners and perform unannounced,

---

[66] 779 F.2d 491 (9th Cir. 1985)

[67] Ibid., pp. 494-495.

[68] 986 F.2d 1521 (9th Cir. 1993).

[69] California Department of Corrections, Operations Manual, December 28, 1989, p. 52050-13.

[70] *Commission Report*, p. 37.

[71] 15 California Administrative Code, Section 3287(4)(b)(1), "Cell, Property and Body Inspections."

random inspections, including of a prisoner's cell and living area.[72] While "living area" is not defined, our interviews indicate that it is understood to include shower and toilet facilities. Title 15 also requires that strip searches should be conducted in a professional manner that avoids embarrassment and indignity to prisoners and that such searches should be conducted outside the view of others whenever possible.[73] Nonetheless, these rules leave too much to officer discretion with respect to the prisoner's right to privacy and create unnecessary opportunities for privacy-related sexual misconduct to occur.

Strip Searches

As stated above, California law prohibits male officers from conducting cross-gender strip searches. However, this protection is meaningless if strip searches are carried out by female officers while in the presence of male colleagues. Yet, we have received reports that women incarcerated at CCWF have been forced to strip and be searched in the presence of male corrections employees. Ellen Barry, of LSPC, told us that she received a letter from a prisoner in February 1995 alleging that women prisoners were required to submit to strip searches while in the receiving area at CCWF in a location where male corrections officers were working and while male transportation officers were passing through. The prisoner who contacted the attorney included her name and identification number and those of two other women prisoners who were stripped under the same conditions. She also attached a petition signed by over fifty women prisoners alleging they were stripped under similarly invasive conditions. One male guard, in particular, was mentioned by several women in CCWF as being known for standing in the doorway and leering during strip searches.[74] The prisoner also filed a grievance about the searches. In response, a sergeant at CCWF conceded that the searches occurred as described, but stated that male officers and employees were not obligated to alter their movements to avoid being present while the searches were conducted and, thus, that no misconduct occurred.

A woman placed in administrative segregation in VSPW wrote a prisoner advocacy organization that prior to taking a shower she had to strip naked, bend over at the waist and spread her cheeks, in the full view of all staff, including men

---

[72] Ibid., Section 3287(4)(c)

[73] Ibid.

[74] Memorandum from Ellen Barry and Cassandra Shaylor, Legal Services for Prisoners with Children, to Human Rights Watch, March 15, 1996.

and women.[75] In addition, she wrote that guards would make rude comments about prisoners' bodies during strip searches and at other times.

Inappropriate Visual Surveillance

A number of prisoners also told us they had been subjected to inappropriate visual surveillance by male officers. At CIW, current and former prisoners told us they are permitted to cover their cell windows when using the toilet or changing.[76] However, not all corrections officers respect this practice. Our interviews indicate that some male corrections officers have instructed women to leave their window clear while others have removed towels or other items used to cover the window. When Nancy C. was at CIW, she told us, a male corrections officer used to peek through her window to watch her or her cellmate change. In other cases, according to Ximena L., male officers enter the women's cells even when the window is covered.

At CCWF, the structure of the living units reportedly contributes to unnecessary viewing by male corrections officers. Prisoners told us that each living unit, which houses up to eight women, has a wide window that opens to the corridor.[77] Unlike at CIW, prisoners at CCWF told us they may not cover this window for short intervals while changing. Male officers, who are routinely stationed on the housing units, wander the corridors at all hours and do not always announce their presence. A large majority of officers in the CCWF housing units are men, and female prisoners sometimes go twenty-four hours without seeing a female officer. A number of women reported that male corrections officers enter living units while women are dressing or showering, on the pretense of conducting a search. At CCWF, male guards routinely watch women use the toilets and showers. Afterwards the guards make degrading remarks about the prisoners'

---

[75] "Women Prisoners Speak Out. . .," *Pelican Bay Prison Express.*

[76] At CIW, each prisoner shares her cell with another woman. The cell has one toilet and a wooden door with a narrow window, or wicket.

[77] When constructed, these cells were designed to house only four women. As the population of incarcerated women rose, so has the number of women housed in each unit. At the time of our visit, prisoners were double-bunked and there were eight women per cell, sharing one toilet and one shower.

bodies.[78] According to Olga G., "You are never sure when you will get walked in on." Vanessa B. told us:

> When you take a shower, they'll come in and talk to you . . .
> When they walk down the hall, they can see you depending on
> your height through the window. They will stand outside your
> window or flash their lights, or they will come in and search the
> room while you are in the shower and tell you to come out.[79]

The shower doors are constructed to cover the body only partially, concealing the women from her shoulders to knees.

Women in VSPW are accorded virtually no bodily privacy in administrative segregation. If a female prisoner has to use the bathroom during her three-hour exercise period, she must use a toilet that is directly below the guard tower, which usually is staffed by a male guard.[80] Often, the woman must request toilet paper from this same guard. In addition, male guards regularly watch women prisoners shower. The showers are positioned such that all male guards have an unobstructed view of the women showering. The guards reportedly try to engage the women in conversation while they are showering, and if they fail, the guards often will make degrading comments about the women.[81] We have also received reports that female prisoners in VSPW often must receive their medical exams, including gynecological exams, in the presence of male guards.[82]

---

[78] Janis Fonseca, "Report of Dec. 1995 Investigation of California Central Women's Facility (CCWF) Chowchilla," *Pelican Bay Prison Express*, April 1996, p. 21.

[79] Interview, California, July 1994.

[80] Murphy, "Inhumane and Degrading Treatment . . . ."

[81] Ibid.

[82] Ibid.

Avenal

Seven former prisoners sued the CDC for violations of privacy between December 1988 and March 1991.[83] The CDC opened two sections for women at Avenal, then a men's prison, on a temporary basis to alleviate overcrowding at CIW. Avenal was structured as an open dormitory environment with few physical or privacy barriers. Prior to their arrival, the only structural change was the installation of opaque screens along the walkways. These screens provided only limited protection—they were approximately three feet high, and were placed off the ground allowing for visibility from underneath. From certain areas in the facility, male corrections officers had an unobstructed view into the showers, enabling them to observe a woman's naked body from her neck to below her knee. Women's cubicles similarly offered limited protection from being viewed while naked—doors were not installed in the housing units of one section, and many of the doors were removed from housing units in the second section. Women could also be viewed while using the toilet. One common toilet facility abutted the guards' office, separated only by a large plate glass window. This gave the officers an unobstructed view of the women using the facilities. Paper was only irregularly put on the window to shield the toilets from viewing by the male officers. In another area, the women's toilets were visible from the officers' platform.

The overwhelming majority of officers at Avenal were men— approximately 90 percent. These officers were directly counseled by the program administrator, one of whom was assigned to each yard, to enter and patrol regularly the showers, sleeping areas and toilets to check for any "misconduct." The program administrators rejected, "for security reasons," proposals to have officers announce their presence prior to entering an area. The women were not only subjected to constant viewing by male officers, but were also viewed by nonsecurity personnel and visitors to the prison on tours. On a number of occasions, such persons were brought through the women's yards even when the women were undressed or using the toilets.

Within this environment, women were exposed to constant physical observation and harassment by male staff. We interviewed two women formerly held at Avenal. According to Quintin N., at times officers would walk into the showers or "they would watch you change your Kotex or go to the bathroom. At times, they would come and talk to you when you were on the toilet."[84]

---

[83] Many of the descriptions of Avenal herein are based on their complaint, discovery obtained during the suit, and our own interviews with two of the women.

[84] Interview, California, July 1994.

The privacy panels did little to conceal the women from the male correctional officers. According to Quintin N., the officers intentionally sat in certain locations so they could watch the women showering and used to play a game—"name those buns"—trying to identify a particular woman by looking at her naked buttocks. She also told us that when women tried to hang a towel to provide some privacy while dressing, officers would pull it down, smile and remark, "You know you can't do that."

Tammy P. supported Quintin N.'s observations. She told us, "I felt like I had no privacy, nowhere to go. I felt exposed at all times . . . I almost lost my mind."[85] The officers, she said, would walk through the sleeping areas at night and in the morning when women were dressing and undressing.

Conditions at Avenal were further exacerbated by the fact that the CDC issued extremely revealing nightgowns to the women imprisoned there. The gown, which we saw, had a low scoop neck, was cut to fit tightly against the body, and was virtually transparent. It did not reach the knees.

Both women we interviewed also experienced problems with abusive pat-frisks by male officers. Tammy P. told us, "They would use their palms. One guard would get real close, lean against you when he did the search. They all used their palms going over the breasts and through the crotch."[86] Quintin N., similarly, told us she was groped by an officer during a frisk. As she described it, "Officer E put his hands on me . . . At first I didn't believe it and just looked back at him. . . This kind of stuff went on together with everything."[87]

THE SYSTEM'S RESPONSE

The CDC told us that it investigates every allegation of sexual misconduct and refers reports of alleged felonies to the local District Attorney's Office.[88] According to the CDC, in 1994-95 it received only ten reports of sexual misconduct in its facilities, half of which were closed because of insufficient

---

[85] Interview, California, July 1994.

[86] Interview, California, July 1994.

[87] Interview, California, July 1994.

[88] Letter from William B. Anderson, chief, Institution Services Unit, California Department of Corrections, to Human Rights Watch, June 5, 1996.

evidence. Of the remaining five reports, three resulted in firing of the abusive employees. Despite these welcome disciplinary actions, our investigation suggests that they address only a fraction of the sexual misconduct occurring in California's facilities. At present, the mechanisms for reporting and investigating such abuse are seriously flawed. In addition, potential complainants perceive that they could face retaliation and thus, are reluctant to come forward. Until these problems are addressed, it will be difficult fully to expose and eliminate sexual misconduct in California's prisons. Only one case was referred to the local District Attorney.[89]

Denial of an Effective Remedy

International human rights law obligates national governments to ensure that when prison abuses occur they can be reported and investigated without the complainant fearing undue punishment or retaliation. Moreover, in the United States, prisoners are guaranteed access to the courts to challenge prison conditions or other prison problems.[90]

Grievance Procedure

Under California's administrative code, prisoners may complain about "any departmental decision, action, condition or policy perceived by [the prisoner] as adversely affecting their welfare."[91] These complaints are known as 602s, the number on the grievance form that a prisoner must file. Both prisoners and attorneys observed, however, that in practice 602s are generally ineffective in addressing complaints of sexual misconduct by corrections officers. According to Professor Jurado, the grievance mechanism functions adequately for routine or clear-cut complaints regarding property or problems with a prisoner's account, but not for what she characterized as "interpersonal" issues.[92] Ximena L. also told us that the grievance procedure works well with technical things: "At the first level, you usually get some idiotic response. You usually need to get to [the second level] to get it fixed." But, she told us, if the grievance raises a problem with an institutional policy or sexual harassment, it generally will be denied.

---

[89] Ibid.

[90] For a more detailed discussion of the due process rights accorded prisoners under international and U.S. law, see the legal background section.

[91] 15 California Administrative Code, Section 3084.

[92] Telephone interview, Rebecca Jurado, Western State University, March 21, 1995.

Our interviews indicate that the grievance procedure is difficult for women to access. First, prisoners entering the system receive no training on how to use the procedure and many women do not know how to file a grievance. Some California prison administrators have inhibited or obstructed efforts by women prisoners to provide training or instructions to other prisoners through prison law libraries. The law librarian at one prison, for example, reportedly would not allow Quintin N. to make copies of the 602 form or of an information sheet that she prepared for the prisoners on how to file a grievance, despite a provision of Title 15 which states that "an inmate, parolee or other person may assist another inmate or parolee with preparation of an appeal unless the act of providing such assistance would create an unsafe or unmanageable situation."[93] Second, while Title 15 mandates that appeals forms be "readily available," this was not the case in at least one California prison that we visited.

The grievance process further requires corrections officers to participate willingly in the grievance process and to respond in a responsible and professional manner to a prisoner's complaint.[94] Officers do not, however, always respect the procedure. Prisoners we interviewed told us that some corrections officers, when presented with a 602 form, have simply thrown the grievance out and/or mocked the prisoner who filed it. According to Susan S.:

> [Corrections officers] will tear it up and throw it in the garbage
> . . . Or, [they] will say, "Go ahead and 602 me because I know
> it won't go nowhere." Most 602s will get thrown in the garbage
> before you go away. It's a joke to them.[95]

California, like Michigan, requires the prisoner to speak with the offending staff member prior to filing a formal appeal.[96] This informal level is

---

[93] 15 California Administrative Code, Section 3084.2(2)(d).

[94] Ibid., Section 3084.3(c)(4).

[95] Interview, California, July 1994.

[96] 15 California Administrative Code, Section 3084.2(b). Title 15 requires prisoners to file their grievances within fifteen working days after the alleged incident. Similarly, they have fifteen working days to appeal an adverse decision on their grievance to a higher level of review. There is a three-year time limit on appeals alleging staff misconduct. Ibid., Section 3084.6. Staff are required to respond within five days at the informal level, within fifteen

waived in limited circumstances, such as actions that the appeals coordinator determines cannot be resolved informally and alleged misconduct by a "departmental peace officer."[97] Misconduct and "departmental peace officer" are not defined. Even though incarcerated women may bypass this informal level, in Professor Jurado's experience and in the experience of other attorney advisors, the grievance eventually filters back to the officer. As a result, women feel threatened or afraid to lodge grievances because corrections officers ultimately will know that they complained.[98] The U.S. Department of Justice, in reviewing a similar requirement in the Michigan grievance procedure, stated that "this requirement has the purpose, intent or effect of intimidating the inmates and discouraging the filing of grievances."[99]

Even when women have filed grievances, they have often faced official bias against prisoner testimony. After the assault on Uma M. detailed in the section on rape and sexual assault above, she told us that she informed a prison investigator about Officer G's previous harassment, his visit to her family's home and his offer to bring her certain items. An investigation was subsequently initiated into Officer G's conduct. According to Uma M., the investigator opened her interview by asserting that she would not believe any charges of sexual misconduct, stating, "Do you know how many girls say they've been sexually harassed? What do you want, to go home early?"

This bias against prisoners has also manifested itself in prison officials' selective enforcement of grievance procedures. In one case we investigated, a sergeant did not respond to a prisoner's grievance concerning an inappropriate strip

---

days at the first level of review, and within twenty days at the third level of review. This informal step means that the prisoner must often physically present the grievance form to the officer whom she is reporting, a procedure that can be extremely intimidating to women who are submitting grievances about sexual misconduct. He then responds to her in writing and returns the form to her. If a prisoner is dissatisfied with the response, she may appeal the grievance to the "formal level" and submit the 602 form, with the officer's response, to the institution's appeals coordinator. A prisoner may not appeal to this formal level unless she demonstrates her attempt to resolve the grievance informally and provides the corrections officer's response to her informal grievance.

[97] Ibid, Section 3084.5(a)(3).

[98] Telephone interview, Rebecca Jurado, Western State University, March 21, 1995.

[99] Letter from Deval Patrick, assistant attorney general, U.S. Department of Justice, to John Engler, governor, State of Michigan, March 27, 1995.

search mentioned above for nearly four weeks, more than three weeks beyond the statutorily mandated period for his response. The authorities nonetheless accepted his response. However, when the prisoner subsequently appealed the sergeant's response to the first level of review, the CCWF's appeals coordinator denied the appeal solely because it was received after the fifteen-day period set forth in Title 15. He never reached the merits of her complaint.[100] The appeals coordinator then denied a second grievance filed by the prisoner regarding the sergeant's initial delay in responding to her grievance on the basis that it was "not an appeal issue."

Corrections officials, in reviewing prisoner grievances, often use a prisoner's prior receipt of disciplinary tickets to deny her grievance or to argue that she is lying. This occurs even when the officer's conduct and his issuing the disciplinary ticket itself are at issue. In one grievance we reviewed, a prisoner reported an officer who, she alleged, pulled her into the guards' office and repeatedly called her a "bitch" and a "fucking bitch." According to the prisoner, the officer then handcuffed her and removed her from the unit. On appeal, CDC officials determined there was no merit to the prisoner's claim because the officer had placed her in administrative segregation following the alleged incident and because her "file [was] replete with misconduct reports which depict a serious pattern of misbehavior." In other words, because the officer disciplined the prisoner at the time of the incident and because she had received disciplinary tickets in the past, her allegation of wrongdoing was deemed meritless.

Investigations

In general, we found that CDC's investigative procedures are fairly *ad hoc*. Moreover, they often are punitive against the complainant, lack any pretense of confidentiality, are largely closed to outside monitors, including the complainants' attorneys, and often expose the prisoners to retaliation and, in some cases, punishment.

As mentioned in the background section above, international human rights law obligates the United States to investigate complaints of ill-treatment effectively. However, California's Title 15 neither specifies a mechanism for investigating allegations of staff misconduct nor indicates when an investigation

---

[100] The appeals coordinator's position on the time limit issue appears to violate the provision, set forth above, that states that there is a three-year window of time for prisoners to report staff misconduct.

is required.[101] Instead, the CDC's operations manual, which consists of internal guidelines and not law, governs investigations.[102] The operations manual indicates that allegations of employee misconduct should first be investigated by the Internal Affairs Division of the CDC as a prerequisite to disciplinary action against an employee. However, the manual does not identify what triggers an investigation into alleged staff misconduct or any procedures or time frame for the conduct of such inquiries.[103] We found that investigations are usually conducted at the institutional level by an investigator based at the prison in question.[104]

Lack of Confidentiality

Effective protection of the confidentiality, and hence safety, of complainants and witnesses is essential to the integrity of any grievance or investigative process. Absent such a guarantee, the fear of retaliation against complainants has a chilling effect on those who might report alleged sexual misconduct. In California, a woman's identity may initially be protected when corrections officials question an implicated officer, but her identity is not always

---

[101] In September 1994, the California legislature created the position of Inspector General (IG) at the Youth and Adult Correctional Agency (YACA), which is part of the department of corrections. Ken O'Brien, a thirty-year veteran of the San Diego Police Department's Internal Affairs Division and a former investigator for the State Bar Association, was appointed to the position by Governor Pete Wilson. The IG has authority to oversee and monitor existing procedures for the investigation of prison staff misconduct. The IG is not now empowered to investigate instances of staff misconduct and can do so only if directed by legislation or by the Secretary of the YACA. In monitoring investigation procedures, the IG is able to interview staff and may receive confidential information from employees. His findings will be reported to the Secretary but will not be released publicly. There is no mechanism by which prisoners are able to report staff misconduct to the IG.

[102] We requested from the CDC a copy of any policy, procedure or other information on how investigations are conducted into alleged overfamiliarity or sexual misconduct between corrections employees and prisoners, and similar information on how a prisoner or officer should report such allegations. In response, we received several pages from the CDC's operations manual.

[103] California Department of Corrections, Operations Manual, February 16, 1990, pp. 33030-1—33030-39.

[104] In Georgia, New York and Illinois, investigators appear to be based centrally rather than at the institution itself. In Michigan, some investigators are also based at the institution.

concealed as the investigation progresses or once it concludes. From our interviews, it appears that some corrections officers under investigation for alleged sexual misconduct were provided with the name of the prisoner or prisoners during the course of the investigation. Provisions of the CDC's operations manual, which governs employee discipline, in fact provide that employees be given a copy of the investigation report, including a summary of the witnesses' statements and their full names, before any disciplinary action may be taken. This procedure is not problematic where an implicated officer has been suspended and is no longer in direct contact with a prisoner, but such precaution is not always taken. Thus, the revelation of the complainant's identity can expose her to the possibility of continued abuse.

Confidentiality is also jeopardized by a provision in Title 15 of the administrative code that encourages corrections officers to review a prisoner's central file "for assistance in better understanding the [prisoner]."[105] A prisoner's central file contains personal information regarding the prisoner, including her criminal and personal history, as well as copies of grievances and documents relating to her role in an investigation. While Title 15 counsels officers that the information is "private and privileged," the access, in and of itself, abrogates any privacy or privilege the prisoner may have with respect to this information. Title 15 also provides that the contents of a prisoner's central file "will not be the subject of banter between employees or between employees and the [prisoner] to whom it pertains or with other [prisoners]."[106] Our interviews indicate, however, that corrections officers have disregarded this provision and have exploited their knowledge of information contained in the central file to harass and badger prisoners.

Two women we interviewed reported that corrections officers knew things about previous investigations or grievances that could only be learned through their central files. This information was then used by the officer to harass the prisoners. According to Patty T., a correctional officer on her unit made a comment to her and her roommate about her pregnancy and the abortion she had undergone.[107] Quintin N. told us that she grew suspicious that officers were looking into her files when one or two began questioning her about her role in the Avenal litigation. She subsequently requested permission to see her central file and told us that she

---

[105] 15 California Administrative Code, Section 3402(a).

[106] Ibid.

[107] Interview, California, July 1994.

discovered that grievances and other information related to the Avenal lawsuit had tabs placed on them indicating that someone had reviewed her files and particularly her past complaints.[108]

In both Rose S.'s and Uma M.'s cases, other corrections officers also obtained information about the investigation. Rose S. remained at the prison during the investigation, and her participation became known because she was repeatedly interviewed and called to meet the prison investigator.[109] According to Uma M., officers at a second prison were aware of her role in the investigation into Officer G and made specific reference to Officer G's suspension.[110] Ximena L. made similar observations to us. She told us that it is "a very dangerous thing to do" to make a report of sexual misconduct against a corrections officer. Prisoners, she said, lacked someone to "run to," they are "without credibility, [without] people who will help [them] or believe in [them]." In her experience, "An awful lot of [women] just silently endure it . . . [They] keep quiet and serve out their term."[111]

Retaliation

The absence of confidentiality, both with respect to the employee when he holds a contact position over the prisoner and with respect to the prison population more generally, enhance the risk that complainants will face retaliatory actions without redress, despite Title 15's clear statement that "no reprisal shall be taken against an inmate . . . for filing an appeal." Our interviews indicate that women who have filed grievances and women who participate in investigations are harassed by corrections staff. According to Quintin N., "Most of the women here are afraid to file a 602 because they think they'll get in trouble. Most women here do not know the procedure and the cops [guards] will take reprisals."[112] Tammy M. resisted a friend's suggestion to come forward after Officer A groped her in the bathroom. "[M]y friend tried to get me to go tell. I wouldn't do it, out of fear. I envisioned them putting me in the hole [segregation]. People were thrown in the

---

[108] Interview, California, July 1994.

[109] Interview, California, July 1994.

[110] Interview, California, July 1994.

[111] Interview, California, August 1994.

[112] Interview, California, July 1994.

hole there all the time, for anything."[113] The officers fuel this fear. Ximena L. told us, "It is easy to intimidate those with no education or those with shorter sentences . . . People are very leery about raising allegations."[114]

Women who have assisted prison officials in investigating sexual misconduct have faced harassment and retaliation. Uma M. told us that after she alleged sexual misconduct, she was repeatedly harassed by staff as well as prisoners sympathetic to the staff. Corrections officers, she reported, repeatedly questioned her about her role in the investigation and called her out of her cell to tell her such things as, "You think that was bad, now you're in my unit. Wait until you see what we do with you here." Everyone, she said, knew she played a role in having Officer G suspended. The harassment from corrections officers continued even after she was transferred to a different facility. At the second prison two officers pulled her from her room, handcuffed her and took her into their office, where they proceeded to badger her. In an apparent reference to Officer G, they reportedly asked her whether she was going to get one of their colleagues suspended.[115]

Rose S. experienced harassment from other officers that she believes stemmed from the investigation into her allegation of attempted rape. Corrections officers allegedly searched her cell repeatedly and made snide remarks such as, "The best thing is to squash this." She told us, "Every day you hear it—'you rat,' 'you slut' . . . They are harassing me to the point where it's getting ridiculous."[116] The female prisoner at CCWF, who was allegedly assaulted by a male nurse, has also experienced harassment from other guards and her fellow prisoners. The harassment reportedly stemmed from the fact that she reported the guard's behavior even though they were both African American.[117]

Rebecca Jurado corroborated the prisoners' accounts of reprisal. She told us that the environment within the women's prisons serves as a strong deterrent to raising complaints and filing grievances, particularly about issues such as sexual

---

[113] Interview, California, July 1994.

[114] Interview, California, August 1994.

[115] Interview, California, July 1994.

[116] Interview, California, July 1994.

[117] Telephone interview, Cassandra Shaylor, Legal Services for Prisoners with Children, April 9, 1996.

misconduct. Since both corrections officers and prisoners appear to profit from the most pervasive form of this abuse—the exchange of sexual favors for preferential treatment, money or goods—they oppose anyone who challenges the status quo. This, Jurado told us, gives rise to a climate hostile to complaints of sexual misconduct. Prisoners who tell get a "snitch jacket" from officers and other prisoners—they are labeled and thereby isolated from the prison community.[118]

Abuse of Administrative Segregation

Efforts by California to remedy the lack of appropriate confidentiality in its grievance and investigatory procedures and to ensure that complainants will not be retaliated against will be of little value unless they are accompanied by the assurance that the state will not punish prisoners if they speak out. At present, no such assurance exists and, in fact, women who complain of sexual misconduct are often punished. Of particular concern to us is the placement of prisoners who report sexual misconduct in administrative segregation while an investigation is pending. In VSPW, according to Millard Murphy, a law professor at the University of California, Davis, many of the women in administrative segregation are there because they resisted pat searches that they perceived as sexually degrading.[119]

We also are concerned about reports of women who have complained about the medical staff at CCWF and were then placed in administrative segregation.[120] Title 15 of California's administrative code contains a vague provision which corrections officials exploit to segregate prisoners even when they have done no wrong. The provision states that a prisoner may be placed in administrative segregation if her "presence [in the general population] presents an immediate threat to the safety of the inmate or others, endangers institution security or jeopardizes the integrity of an investigation of an alleged serious misconduct or criminal activity."[121] Title 15 also provides that the prisoner may be held in administrative segregation for ten days without a hearing, and the prisoner receives

---

[118] Telephone interview, Rebecca Jurado, Western State University, March 21, 1995.

[119] Telephone interview, Millard Murphy, professor of law, University of California, Davis, March 18, 1996.

[120] Memorandum from Ellen Barry and Cassandra Shaylor, Legal Services for Prisoners with Children, to Human Rights Watch, March 15, 1996.

[121] 15 California Administrative Code, Section 3335(a).

a review of the segregation order every thirty days thereafter. There is no outside limit on the time spent in segregation.[122]

While administrative segregation is clearly intended as a legitimate means to isolate prisoners who pose a risk to others or who have violated the rules, this provision also has been used to isolate rule-abiding prisoners who have reported abuse by corrections employees. Moreover, Title 15 requires that the conditions of administrative segregation "approximate" those of the general population. However, we found that women housed in administrative segregation pending an investigation have been kept there for extensive periods of time and denied access to the telephone and visits with their attorneys. They were permitted to leave their rooms for shorter periods than those in general population and reported receiving inadequate and inedible food. Prisoners held in administrative segregation at CIW reported that there were rats and bugs in the cells and that the food arrived cold, with bird droppings in it.[123]

Carrie Hempel, an attorney and law professor, told us that one of her clients was kept in administrative segregation for over three months.[124] The prisoner was sent to administrative segregation after another prisoner, who was impregnated by a staff member, attempted to self-administer an abortion. Hempel's client was one of three prisoners placed in administrative segregation at the prison for allegedly having knowledge of the incident, while prison officials purportedly investigated. While in administrative segregation, the prisoner was not permitted to telephone an attorney. In addition, upon the prisoner's placement in administrative segregation, her personal property was confiscated and her space within the general population reassigned. At the time we spoke with Hempel, prison officials had returned only certain items to the prisoner and she was experiencing difficulties obtaining the rest. No charges were ever filed against Hempel's client, or the other two women, who both spent more than thirty days in segregation. The male staff member was reportedly suspended.

Uma M., who reported having been raped by an officer, was repeatedly placed in administrative segregation for long periods of time throughout the first half of 1994. According to Uma M., after she came forward, she was transferred to a second prison while officials at the first prison conducted an investigation. At

---

[122] Ibid., Section 3335 (c).

[123] Interviews, California, July 1994.

[124] Interview, Carrie Hempel, University of Southern California Law School, California, July 25, 1994.

this second prison, she was initially placed in the general population and then moved by an assistant warden to administrative segregation, where she was housed for over a month. She told us prison officials denied her privileges of the general population even though she was sent to administrative segregation "for the security of the institution" and not on a disciplinary offense. Uma M. was subsequently transferred a second time and once again placed in administrative segregation for nearly six weeks for the "security of the institution," again due to her role in the investigation at the first facility.[125]

This punitive use of administrative segregation during investigations strongly deters prisoners from bringing allegations of misconduct by correctional officers. Prisoners believe that if they come forward, they will be placed in segregation while the institution decides how to respond to the complaint. According to Ximena L., "People can't really come forward. If it's an allegation of substantial wrongdoing by an officer against a prisoner, you can count on going to jail [administrative segregation]."

Lack of Accountability to Prisoners and External Monitors

Improvements in California's response to prisoner complaints of sexual misconduct would be that much more likely, and effective, if they were adopted in cooperation with external, independent monitors, including prisoners' attorneys. At present, however, such external advocates have inadequate access to prison facilities and to prisoners, and are consulted infrequently, if at all, with respect to these issues. Moreover, significant barriers exist to prisoners' communication with those outside the system. Prisoners are permitted only one collect telephone call every two weeks unless they obtain special privileges through their work details or through the willingness of particular staff. Legal visits are also restricted to certain days and times, and legal calls are difficult to arrange.[126] When we contacted one prison to obtain information about the procedure for arranging legal visits, we were given the procedure but informed that we would have to give additional notice if we were with the American Civil Liberties Union (ACLU) and looking into medical care issues.

California enacted legislation in August 1994 to restrict prisoners' rights and their access to those outside the prisons even further. Under Title 15, a prisoner's visits may only be restricted "as is necessary for the reasonable security

---

[125] Interview, California, July 1994.

[126] Fax from Ellen Barry, Legal Services for Prisoners with Children, to Human Rights Watch, March 15, 1996.

of the institution and safety of persons."[127] The legislation amended Section 2601 of the California Penal Code to grant prison officials broader authority to limit visits, allowing the denial of visitation if they determine that this would serve a "legitimate penological interest."[128]   The provision appears to permit prison officials the same, broad discretion in denying legal as well as family visits. Although the language may be unconstitutional (plans to challenge it are underway), prior to a court ruling it could lead to severe limitations on the rights of prisoners to access the court.

Prisoners housed in administrative segregation are further limited in their ability to contact their attorneys. As mentioned above, according to Carrie Hempel, one of her clients was denied telephone calls completely after she was sent to administrative segregation and was forced to contact Hempel in writing. This delayed Hempel's efforts to pursue her client's case with prison officials. Hempel experienced even more difficulties when she attempted to visit her client. She told us that, contrary to Title 15, prison officials initially would allow her to see the prisoner only in a noncontact, nonconfidential setting.[129] Prison officials eventually granted the prisoner a confidential, noncontact visit only after she persisted and waited approximately two and one-half hours.

According to Hempel, who directs a legal clinic at the University of Southern California that provides legal representation to women at CIW, officials at the prison have not been open to meeting with clinic representatives. In contrast, prison officials at the Terminal Island men's prison had been receptive to the legal clinic and they were able to establish a good working relationship.[130]

California also has taken steps to reduce journalists' access to prisoners by prohibiting reporters from interviewing prisoners in the prison.[131] According to J.P. Tremblay, assistant secretary of the Youth and Adult Correctional Agency (an executive body), as of December 1995 the ban was a temporary measure to

---

[127] 15 California Administrative Code, Section 3107 (b).

[128] Senate Bill 1260, Section 2601.

[129] Senate Bill 1260, Section 2601.

[130] Telephone interview, Carrie Hempel, University of Southern California Law School, March 6, 1996.

[131] Michael Taylor, "State Inmates Barred From Media Interviews," *San Francisco Chronicle*, December 28, 1995.

discourage the media glamorization of certain prisoners. The ban would be in force until new guidelines could be drafted that distinguished between "legitimate news and entertainment news."[132] However, when justifying the prohibition on reporters, Tremblay cited Vaughn Dortch, whose media exposure had been limited to recounting his experience of being scalded during a forced bath while in prison. This suggests that part of the ban's rationale was to prevent prisoners from publicizing certain prison conditions. On March 29, 1996, the CDC further restricted prisoners' ability to correspond confidentially with reporters by filing proposed revisions to prison regulations that would make the media ban permanent and allow the CDC to read prisoners' letters to reporters.[133] Tremblay stated the latter revision was designed to prevent prisoners from requesting help for escapes.[134] Prisoners may still call reporters on the phone, but such conversations are monitored randomly.

Impunity

One of the most troubling aspects of the CDC's failure to respond adequately to sexual misconduct is its consistent unwillingness adequately to discipline or punish correctional officers who engage in such abuse. As noted above, California does have a law criminalizing actual sexual misconduct in custody. However, according to the CDC's own figures, this only rarely results in referral for prosecution. Of the total of ten reported complaints of sexual misconduct in 1994-95, only one case was referred to the district attorney.[135]

Testimony we received from prisoners indicates that, in some cases, corrections officers and other employees allegedly involved in sexual relations with

---

[132] Ibid.

[133] A reporter may still interview a prisoner through getting on his official visiting list, which could take weeks and restricts reporters to the same visiting hours and conditions as routine visitors. Michael Taylor, "Prisoners' Missives to Media Restricted," *San Francisco Chronicle*, March 30, 1996.

[134] Ibid.

[135] Letter from William B. Anderson, chief, Institutional Services Unit, California Department of Corrections, to Human Rights Watch, June 5, 1996.

prisoners are suspended or moved to noncontact positions pending investigation.[136] Quintin N. provided us with the names of seven male officers—including Officers G and R—who were reportedly suspended from the prison where she was incarcerated amid, she believed, allegations of sexual misconduct. However, according to the testimony we received, although the officers are temporarily suspended, they often return to the facility after an investigation ends, or are transferred to another prison. Investigators reportedly told Rose S. that if she was transferred to another facility, Officer R would return to the prison.

We learned, moreover, that the CDC does not always respond promptly with disciplinary action. As mentioned above, in 1993 seven women formerly incarcerated at Avenal sued several corrections officers and the CDC for alleged violations of their constitutional rights. Some of these officers remained at Avenal after the women left; others, including Officer G, were transferred to CCWF. Once at CCWF, Officer G was suspended after he was reportedly discovered bringing women's lingerie and other contraband into the facility. Shortly after this incident, CDC settled the Avenal suit. However, an attorney representing the women knew of no disciplinary action taken against any of the corrections officers named in the suit. He told us the CDC "took pains not to admit any liability as part of the settlement."[137] In addition, to our knowledge, the doctor at CCWF, who reportedly sexually assaulted several women prisoners, continues to practice there.

RECOMMENDATIONS

I. Prohibiting Sex in Custody

A. California should enforce its law criminalizing all instances of sexual intercourse between prison staff and prisoners by investigating all reports of such incidents and prosecuting responsible prison staff to the full extent of the law.

B. The California Legislature also should amend Title 15 of the Administrative Code to explicitly ban sexual intercourse, sexual touching or any other form of sexual contact between corrections employees and prisoners and to require that prisoners are free from torture or cruel,

---

[136] Memorandum from Ellen Barry and Cassandra Shaylor, Legal Services for Prisoners with Children, to Human Rights Watch, March 15, 1996.

[137] Telephone interview, Rick Seltzer, attorney, Seltzer & Cody, Oakland, California, September 15, 1994.

inhuman, or degrading treatment as a matter of compliance with U.S. obligations under international law. Such contact not only constitutes a violation of the corrections official's professional duty; it is also a criminal offense and should be prosecuted as a felony.

C.   The CDC should remove all administrative provisions that allow for the punishment of prisoners who engage in sexual intercourse, sexual contact or any other form of sexual conduct with corrections staff, and cease punishing prisoners found to have engaged in such behavior. Punishment of prisoners has the effect of deterring their reporting of sexual abuse by corrections staff.

D.   The CDC should cease using administrative segregation as de facto punishment when prisoners report sexual misconduct by guards.

II.   Safeguarding Prisoners Impregnated by Guards
A.   The CDC should stop punishing or harassing in any way prisoners who are impregnated by officers. The CDC should also refrain from administratively segregating pregnant prisoners, unless they expressly request it. Administrative segregation should provide for the provision of adequate medical and hygienic requirements necessary for a safe pregnancy.

B.   The CDC should ensure that female prisoners impregnated by corrections staff are not pressured in any way to undergo an abortion. Prisoners also should receive neutral counseling on the options available to them.

C.   The CDC should ensure that pregnant women receive timely and adequate medical care, and that medical treatment recommended by physicians is provided as prescribed.

D.   Medical care should include psychiatric counseling for prisoners who are impregnated as a consequence of rape or sexual abuse.

III.   Prohibiting Abusive and Degrading Language
The CDC should enforce provisions of Title 15 that mandate humane treatment and prohibit derogatory language. Corrections staff must be made aware, through enforcement, that they are obligated to comply with such provisions or be subjected to disciplinary sanctions.

IV.   Protecting Privacy: The Need for a Policy

A.   The CDC should institute a policy to protect the privacy of women prisoners consistent with several federal court decisions recognizing that prisoners have a constitutionally protected right to privacy. Corrections employees should be fully trained in this policy, and it should be enforced strictly. Such a policy should include, among other things:

1.   a requirement that male officers announce their presence before entering a women's housing unit, toilet or shower area;

2.   permission for prisoners to cover their cell windows for limited intervals while undressing or using the toilets in their cells; and

3.   a rule that only female officers should be present during gynecological examinations.

B.   Consistent with Title 15, Section 3287, the CDC should cease "unclothed body searches" of women prisoners either by or in the presence of male employees, or under circumstances where a male employee may be in a position to observe the prisoner while she is undressed. Strip searches should be administered in a location that limits access by other prisoners or employees.

C.   The CDC should use female officers to pat-search female prisoners whenever possible. All officers should be trained in the appropriate conduct of pat frisks and in the disciplinary sanctions associated with improperly performed searches. Women prisoners who either pull away during offensive pat-searches or request that the search be conducted by a female officer should not be subjected automatically to disciplinary action.

V.   Ensuring an Effective Remedy
Grievances

A.   In cases of alleged sexual misconduct by corrections employees, prisoners should be authorized to bypass the informal level of review and file their complaints directly with the prison superintendent or investigator. The CDC should amend Title 15 to encourage the use of an informal stage rather than to require such a stage.

B.   The CDC should also introduce into Title 15 protections that require prompt and impartial investigations into complaints of sexual misconduct by corrections employees. The grievance procedure should, among other things, protect the confidentiality of the complainant and witnesses during the time that the officer is potentially in contact with them, ensure that prisoner testimony is give due weight, and prohibit the implicated officer from conducting the investigation.

C.   The CDC should make grievance forms readily available in the prison library or some other neutral place.

D.   The CDC should enforce provisions of Title 15 that permit prisoners to assist each other in the preparation of grievances.

Investigations

A.   The CDC should promulgate a written, public procedure for conducting investigations into sexual misconduct. The investigative procedure should, at a minimum:
1.   specify the circumstances necessary to initiate an investigation;
2.   provide for a special investigator trained to handle such issues, with the necessary human and material resources to do so;
3.   set forth a clear structure and time frame for conducting investigations;
4.   protect as much as possible the anonymity of the complainant;
5.   guard complainants and witnesses from retaliation and harassment; and
6.   ensure accountability to outside monitors. The complainant's legal counsel, upon request, should be provided a written record of the investigation, including all statements made by the complainants and witnesses.

B.   The CDC should integrate the investigative procedure into its operations manual and make it available as a public document.

C.   The CDC should require all corrections employees to report promptly any allegations, including rumors, of sexual misconduct or other overfamiliar conduct to the prison warden. Failure to do so should be a punishable offense.

D.   The CDC should not, under any circumstances, assign implicated officers to investigate allegations of their own misconduct. Officers alleged to have committed rape, sexual assault or criminal sexual contact should be assigned to noncontact positions or suspended until the circumstances are clarified and the investigation completed.

E.   The CDC should refer promptly all allegations of rape, sexual assault and other alleged criminal conduct to the state police for criminal investigation. When a referral is made to the state police, the CDC should continue, not cease, its own internal investigation into possible employee misconduct and proceed with disciplinary action when appropriate.

VI.   Preventing Retaliation Against Complainants

A.   Investigators should not recommend a disciplinary report, and wardens should not impose one, as punishment for a complaint of sexual abuse found to be unsubstantiated, unless the complaint is manifestly frivolous or made in bad faith.

B.   The CDC should ensure, as much as possible, the confidentiality of allegations of sexual misconduct by prison staff and the anonymity of both complainant and witnesses; their names should not be given to the accused officer while he or she remains in a contact position with the complainant or is assigned to the facility where the complainant resides. The CDC should also prevent the complainant's name from being revealed generally within the facility.

C.   The California Legislature should review Title 15, Section 3402, of the administrative code and amend it further to restrict access to files not already protected and to ensure that better protections for the confidentiality of records are provided. We believe that in order to be prepared to work with women prisoners, corrections investigators should receive increased staff training and supervision, rather than unfettered access to prisoner files.

D.   In accordance with its operations manual, the CDC should suspend (place on administrative leave) any employee accused of sexual misconduct, including "unacceptable familiarity," with a prisoner, if such misconduct once proven would result in dismissal.

E.   The CDC should investigate reports of retribution promptly and vigorously and should discipline transgressing employees appropriately.

VII.   Curtailing the Use of Administrative Segregation

The CDC should authorize the use of administrative segregation during an investigation only at the prisoner's explicit request. Since a prisoner placed in administrative segregation for her own protection has not committed a disciplinary offense, she should retain the rights of the general population (e.g., telephone calls, visits, access to recreation, etc.). She should be returned to the general population when she requests to be. The CDC should train employees assigned to segregated housing units regarding such provisions.

VIII.   Ensuring Discipline

A.   The CDC should create a clear policy on disciplinary action against abusive corrections employees. This policy should state explicitly that an employee found to have engaged in sexual relations or sexual contact with prisoners will be dismissed. Transfer of such employees to other positions or facilities does not constitute appropriate punishment.

B.   The CDC should also discipline officers who have violated Title 15 provisions mandating the humane treatment of prisoners.

C.   The CDC should publish, at least quarterly, a report on disciplinary actions taken against corrections employees responsible for misconduct or abuse. The reports should omit the names of prisoners and, if necessary, of employees. But they should include dates, locations, and other relevant details about the reported incidents and the types of punishment applied.

IX.   Hiring and Training Corrections Employees

A.   The CDC should improve its screening procedures for applicants for corrections positions. Background checks should be completed before new employees are sent into correctional facilities. In no case should the CDC rehire an employee who has been convicted of an offense related to sexual misconduct in custody or who resigned in order to avoid such investigation.

B.   The CDC should, as soon as possible, implement comprehensive and mandatory training on issues specific to incarcerated women for all current and future corrections employees assigned to women's prisons. This training should include, among other things:

1.   a general discussion or profile of female prisoners and their potential vulnerability to sexual misconduct;

2.   CDC policies on privacy and the prohibition on sexual relations, degrading language, and other sexually oriented or degrading behavior toward incarcerated women and the disciplinary or criminal sanctions associated with this behavior; and

3.   appropriate methods for conducting pat-searches, strip searches, and searches of women's cells. The CDC should collaborate with local nongovernmental organizations experienced in working on issues affecting incarcerated women, including rape and sexual assault.

X.   Educating Prisoners

A.   The CDC should advise incarcerated women, as part of their orientation to the corrections system, as well as prisoners already serving their sentences, of the following:

1.   Corrections officers are strictly prohibited from having any form of sexual contact with prisoners. The orientation should also include a thorough review of departmental process regarding privacy and humane treatment; the procedures for reporting and investigating sexual misconduct; and the departmental or criminal law sanctions associated with it.

2.   Grievances relating to sexual misconduct may be filed directly and confidentially with the prison investigator. All grievances should be acknowledged and resolved as soon as possible. Prisoners should be informed about the issues that may be dealt with through the grievance procedure, with a particular emphasis on instances of sexual misconduct; the location of grievance forms; any specific procedures for reporting sexual misconduct; the recourse available when corrections officers fail to respond; and the potential to resolve complaints through the internal investigation procedure and the independent review board when one is established.

3.   The CDC should also acquaint prisoners with their rights under international human rights treaties ratified by the U.S. as well as under U.S. constitutional law.

B.   The above information should be included in the prisoner handbook.

XI.   Allocating Supplies
The CDC should ensure that incarcerated women, including those in administrative segregation, receive sufficient and appropriate supplies, especially sanitary napkins and toilet paper. These items should be available in a neutral location.

XII.   Ensuring Accountability to Outside Monitors
A.   The CDC should provide timely and written information about an investigation to the complainant and the people she designates, such as her attorney and her family, upon their request.

B.   The California Legislature should create a fully empowered and independent review board to investigate, among other things, complaints of sexual misconduct. The review board should have the authority to turn over evidence of possible criminal wrongdoing to prosecutorial authorities. The board should also be able to recommend remedial action to stop abuses or other problems during an investigation. The review board also should
1.   develop a system whereby the records of any corrections employee who has been the subject of repeated sexual misconduct complaints are reviewed by the appropriate authorities; and
2.   further provide a toll-free telephone number that prisoners can use to contact investigators or to file anonymous complaints of misconduct, including retaliation against complainants.

IV. THE DISTRICT OF COLUMBIA

Sexual abuse and degrading treatment have been persistent problems for women incarcerated in the District of Columbia. In October 1993 women in Washington, D.C. prisons filed suit in district court against the District of Columbia Department of Corrections (DCDC) alleging sexual misconduct by guards, along with other violations of their constitutional rights. On December 14, 1994, the district court found that the rape, sexual assault and degrading language in the DCDC violated the eighth amendment's prohibition against cruel and unusual punishment.[1] The district court also found that the DCDC had not made adequate efforts to prevent and punish such sexual misconduct. The case was overturned by D.C. Circuit Court in August 1996 on other issues.[2]

In light of the litigation, we were unable to conduct personal interviews with women incarcerated in the District of Columbia.[3] Our discussion of sexual misconduct in Washington, D.C. is, therefore, based on our observations at trial, press accounts, public documents relating to the litigation, the judge's decision and order in the case, and interviews with attorneys working with prisoners. Because the decision and court order arising from this class action offer an important example for providing redress for custodial sexual abuse, we include the case in this report even though Human Rights Watch did not conduct firsthand interviews in the D.C. prisons for women.

---

[1] *Women Prisoners of the District of Columbia Department of Corrections v. District of Columbia*, 877 F. Supp. 634 (D.D.C. 1994). Hereafter *Women Prisoners*.

[2] As of October 1996, attorneys for the women prisoners were petitioning the D.C. Circuit Court for a rehearing by all judges on the circuit.

[3] Under this litigation, the women plaintiffs are covered by a protective order that conceals their identities and attorneys on both sides of the litigation are barred from revealing the women's names or using their testimony for purposes outside the scope of the litigation. Interview, Brenda Smith, National Women's Law Center, Washington, D.C., February 27, 1995.

CONTEXT

The overwhelmingly African American—96 percent—female prison population in the District of Columbia is growing at an enormous rate. Most of the growth is fueled by mandatory sentencing laws for drug-related crimes; over 78 percent of female prisoners in D.C. are incarcerated for nonviolent offenses, and over 58 percent were sentenced for drug-related crimes.[4] In addition, 80 percent of women incarcerated in the district have children and two-thirds have legal custody.[5] These women are primarily guarded by male officers. As of 1994, in each facility that houses women, the majority of the prison staff was male.[6] However, the DCDC houses female prisoners in the same facilities as male prisoners, therefore it is difficult to establish the gender breakdowns for the female housing areas.

State Legal and Regulatory Framework

When women prisoners in Washington, D.C. filed suit in 1993, sexual intercourse and sexual contact with prisoners were not prohibited under Washington D.C.'s criminal law beyond the general prohibition against rape and sexual assault. In December 1994, subsequent to the suit, the D.C. City Council modified its rape law (defined as "sexual abuse" in D.C. law) to make both sexual intercourse and sexual contact with a person in the custody of the District of Columbia explicitly felony offenses. Under the amended statute, a person commits "first degree sexual abuse of a ward" if he or she "engages in a sexual *act* with another person or causes another person to engage in or submit to a sexual act when that other person . . . is in official custody."[7] This felony is punishable by up to ten years in prison and a fine not to exceed $100,000. A person commits "second degree sexual abuse of a ward" if he or she "engages in sexual *contact* with another person or causes another person to engage in or submit to a sexual contact when that other person . . . is in official custody."[8] This charge carries a

---

[4] National Women's Law Center, "Women in Prison Project," March 1995.

[5] Ibid.

[6] DCDC, "Cumulative Staff Demographic Breakdown (by Institution)," March 24, 1994.

[7] D.C. Code, 22-4113(1). Emphasis added.

[8] D.C. Code, 22-4114(1). Emphasis added.

penalty of up to five years in prison and a fine not to exceed $50,000. Consent of the prisoner is not a defense to either provision. The law went into effect on May 23, 1995.

National and International Law Protections

As discussed in the legal background chapter of this report, sexual misconduct is clearly prohibited under both U.S. constitutional law and international and international treaty and customary law that is binding on the U.S. federal government as well as its constituent states.[9] The eighth amendment to the Constitution, which bars cruel and unusual punishment, has been interpreted by U.S. courts to protect prisoners against rape and sexual assault. This constitutional shield is augmented by the Fourth Amendment's guarantee of the right to privacy and personal integrity, which, in a series of lower court cases, has been interpreted to prohibit male guards from inappropriately viewing or strip searching female prisoners or conducting intrusive pat-frisks on female prisoners.

Constitutional protections for prisoners' rights are enforceable via lawsuits filed by or on behalf of prisoners, or by the U.S. Department of Justice (DOJ). Historically, U.S. prisoners have achieved most of their landmark victories through private litigation, particularly suits litigated by prisoners' rights groups such as the National Prison Project of the American Civil Liberties Union. However, if stringent intent requirements are met, the DOJ may criminally prosecute abusive prison officials under federal civil rights provisions. In addition, the DOJ has the statutory right to investigate and institute civil actions under the Civil Rights of Institutionalized Persons Act (CRIPA) whenever it finds that a state facility engages in a pattern or practice of subjecting prisoners to "egregious or flagrant conditions" in violation of the Constitution.

In addition to constitutional protections, prisoners' rights are protected under international human rights treaties that are legally binding on the United States. The primary international legal instruments protecting the rights of U.S. prisoners are the International Covenant on Civil and Political Rights (ICCPR), ratified by the United States in 1993, and the Convention Against Torture and Other Cruel, Inhuman or Degrading Treatment or Punishment, ratified in 1994. The ICCPR guarantees prisoners' rights to privacy, except when limitations on this right are demonstrably necessary to maintain prison security. Both treaties bar torture and cruel, inhuman or degrading treatment or punishment, which

---

[9] For a detailed discussion of United States obligations under U.S. constitutional law and international law pertaining to the treatment of prisoners, see the legal background chapter of this report.

authoritative international bodies have interpreted as including sexual abuse. To constitute torture, an act must cause severe physical or mental suffering and must be committed for a purpose such as obtaining information from a victim, punishing her or intimidating or coercing her or for any reason based on discrimination of any kind. Cruel, inhuman or degrading treatment or punishment includes acts causing a lesser degree of suffering that need not be committed for a particular purpose.

When prison staff members use force, the threat of force, or other means of coercion to compel a prisoner to engage in sexual intercourse, their acts constitute rape and, therefore, torture. Torture also occurs when prison staff use force or coercion to engage in sexual touching of prisoners where such acts cause serious physical or mental suffering. Instances of sexual touching or of sexual intercourse that does not amount to rape may constitute torture or cruel or inhuman treatment, depending on the level of physical or mental suffering involved. Other forms of sexual misconduct, such as inappropriate pat or strip searches or verbal harassment, that do not rise to the level of torture or of cruel or inhuman treatment, may be condemned as degrading treatment.[10]

Legal Action to Expose and Remedy Abuses

As stated above, in 1993 women prisoners in the District of Columbia sued the DCDC. Their complaint asserted that the DCDC failed to protect them from rape, sexual assault and sexual harassment by corrections officers, provided them with inadequate medical care, subjected them to poor conditions of confinement, and offered them educational, work, religious and recreational programs inferior to those provided to male prisoners. Brenda Smith of the National Women's Law Center (NWLC), an attorney on that lawsuit, told Human Rights Watch that through her work providing legal services and programming to incarcerated women since 1990, she had received reports of sexual assaults and pregnancies within the prisons and assisted several women on an individual basis. However, it was not until the lawsuit was filed that the magnitude and pattern of the abuses were exposed. She told us, "It is really like this dirty little secret that everyone in corrections knows about and doesn't want to talk about. It is a huge problem."[11] According to Smith, attorney on the lawsuit, over ninety women came

---

[10] For a detailed discussion of the prohibition against torture and other cruel, inhuman or degrading treatment or punishment under international law and its applicability to custodial sexual misconduct, see the legal background chapter of this report.

[11] Interview, Brenda Smith, senior counsel, National Women's Law Center, Washington, D.C., February 27, 1995.

forward and many, although not all of them, complained of sexual misconduct by prison staff.[12] All of these women were incarcerated in one of three facilities operated by the DCDC: D.C. Central Facility (Jail), the D.C. Correctional Treatment Facility (CTF), and the Lorton Minimum Security Annex (Annex).

A three-week trial was held in June 1994, before June Green, a senior district court judge for the District of Columbia. In her December 1994 ruling, Judge Green found a general acceptance within the DCDC of sexual relationships between staff and prisoners that gave rise to a "sexualized environment."[13] As to the legal claim, she concluded that there was a pattern of sexual harassment of incarcerated women by male corrections staff that violated the eighth amendment's prohibition against cruel and unusual punishments.[14]

Subsequent to her findings, Judge Green issued an extensive order directing the DCDC to remedy constitutional violations within its corrections system. Her order addressed a range of problems that contributed to the sexual abuse and degrading treatment of incarcerated women, including: the absence of a clear prohibition on sexual activity and sexualized language, the failure to report and investigate allegations of such misconduct, and the lack of training for corrections staff and for female prisoners.[15]

Within the order, the judge appointed an independent special monitor[16] to receive and investigate complaints of sexual misconduct at the three facilities housing women and to report her findings to the warden at each institution. The special monitor was also instructed to investigate any outstanding allegations of sexual misconduct and to oversee the DCDC's resolution of sexual misconduct complaints. The special monitor, Grace Lopes, who has a three-person staff, began her duties on December 1, 1995. While the special monitor has improved the

---

[12] To protect the women from retaliation or harassment, women who were deposed or who testified in the class action as witnesses were identified as Jane Does. Smith said that the Jane Does were first numbered 1 to 13, then with letters of the alphabet, then doubled and tripled letters of the alphabet, such as Jane Doe AA and Jane Doe AAA.

[13] *Women Prisoners*, p. 639.

[14] Ibid., p. 667.

[15] *Women Prisoners v. District of Columbia*, Civil Action File No. 93-2052 (JLG), Order for Declaratory and Declarative Relief, December 13, 1994.

[16] The special monitor is a special officer, a federal court official with judicial powers.

complaints process, she is responsible for monitoring several other court orders in D.C. prisons and is extremely busy.[17] In addition, Lopes has not taken many affirmative steps to contact women prisoners. Smith of NWLC asked Lopes to explain her job and responsibilities at a session of NWLC's training for women prisoners in D.C. She declined.[18]

The order also requires the DCDC to institute training for corrections employees specifically addressing issues arising in a women's institution as well as training on sexual harassment for female prisoners. Corrections employees have already begun to receive training provided by the DCDC, although without any contributions from local nongovernmental organizations working on the issue.

The judge further directed the DCDC to write and institute a policy prohibiting sexual harassment of female prisoners by corrections employees. This policy, which went into effect on May 15, 1995, prohibits sexual misconduct against prisoners by any employee or agent of the DCDC.[19] Sexual misconduct is defined broadly in the policy to include: any act of sexual abuse, sexual assault, physical contact of a sexual nature, sexual harassment,[20] and invasion of privacy (including observing prisoners' personal affairs without a sound penological reason), and any "conversations or correspondence which demonstrates or suggests a romantic or intimate relationship between an inmate and employee."[21] Penalties range from reprimands for some first offenses to termination for a first offense of sexual assault or sexual abuse. But, even though the new D.C. sexual abuse law criminalizes any sexual contact between prisoners and prison officials regardless

---

[17] Bruce D. Brown, "Confronting the Cruel and the Unusual," *Legal Times* (Washington, D.C.), March 11, 1996.

[18] Interview, Brenda Smith, National Women's Law Center, Washington, D.C., February 5, 1996.

[19] District of Columbia Department of Corrections, "Sexual Misconduct Against Inmates," Department Order 3350.2A, May 15, 1995.

[20] Sexual harassment is defined to encompass degrading language and any threats or promises used to influence prisoners' behavior and "[m]aking sexually offensive comments or gestures, or engaging in physical contact of a sexual nature with an inmate." Ibid., Section VI, E (1)(b).

[21] Ibid.

of evidence of coercion, the DCDC policy requires that only allegations of unwelcome sexual intercourse or sexual touching be reported to the police.[22]

The policy also contains many additional safeguards for female prisoners. The policy strictly prohibits overt or covert retaliation against prisoners, sets a time frame for investigations[23] and imposes a positive obligation on DCDC and its employees to report in writing sexual misconduct, either witnessed or suspected. Failure to report shall subject the employee to disciplinary action, up to termination.[24] Another innovation is a confidential twenty-four-hour telephone hotline for female prisoners to report sexual misconduct, which became operational in 1996. Under the new policy, information and documentation of sexual misconduct complaints must be kept confidential and only released to relevant parties on a "need to know basis." Moreover, any prisoner who reports sexual misconduct "may request and be treated as a anonymous informant."[25]

The DCDC appealed the court's appointment of a special monitor to investigate allegations of sexual misconduct, and certain programming requirements,[26] but not the court's finding of an eighth amendment violation. The DCDC's appeal was argued in front of the D.C. Circuit Court of Appeals in February 1995. However, after the April 1996 passage of Prison Litigation Reform

---

[22] The policy only requires the DCDC to forward allegations of sexual assault, as defined by the policy to the relevant law enforcement agencies. Sexual assault is defined in the policy as "forced, nonconsensual or coerced sexual conduct." "Sexual Misconduct Against Inmates," Section VI, E(2).

[23] Each complaint must be thoroughly investigated and a final written report must be submitted within thirty days of department knowledge of the complaint. The prisoner complainant must be informed of the findings and conclusion within forty-eight hours. She then has five days to appeal the ruling to the director of the DCDC, and her appeal must be responded to within ten days. The warden must take appropriate disciplinary action against the official within fifteen days. Ibid., Section VII, B(7)-(8).

[24] Ibid., Section VII, A(1)(b).

[25] Ibid., Section VII, B(5)(b).

[26] *Women Prisoners v. District of Columbia,* Civil Action File No. 93-2052 (JLG), Brief of Appellants District of Columbia, December 11, 1995.

Act, federal legislation which limits the available remedies for custodial abuse,[27] the DCDC filed a brief requesting that certain provisions of the district court's decision, including the appointment of a special monitor to investigate sexual misconduct, be removed.[28] On August 30, 1996, a three-judge panel of the Circuit Court released its decision overturning most provisions of the district court's decision, including the appointment of a special monitor to investigate sexual misconduct. The eighth amendment finding, however, was not affected. The women prisoners have filed an appeal to have the case heard by the entire D.C. Circuit.[29]

Female employees at DCDC also sued the department for sexually degrading conduct by staff at all levels in women's prisons, including high-ranking officials.[30] In January 1994 eight current and former female employees filed a sexual harassment lawsuit against the DCDC alleging a pattern of sexual harassment against female staff.[31] The trial, which concluded August 9, 1995, was bifurcated into a liability phase and a separate damages phase. Under the liability phase, the jury found that there was a pattern of sexual harassment of female corrections officers and retaliation against those officers who tried to protect

---

[27] For a more detailed discussion of the Prison Litigation Reform Act and its implication for sexual misconduct against women in prison, see the legal background chapter of this report.

[28] *Women Prisoners v. District of Columbia*, Civil Action File Nos. 95-7041 and 95-7205, Supplemental Brief of Appellants.

[29] *Women Prisoners v. District of Columbia*, Civil Action File Nos. 95-7041 and 95-7205, Concise Statement of Issue and its Importance, September 30, 1996.

[30] *Neal et al v. Director, District of Columbia Department of Corrections*, Civil Action File No. 93-2420 (RCL). A DCDC task force created to study allegations of sexual harassment against female staff found that DCDC employees were not trained about sexual harassment and victims feared reprisals if they filed a sexual harassment complaint. Employees were concerned that those found guilty of sexual harassment would not be punished while supervisors were more concerned about disciplining employees for filing false reports. Keith A. Harriston, "D.C. Corrections Gets Sex Harassment Report," *Washington Post*, March 24, 1994.

[31] Keith A. Harriston, "D.C. Agency Accused of Harassment: Suit says sexual demands are the rule in corrections," *Washington Post*, January 7, 1994.

women from sexual harassment.[32] It also found that the DCDC constituted a hostile work environment whereby supervisors and employees engaged in offensive conduct of a sexual nature.[33] The jury then awarded the original six plaintiffs more than $1.4 million in damages.[34] The DCDC appealed the jury verdicts and court findings. Oral arguments for the appeal were held on May 14, 1996. On May 20, 1996, the circuit court remanded the case to the district court for additional findings of fact on the district court's finding that defendants had not complied with discovery rules and court orders. The district court complied with this request on June 19, 1996,[35] and on August 23, 1996, the Circuit Court overturned the District Court's decision to prohibit the DCDC's witnesses from testifying.[36] The case will be tried again with the additional testimony from the defense.

In addition to the two class action suits, at least one civil suit has been pursued in the District of Columbia by a female prisoner raped and impregnated by a guard. The prisoner filed suit in 1993 against the DCDC and Lt. Joseph Willis who worked at the Correctional Detention Facility.[37] The plaintiff's suit alleged that the DCDC was liable for Willis's actions because it had failed to take sufficient action to discourage or prevent guards from having sex with prisoners. The DCDC withdrew its legal support of Willis in July 1994 after firing him for reasons unrelated to the suit. The DCDC then asserted that once Willis became involved with the plaintiff he violated DCDC policy and therefore, the DCDC had no responsibility for his actions. Willis, on the other hand, argued that he had a consensual relationship with the plaintiff and as a result, she suffered no injury. Willis submitted alleged love letters from the plaintiff to support that defense. In response, the plaintiff alleged that there was no possibility of consent in prison. In

---

[32] *Neal v. Director, District of Columbia Department of Corrections*, Civil Action File No. 93-2420 (RCL), Memorandum Opinion I, August 9, 1995.

[33] Ibid.

[34] *Neal v. Director, District of Columbia Department of Corrections*, Civil Action File No. 93-2420 (RCL), Final Judgment and Order I, August 9, 1995.

[35] *Neal v. Director, District of Columbia Department of Corrections*, Civil Action File No. 93-2420 (RCL), Statement of Reasons on Remand, June 19, 1996.

[36] Toni Locy, "Judges Void Harassment Suit Verdict," *Washington Post,* August 24, 1996.

[37] Telephone interview, Steven Kupferburg, attorney, February 26, 1996.

October 1995, the jury rejected the defenses of the DCDC and Willis and found the DCDC liable for $5,000 in damages, which as of February 1996 they still had not paid. The jury also found Willis liable for $25,000 in damages.

ABUSES[38]

Rape, Sexual Assault or Abuse, and Criminal Sexual Contact

During the *Women Prisoners* case, the district court heard from many women incarcerated in Washington, D.C. who were sexually assaulted and sexually harassed by prison staff, including corrections officers as well as civilian staff.[39] The judge cited the testimony of Jane Doe RR, Jane Doe Q, and Jane Doe W, all of whom were raped or sexually assaulted by male corrections staff. Jane Doe RR was forced to perform oral sex on a corrections officer at CTF, Jane Doe Q was raped by a corrections officer while housed in the prison infirmary at the Jail, and Jane Doe W was sexually assaulted by a sergeant while incarcerated at CTF. In addition, a CTF officer tried on several occasions to fondle Jane Doe K's breasts, vagina, and buttocks; male officers and employees fondled women's breasts, legs, arms, and buttocks; and a teacher at the print shop often tried to kiss Jane Doe OOO.[40]

More recently, complaints were filed against L.C. Jones, acting deputy warden for operations at the CTF, alleging that he anally raped a female prisoner

---

[38] By rape, we mean sexual intercourse between a prison employee and a prisoner that is accompanied by the use or threat of force or coercion which, under certain circumstances, can take the form of the provision or denial of privileges, money, or goods. Sexual assault is sexual touching, short of intercourse, involving the same coercive influences. Sexual abuse is sexual intercourse or touching involving the offer of goods or privileges absent any actual or perceived threat to the prisoner. Criminal sexual contact refers to sexual intercourse or sexual touching that cannot be shown to involve any of the above elements but which nonetheless constitutes a gross breach of official duty. Rape, sexual assault or abuse, and criminal sexual contact should all be prosecuted as felonies. For a more detailed discussion, see the legal background chapter.

[39] Judge Green identified incidents of sexual assault as part of the overall sexual harassment within the D.C. system.

[40] *Women Prisoners*, p. 640.

in November 1995.[41] Reportedly, the prisoner went to Jones's office to get his signature on an official order. Jones, according to the prisoner, refused to sign the order until the woman had sex with him. The prisoner asserted that although she agreed to have sex with Jones, he forced her to have anal sex. The authorities became aware of the rape when the woman was treated at D.C. General Hospital for a ruptured rectum.[42] Jones, who was the first individual to be charged under D.C.'s new "anti-sexual abuse" law, was placed on administrative leave with pay during the criminal proceedings. The case was presented to a grand jury for an indictment, and the grand jury declined to press charges.[43] In addition, the special monitor, in a separate, concurrent investigation, cleared Jones of all charges.[44] To our knowledge, no other cases have been pursued under the "anti-sexual abuse" statute as of this writing.[45]

Attorneys in the *Women Prisoners* case also argued that women incarcerated in D.C. prisons were coerced into sexual activity with prison staff through the use of threats, including the use of disciplinary reports.[46] According to the court papers and testimony at trial, corrections employees also compelled women into sexual relationships in exchange for favorable treatment and goods, including cigarettes, candy, food, and money.[47] In some cases, women became pregnant as a result of these liaisons.[48] The district court found that these allegations were proved during the trial.

---

[41] Toni Locy, "Inmate Accuses D.C. Corrections Official of Sexual Assault," *Washington Post,* November 21, 1995.

[42] Ibid.

[43] Toni Locy, "Inquiry Clears Correction Official of Rape Allegation," *Washington Post,* March 14, 1996.

[44] Ibid.

[45] Telephone interview, Assistant U.S. Attorney for District Of Columbia, August 9, 1996.

[46] *Women Prisoners v. District of Columbia Department of Corrections*, Civil Action File No. 93-2052 (JLG), Plaintiffs' Proposed Findings of Fact, June 8, 1994.

[47] "Female Inmates Tell of Sex for Favors in Jail," *Washington Post*, June 17, 1994.

[48] Toni Locy, "Officer Describes 'Auction' of Female Inmates at D.C. Jail," *Washington Post*, March 9, 1995.

Abusive and Degrading Language

Several plaintiffs testified that women prisoners in the District of Columbia are constantly subjected to degrading, sexualized language. One Jane Doe testified that when she informed an officer that she was going to take a shower, he responded, "Well, you go ahead and do that, and I'll be in there to stick my rod up in you."[49] The court also found that male corrections staff and male prisoners frequently made derogatory comments about the women's breasts and buttocks.[50] Testimony at trial revealed that some staff at the Annex were aware of and witnessed the male prisoners' conduct but failed to take any disciplinary action. Since the court decision, as discussed later in this chapter, the degrading treatment continues at D.C. correctional facilities.

Further, one former employee testified at the corrections employees trial that in the early 1980s female prisoners at the D.C. jail were lined up by several high-ranking male officials who:

> looked them over and picked the women they wanted to work in their offices. Lower ranking officers picked from the inmates who were left over . . . and those women were assigned to do special duties for them.[51]

The former employee also testified that several of these prisoners told her that the male employees used the work assignments as an opportunity to have sex with the prisoners.[52]

These abuses took place in a context that is largely devoid of privacy protections for women from viewing by male guards and prisoners.[53] According to Judge Green's opinion, male officers did not announce themselves in the

---

[49] *Women Prisoners*, p. 640.

[50] Ibid.

[51] Locy, "Officer Describes 'Auction'. . ." *Washington Post.*

[52] Ibid.

[53] All three facilities run by the DCDC that hold women are co-correctional, meaning they house both female and male prisoners.

housing areas, and the structural design of CTF permitted male prisoners to view the women's cells from a number of locations inside the facility.[54]

THE SYSTEM'S RESPONSE

Prior to the filing of the class action suit in 1993, the DCDC had been very slow to respond to allegations of sexual misconduct and degrading treatment within its facilities. Judge Green found that while the DCDC had several policies ostensibly intended to respond to allegations of sexual misconduct and criminal behavior, including a grievance procedure, these were "of little value since the [DCDC] address[ed] the problem of sexual harassment of women prisoners with no specific staff training, inconsistent reporting practices, cursory investigations and timid sanctions."[55]

The district court found that there was no clear procedure for reporting and investigating complaints of sexual misconduct. Investigations were handled inconsistently among the three facilities, and staff did not routinely report abuses that came to their attention. In some cases, the DCDC failed entirely to investigate, while in other instances investigations lingered and remained unresolved. Judge Green also found that the investigative process was biased in favor of corrections staff; where an allegation amounted to the word of a prisoner against the word of an employee, the DCDC sided with the employee and summarily dismissed the prisoner's claim.[56]

The DCDC also generally failed to discipline employees for sexual misconduct. Some officers were reassigned to other facilities while others remained at the same institution and were even assigned to work in the unit where the complainants were housed. In one case cited by the district court, several prisoners complained to the prison administration about sexually explicit harassment from a teacher, but "there [was] no evidence that the administration

---

[54] The district court did not address these abuses as violations of the prisoners' constitutional right to privacy, because it found them prohibited under the eighth amendment. *Women Prisoners*, p. 665.

[55] Ibid., p. 640.

[56] Ibid., p. 642.

took corrective action."[57]   In another instance, Deputy Warden L.C. Jones, discussed elsewhere in this chapter, reportedly discouraged a prisoner from pressing a complaint or discussing it with attorneys on the suit.[58] In exchange, he promised to assist her in getting released from prison. Jones himself was cited for sexual misconduct in both the *Women Prisoners* litigation[59] and the women corrections officers' suit, yet, to our knowledge, he has never been disciplined by the DCDC. Attorney Brenda Smith reiterated this point. She found very few instances of disciplinary action against abusive officers, and even when such actions were taken, the penalties were disproportionately mild, limited often to a brief suspension.[60] The corrections department seldom referred cases of sexual assault or rape to the D.C. police; when the police did investigate, the DCDC automatically ceased its own internal inquiry.

There was no effective mechanism in the DCDC for protecting the complainants' confidentiality. The judge found that reported incidents "quickly became a matter of public knowledge among prisoners and staff," who then retaliated against and harassed the complainants.[61] Judge Green concluded that "those who report the [sexual] harassment often experience increased stress and may end up becoming isolated from other women in the institution."[62] She was persuaded by testimony at the trial that the department's failure to respond to abuses, combined with the women's history of sexual abuse, compounded the women's ordeal. Attorney Smith agreed with the judge's conclusion. In investigating the abuses, she found a serious problem of underreporting of sexual misconduct because many women had a well-founded fear of filing complaints.[63]

---

[57] Ibid.

[58] Ibid., p. 641.

[59] Ibid.

[60] Interview, Brenda Smith, National Women's Law Center, Washington, D.C., February 27, 1995.

[61] *Women Prisoners*, p. 641.

[62] Ibid., p. 643.

[63] Interview, Brenda Smith, National Women's Law Center, Washington, D.C., February 27, 1995.

Retaliation by staff within the DCDC assumed many forms: complainants were placed in administrative segregation; targeted for disciplinary reports, which affected their parole; removed from programs which they needed; and denied work assignments.[64] Women who spoke out also received a "snitch jacket" or reputation within the prison community that they were untrustworthy. This label then exposed them to abuse from other prisoners.

The Effect of *Women Prisoners v. District of Columbia*

In response to the order issued in the *Women Prisoners* suit and the accompanying policy, the DCDC response to sexual misconduct has improved. For example, in August 1995, the DCDC suspended seven corrections officers for attending a party at the city jail where two female prisoners did a striptease.[65] In addition, Smith reports that since the new policy went into effect, more officers have been reporting sexual misconduct by their fellow guards.[66] She attributes this improvement to the policy's reporting requirement and to the increased awareness of the problem of sexual misconduct raised by the suit. Nonetheless, according to Smith, a "significant core" of the corrections officers continues to not take sexual misconduct seriously, and she continues to receive allegations of sexual misconduct by DCDC staff.[67]

Moreover, it is particularly problematic that, in regard to the anal rape allegation against L.C. Jones that was rejected by the grand jury and special monitor, the special monitor reportedly planned to explore the possibility of filing perjury charges against the prisoner.[68] Brenda Smith told us that she credits her client's testimony and is concerned more generally that prosecution for perjury in this instance will discourage women prisoners from coming forward in the future.[69]

---

[64] *Women Prisoners*, p. 666.

[65] Toni Locy, "7 D.C. Jail Guards Suspended in Cellblock Striptease," *Washington Post*, August 4, 1995.

[66] Interview, Brenda Smith, National Women's Law Center, Washington, D.C., February 5, 1996.

[67] Ibid.

[68] Locy, "Inquiry Clears Corrections Official . . .," *Washington Post*.

[69] Telephone interview, Brenda Smith, National Women's Law Center, March 21, 1996.

Human Rights Watch shares this concern. While we oppose false allegations, we believe prosecution should be used only in extreme cases where such accusations are manifestly malicious or in bad faith. This caution takes into account the chilling effect such punishments have on prisoners reporting sexual misconduct.

In addition, neither Smith nor her client was officially informed of the grand jury's decision or the conclusions of the special monitor. Indeed, Smith learned of the grand jury's decision and the special monitor's report from a *Washington Post* reporter.[70] She then notified her client. As of March 21, 1996, neither Smith nor her client had received written notice of the special monitor's decision or a copy of the special monitor's report. Smith later received a copy of the decision after specifically requesting it. Without a copy of the report being provided automatically, the right to appeal guaranteed by the new DCDC policy had been rendered virtually meaningless because neither Smith nor her client were aware of the rationale for the decision. The client has appealed the decisions.[71]

RECOMMENDATIONS

I.   The U.S. attorney should strictly enforce the anti-sexual abuse law of the District of Columbia prohibiting sexual intercourse and contact with a person in custody. The consent of the victim, which is not a legal defense to a prosecution under this section, should not be a *de facto* bar to prosecution.

II.   The DCDC should revise its sexual misconduct policy to require that all complaints of sexual contact between a prisoner and a corrections official be forwarded to the police, pursuant to the D.C. anti-sexual abuse law, rather than the current requirement of forwarding only allegations of "unwelcome" sexual intercourse or touching.

III.   The DCDC should notify prisoners and their legal representatives of the results of investigations into their complaints and forward their findings to them promptly in order to permit prisoners to file well-grounded appeals in accordance with the DCDC policy.

---

[70] Ibid.

[71] Telephone interview, Joanna Grossman, staff attorney, National Women's Law Center, August 7, 1996.

IV.   Prisoners who file sexual misconduct complaints that either the criminal authorities or the DCDC decide not to pursue, should not automatically be subject to a perjury investigation, without any additional evidence that the prisoner filed a false statement maliciously or in bad faith.

V.   The D.C. City Council should create a fully empowered and independent review board to investigate, among other things, complaints of sexual misconduct that are not satisfactorily resolved by the grievance or investigative mechanisms.

A.   The review board should have the authority to turn over evidence of wrongdoing for criminal investigation and prosecution. The board should also be able to recommend remedial action—including temporary reassignment or suspension of the accused—to end abuses or other problems uncovered during an investigation.

B.   The review board should develop a system whereby the records of corrections employees who have been the subject of repeated complaints are reviewed by the appropriate authorities.

C.   The review board should provide a toll-free telephone number that prisoners can use to contact investigators or to file anonymous complaints of employee misconduct, including retaliation against complainants.

V. GEORGIA

In Georgia prison officials entrusted with custodial power over the women's prison population have engaged in serious sexual misconduct. Indeed, prior to 1992, officers raped, sexually assaulted and sexually harassed female prisoners with little regard for legal or institutional constraints. Although Georgia criminal law formally prohibited sexual contact between prison officials and prisoners, the law was not enforced. Similarly, the departmental policies arguably barring such abuses were belied by the impunity with which prison staff, including supervisory staff, engaged in sexual relations with prisoners.

Unlike most other states, however, Georgia has been forced to take meaningful steps to put a stop to these abuses. In 1992, because of an amended class action lawsuit filed on behalf of Georgia women prisoners, the problem of custodial sexual misconduct received significant public attention, spurring departmental efforts toward reform. More concretely, the lawsuit resulted in a number of federal court orders requiring the Georgia Department of Corrections (GDC) to rectify many of its past practices. Although at times the GDC responded less than enthusiastically to this persistent judicial prodding, the overall atmosphere in its women's prisons has greatly improved. Nonetheless, even now sexual contact between officers and prisoners occurs and, in some instances, amounts to rape or sexual assault.

Our investigation of custodial sexual misconduct in Georgia was conducted during the pendency of the aforementioned lawsuit, *Cason v. Seckinger*.[1] The case was originally filed in 1984 as a challenge to prison conditions in Georgia and was amended in March 1992 to include allegations that women incarcerated at the Georgia Women's Correctional Institution (GWCI) were being subjected to custodial sexual abuse. In conducting our investigation, we interviewed nine current and former prisoners, all of whom served time at GWCI;[2] attorneys and a clinical social worker active on the suit and on the civil damages suits spawned by the abuses at GWCI; the former Baldwin County prosecutor, responsible for trying prison staff indicted for criminal sexual contact with prisoners; the former GDC assistant deputy commissioner for women's services; and other individuals with firsthand knowledge of the conditions at GWCI, including a former GDC

---

[1] *Cason v. Seckinger*, Civil Action File No. 84-313-1-MAC.

[2] In accordance with a protective court order in the class action suit, all of the women we interviewed are identified in this chapter by pseudonyms or by their Jane Doe number.

employee.[3] We also reviewed the records of disciplinary hearings of correctional officers that corroborate or augment the testimony of the prisoners we interviewed. While we primarily investigated abuses that occurred prior to March 1992, our investigation also examined incidents of sexual misconduct occurring since March 1992 and the GDC's response to these abuses.

Human Rights Watch urges the Georgia authorities responsible for the corrections and criminal justice systems to intensify their efforts toward preventing and prosecuting custodial sexual misconduct. In particular, we believe that Georgia prosecutors should strictly enforce the state's criminal prohibition on sexual contact with a person in custody and that the GDC, for its part, should refer to prosecution all cases that fall within the statutory definition. The GDC should also use extreme caution in assessing disciplinary reports against prisoners whose complaints of sexual misconduct are found to be unsubstantiated; collaborate with lawyers litigating *Cason*, and with organizations that assist victims of rape, to develop further the training programs for staff and women prisoners regarding sexual misconduct; and publish regular reports of the results of its sexual misconduct

---

[3] Neither the *Cason* lawsuit nor our investigation systematically examined the problem of custodial sexual abuse in Georgia jails. Unfortunately, jail abuses are much more difficult to address than are prison abuses. To begin with, there are over 200 city and county jails in Georgia, each with a separate set of responsible authorities (and thus, for purposes of litigation, a separate set of potential defendants). In addition, jails hold a much more transient population than do prisons—detainees may be held for very short periods—so that, in the absence of constant monitoring, abuses are likely to remain concealed. In short, it would require a large and continuing investment of resources to investigate jail abuses and to initiate legal action to remedy them. Given the absence of an adequate oversight mechanism to monitor jail abuses, however, and given the generally bad state of Georgia jails, we are greatly concerned about the possibility of custodial sexual abuse in the jail system. Indeed, press reports and other sources suggest that such abuse is a recurring problem. See, for example, David Corvette, "Upson County Jailer Charged with Sexual Assault on Inmate," *Atlanta Journal-Constitution*, July 7, 1992; Scott Marshall, "Some Deputies Rehired at Gwinnett County Jail: All Accused of Sexual Improprieties," *Atlanta Journal-Constitution*, January 23, 1993; Doug Payne, "Woman Was Twice Victimized by Jailer, her Lawyer Says," *Atlanta Journal-Constitution*, February 11, 1993 (Marietta City Jail); "Swainsboro: Sheriff Calls for Investigation of Jail-Sex Allegations," *Atlanta Journal-Constitution*, May 29, 1993 (Emanuel County Jail); Scott Marshall, "Former Chief Jailer Indicted on Sex Assault Charges," *Atlanta Journal-Constitution*, September 16, 1993 (Clayton County Jail); *Cason v. Seckinger*, Affidavit, Jane Doe 187, November 4, 1993 (stating that she had sex with a bailiff while held at the Chatham County Jail). In light of the reforms instituted in the Georgia prison system, we urge Georgia officials to accord like attention to addressing the problem of custodial sexual abuse in Georgia jails.

investigations and of disciplinary actions taken as a result of such investigations. Finally, we recommend that the Georgia Legislature create a fully empowered and independent review board to monitor the GDC's compliance with the requirements of *Cason* and to ensure that complaints of sexual misconduct are adequately investigated and remedied.

CONTEXT

Custodial Environment

Mirroring a national pattern, Georgia's female prison population has increased dramatically over the last fifteen years.[4] As of March 1996, women constituted 6 percent—over 2,000 prisoners—of an overall prison population of 35,000.[5] One-third of these women have been convicted of violent crimes, 22 percent of drug offenses. Their average age is thirty-three. Two-thirds of female prisoners are non-white (Georgia's prison statistics do not indicate the racial makeup of the prison population beyond white and non-white). The vast majority have at least one child.

Until 1989 Georgia operated only one prison for women—the Georgia Women's Correctional Institution (GWCI)—in conjunction with a nearby camp facility, Colony Farm. In 1989 the state opened a second women's facility, the Milan Correctional Institution, to ease overcrowding at GWCI (Milan CI has since reverted back to being a male facility). Then, largely in response to the litigation mentioned above, the GDC converted the Washington Correctional Institution (Washington CI) to a women's facility in 1992; also at plaintiffs' request, it began to convert Metro Correctional Institution (Metro CI) to a women's facility in 1993; then in 1994 it opened the Pulaski Correctional Institution as an additional women's facility, as was previously planned. The GWCI was converted to a men's facility in 1993 and renamed the Baldwin Correctional Institution. In mid-1996, as a symbolic element in a "get tough on prisoners" campaign, Georgia changed the names of all of its penal facilities, replacing the designation "correctional

---

[4] The number of prison beds for incarcerated women has more than doubled since 1983. If one includes community corrections facilities, the number of women in custody has nearly tripled. Georgia Department of Corrections, "Ten-Year Trend Analysis: Georgia's Female Offender Population Calendar 1983-1992," October 19, 1993.

[5] Georgia Department of Corrections, "GDC Facts at a Glance," March 1996 Update.

institution" with "state prison," so that Pulaski Correctional Institution, for example, is now Pulaski State Prison.[6]

Georgia, like other states, permits male officers to work in its women's prisons.[7] At GWCI, the prison whose abuses were cited in the amended lawsuit, male guards far outnumbered female guards at the time the suit was revised to cover custodial sexual abuse. In April 1992, immediately after the amended complaint was filed, the GDC promulgated a rule restricting certain staff positions to staff of the same sex as the prisoners supervised. The positions for which cross-gender guarding was deemed inappropriate were those "involving frequent or prolonged physical contact with, and/or visual observation of unclothed inmates, and/or where potential invasion of the inmate's privacy is unavoidable in the course of normal facility operations."[8] In March 1996, the GDC further narrowed the positions for which cross-gender guarding is permissible: it agreed to a consent order in the *Cason* suit by which only female staff will be assigned to women's housing units.[9]

Despite these restrictions on assignment, male guards still outnumber female guards in two of three Georgia women's facilities; only Pulaski has more women than men officers. In March 1996, however, GDC Commissioner Wayne Garner began transferring male guards out of Washington CI and replacing them with female guards. He planned to continue transferring staff—and to effect similar transfers at Georgia's other two women's prisons—until there were no male

---

[6] For a discussion of other aspects of the renewed punitive emphasis of the Georgia correctional system, see the chapter on the treatment of prisoners in *Modern Capital of Human Rights? Abuses in the State of Georgia* (New York: Human Rights Watch, 1996).

[7] Few other countries allow male guards to hold contact positions in women's prisons. Indeed, the U.N. Standard Minimum Rules for the Treatment of Prisoners, an authoritative interpretation of international law norms mandating humane treatment and respect for the human dignity of prisoners, specifically bars the practice. Article 53(3), Standard Minimum Rules for the Treatment of Prisoners, approved by the Economic and Social Council by resolutions 663 C, July 31, 1957 and 2076, May 13, 1977. Human Rights Watch, nonetheless, is not *per se* opposed to the use of male staff in women's prisons, as long as the authorities take appropriate precautions to ensure that women prisoners' rights are not compromised by their use.

[8] GDC Standard Operating Procedures, "'Same Sex Contact' Positions," Ref. No. IV002-005 (effective date April 1, 1992).

[9] *Cason v. Seckinger*, Civil Action File No. 84-313-1-MAC, Consent Order, March 7, 1996.

staff in contact positions with women inmates.[10] The new policy was immediately challenged by the Georgia State Employees Union on anti-discrimination grounds, however.[11] In late August 1996, after the Georgia Equal Employment Opportunity Commission initiated an investigation of the transfers, the GDC reversed itself and returned the transferred women guards back to work in their original facilities.[12]

The potential for abuse inherent in the custodial context—heightened by reliance on cross-gender guarding—is reinforced by the case histories of many women prisoners. A high proportion of incarcerated women—and, according to *Cason* class counsel, an overwhelming proportion of the women singled out for sexual abuse—enter the correctional system with a prior history of sexual victimization. As Darien Bogenholm, a clinical social worker who worked on the *Cason* litigation, described it: "[You] do not have to go far until you hear this train wreck history of sexual abuse."[13]

Accustomed to sexual exploitation, many women prisoners have little awareness of their rights. Indeed, Lisa Burnette, an attorney with Zimring, Ellin & Miller litigating the class action, explained: "These women do not have a clear idea what is rape . . . [They do not] realize what rape [is], let alone sexual harassment."[14] In her view, if abusive custodial relationships are to be stopped, the women must be given education and counseling. Not only must they be told of

---

[10] Telephone interview, Mike Light, spokesman, Georgia Department of Corrections, April 17, 1996.

[11] Because of the transfers, women correctional officers who had had less than a fifteen-mile commute to work found themselves with a forty-five-mile commute. Represented by the employees' union, a number of these women filed suit in Fulton County Superior Court to block the transfers, claiming that gender-based transfers violate their right to equal employment opportunity, protected by state and national anti-discrimination laws. On April 8, 1996, the court denied the women guards' motion for a temporary restraining order to enjoin the transfers. Without reaching the women's substantive claims, it found the transfers would not cause irreparable injury to the women. Six women filed equal employment opportunity claims seeking to have the policy reversed. Telephone interview, David Finz, attorney, Georgia State Employees Union, April 18, 1996.

[12] Telephone interview, David Finz, attorney, Georgia State Employees Union, September 11, 1996.

[13] Interview, Darien Bogenholm, social worker, Atlanta, August 4, 1994.

[14] Telephone interview, Lisa Boardman Burnette, attorney, May 9, 1995.

their right to object to sexual misconduct, many of them would benefit greatly from psychological care regarding their prior sexual abuse.[15]

Corrections staff often targeted the most vulnerable women: those who were younger, emotionally weaker or with lower self-esteem. Attorney Bob Cullen told us that the initial psychological profile of a women will indicate whether she is likely to be a victim or report abuse. This profile is contained in a woman's file and is accessible to prison staff. He found a high correlation between those women who were victimized by corrections staff and those who had a victim profile. In fact, he said, "I haven't seen a file of a woman deemed unlikely to be victimized who was."[16]

Preying on women inmates' vulnerabilities, male officers enticed them into sexual involvement by making them feel special. A number of incarcerated women emphasized this point in their administrative hearing testimonies and in their interviews with us. Jane Doe 85 told us that in order to persuade her into sexual relations, Lt. James Philyaw made her feel like he cared: "Sometimes he would call me to his office to see how I was and he would tell me things, like how pretty I was and that he was there for me." Other prisoners spoke of receiving cards and flowers from staff, personal items, favors—special attention that helped allay their fear of being alone and unprotected in the correctional setting.

State Legal and Regulatory Framework

As a matter of state criminal law, sexual contact with a person in the custody of the Georgia Department of Corrections has been punishable as a felony since 1983. Under Section 16-6-5.1 of Georgia's criminal code, which carries a penalty of one to three years' imprisonment, a person commits sexual assault when:

> he engages in sexual contact with another person who is in the custody of the law . . . or who is detained in [an] institution and

---

[15] Burnette was thus extremely disappointed when the GDC summarily rejected a recent offer from an Emory University psychology professor to provide free counseling to women inmates. The professor and several other researchers wanted to conduct a long-term study to examine whether providing mental health services reduces the recidivism rate of incarcerated women. Interview, Lisa Boardman Burnette, attorney, Atlanta, February 6, 1996.

[16] Interview, Bob Cullen, attorney, Atlanta, August 4, 1994.

such actor has supervisory or disciplinary authority over such other person.[17]

Sexual contact is defined as "any contact for the purpose of sexual gratification of the actor with the intimate parts of a person not married to the actor."[18] The consent of the incarcerated person is irrelevant.

Until January 1995, when new standard operating procedures went into effect pursuant to a consent order in the *Cason* litigation, the statutory ban on sexual contact with a prisoner was not incorporated explicitly into GDC departmental policy. Rather, when seeking to discipline officers and employees for misconduct, the GDC, like many other state correctional agencies, relied on broad provisions regarding personal dealings. One such provision is a short, vague statement on the back of signed employee identification cards which provides: "There shall be no personal or business dealings with prisoners, probationers or parolees."[19] Another is included in the GDC standards of conduct, which states: "It shall be prohibited for any employee to knowingly have personal involvement with . . . known prisoners or active probationers." A third provision, Administrative Regulation 125-2-1.07(d), provides: "Employees shall not . . . maintain personal associations with, engage in personal business or trade with, or engage in non-job-related correspondence with, or correspond in behalf of or for, known prisoners, active probationers, or parolees."[20]

At present, GDC standard operating procedures specifically distinguish sexual misconduct from personal dealings, defining what actions constitute sexual contact, sexual abuse and sexual harassment.[21]

---

[17] G.C.A. Section 2020.1.

[18] Ibid. Intimate parts are defined as the "genital area, groin, inner thigh, buttocks, or breasts of a person."

[19] *Ray Griffin v. Department of Corrections*, before the State Personnel Board for the State of Georgia, No. 92-329, p. 5.

[20] Ibid., p. 4.

[21] For a detailed discussion of these procedures, see the section below titled "Improved Investigations Procedure."

National and International Law Protections

The eighth amendment to the Constitution, which bars cruel and unusual punishment, has been interpreted by U.S. courts to protect prisoners against rape and sexual assault. This constitutional shield is further augmented by the Fourth Amendment's guarantee of the right to privacy and personal integrity, which, in a series of lower court cases, has been interpreted to prohibit male guards from strip-searching female prisoners or conducting intrusive pat-frisks. In one recent case, the Eleventh Circuit Court of Appeals, which has jurisdiction over Georgia, ruled that prisoners retain a constitutional right to bodily privacy protecting them from being viewed while naked by corrections officers of the opposite sex.[22] The case was filed by men incarcerated at the Georgia State Prison to challenge the assignment of female officers to their housing units, where the officers could view the prisoners using the showers and toilets and while they were undressed. The circuit court expressly referred to and followed an emerging trend in other circuits recognizing that prisoners retain a constitutional right to privacy.[23] The decision did not, however, address what specific measures the GDC must implement to protect this right.

Constitutional protections on prisoners' rights are enforceable via lawsuits filed by or on behalf of prisoners, or by the U.S. Department of Justice (DOJ). Historically, U.S. prisoners have achieved most of their landmark victories through private litigation, particularly through suits litigated by prisoners' rights groups such as the National Prison Project of the American Civil Liberties Union.

Yet if certain stringent intent requirements are met, the DOJ may criminally prosecute abusive prison officials under general federal civil rights provisions.[24] In addition, the DOJ has the statutory right to investigate and institute civil actions under the Civil Rights of Institutional Persons Act (CRIPA) whenever it finds that a state facility engages in a pattern or practice of subjecting prisoners to "egregious or flagrant conditions" in violation of the Constitution.[25]

In addition to constitutional protections, prisoners' rights are also protected under international human rights treaties that are legally binding on the United States. The primary international legal instruments protecting the rights of

---

[22] *Fortner v. Thomas*, 983 F.2d 1024 (11th Cir. 1993).

[23] Ibid., p. 1030.

[24] See 18 U.S.C. §§ 241 & 242.

[25] See 42 U.S.C. § 1997 *et seq*.

U.S. prisoners are the International Covenant on Civil and Political Rights (ICCPR), ratified by the United States in 1993, and the Convention Against Torture and Other Cruel, Inhuman or Degrading Treatment or Punishment, ratified in 1994. Both treaties bar torture and cruel, inhuman or degrading treatment or punishment, which authoritative international fora have interpreted as including sexual abuse. To constitute torture, an act must cause severe physical or mental suffering and must be committed for a purpose such as obtaining information from the victim, punishing her, or intimidating or coercing her. Cruel, inhuman or degrading treatment or punishment includes acts causing a lesser degree of suffering that need not be committed for a particular purpose.

When prison staff members use force, the threat of force, or other means of coercion to compel a prisoner to engage in sexual intercourse, their acts constitute rape and, therefore, torture. Torture also occurs when prison staff use force or coercion to engage in sexual touching of prisoners where such acts cause serious physical or mental suffering. Instances of sexual touching or of sexual intercourse that does not amount to rape may constitute torture or cruel or inhuman treatment, depending on the level of physical or mental suffering involved. Other forms of sexual misconduct, such as inappropriate pat or strip searches or verbal harassment, that do not rise to the level of torture or of cruel or inhuman treatment, may be condemned as degrading treatment.

Legal Action to Expose and Prevent Abuses

The amended complaint filed in 1992 in *Cason v. Seckinger*, a federal class action lawsuit against the GDC, marked a turning point in Georgia's handling of custodial sexual misconduct.[26] The complaint alleged rape, sexual assault and coerced sexual activity, involuntary abortions, and retaliation or threats of retaliation against women who refused to participate in sexual activities within the prison. Supporting the complaint were the affidavits of ten women, identified only as Jane Does, who either were forced to engage in sexual relations with prison staff or who had direct knowledge of ongoing sexual misconduct within the prison.[27]

---

[26] The case was originally filed in 1984 by attorneys with Georgia Legal Services to challenge the constitutionality of Georgia prison conditions. (Attorney Bob Cullen, the lead lawyer on *Cason*, is now in private practice, as Georgia Legal Services no longer handles prison litigation.)

[27] Since the complaint was filed, the number of "Jane Does" has risen to over two hundred and the pool of women has broadened to include prisoners incarcerated at other women's prisons in the state. The number of Jane Does does not necessarily reflect the number of

The prisoners' allegations were reported almost immediately in the *Atlanta Journal-Constitution* and other local press. Under intense public scrutiny, the GDC, in negotiation with the plaintiffs' attorneys, launched an investigation of the charges and entered a period of internal review. This internal review, discussed in more detail below, included an investigation into past misconduct, disciplinary action against certain staff, and a number of reforms. In March 1993 the story was aired nationally by "Day One," an ABC television news show that had conducted its own four-month investigation of the problem. Subsequently, the Department of Corrections commissioner, Bobby Whitworth, stepped down and joined the Georgia Parole Board. The deputy commissioner, Lanson Newsome, opted for early retirement.[28]

The lawsuit, which was still pending at the time this report went to print, has never resulted in a full trial, although numerous hearings have been held. Under the supervision of the magistrate judge hearing the case, attorneys representing the women and those representing the GDC have attempted to work together to investigate and address the concerns raised by the suit. The magistrate has also issued a number of orders requiring the GDC to institute reforms. Most notably, in March 1994, he issued an order permanently enjoining sexual contact, sexual abuse, and sexual harassment of all women incarcerated, now and in the future, by any staff, employee, agent or contractor of the GDC.[29] He found that

---

women who have come forward with allegations of abuse or direct knowledge of such abuse, however. Some women have been given more than one Jane Doe number to correspond to separate incidents; other women chose not to go on the record as Jane Does, and not to file a formal complaint. Also, some Jane Doe affidavits correspond to incidents of stripping and restraining of mental health inmates.

[28] In addition, a number of the Jane Does filed civil suits against the GDC for damages stemming from the abuse incurred while at GWCI. These suits are still pending. Some prisoners also received payments for the movie rights to their story.

[29] The order defines sexual contact as any intentional touching, either directly or through the clothing, of the genitalia, anus, groin, breast, inner thighs, or buttocks, intended to abuse, humiliate, harass, degrade, or arouse or gratify the sexual desire of any person. Sexual abuse, as defined in the order, includes subjecting any person to sexual contact when the person is unable to consent as a result of her custodial status; through the use of coercion; physical or mental incapacitation; or any forceful sexual contact. Sexual harassment is broadly defined as "unwelcome sexual advances, requests for sexual favors, and other verbal or physical conduct of a sexual nature." The order specifically permitted pat-downs, strip searches, and other similar action as long as they were for legitimate correctional or security

such an injunction was necessary in light of the past and continuing problems with sexual abuse, and despite efforts being made by the GDC to prevent future misconduct, to guarantee the women's constitutional rights under the eighth and fourteenth amendments of the U.S. Constitution.

ABUSES[30]

Custodial sexual misconduct in Georgia has involved a range of offenses. Corrections officials have raped, sexually assaulted and engaged in criminal sexual contact with prisoners. They have also degraded female prisoners verbally, using highly sexualized language, and violated their right to privacy. While Georgia's criminal law bans sexual contact in custody, prisoners and advocates for prisoners rights have had to wage a long battle to ensure its enforcement. And, our investigation found, past practices linger.

Before *Cason*

Abuses prior to March 1992 included forced sexual intercourse and other misconduct likely to result in severe physical and psychological harm to the prisoner. Moreover, the perpetrators engaged in such abuses with impunity.

Unless indicated by the use of a full name, the names of the prisoners have been changed to protect their anonymity. In some cases, the location and exact date of prisoner interviews have also been withheld.

---

needs. *Cason v. Seckinger*, Civil Action File No. 84-313-1-MAC, Permanent Injunction, March 7, 1994.

[30] By rape, we mean sexual intercourse between a prison employee and a prisoner that is accompanied by the use or threat of force or coercion which, under certain circumstances, can take the form of the provision or denial of privileges, money, or goods. Sexual assault is sexual touching, short of intercourse, involving the same coercive influences. Sexual abuse is sexual intercourse or touching involving the offer of goods or privileges absent any actual or perceived threat to the prisoner. Criminal sexual contact refers to sexual intercourse or sexual touching that cannot be shown to involve any of the above elements but which nonetheless constitutes a gross breach of official duty. Rape, sexual assault or abuse, and criminal sexual contact should all be prosecuted as felonies. For a more detailed discussion, see the legal background chapter.

Rape, Sexual Assault or Abuse, and Criminal Sexual Contact

Until March 1992 an environment existed within Georgia women's prisons such that sexual relations between staff and prisoners were an accepted occurrence. Within GWCI and Colony Farm, members of the prison staff fondled and groped female prisoners, sexually propositioned them, and coerced them into sexual relationships either upon threat of retaliation or in exchange for contraband, favorable treatment and attention. They manipulated women's work schedules and freely called women from their units or work details for sex. As Bob Cullen, *Cason* class counsel, put it, "You get the impression from the staff at GWCI that it was a sexual smorgasbord and they could pick and choose whom they wanted."[31] Other corrections employees at the prison turned a blind eye to the ongoing sexual misconduct.

Disciplinary hearings conducted by the GDC reveal that it was often those in supervisory positions at GWCI who exploited their positions to coerce prisoners into sexual relations over a period of years. In particular, the hearings showed that three men—Lt. James Philyaw, Deputy Warden Cornelius Stanley, and Ray Griffin, then senior ranking officer at Colony Farm—used their positions of authority to abuse sexually a number of female prisoners under their supervision. Many of the descriptions of abuses below are based on the decisions of administrative law judges in state disciplinary hearings and the testimony of incarcerated women at those hearings. The Department of Corrections called the prisoners to testify as witnesses against the employees to substantiate charges of sexual misconduct.

The most notable among those charged was Lt. James Philyaw, who worked as the night shift supervisor for security at GWCI. According to testimonies at his disciplinary hearing, Philyaw had sex with at least seven prisoners over a five-year period, from 1987 to 1991, while employed at GWCI and Colony Farm. Philyaw appeared to follow a pattern. He would approach certain prisoners, compliment them by telling them how pretty they were and offer them his assistance. He would tell them to come to him if they needed anything, including assistance with a disciplinary report, and he offered to bring them things such as cigarettes and alcohol. He then pushed them into having sexual relations with him, threatening them if they did not comply.

Philyaw directed women to meet him in various locations around the prison, particularly offices in the administration building which were empty in the evenings. Each time, he apparently assigned officers under his supervision to locations where they would not discover his activities. The administrative law

---

[31] Interview, Bob Cullen, attorney, Atlanta, August 4, 1994.

judge in the hearing concluded that Philyaw had the power to call prisoners to certain locations and "knew precisely where all of his subordinates were at any given time and had the power to position them where he wanted and at times as he wished."[32]

Jane Doe 14 was reassigned in the summer of 1990 by Philyaw to buff the floors in the administration building (A-building) at night. This switch reportedly occurred a few days after he called her into his office and complimented her on her appearance. According to Jane Doe 14, on her first night on duty, Philyaw told her to follow him into the bathroom, where he kissed her and told her he was attracted to her and wanted to have sex. She told him she was menstruating and nothing else occurred that evening. Philyaw continued to pressure Jane Doe 14 for sex on subsequent evenings. A few evenings later, Philyaw called Jane Doe 14 into the men's bathroom, where he had spread a sheet on the floor, and raped her. Over the next three months, Jane Doe 14 had sex—anal, oral and vaginal—with Philyaw on repeated occasions. Jane Doe 14 stated at the disciplinary hearing that Philyaw's status within the institution not only prompted her to submit to his advances, it prevented her from coming forward. When asked why she allowed Philyaw to have sex with her, she replied, "because he was a lieutenant and he was over that shift, he was like the warden of that shift, and he could do anything he wanted to me, and no one was going to believe me just like he said." The situation ended when Lieutenant Philyaw was transferred to Colony Farm.[33]

Philyaw also manipulated at least one prisoner's dependency on alcohol to entice her into sexual relations. Jane Doe 85 had a drinking problem prior to incarceration; she submitted to sexual relations with Philyaw because, she said, he gave her alcohol and made her believe he cared. He allegedly also suggested items such as marijuana, alcohol and cigarettes. She testified:

> I drank, and I would smoke marijuana. . . . When I got locked up
> I didn't know how to deal with my problems without getting
> high, I was real vulnerable and depressed at that time. I had not
> been locked up very long, and I didn't go outside much, so when
> he came along it was comforting to know that someone in blue

---

[32] *Philyaw v. Department of Corrections*, before the State Personnel Board for the State of Georgia, p. 68.

[33] Interview, Bob Cullen, attorney, Atlanta, August 4, 1994.

could help me, so I believed in him. I believed he could help me, and he gave me alcohol.[34]

In exchange for having sexual relations with him, Philyaw provided prisoners with certain items and granted them special privileges that often violated prison policy. The first time Jane Doe 85 had sex with Philyaw, he called her into the room, locked the door and gave her a bottle of Jack Daniels which they drank, and she submitted to sexual intercourse. Jane Doe 85 told us that she and Philyaw had sexual relations on four or five occasions over a two-month period, either in a counselor's office at Colony Farm or at her work assignment. He would come to her dorm and put cigarettes in her locker or under her mattress. Philyaw promised Jane Doe 14 "that if she received any DRs [disciplinary reports] to let him know so that he could take care of them; and . . . he would write a letter in her behalf to the parole board."[35] When a friend received a DR, Jane Doe 14 raised the issue with Philyaw and performed oral sex on him; the friend was never called on the DR. Jane Doe 15, according to the disciplinary hearing, had sexual intercourse with Philyaw seven to eleven times over a three-month period. In return, he did favors for her, such as moving prisoners at her request and permitting her to see her prison file, contrary to prison policy.[36]

In another incident, Jane Doe 88 witnessed Philyaw having sexual intercourse with Jane Doe 111 in a secretary's office; he later approached her and "told [her] not to repeat what [she] had seen and he asked [her] was there anything he could do for [her]."[37] Philyaw subsequently put money in her prison account. Jane Doe 88 testified that she wrote to Internal Affairs about the incident but received no response.[38]

Philyaw often targeted prisoners who were loners or emotionally vulnerable. According to testimony at his disciplinary hearing, Philyaw called Jane Doe 13 from the prison yard to the control area and told her "he had noticed that she did not hang around with a lot of other people and therefore felt he could trust

---

[34] *Philyaw v. Department of Corrections*, p. 292 (testimony of Jane Doe 85).

[35] Ibid., p. 14.

[36] Ibid., p. 9 (testimony of Jane Doe 14).

[37] Ibid., p. 18.

[38] Ibid.

her. . . . He told her he was attracted to her and would like to have sex with her."[39]
Philyaw proceeded to kiss and undress the prisoner, then to have sexual intercourse
with her. Following this, Philyaw gave Jane Doe 13 special privileges and
interceded on her behalf when she was disciplined by another officer.[40]

Philyaw pursued a similar pattern with Jane Doe 64. He counseled Jane
Doe 64 one evening when she was upset about a broken relationship with a male
prisoner, then continued to pay her special attention. According to Jane Doe 64's
testimony at his disciplinary hearing:

> I liked the feeling that I had of being special and important to
> someone, and he made me believe that I was special. . . . He
> made me feel like I was the only person that he was involved
> with, by telling me so many things . . . that made me think it was
> special.[41]

She testified that she started spending extended periods of time in the prison library
so she could see or talk to Philyaw. Then, on one occasion, Philyaw brought her
to the administrative offices to "do some filing" and, she testified:

> [I] went back to the office where he was, and he shut the door
> and we began to kiss and fondle, and at that time is the first time
> that I performed oral sex on him, but we did not finish because
> he told me to stop, and I suppose he told me to stop because he
> hadn't made arrangements for that particular meeting, and
> perhaps didn't know where all of his officers were, or if someone
> was due to come back, and so he made me stop.[42]

He arranged for them to meet and have either oral or vaginal intercourse on two
additional occasions. The abuses ended when Philyaw canceled a prearranged

---

[39] Ibid., p. 13.

[40] Ibid., p. 14.

[41] Ibid., p. 335.

[42] Ibid., p. 334.

meeting, and Jane Doe 64 learned that he had sex with another prisoner earlier that day.[43]

The disciplinary hearings we reviewed also showed that Deputy Warden Cornelius Stanley raped at least one inmate, Jane Doe 39, and attempted to intimidate another, Jane Doe 15, to prevent her from repeating her allegations of sexual misconduct against Philyaw. According to his disciplinary hearing, Stanley called Jane Doe 39 into his office to discuss problems she was having, then groped her breasts and genitals, and told her, "I want to fuck you." He then pulled down Jane Doe 39's pants and forced her to have sexual intercourse with him. Stanley reportedly told her "there was nothing she could do and that she would not be believed if she told any one about his actions."[44] On two other occasions, while Jane Doe 39 was in lockdown in the Mental Health Unit (MHU) without clothing, Stanley came into her cell and groped her. On one of these occasions, he also raped her. According to Jane Doe 39, Stanley said, "You should give up. You're going to have sex with me whether you want it or not."[45]

A third employee in a supervisory position, Baby Ray Griffin, maintained a sexual relationship with Jane Doe 11 both while she was incarcerated and during her parole. Griffin was a correctional institutional manager at GWCI, assigned to Colony Farm as its highest ranking officer.[46] According to the disciplinary decision, Griffin had sexual intercourse with Jane Doe 11 on a regular basis at Colony Farm, in places such as the storage closet, the officer's restroom, or an office. When Jane Doe 11 was transferred to the Macon Transitional Center, Griffin would pick her up either on her weekend leaves and take her to a hotel, or drive her to or from her work assignment, and they would engage in sexual intercourse in his car. Upon her release, Jane Doe 11 moved into Griffin's home near the prison until she was seen driving his car by another prison employee in September 1990.[47]

---

[43] Ibid., p. 26.

[44] *Stanley v. Department of Corrections*, before the State Personnel Board for the State of Georgia, p. 3.

[45] Ibid.

[46] *Griffin v. Department of Corrections*, before the State Personnel Board for the State of Georgia, p. 5.

[47] Ibid.

In another case at GWCI, a first-time prisoner, Felicia J., was sexually involved for several months with Officer A, the male supervisor on her work assignment.[48] According to Felicia J., Officer A would talk to her and, she said, make her laugh and feel good. One day, she and Officer A had sexual intercourse. They continued to meet for nearly a year at various locations he designated—the dining hall, the gym, the warehouse, the clinic—knowing others would not be present. She told us the relationship over time became increasingly intense and Officer A began requesting her to perform "strange sex acts," like putting on handcuffs, biting her, and roughhousing. She reportedly tried to get out of the relationship and began to stay close to officers whom she knew would not tolerate Officer A's behavior. The relationship came to the attention of officials within the prison, and an investigation was initiated. Felicia J. told us that she repeatedly denied any sexual involvement with the officer because she feared that she would be disciplined if she told the truth. According to Felicia J., then Warden Black ultimately called her into his office and told her to avoid the officer. Documentation we obtained indicates that Black similarly counseled the officer to avoid Felicia J. Eventually, she and the officer were discovered by a nurse having sex in a closet, and the officer was transferred to a men's prison.

After her relationship with Officer A ended, Felicia J. became involved with Officer B who reportedly brought her certain things, such as gum and stamps, which she either could not afford or could not obtain within the prison. She told us that she has no family in Georgia and the relationship was "the way to make my life."[49]

Philyaw, Stanley, Griffin, and Officer A were not the only employees at GWCI sexually involved with female prisoners. A number of other employees were later indicted for such misconduct under Georgia criminal statutes covering sexual assault, sodomy and rape. Not all of the officers indicted were men. Four women, Jackie Lee, Sandra Floyd, Rachel Durden, and Pam Saulsbury, were charged with sexual contact against a person in custody for their alleged relationships with different Jane Does between 1987 and 1990.[50]

---

[48] Interview, Georgia, March 1994.

[49] Ibid.

[50] Jackie Lee, a female officer at GWCI, was indicted for sexual involvement with Jane Doe 36 between January and December 1987. Sandra Floyd, another female officer, was indicted for alleged sexual involvement with Jane Doe 18 at Colony Farm between May 1988 and March 1989. The sexual encounters reportedly occurred in various locations at

Allegations of sexual misconduct also arose at the Milan Correctional Institution, which was opened in 1989. The record of one disciplinary hearing reveals that the store manager at Milan, Samuel Evans, between 1990 and 1991, offered prisoners store goods in exchange for fondling their breasts or asking them to undress, while other prisoners served as lookouts.[51] GDC documents also indicate that in 1991 an athletics coach at Milan CI groped one prisoner's breasts and pulled down her pants, while he cornered and "engaged in a sex act in a standing position" with another prisoner. He repeatedly commented on a third prisoner's breasts and asked her to do a "table dance" for him.

Mistreatment of Prisoners Impregnated by Guards

In at least one instance prior to March 1992, a prisoner at GWCI became pregnant by a corrections officer.[52] According to Jane Doe 1, the supervisor on her work assignment had been repeatedly "coming on" to her. Then, one day, the supervisor allegedly cornered and raped her. Both before and after this incident, she reportedly spoke to her counselor on at least three occasions to request a change of assignment, but her request was denied by the warden. At one time, she said, she stopped reporting to work but returned after she was threatened by prison officials with segregation. When she missed a menstrual period after her rape, Jane Doe 1 told her supervisor she thought she was pregnant. She told us he responded, "I could always beat it out of you."[53]

Days later, in May 1989, approximately seven weeks after the rape, Jane Doe 1 reportedly was called into the warden's office early in the morning. She alleges that the warden at the time, Gary Black, "told me if I did not get an abortion then I would not get parole." Jane Doe 1 stated that she never consented to the

---

the prison, including in a bathroom and behind a screen in Floyd's office. Pam Saulsbury was indicted for fondling Jane Doe 6 over several months in 1990.

[51] *Evans v. Department of Corrections*, before the State Personnel Board for the State of Georgia.

[52] The *Atlanta Journal-Constitution* found that the state paid for twenty-eight abortions between 1989 and 1991, but could not obtain a breakdown between abortions for women who came into the system pregnant and those impregnated by staff. Rhonda Cook, "Prisoners allege frequent sex with staff: Prisoners claims state paid for coerced abortion," *Atlanta Journal-Constitution*, March 11, 1992.

[53] Interview, Georgia, March 1994.

abortion but was forced to have one by then Warden Black. She told us, "I never consented to Black. I never signed anything indicating consent." The conversation was reportedly overheard by Black's secretary who, according to Jane Doe 1, came forward as a witness in Jane Doe 1's civil suit against the state.

Despite her unwillingness to undergo the abortion, she was taken out of the prison at 4:00 a.m. and driven to an Atlanta clinic where the procedure was performed. At the clinic, she was "dragged through a picketing group of anti-abortion activists." She described the whole experience as emotionally wrenching. She was very depressed following the abortion, but was not offered therapy for over five years. Another former employee, who escorted Jane Doe 1 to the hospital for the procedure, kept copies of the check written by the GDC and Jane Doe 1's medical record to support Jane Doe 1's allegations.

Privacy Violations and Mentally Ill Prisoners
Women prisoners with mental illnesses have been particularly vulnerable to privacy violations, in some instances so severe that they amounted to torture or cruel, inhuman or degrading treatment. Women incarcerated in the Mental Health Unit at GWCI, perceived to be suicide risks, were forcibly stripped by male and female staff and placed in restraints, including straightjackets or four-point restraints. In some cases, women were stripped and left hog-tied in their cells.[54] The women were then left naked for up to three days where they could be viewed by members of the opposite sex. Videotapes of women being stripped sometimes revealed discrepancies between officers' reports of their treatment of prisoners and the visual record. In one incident, the officer's report neglected to reveal that a prisoner's hands and feet were shackled, a point made clear by the video.[55]

The GDC policy in place required prison personnel to employ the least restrictive means possible to restrain disruptive or mentally ill prisoners but was silent on the stripping of prisoners, the use of videotapes, and the presence of

---

[54] Rhonda Cook, "Official directive to stop hog-tying prisoners ignored," *Atlanta Journal-Constitution*, September 16, 1992. According to Lisa Burnette, this method of restraining prisoners is called hog-tying because the women were tied like cattle at a rodeo: their hands are tied behind their backs at the wrists, their knees are bent and their legs are tied around the ankles. Then, the ankles are tied to the wrists. Women restrained in this manner were left straightjacketed on their stomachs, or, many times, completely nude. Telephone interview, Lisa Boardman Burnette, attorney, June 6, 1995.

[55] Cook, "Official directive to stop . . .." *Atlanta Journal-Constitution*.

correctional officers of the opposite sex.[56] According to press reports, the then deputy commissioner of the GDC, Lanson Newsome, told wardens in November 1991 never to hog-tie psychiatric patients. The practice, however, continued at the women's prison until April 1992, when a new warden and administration were installed.[57]

Attorney Bob Cullen told us that it is virtually impossible to obtain an accurate assessment of the number of women who were victimized in this way, since many of the GDC's logbooks vanished. Based upon the remaining logbooks, Cullen found that at least sixty-four women incarcerated at GWCI were forcibly stripped and restrained over an eight-month period from 1991-1992.

After *Cason*

Our inquiry focused not only on past abuses but also on more current instances of sexual misconduct in Georgia women's prisons. We recognize that since the *Cason* lawsuit was amended in 1992, the GDC has taken important steps to improve its investigation of and response to allegations of custodial sexual misconduct. Nonetheless, on many issues, the necessary reforms were only instituted after persistent prodding from *Cason* class counsel, supported by the court, raising concerns regarding whether such improvements will prove to be deep-rooted and permanent.

Rape, Sexual Assault or Abuse, and Criminal Sexual Contact

The initial publicity and subsequent court orders stemming from the *Cason* lawsuit had a noticeable effect in reducing the level of abuse. Advocates monitoring the women's prisons noted a decline in the frequency and severity of sexual misconduct and what they describe as "perverse sexual behavior."[58] Most notably, incidents of forced sexual intercourse have declined precipitously.

---

[56] See Georgia Department of Corrections Standard Operating Procedures, "Mental Health Services: Physical Restraints," Ref. No. VCO1-0014 (effective date May 1, 1988); Georgia Department of Corrections Standard Operating Procedures, "Stripped Cells and Temporary Confiscation of Personal Property," Ref. No. IIBO8-0005 (effective date October 1, 1989); Georgia Department of Corrections Standard Operating Procedures, "Use of Force and Restraint For Inmate Control," Ref. No. IIBO8-0001 (effective date October 1, 1991).

[57] Cook, "Official Directive to stop . . .." *Atlanta Journal-Constitution.*

[58] Interview, Lisa Boardman Burnette, attorney, Atlanta, August 4, 1994.

Instances of rape, sexual assault or abuse, and sexual harassment by corrections staff have nonetheless continued to occur, though the climate of impunity that existed prior to the suit has dissipated. Bob Cullen told us that he has learned of approximately 370 reported incidents of sexual misconduct since March 1992, a number of which have been detailed in press reports.[59]

In one case a female prisoner, Dolores T., reported that she was sexually involved with a religious leader employed by the GDC who provided her with marriage counseling. After several prior counseling meetings, the religious leader arrived at the prison one evening in August 1992 and called her to the chapel. When she got ready to leave, he reportedly embraced her and made a move to kiss her, but she pulled away. She told us, "It was too long . . . I was uncomfortable and felt threatened."[60]

Approximately two weeks later, Dolores T. saw him again during a scheduled service that, she said, only she attended. He had allegedly told the other women that the service for the evening was canceled. That night, he reportedly grabbed her ankle and wanted to know why she pulled away on the other occasion; they kissed and he fondled her. She subsequently had three "sexual encounters" with the religious leader over the next two months. The relationship ended when she discovered he was involved with two other prisoners. Dolores T. told us that he was fired after his wife discovered collect phone calls that Dolores T. and other prisoners had made and letters they had written to him.

In May 1993 two kitchen workers at Washington CI were suspended for alleged sexual misconduct with incarcerated prisoners.[61] Describing sexual misconduct by staff there, social worker Darien Bogenholm said, "You go there to meet a mate and have a baby," and "It's an atmosphere of a middle school bus in the summer time."[62] She told us:

> There is sex all over—the kitchen, the utility room—it seems.
> The guards are known to be touchers and sexually inappropriate.

---

[59] Interview, Bob Cullen, attorney, Atlanta, February 7, 1996.

[60] Interview, Georgia, March 1994.

[61] Rhonda Cook, "2 employees suspended over new claims of inmate sex," *Atlanta Journal-Constitution*, May 1, 1993.

[62] Interview, Darien Bogenholm, social worker, Georgia, August 4, 1994.

There is a lot of discussion of the women's sex lives in the free world.[63]

Sexual misconduct persisted at other facilities as well. In June 1993 a teacher at GWCI/Baldwin was suspended and ultimately fired after he raped a prisoner.[64] In September 1993 one corrections officer was fired from GWCI/Baldwin, and another was transferred to a men's facility for sexual misconduct with prisoners. The first officer, according to press reports, allegedly had "sexually explicit and suggestive" conversations with a prisoner, sent her cards and flowers, and gave her his home phone number. The second officer, accused of impregnating a prisoner at GWCI/Baldwin, was transferred pending DNA testing to determine paternity, and later fired.[65]

At Metro CI, another prisoner told a number of corrections employees of her sexual involvement with male staff but received no response for months. According to her affidavit, she was approached by a male corrections officer and a maintenance employee around Christmas 1993 and began to have sexual relations with them in March and April 1994.[66] During this time, the woman discussed her sexual relations with an athletics coach at Metro CI and also told a number of corrections officers. At one point, she reportedly informed an officer that she believed she was pregnant, and he told her to "pray about it." She also allegedly requested a pregnancy test from the medical clinic, but no test was given, nor did anyone ask any questions. The situation was finally revealed in April 1994, when the woman told the warden and her attorney, yet she reportedly had sexual intercourse with one of the male staff days later.

Prisoners' difficulties in obtaining goods, even relatively minor items, enhance their vulnerability to sexual misconduct. Unlike other states we visited, Georgia does not provide prisoners with a stipend for their work. As a result, prisoners are financially dependent: they must rely on state allocations to obtain personal items, including clothing and personal hygiene supplies, or they must

---

[63] Ibid.

[64] Rhonda Cook, "Prison guard acquitted on all counts: Prisoners who alleged abuse 'unbelievably upset,'" *Atlanta Journal-Constitution*, June 24, 1993.

[65] Rhonda Cook, "2 guards disciplined at prison for women: Charges involving sex lead to firing, transfer," *Atlanta Journal-Constitution*, September 30, 1993.

[66] Telephone interview, Robin Hutchinson, attorney, February 16, 1995.

depend on their families or friends to purchase them. Until the last couple of years, the GDC provided a very limited supply of sanitary products, including toilet paper. Cullen told us that when he began the case, he "couldn't go through a day of interviewing without hearing complaints about this." These restrictions, said Cullen, "encouraged problems because the women will do whatever they have to, to get what they need."[67] Similarly, a surprising proportion of the reported instances of sexual misconduct during 1995 stemmed from a new state prison policy banning cigarettes. Imposed in July 1995, it immediately created a tremendous black market in cigarettes and a trade in sex for cigarettes. As of February 1, 1996, however, the ban was lifted: all facilities now permit smoking in the outdoor areas.

Mistreatment of Prisoners Impregnated by Guards

There has been at least one case of a prison employee impregnating an inmate at Washington CI since the *Cason* suit was filed. In 1994 a prisoner at Washington CI was impregnated by a male teacher on staff.[68] The teacher reportedly asked the woman to remain after class, then took her into the bathroom. She allegedly took off her pants, bent over and he entered her from behind. The woman informed the teacher when she discovered she was pregnant. He reportedly brought her, over a period of days, a substance thought to be quinine to induce a miscarriage. Attorneys on *Cason* assert that the woman was given a pregnancy test and a sonogram in mid-March 1994, after another prisoner reported the incident. Bob Cullen told us this sonogram revealed that the fetus was dead, but no action was taken for approximately a month to give the woman an abortion.[69] Medical records we reviewed did not indicate when the woman was first given a pregnancy test or a sonogram. The records did show that on the day the abortion was conducted, nearly a month after Cullen states the incident came to the attention of authorities, the woman received a sonogram.

Privacy Violations and Mentally Ill Prisoners

GDC policy permits male correctional officers to conduct pat-searches, although it stipulates that such searches "be conducted, when possible, by an

---

[67] Telephone interview, Bob Cullen, attorney, February 16, 1995.

[68] Interview, Bob Cullen, attorney, Atlanta, August 4, 1994.

[69] Ibid.

officer of the same sex."[70]   The policy also states that strip searches of female prisoners should be conducted by female corrections officers, except in case of emergency and "only if a correctional officer of the same sex is not available."[71] In practice, we were told, in the last few years only women guards conduct pat- and strip searches of women prisoners. Attorney Burnette on *Cason* believes that this *de facto* ban is of critical importance in protecting female prisoners from abuse.[72] She notes, however, that over one-tenth of recent misconduct complaints involve women staff and that a high proportion of such allegations involve abusive searches.

Until March 1996, there was no statewide policy restricting the use of male officers in women's housing units; different prisons had different rules on the subject. At GWCI, only female corrections officers were assigned to work the women's housing units and dorms. In addition, GDC rules required that male officers be escorted while in the dorms.[73]   However, according to testimony presented at several disciplinary hearings, this policy was "not consistently enforced" and was often ignored by high ranking male supervisors.[74] At Pulaski, which had the highest proportion of female officers of any Georgia women's prison, male officers were not assigned to housing units. But even there, we were told, men would walk around the units and the day rooms without announcing their presence.[75] Women we interviewed at Metro reported that a large number of male officers were assigned to their living units, including segregation units. While they said some officers called out "man on the hall" before entering, others did not announce their presence.[76] Some women told us that male officers at Metro would

---

[70] Georgia Department of Corrections, "Searches, Security Inspections and Use of Permanent Logs," Reference No. IIB01-0013 effective date December 1, 1991.

[71] Ibid.

[72] Interview, Lisa Boardman Burnette, Atlanta, February 6, 1996.

[73] *Stanley v. Department of Corrections*, before the State Personnel Board, Appeal No. 93-53, p. 6.

[74] Ibid., p. 13.

[75] Telephone interview, Lisa Boardman Burnette, attorney, May 9, 1995.

[76] Interviews, Atlanta, March 1994.

enter their cells, even when they placed paper over the window, and stand outside the showers when they were naked. Since a consent order signed in March, however, only female staff can be assigned to women's housing units, reducing the likelihood of privacy violations.[77] In addition, pursuant to *Cason*, the GDC promulgated a new policy—made part of another consent order[78]—requiring all male staff members to announce themselves before entering any area where women prisoners might be undressed, and to allow the prisoners an appropriate amount of time to dress.[79]

As another consequence of the *Cason* suit, the GDC entered into a consent decree on September 15, 1994 to change its policy on restraining and stripping mentally ill prisoners. The new policy specifically prohibits the "tethering or restraint in a hog-tied position,"[80] as well as the stripping of mentally ill inmates, unless the clothing could be used for self-injury or destruction of property. Even then, stripping is only allowed upon a doctor's order.[81] Prisoners who are stripped are to be offered a paper gown and panties. According to Bob Cullen, the GDC appears to be adhering to this policy.

THE SYSTEM'S RESPONSE

International human rights law obligates national governments not only to prohibit torture and cruel, inhuman or degrading treatment but also to ensure that when such abuses occur they can be reported and fully and fairly investigated without the complainant fearing punishment or retaliation from the authorities. U.S. law, additionally, guarantees prisoners access to the courts to challenge abusive prison conditions and other problems.

---

[77] *Cason v. Seckinger*, Consent Order, March 8, 1996.

[78] *Cason v. Seckinger*, Consent Order, December 12, 1995.

[79] Georgia Department of Corrections Standard Operating Procedures, "Bodily Privacy," Ref. No. VG01-00-77 (effective date March 28, 1996).

[80] Georgia Department of Corrections Standard Operating Procedures, "Mental Health Services: Physical Restraints," Ref. No. VH01-0014 (effective date May 1, 1994).

[81] Ibid., "Mental Health Services: Seclusion Cell, Stripping of Inmates, and Temporary Confiscation of Personal Property," Ref. No. VH01-0023 (effective date May 1, 1994).

Without question, the prison context, in which officers are granted significant power over the daily lives and welfare of their charges, carries with it an inherent potential for custodial abuse.   The state, having established a fundamentally unequal relationship between prison staff and prisoners, is responsible for ensuring that staff members do not wrongfully exploit this inequality. Particularly given the reliance on cross-gender guarding, the authorities must formulate policies and procedures to ensure against custodial sexual misconduct and to facilitate the reporting and investigation of such abuse when it occurs.

Prior to *Cason*, the mechanisms available for reporting and investigating custodial sexual abuse in Georgia were so seriously flawed as to be almost useless. At that time, in addition, the environment within the correctional system made it difficult for women to come forward with such complaints without fear of retribution.   Even now, after procedures have been substantially reformed, obstacles still exist that hinder women from fully enjoying their right to report abuses and to see them remedied.

Before *Cason*

Failure of the complaint mechanisms within Georgia women's prisons and routine blindness by the leadership at GWCI and within the GDC more generally to allegations of rape and sexual assault or abuse contributed to the perpetuation of sexual misconduct by prison staff. In the period preceding the *Cason* amended complaint, that is, until March 1992, the environment within Georgia women's prisons was hostile to women and staff coming forward with allegations of misconduct.

Prison employees at GWCI freely engaged in sexual relations with incarcerated women with the knowledge that the women had little, if any, ability to report such behavior. Where women attempted to report abuse, they were targeted for retaliation by prison staff and thwarted by a general GDC presumption that prisoners lie and that, without staff corroboration, their assertions should automatically be dismissed. Fellow officers, furthermore, turned a blind eye to sexual relations as long as the staff member maintained a minimal level of discretion. Those employees who attempted to report sexual misconduct by their colleagues were often ignored and even harassed at the institutional level. Only in cases where the abuse simply could not be ignored, as in cases of pregnancy or where another member of the staff happened upon a colleague in the act, was any action taken. However, even in these cases, the GDC either permitted the guilty individual to resign or transferred him to another facility rather than take appropriate disciplinary action, including dismissing the staff person in question and referring the case to the district attorney for possible criminal prosecution.

Grievance Procedure

The GDC has a grievance procedure that in principle enables prisoners to complain about "any condition, policy, procedure or action over which the department of corrections has control."[82] In practice, however, this mechanism was largely unavailable to women prior to 1992. As a result of either their direct personal experiences or their general impression that the procedure was ineffective, incarcerated women seldom resorted to it.

The problems with the grievance mechanism stem from both its design and its implementation. The procedure itself, which stipulates that "whenever possible, inmate complaints and grievances should be resolved on an informal basis without the filing of a formal grievance,"[83] discourages the actual filing of grievances. Instead, priority is placed on conciliation and negotiated solutions. Whatever the advantages of this approach with regard to ordinary complaints, it is utterly inappropriate for complaints of custodial sexual misconduct. Women prisoners' concern that offending staff members would learn of their grievances deterred them from reporting abuses.

Moreover, the grievance mechanism's bias against the formal institution of complaints was greatly reinforced before 1992 in practice. According to one institutional counselor:

> The grievance procedure was a joke. My job was to convince the inmate not to file the complaint. I would try to resolve the situation without it. Really though, I was not to give the prisoners grievances. If one was filed, I was responsible for investigating it. The supervisors would not. Nothing happened with the grievances and the women were often retaliated against.[84]

---

[82] Georgia Department of Corrections, Standard Operating Procedures, Reference No. IIB05-0001, November 1, 1990.

[83] Ibid.

[84] Interview, Atlanta, March 1994.

Bob Cullen echoed these comments. He told us, "The grievance procedure is irrelevant to the women reporting [sexual misconduct]. The women must get permission from their counselors to grieve."[85] Cullen reviewed the records of many of the women involved in the *Cason* suit and was active in bringing their allegations to light. By reviewing these records, he learned that counselors at the prison often talked women out of filing grievances.

One of the few occasions in which the counselor cited above allowed a prisoner to file a grievance was when the prisoner reported that a staff member in the dental lab had propositioned her. When the counselor consulted a supervisor to inquire how to proceed, the supervisor told the counselor to "investigate" the grievance and to state that it was unfounded. According to the counselor, the supervisor said, "Did anyone see [the incident]? Since he denied it, without a witness, there's your answer."

Internal Investigations

Prior to March 1992, in a limited number of cases, the GDC conducted internal investigations into allegations of sexual misconduct by prison staff at the women's prisons. There was no written policy or procedure for conducting these investigations. Allegations were generally raised at the institutional level, through letters or complaints to staff, or by staff observations and reports. The warden often conducted the investigation himself by interviewing the prisoner raising the allegation or the implicated officers.[86] In some cases, it was then turned over to the GDC Internal Affairs division (IAD), which is located in Atlanta.[87] Investigations appeared to be conducted promptly by the IAD, but charges against officers were rarely substantiated because the testimonies of incarcerated women were rarely deemed credible. Where an allegation involved the prisoner's word against the employee's, the GDC seldom took disciplinary action.[88]

Many allegations of sexual misconduct were simply never investigated. A GDC senior investigator and the current and former directors of Internal Affairs testified in February 1994, in a disciplinary hearing, that prior to March 1992 it was

---

[85] Interview, Bob Cullen, attorney, Atlanta, August 4, 1994.

[86] Deposition of Gary Black, former warden, Georgia Women's Correctional Institution, February 21, 1994.

[87] Interview, Lisa Boardman Burnette, attorney, Atlanta, August 5, 1994.

[88] Ibid.

the policy or practice of the GDC to cease an investigation if an employee resigned voluntarily.[89] According to attorney Lisa Burnette, this approach did not necessarily prevent the GDC from rehiring the employee at a future date. She explained that a code is placed in an employee's personnel file to indicate whether the GDC could rehire him. If a person resigns, a "no rehire" code was not necessarily entered into the file.[90]

Intimidation

Prisoners who reported sexual misconduct risked not only disbelief by the prison administration but also intimidation by the employees they implicated. According to the testimony at Philyaw's disciplinary hearing of Anne Collins, a counselor at GWCI/Baldwin, Philyaw attempted to intimidate both Collins and a Jane Doe she was assisting. Collins testified that Jane Doe 15 approached her one afternoon to discuss a disciplinary report she received for contraband. She told Collins that she had received the contraband from Philyaw. She also informed Collins that she was afraid that Philyaw and other prisoners might retaliate against her for speaking out because Philyaw "did them favors."[91] After this conversation, Jane Doe 15 prepared a written statement implicating Philyaw.

The harassment allegedly occurred the evening after Jane Doe 15 prepared the report. Collins testified that Jane Doe 15 returned to her office in an agitated state, disheveled and crying because she feared Philyaw would learn about her report. Collins was working a late night shift and was the only counselor on staff at the time. During this meeting, Philyaw appeared and began walking through the office and loitering outside the doorway. After Philyaw passed through the office several times, Collins became extremely concerned, both regarding her own safety and that of Jane Doe 15. Indeed, she tried to try to place Jane Doe 15 in protective custody but was unable to reach the security supervisor.

Staff Reporting

In addition to obstacles in their own reporting of sexual misconduct, incarcerated women could not rely on prison staff either to report sexual misconduct or to protect prisoners from retaliation if the latter raised complaints.

---

[89] Testimony of Richard Richards, Edward Walker and Thomas Walton, in the disciplinary hearing of Thomas Walton, February 9, 1994.

[90] Interview, Lisa Boardman Burnette, attorney, Atlanta, August 5, 1994.

[91] *Philyaw v. Department of Corrections*, p. 161.

As one former employee told us, "That's the way the system was—you keep your mouth shut about the rumors and allegations." This person knew one colleague who avoided the administration building when she worked late at night for fear of seeing a staff person engaging in sex with a prisoner.[92]

According to the disciplinary decision against Deputy Warden Cornelius Stanley, even where staff reported misconduct, their allegations often were not treated any more seriously than those of prisoners, and an investigation was not necessarily launched. Stanley's disciplinary record reveals that in September 1991, Collins informed her superiors about Philyaw's involvement with Jane Doe 15. Both Collins and Jane Doe 15 submitted written statements that were then given to Stanley.[93] Collins testified that Stanley approached her a week later and told her that he was handling the investigation and that she need not concern herself with the matter any further. No investigation, however, was initiated until three months later, in January 1992, when the warden directed someone to look into the allegations.[94]

Impunity

The failure to discipline officers for sexual misconduct and, where appropriate, pursue criminal charges against them, was intimately connected to the GDC's faulty policy and procedure for conducting investigations. Prior to March 1992, in those instances where employees agreed to resign, the GDC ceased investigating the allegations and made no referral to the district attorney, even where the employee admitted to sexual contact with an inmate in violation of the state's felony provision. The law's disuse was apparently not a matter of oversight but of design. Indeed, Bobby Whitworth, then commissioner of corrections, stated that it was departmental policy not to enforce the felony provision.[95] Whitworth told ABC's "Day One" that it was "the policy of this agency prior to 1990 really not to press for prosecution. It was a policy that if we had an officer or a staff member

---

[92] Interview, former Georgia prison employee, Atlanta, March 1994.

[93] *Stanley v. Department of Corrections*, p. 6.

[94] Ibid., pp. 7-8.

[95] A senior investigator and former director of Internal Investigations similarly testified in February 1994 that it was the policy or practice of the department to cease investigations when an employee resigned.

who engaged in sexual relations with a prisoner [they] were either terminated or fired."

In other words, the GDC actively and knowingly failed to protect women in its custody from the criminal acts of its employees. Department employees, as a result, were able to sexually assault prisoners at the risk only of losing their jobs. Even then, it appears they may have risked only a temporary loss of employment. During the period preceding *Cason*, corrections staff caught engaging in sexual misconduct were generally let off with minor chastisement, transferred to other facilities, or permitted to resign rather than face investigation or be demoted. The employee who impregnated Jane Doe 1, one of the Jane Does, was permitted to resign with no admission of guilt, rather than face a departmental investigation. Warden Black told GDC leadership that he hoped the employee could find a new position in another Georgia corrections facility.

The decision to retain staff and close investigations, even in the presence of substantiating evidence, was upheld at the highest levels of the GDC. In numerous incidents, the deputy commissioner closed investigations where charges of misconduct were substantiated, upheld minor disciplinary sanctions and failed to refer credible allegations to the district attorney for prosecution.[96] Throughout his tenure, the former commissioner of the GDC was regularly kept appraised of the findings and disposition of such investigations.

The GDC's failure to sanction employees appropriately, by dismissing them and referring their cases as appropriate to the district attorney, amounted to complicity in the staff's misconduct and abuse. In at least two circumstances, employees who received only minor reprimands persisted in their misconduct. As noted earlier, a 1990 investigation found that Baby Ray Griffin was found cohabitating with Jane Doe 11, a recent parolee. Griffin was not punished. Rather, the deputy commissioner closed the investigation and retained Griffin in his position following "extensive counseling" for his "questionable judgment and conduct."[97] According to Griffin's disciplinary hearing, the reprimand had no impact on Griffin's behavior. He continued his relationship with Jane Doe 11 and,

---

[96] Until March 1992 sexual misconduct was investigated and referred to under the catchall term "misconduct." Following the amended complaint filed in *Cason*, the terminology for such investigations changed.

[97] *Griffin v. Department of Correction*, p. 8.

she testified, he became verbally and physically abusive, threatening to have her parole revoked if she left him.[98]

In 1990 an investigation substantiated charges that the store manager at Milan, Samuel Evans, was trading store goods for sexual favors. The employee initially received only a salary reduction and verbal instructions on how to conduct his job.[99] He was only dismissed two years later, after *Cason* was filed, when he was found to be engaging in the same conduct with additional prisoners.

After *Cason*

When the *Cason* suit was amended in 1992, the GDC entered a period of internal review of the past allegations of sexual misconduct raised by the amended complaint. Old investigations were reopened and reexamined, and a number of corrections officers and other prison staff were disciplined. Changes were also made regarding the supervision of incarcerated women.

Investigations and Disciplinary Action

In March 1992, the GDC deployed an investigator, Andie Moss, to GWCI to examine the allegations raised by the *Cason* suit and to give her assessment to the deputy commissioner and commissioner.[100] While the prisoners' names were otherwise protected by court order, according to which they were identified only as Jane Does, both Moss and the GDC leadership knew who each woman was. The Georgia Bureau of Investigations (GBI) was also called in to interview those prisoners who had filed affidavits.

Moss's investigation focused on allegations raised by and predating the *Cason* suit. Many of these allegations, found unsubstantiated prior to March 1992, were, upon reinvestigation, substantiated and found sufficient for disciplinary

---

[98] The investigation was reopened the following year, after the lawsuit was filed. The department charged that the employee, Baby Ray Griffin, "would physically and verbally abuse and intimidate [the woman] and would threaten to have her parole status revoked if she revealed to other parties . . . the nature of [his] relationship with her." Griffin was dismissed in March 1992 and indicted in November 1992 for violating the Georgia felony provision outlawing sexual contact with a prisoner or parolee. Griffin was never tried; the district attorney, as in other cases from GWCI, eventually dropped the charges against him.

[99] *Evans v. Department of Corrections*, before the State Personnel Board for the State of Georgia, Appeal No. 93-29, p. 5.

[100] Interview, Andie Moss, then assistant deputy commissioner for women's services, Georgia Department of Corrections, Atlanta, March 22, 1994.

action. According to Bob Cullen, the differing results in response to the same allegations were due in large part to the GDC's new willingness to give weight to prisoner testimony.[101]

Fifteen employees, including Philyaw, Griffin and Stanley, were suspended and eventually fired, or otherwise disciplined for sexual misconduct or misconduct associated with the *Cason* litigation. Pursuant to civil service regulations governing the terms of their employment, Philyaw, Stanley, Griffin, and several others appealed their dismissals, which were upheld by the reviewing administrative judge.

Not all dismissals sought by the GDC were granted, however. Art Gavin, the warden who succeeded Gary Black, was disciplined but not fired. Gavin was discovered copying and providing confidential information about certain Jane Does to Jackie Lee, a female correctional officer at GWCI who was, at the time, suspended amidst allegations of sexual misconduct. The GDC also did not seek to terminate Gary Black. Rather, in January 1993, Black was demoted and reassigned as a program coordinator to the northeastern regional office.[102] He later filed suit in federal court seeking his job back, as well as $500,000 in pain and suffering and $1 million in punitive damages.[103] The case has not yet gone to trial.[104]

Criminal Indictments—Failed Prosecutions

For the first time, the GDC also referred many cases of sexual misconduct to local prosecutors for criminal action.[105] In October and November 1992, indictments were handed down against fourteen former GWCI or Colony Farm employees on state criminal law charges ranging from sodomy and sexual assault

---

[101] Interview, Bob Cullen, attorney, Atlanta, August 4, 1994.

[102] Deposition of Gary Black, former warden, Georgia Women's Correctional Institution, February 24, 1994.

[103] "Prison System Sued," *Atlanta Journal-Constitution*, December 30, 1994.

[104] Telephone interview, Joseph Ferraro, attorney, Georgia Department of Corrections, February 29, 1996.

[105] According to Joe Briley, then Baldwin County prosecutor, the law had been invoked only twice before and both times for incidents in county jails, not state prisons. Interview, Joe Briley, former district attorney, Gray, Georgia, March 24, 1994.

against a person in custody to rape.[106] A fifteenth defendant was later indicted after DNA testing showed him to be the father of a prisoner's baby. The sexual acts alleged in the indictments took place between 1983 and 1992 and involved more than twenty-five prisoners.

Only two defendants were actually brought to trial on these charges, although two others pled guilty and were sentenced to terms of probation. The first to be tried, Lt. James Philyaw, was charged with twenty-one counts of sexual assault and sodomy involving eight women, for incidents which occurred over a period of five years. He was acquitted in June 1993, despite extensive testimony against him.[107] The jury deliberated only twenty minutes.

Philyaw's trial was marred by a number of irregularities that contributed to his acquittal. First, there were difficulties seating an impartial jury. The criminal trial was held, pursuant to Georgia law, in the same county where GWCI was located. The county is heavily dependent on the state correctional system for employment—it is home to four other state institutions, including three prisons. Of the fifty-six people from whom the jury was selected, twenty-eight either had a friend or relative working for the GDC.[108] At least another ten members of the jury pool were then presently or formerly employed at a correctional institution. The jury itself included a man whose son worked at a correctional institution, another whose uncle worked in one and a woman, who served as the jury foreman,

---

[106] Under Georgia's penal code, rape, sexual assault against a person in custody, and sodomy are three distinct criminal offenses. Oral and anal intercourse are criminalized as sodomy. Where an employee allegedly engages in oral or anal intercourse with a prisoner, the employee is charged with sodomy as well as sexual assault against a person in custody.

Although Human Rights Watch supports the criminal prosecution of prison staff guilty of sexual contact with prisoners, we believe that the crime is predicated on the abuse of custodial authority, not on the irrelevant distinctions between oral, anal and vaginal sex. We are also sensitive to the abuse of sodomy laws against sexual minorities. For that reason, we believe that instances of custodial sexual abuse should be prosecuted under Georgia's sexual assault law—or, where applicable, its rape law—but not under its sodomy law.

[107] Cook, "Prison guard acquitted . . . ." *Atlanta Journal-Constitution.*

[108] Interview, Robin Hutchinson, attorney, Bondurant Mixson & Elmore, Atlanta, August 5, 1994. See also Rhonda Cook, "First trial underway in prison sex scandal: Finding jurors with no connection to corrections system was difficult," *Atlanta Journal-Constitution,* June 15, 1993.

whose cousin was one of those indicted.[109]   One of the alternates was a former GDC employee who knew three of the indicted defendants.

Secondly, then District Attorney Joseph Briley, who oversaw GWCI-related prosecutions, did not engage in a vigorous prosecution of the defendant. Briley believed that the felony of sexual contact with a prisoner was a crime without a victim.   He viewed the women prisoners as accomplices and contemplated trying for sodomy those prisoners who engaged in oral sex with corrections officers; in fact, he told us, "the women themselves could have been charged as aiding and abetting the commission of a crime."[110]   In his opinion, sexual relations between prisoners and prison staff are inevitable when "pretty young things" are locked up and deprived of sex; the officers, he said, were merely guilty of giving in to temptation.[111]

Witnesses called to testify by the prosecution report that Briley did not prepare them for trial and did not present relevant testimony. One witness told us that, when she was on the witness stand, Briley never questioned her about sexual abuse of which she had firsthand knowledge. He reportedly cut her off when she tried to highlight such information in her testimony.[112]

After Philyaw's acquittal, indictments in other cases languished: some were expressly dismissed, others expired. At the time of our interview in March 1994, Briley had no timetable to proceed with prosecution, blaming the slow pace on an absence of available judges. In June 1994, Briley dropped charges of rape and sodomy against former Deputy Warden Cornelius Stanley.[113] Briley himself was forced to resign in August 1994 after he was caught on tape making sexual

---

[109] Ibid.

[110] Interview, former district attorney, Joe Briley, Gray, Georgia, March 24, 1994. A similar willingness to punish women prisoners who had sexual contact with guards had previously been voiced by Georgia State Representative Terry Coleman (Democrat-Eastman), whose legislative district included a women's facility. Rhonda Cook, "Legislator: Guards not sole culprits in sex case," *Atlanta Journal-Constitution*, October 28, 1992.

[111] Ibid.

[112] Interview, Georgia, March 1994.

[113] "Guard in sex case gets job back," *Atlanta Journal-Constitution*, December 9, 1994.

advances to a female staff member.[114] Press reports indicate that a second woman also came forward with similar charges.[115]

The original indictments resulted in only two convictions: both were based on guilty pleas, and both men were sentenced to probation in 1994. Indeed, to our knowledge, no custodial sexual misconduct prosecution to date has resulted in prison time for the guilty party. The only other case that went to trial, that of Julien Edwards, ended in acquittal in April 1996 despite the fact that DNA evidence, indicating a match of one in 57,000, showed that he was the father of a prisoner's baby.

With later indictments, prosecutors have only obtained convictions via plea bargaining and have always settled for imposing terms of probation. A typical case is that of two maintenance workers at GWCI. Convicted in 1994 of three counts of sodomy, one count of sexual assault on a person in custody, and one count of aggravated sodomy, the first defendant was sentenced to five years' probation and a $1,000 fine. The other defendant, who was convicted of one count of sodomy and one count of sexual assault against a person in custody, received twenty months' probation and a $1,000 fine.[116]

Not all GDC employees implicated in pre-1992 incidents of sexual misconduct were even indicted. The district attorney in Telfair County, home to Milan CI, was unable to secure indictments and prosecute GDC employees for allegations arising there. According to press reports, shortly after Philyaw was acquitted in June 1993, a Telfair County grand jury declined to indict eight GDC employees accused of sexually abusing women incarcerated at Milan.[117] Briley ascribed these unsuccessful prosecutions to jurors' extreme reluctance to prosecute or punish corrections employees for acts against convicted criminals.[118]

---

[114] "Ocmulgee DA was told to quit, GBI report says," *Atlanta Journal-Constitution*, October 11, 1994.

[115] Ibid.

[116] "Milledgeville: Ex-prison workers are sentenced," *Atlanta Journal-Constitution*, September 21, 1994.

[117] Rhonda Cook, "Federal civil rights probe targets ex-prison worker," *Atlanta Journal-Constitution*, August 10, 1993.

[118] Interview, Joe Briley, former district attorney, Gray, Georgia, March 24, 1994.

The GDC's practice of not referring allegations of sexual misconduct promptly to local prosecutors resulted in impunity for many abuses that occurred at GWCI prior to March 1992 because the charges were filed after the statute of limitations had expired. For this reason, in November 1994 the state dropped nineteen counts of sodomy and sexual assault against a person in custody against Jackie Lee, a female officer at GWCI. The indictment had stemmed from incidents at GWCI in 1987.[119]

Retaliation Against "Jane Does"

Our interviews reveal that corrections officers and prisoners have retaliated against women involved in the *Cason* lawsuit as Jane Does. According to Cullen, this harassment fuels the women's insecurities and has discouraged them from speaking out about subsequent incidents. The "Jane Does" represented a threat to many incarcerated women who had come to accept and even benefit from the exchange of sex for things such as alcohol, cigarettes, gum and stamps in the prisons. Even though their identities were ostensibly concealed by a protective order, the Jane Does were easily identified by prison staff and other prisoners.[120] After the suit was filed, the women were called "Jane Doe hos" and "Jane Doe sluts." According to inmate Carrie Johnson:

> It was hard to deal with the other prisoners who weren't Jane Does. They are hateful and mean and give the Jane Does a hard time. Everywhere you went, they would call you "Jane Doe ho." ... The officers would be with the prisoners and join them in the teasing.[121]

Some of the women we interviewed indicated that, at one point or another, they could no longer bear the pressure related to their Jane Doe status and tried to end their participation in *Cason*. Corrections officers have on occasion been hostile towards other prisoners, besides the Jane Does, whom they think may report

---

[119] Cook, "Prison guard accused . . .." *Atlanta Journal-Constitution.*

[120] One former warden at GWCI, Art Gavin, provided confidential information about the various Jane Does to Jackie Lee, a GWCI employee who was suspended amid charges of sexual misconduct with prisoners. Memorandum from Commissioner's Designee for Adverse Action to Arthur B. Gavin, December 22, 1992.

[121] Interview, Georgia, March 1994.

instances of abuse or threaten the status quo, and they have pressured prisoners not to speak to the administration and especially to class counsel. In the words of one Jane Doe, "Once, here at Metro, an officer told me I had been up here snitching after I talked to the warden."[122] Jackson similarly told us that she gets "strange looks" whenever she meets with her attorney.

Changes in Leadership and Administration

The GDC has undergone various changes in leadership since March 1992. In April of that year, a female warden, Mary Esposito, was installed at GWCI—the first female warden of a women's prison in Georgia.[123] After GWCI was converted into a men's facility, she was reassigned to serve as warden at Metro CI.[124] The GDC also created a new supervisory post, an assistant deputy commissioner for women's services, to oversee female prisoners under the department's jurisdiction. Andie Moss was installed in that position, but her jurisdiction over the female prisons was only temporary. In 1994 the GDC removed oversight of the women's prisons from Moss's direct administration and returned it to the regional offices of the GDC. In late 1995, Andie Moss left the GDC, and her remaining responsibilities with regard to the female correctional population shifted to someone lower in the GDC hierarchy.

In July 1993, following the airing of the "Day One" segment on sexual abuse at GWCI, Deputy Commissioner Lanson Newsome resigned and Commissioner Bobby Whitworth was reassigned to the parole board by the

---

[122] Ibid.

[123] A memorandum that Warden Esposito circulated to the prisoner population at GWCI in January 1993 suggests that she blamed prisoners, rather than staff, for the problem of custodial sexual abuse. The memorandum notes, in an evident allusion to the abuse allegations then receiving widespread publicity, that "in the past we had several serious incidents which involved not only the prisoner population, but staff as well." After warning prisoners that "serious incidents"—including "sexual activity"—would result in criminal prosecution, her memorandum emphasizes in closing that the facility "cannot tolerate *inmates who abuse staff,* or who cause serious incidents." Memorandum to inmate population, Georgia Women's Correctional Institution, January 8, 1993 (emphasis added).

[124] Esposito has since left Metro and a new female warden named Wendy Thompson was installed. Thompson formerly served as a warden at a men's prison in the state, and at GWCI as deputy for security. Certain women prisoners are wary of her background at GWCI and feel she has a "vengeful" attitude. Interview, Lisa Boardman Burnette, attorney, Atlanta, February 6, 1996.

governor.[125] Dr. Allen Ault, who had served as commissioner of the GDC years earlier, became the new commissioner.

Whitworth's position on the parole board raises concern. A number of prominent Jane Does, including Jane Doe 1, who have come before the parole board since 1993 have had their parole denied while other less prominent Jane Does have received parole. According to Cullen, it is impossible to attribute the parole denials directly to Whitworth's new position. The denial of parole to Jane Doe 1 and another Jane Doe followed a change in parole board policy regarding the granting of parole more generally.[126] Cullen added, however, that a general perception exists within the women's prisons that because of Whitworth's position, women are or will be denied parole because of their involvement in the lawsuit.[127] Jane Doe 1 told us she believed her parole was denied because of her involvement as a Jane Doe and a pending civil suit in which Whitworth is a defendant.[128] Such a perception is likely to have a chilling effect on prisoners who may wish to file complaints.

In December 1995 a new commissioner, Wayne Garner, was appointed after Ault resigned. Judging from his early policies and public statements, his primary goals in running the Georgia correctional system are to cut costs and toughen punishments. Prisoners have raised concerns that the new punitive atmosphere prevailing at the prisons only encourages sexual misconduct, as women prisoners feel further intimidated by the prison environment and, faced with losing basic privileges, have more incentive to seek "special treatment" from prison staff.[129]

Since Commissioner Garner's arrival, Bernadette Hernandez, the GDC's lead sexual misconduct investigator, has left the department. Her replacement is Jane Roulain, a former investigator with the GDC Internal Affairs division.

---

[125] Interview, Andie Moss, then assistant deputy commissioner for women's services, Atlanta, March 22, 1994.

[126] Interview, Bob Cullen, attorney, Atlanta, August 4, 1994.

[127] Ibid.

[128] Interview, Georgia, March 1994.

[129] Telephone interview, Lisa Boardman Burnette, attorney, August 12, 1996.

Failure to Comply with the Court's Orders

Until mid-1995, the GDC failed fully to comply with the March 1994 court order that permanently enjoined sexual misconduct, discussed at the beginning of this chapter. To ensure enforcement of the ban, the court required the GDC to notify its staff about the order and obtain a statement from them acknowledging that they had read and understood the order.[130] In April 1995, attorneys on the *Cason* litigation filed a contempt motion that the GDC had not obtained the requisite acknowledgments from many of the employees working in the women's prisons and was seeking unilaterally to limit the scope of the court order. They cited an April 6, 1995 letter from the GDC's counsel to an institutional administrator informing the administrator that the GDC's attorneys would "decide on a case-by-case basis whether someone should be exempted from the judge's requirement."[131] Similarly, on April 7, 1995, the GDC informed all wardens and superintendents that it would be seeking an exemption from the order for hospital personnel. The GDC's actions led the attorneys to conclude in their motion that the GDC had "no intention of fully complying with the court's order in the future."[132]

The genesis of the April contempt motion suggests the importance of notification. *Cason* class counsel learned of the department's low level of compliance upon investigating a case of custodial sexual assault that occurred at Metro CI. The prison employee, a member of the print shop staff, admitted having sex with an inmate but claimed that he had never received notice of the March 1994 court order. Because he had no notice of the order, he could not be held in contempt of court for violating it.[133]

Plaintiffs' pressure led the GDC to greatly improve its notification procedures. At present, no one can enter a women's facility without signing a form acknowledging awareness of the rules and of the *Cason* suit. In addition, notices informing visitors of the case are now posted on the outer gates of the facilities.

---

[130] Ibid.

[131] *Cason v. Seckinger*, Civil Action File No. 84-313-1-MAC, Plaintiff's Motion for Contempt and Further Relief, April 26, 1995.

[132] Ibid.

[133] He did, however, plead guilty to sexual assault under Section 16-6-5.1 and was sentenced to first offender probation. He was also fired from his employment with the GDC, receiving a hiring code that bars him from ever again being employed by the GDC or any other state agency. Interview, Lisa Boardman Burnette, attorney, Atlanta, February 6, 1996.

Failure to Train

The contempt motion cited above also argued that the GDC had largely failed to implement mandatory and effective training for its employees assigned to work in the women's prisons on sexual harassment and sexual abuse of prisoners. Class counsel asserted that "upon information and belief, some supervisors may be discouraging their subordinates from attending [the sexual misconduct] portion of the training."[134]

Even where the training was provided, it did not appear directly to address and confront the problem of sexual misconduct and inappropriate relationships. Our review of a training session conducted by the GDC in February 1993 on staff-prisoner relationships found that it focused heavily on homosexuality between prisoners and on prisoners' adaptation to incarceration, but said little about sexual relations between corrections employees and prisoners.

As a result of a stipulation resolving the contempt motion, however, the training has since been improved, at least with regard to the requirements ordered under *Cason*. We were told that it now lasts about a half-day and at the end of the session the employee must take a test on the material. Employees who pass the test receive a sticker for their I.D. cards; without such a sticker, they are barred from entering the women's prisons.[135]

An additional element of the stipulation was that the GDC agreed to develop training for women prisoners to educate them about their right not be sexually abused and to teach them how to report instances of misconduct. Women who enter the prison system, while they are in the "diagnostics" or entry stage, now watch a video on the subject. Though attorney Lisa Burnette thinks that the video itself is "not the best," she believes that efforts to educate women inmates regarding their rights are of critical importance.[136]

Handling of Investigations

As stated above, the review conducted by the GDC in 1992 focused solely on actions predating the *Cason* suit, resulting in the reopening of old investigations. Allegations which arose afterwards were addressed separately.

---

[134] *Cason v. Seckinger*, Civil Action File No. 84-313-1-MAC, Plaintiff's Motion for Contempt and Further Relief, April 26, 1995.

[135] Interview, Lisa Boardman Burnette, attorney, Atlanta, February 6, 1996.

[136] Ibid.

For over two years after the allegations in *Cason* surfaced, the GDC failed to develop an adequate policy or mechanism for investigating sexual misconduct and revealed a continued lack of interest and commitment to addressing allegations of sexual abuse by prison staff. In mid-1993 the GDC assigned to the Internal Affairs division a special investigator solely responsible for examining allegations of sexual assault, personal dealings, and sexual misconduct in the prisons. However, the person hired, Bernadette Hernandez, had no experience or specialized training in investigating sexual assault or rape.[137] Although she was the only investigator, she received no training from the GDC in this area before starting her job,[138] no written guidelines for conducting her work, [139]and no car to get around to the four GDC women's facilities for which she was responsible.

The absence of a written and clear GDC procedure for conducting investigations contributed to irregularities and delays in the reporting and investigation of sexual misconduct allegations. According to Cullen, who deposed Hernandez on two occasions as part of *Cason*, Hernandez was left to cobble together her own method for conducting investigations on a case-by-case basis. The GDC failed to provide timetables and predetermined procedures for interviewing prisoners and investigating allegations.[140] As a result, Cullen told us, investigations under Hernandez initially languished unresolved for extended periods of time. Her deposition revealed that of the fifty-two investigations initiated since she started in mid-1993, over twenty were still unresolved in July 1994.

The absence of a clear investigations policy, furthermore, contributed to *ad hoc* decisions regarding the use of administrative segregation for several months in 1994. In early 1994 some prisoners who alleged sexual misconduct or sexual assault were involuntarily "separated administratively" or placed in segregation

---

[137] Hernandez formerly worked with the Atlanta Police Department, with their narcotics investigation unit and as patrol officer. Deposition of Bernadette Hernandez, May 20, 1994.

[138] According to a July 20, 1994 deposition, Hernandez received three hours of training in sex crimes investigations in June 1994, or almost a year after she started her position as an investigator with the GDC. She received this training after she was questioned during a May 20, 1994 deposition by *Cason* attorneys about her experience and training working on sexual assault or rape cases.

[139] Telephone interview, Bob Cullen, attorney, February 16, 1995.

[140] Ibid.

pending an investigation into their charges. At the same time, the implicated staff member remained at the institution. Hernandez seemed unaware of how the use of administrative segregation would negatively impact the investigative process, particularly the willingness of incarcerated women to report abuse. While Hernandez acknowledged that being placed in segregation was "automatically punitive," she did not think it would inhibit women from reporting abuse. Rather, Hernandez asserted that the prisoners "who are telling the truth don't worry about that [being placed in segregation]" and would simply know they were not being punished for coming forward since she told them they would not get in trouble for talking to her.

Rehired Former Employees

In July 1994 the GDC rehired Cornelius Stanley, the former deputy warden for security at GWCI who was fired in July 1992 on the grounds of rape and intimidation of prisoners.[141] The GDC had successfully justified his dismissal on appeal before an administrative law judge. The judge found, by a preponderance of the evidence, that Stanley was guilty of misconduct and had "demonstrated . . . unfitness to perform duties in a Correctional Institution."[142] In fact, this was not the first occasion Stanley had been reprimanded for inappropriate conduct as a correctional employee. In January 1990, two years before his dismissal, Stanley was demoted from correctional manager to captain after an incident at a men's facility where a prisoner was beaten by officers under Stanley's supervision.[143]

Despite his record of abusive behavior, Stanley was rehired in July 1994 as a lieutenant at the Hancock Correctional Institution, a prison for men, at the pay of a captain, which was the rank he held when he was fired.[144] His dismissal for sexual misconduct against female prisoners, therefore, had no impact on his

---

[141] Rhonda Cook, "Prison guard accused of abusing female prisoners is rehired," *Atlanta Journal-Constitution*, July 12, 1994.

[142] *Stanley v. Department of Corrections*, p. 27.

[143] According to Stanley's disciplinary hearing for events at GWCI, he was given a written reprimand following the earlier incident "for failure to properly supervise subordinates during an incident in which abuse of a prisoner did occur." Stanley was also suspended without pay for seven days in 1979 for sleeping while on duty. Ibid., p. 15.

[144] Cook, "Prison guard accused . . .," *Atlanta Journal-Constitution*.

employment or his pay scale. In fact, he received over $58,000 in back pay, plus damages, when he was rehired. The criminal charges against him were dropped.

Rehiring Stanley, according to Bob Cullen, sent a message that the GDC does not take the issue of sexual misconduct in its facilities seriously. He told us, "[It] hurts big time. It lowers the faith of the women in the new system for reporting these kind of cases. If Stanley is fit to come back, then why not the others?"[145] In fact, in December 1994, the GDC reinstated Jackie Lee, who had been suspended for nearly two years on charges of sodomy and sexual assault against a person in custody; she too claimed the right to back pay and damages (in a negotiated settlement, she received just over $10,000 in back pay, along with leave and retirement benefits).[146]

Improved Investigations Procedure

In November 1994, more than a year after plaintiffs drafted and submitted a policy to the GDC, the department finally agreed to adopt new standard operating procedures for investigating allegations of sexual contact, sexual abuse, and sexual harassment within the prisons, for handling suspected cases of sexual abuse by the medical staff, and for providing counseling to victims of abuse.[147] In addition, the GDC employed three additional special investigators to implement the new policies under the supervision of the lead investigator.

The investigative procedure that went into effect in January 1995 distinguishes, for the first time, between personal dealings and sexual misconduct, specifically defining what constitutes sexual contact, sexual abuse, sexual harassment, and personal dealings.[148] It imposes a strict obligation on staff

---

[145] Interview, Bob Cullen, attorney, Atlanta, August 4, 1994.

[146] "Guard in sex case gets job back," *Atlanta Journal-Constitution*, December 9, 1994; telephone interview, Karen Kirk, spokesperson, Georgia Department of Corrections, April 30, 1996.

[147] *Cason v. Seckinger*, Civil Action File No. 84-313-1-MAC, Consent Order, November 23, 1994. The GDC agreed to do so after one week before a trial on the issue, and after a pre-trial order was filed.

[148] The policy provides that sexual contact includes, but is not limited to: "the intentional touching, either directly or through clothing, of the genitalia, anus, groin, breast, inner thighs, or buttocks of any person with an intent to abuse, humiliate, harass, degrade, or arouse or gratify the sexual desire of any person." Sexual abuse includes, but is not limited to: "subjecting another person to sexual contact by persuasion, inducement, enticement, or

immediately to report incidents of sexual misconduct, including rumors, to the warden or other designated persons and provides for disciplinary action, up to and including dismissal, for failing to do so. Confidentiality is provided for the complainant as well as the alleged victim. The procedure, furthermore, specifically bans any retaliation against the victim or complainant, limits the use of administrative segregation to "necessary" circumstances and only allows its use for up to seven days. It allows specially trained counselors to meet with the prisoner before she is interviewed and, in certain circumstances, to attend interviews between the prisoner and special investigator. It also introduces a time frame for investigations, review by the GDC commissioner, and notification to concerned attorneys.[149] A prisoner may be disciplined as a result of filing a report of abuse only if it is determined that she "made a false allegation or made a material statement which she, in good faith, could not have believed to be true."

Attorney Bob Cullen told us that the investigators have been "roughly abiding by the guidelines" and that they are doing a decent job in evaluating complaints, despite a marked bias against prisoner testimony described in more detail below.[150] During 1995 (from January 23 to December 31), 156 complaints

---

forcible compulsion; subjecting to sexual contact another person who is incapable of giving consent by reason of her custodial status; subjecting another person to sexual contact who is incapable of consenting by reason of being physically helpless, physically restrained, or mentally incapacitated; and raping, molesting, prostituting, or otherwise sexually exploiting another person." The policy provides that sexual harassment includes, but is not limited to, "unwelcome sexual advances, requests for sexual favors, or other verbal or physical conduct of a sexual nature." Personal dealings are defined as "contact or business dealings with sentenced females in violation of GDC [policy]. This includes, but is not limited to, giving, receiving, selling, buying, trading, bartering or exchanging anything of value with any sentenced female." Georgia Department of Corrections Standard Operating Procedures, "Investigations of Allegations of Sexual Contact, Sexual Abuse and Sexual Harassment," November 23, 1994.

[149] Under the policy, investigators are required to prepare a preliminary investigative report within fourteen calendar days of receiving a complaint, with a recommendation for additional action. Attorneys working on *Cason*, the district attorney and other interested attorneys must be notified of the GDC's decision on the preliminary investigation within twenty-one days. The GDC commissioner or his designee, furthermore, must review the investigator's recommendation and decide how to proceed. If he or she decides to continue the investigation, the final investigation must be completed within twenty-eight days of the allegation.

[150] Interview, Bob Cullen, attorney, Atlanta, February 7, 1996.

of sexual misconduct were filed under the new investigative procedure. The resulting investigations had the following outcomes: three cases were referred to the district attorney for prosecution, nine staff were terminated, thirteen staff resigned, five were transferred to a male institution, one received a written reprimand, and three were subject to other disciplinary action.[151] Counsel on *Cason* have the sense that investigators' recommendations for these cases have generally been followed.

Persistent Bias Against Prisoner Testimony

Unfortunately, the improved investigatory procedure has to some extent been compromised by a renewed bias against prisoner testimony within the GDC. According to Cullen, the GDC has moved away from viewing prisoner allegations and testimony as credible. Immediately following *Cason*, the GDC relied on prisoner testimony to support charges of misconduct against staff and called prisoners as witnesses in disciplinary hearings. The administrative law judges, in upholding the dismissals, noted that merely because one violated the law in the past did not mean that person was not credible in the present. In more current investigations, however, the GDC has reverted to its previous practice of discounting prisoner testimony, even in instances where the prisoner passes a polygraph test and the employee fails. Cullen told us that in his estimation investigators presently assess prisoners' reports of abuse using an extremely exacting standard: prisoners must prove their allegations "beyond a reasonable doubt," and prisoner testimony alone is almost never sufficient.[152]

One serious problem related to the reluctance to credit prisoner testimony, which began to crop up in late 1995, is a trend toward assessing disciplinary reports (DRs) when prisoners' reports of sexual misconduct are found to be unsubstantiated. Obviously the possibility of receiving a DR—which can result in a week or more of disciplinary segregation—works to discourage women inmates from filing complaints.

Given the high standards used in evaluating prisoners' complaints, it is clear that not only frivolous complaints result in DRs. Indeed, class counsel in *Cason* have already had DRs expunged that involved reasonable complaints. In one instance, for example, the warden imposed a DR even though the investigator recommended against it. In another, in which an inmate reported sexual activity that she had witnessed, there was corroborating evidence of such activity—and

---

[151] Interview, Lisa Boardman Burnette, attorney, Atlanta, February 6, 1996.

[152] Interview, Bob Cullen, attorney, Atlanta, February 7, 1996.

both the named prisoner victim and the accused staff member failed polygraph examinations regarding the incident—but the investigator found the complaint to be unsubstantiated, and a DR was imposed. Class counsel are carefully monitoring the use of DRs against complainants and will consider filing a contempt motion with the court if they conclude that DRs are being used abusively.[153]

Lack of Independent Oversight

The federal government has not invoked its authority under the Civil Rights of Institutionalized Persons Act (CRIPA) to investigate Georgia women's prisons for violations of federal civil rights. It also has not filed any criminal indictments against any corrections officers or other GDC employees for federal civil rights violations. GDC Commissioner Allen Ault reportedly asked the Department of Justice to conduct a federal inquiry into the situation in Georgia's women's prisons in July 1993, a month after Philyaw's acquittal.[154] Local attorneys informed us that while the DOJ apparently made some preliminary inquiries and requests for information, no indictments were ever handed down.[155]

Even were the will to investigate ever mustered, the DOJ's slow response has already effectively foreclosed possible federal criminal action on many allegations in Georgia predating *Cason*, as there is a five-year statute of limitations on bringing criminal charges. It has already been four years since *Cason* was amended to include allegations of sexual misconduct and three years since the Philyaw trial, and most of the incidents alleged in both instances occurred before 1992.

---

[153] Interview, Lisa Boardman Burnette, attorney, Atlanta, February 6, 1996.

[154] Interview, Andie Moss, then assistant deputy commissioner for women's services, Atlanta, March 22, 1994. Press reports indicate that Dr. Ault requested the DOJ to investigate allegations that Philyaw sexually abused women incarcerated at GWCI, as well as other allegations emanating from Washington CI and Milan CI. The broadened request followed the failure of a grand jury in Telfair County, Georgia to indict eight people accused of abusing incarcerated women at Milan CI. Rhonda Cook, "Federal civil rights probe targets ex-prison worker." *Atlanta Journal-Constitution*, August 10, 1993.

[155] Interview, Atlanta, March 1994.

RECOMMENDATIONS

I.   **Ensuring Compliance with Judicial Order**

A.   The Georgia Department of Corrections should take all action necessary to comply with the March 1994 judicial order issued in *Cason v. Seckinger* that requires the GDC to prohibit all sexual abuse, sexual contact and sexual harassment of female prisoners. The GDC should also ensure that its employees desist from other forms of degrading treatment of incarcerated women.

B.   The Georgia Legislature should create a fully empowered and independent review board to monitor the GDC's compliance with *Cason's* mandates and to ensure that complaints of sexual misconduct are adequately investigated and remedied. The review board should be guaranteed full and unhindered access to GDC facilities and records, including all records collected under the new investigative procedure, and should have the authority to turn over evidence of possible criminal wrongdoing for police investigation. The board should also be able to recommend remedial action—including temporary reassignment or suspension of accused officers—to stop abuse or other problems.

     1.   The review board should develop a system whereby the records of corrections employees who have been the subject of repeated complaints are reviewed by the appropriate authorities.

     2.   The review board should provide a toll-free telephone number that prisoners can use to provide information or to file complaints of employee misconduct, including retaliation against complainants.

C.   As a means of additional oversight, the GDC should facilitate the access of outside monitors, such as lawyers and prisoners rights advocates, to its women's correctional facilities.

II.   **Prohibiting Sex in Custody**

A.   Georgia prosecutors should strictly enforce Section 16-5-5.1 of the Georgia Penal Code prohibiting sexual assault, defined as engaging in sexual contact with a person in custody. The consent of the victim, which is not a legal defense to a prosecution under this section, should not be a *de facto* bar to prosecution. Of course, cases which fall within the statutory definition of rape should be prosecuted as such. Yet, since the offense of prison sexual abuse is predicated on the abuse of custodial authority, not on distinctions between oral, anal and vaginal sex that are entirely irrelevant to this key issue, we recommend against prosecution under the Georgia sodomy law.

B.   For its part, the GDC should refer all cases of sexual misconduct that fall within the statutory definition to the local authorities for prosecution.

C.   The GDC should include in its standard operating procedures a requirement that prisoners be treated humanely and be free from torture and cruel, inhuman or degrading treatment as a matter of compliance with U.S. obligations under international law, in particular the International Covenant on Civil and Political Rights and the Torture Convention.

III.   Safeguarding Prisoners Impregnated by Guards

A.   The GDC should make every effort to protect women who are impregnated by corrections employees from being accosted further by those employees.

B.   The GDC should not punish prisoners, either as a matter of informal practice or of official policy, who are impregnated by officers. The GDC should also refrain from administratively segregating pregnant prisoners, unless they expressly request it.

C.   The GDC should ensure that corrections staff do not employ coercion to persuade pregnant prisoners to have abortions.

D.   The GDC should ensure that pregnant prisoners receive timely and adequate medical care, and that medical treatment recommended by physicians is provided as prescribed. Medical care should include professional psychiatric counseling for prisoners who are impregnated as a consequence of rape or sexual abuse. Prisoners also should receive neutral counseling on the options available to them. Administrative segregation should not preclude the provision of adequate medical and hygienic requirements for a safe pregnancy.

IV.   Ensuring an Effective Remedy
        Grievances
A.   The GDC should make grievance forms readily available to prisoners at
        a neutral location, such as a prison library or other similar place. It should
        also enable prisoners to file complaints without seeking the permission of
        any GDC employee.

B.   The GDC should ensure that institutional counselors do not, under any
        circumstances, attempt to talk prisoners out of filing their grievances.

        Investigations
A.   The GDC should take all action necessary to comply with the November
        23, 1994 court order that resulted in new standard operating procedure,
        adopted in January 1995, for investigating allegations of sexual
        misconduct.   Additionally, it should ensure that investigators have
        adequate human and material resources to investigate fully and
        expeditiously all complaints of sexual misconduct.

B.   In addition to training all persons hired to investigate allegations of sexual
        misconduct on the requirements of the investigative procedure, the GDC
        also should ensure that they fully understand the coercive dynamics of the
        prison environment and the inherently punitive nature of administrative
        segregation.

V.   Preventing Retaliation Against Complainants
A.   Investigators should not recommend disciplinary reports, and wardens
        should not impose them, as punishment for a complaint of sexual abuse
        found to be unsubstantiated, unless the complaint is manifestly frivolous
        or made in bad faith.

B.   The GDC should investigate promptly and vigorously all charges of
        harassment and retaliation against prisoners who report wrongdoing. The
        GDC must effectively inform corrections employees that reprisal against
        prisoners will not be tolerated, that complaints of such conduct will be
        treated seriously and expeditiously, and that staff found guilty of
        retaliation will be sanctioned.

VI.   Ensuring Discipline

A.   Human Rights Watch is extremely troubled that the governor of Georgia
        appointed Bobby Whitworth, former commissioner of corrections, to the
        state parole board, after he stated on national television that it was his
        agency's general policy not to enforce the law against custodial sexual
        assault. We call on the governor of Georgia to remove Bobby Whitworth
        from the parole board and not to appoint him to any position of authority
        over prisoners in Georgia.

B.   Human Rights Watch is also extremely concerned by the GDC's decision
        to rehire Cornelius Stanley and to return Jackie Lee to her post. The GDC
        should proceed with investigations into employee misconduct while
        allegations are pending before the appropriate police or prosecutorial
        authorities, and take appropriate disciplinary action. Investigations should
        examine possible criminal law violations as well as administrative
        infractions of GDC's employee code of conduct. Even if a person is
        acquitted of a criminal offense, the GDC should still pursue disciplinary
        action if evidence indicates that the employee violated the rules governing
        his or her employment.

C.   The GDC should dismiss employees found to have engaged in rape,
        sexual assault or sexual abuse of prisoners. There should be no tolerance
        for rehiring employees who have been disciplined and terminated.
        Transfer of such employees to other positions or facilities does not
        constitute appropriate punishment.

D.   The GDC should publish, at least quarterly, a report on disciplinary
        actions taken against corrections employees responsible for misconduct
        or abuse. If necessary, the reports should omit the names of prisoners
        and, if necessary, of employees. But they should include dates, locations,
        and other relevant details about the reported incidents, and the types of
        disciplinary sanctions applied, including referrals to the local prosecutor.

VII.   Hiring and Training Corrections Employees

A.   The GDC should improve its screening procedures for applicants for
        corrections positions. Background checks should be completed before
        new employees are sent into correctional facilities. In no case should an
        employee who has been convicted of an offense related to sexual
        misconduct in custody be rehired.

B.   The GDC should ensure that the training of all corrections employees assigned to work in the women's prisons includes, among other things:

     1.   A general discussion of the profile of female prisoners and their potential vulnerability to sexual misconduct;

     2.   A review of all relevant GDC policies regarding sexual misconduct and their associated disciplinary sanctions, as well as the criminal law prohibition on sexual contact with a person in custody;

     3.   A demonstration of appropriate methods for conducting pat-searches, strip searches and searches of women's cells. In developing this training, the GDC should collaborate with local nongovernmental organizations experienced in working on issues such as rape and sexual assault.

VIII.   Educating Prisoners

A.   The GDC should advise incarcerated women, as part of their orientation to the corrections system, as well as prisoners already serving their sentences, of the following:

     1.   They have the right to be free from all forms of custodial sexual abuse, including all sexual contact or harassment. The orientation should describe in detail what actions may constitute sexual misconduct, and should also include a thorough review of departmental policies regarding privacy and humane treatment; the procedures for reporting and investigating sexual misconduct; and the administrative and criminal sanctions associated with it.

     2.   Grievances related to sexual misconduct may be filed directly and confidentially with the prison superintendent or investigator. Prisoners should be informed about: the issues that may be dealt with through the grievance procedure, with particular emphasis on instances of sexual misconduct; the location of grievance forms; bypass mechanisms available for reporting sexual misconduct; and the recourse available when corrections officers fail to respond.

     3.   Complaints may also be resolved through the investigation procedure and/or the independent review board.

     4.   Prisoners enjoy a range of rights under international human rights treaties ratified by the United States and under U.S. constitutional law.

B.   The above information should be included in the prisoner handbook.

IX.   Allocating Supplies

The GDC should ensure that it always allocates basic sanitary items sufficient to meet female prisoners' needs, to avoid situations where prisoners exchange sexual favors with officers for goods. Adequate supplies should be accessible to prisoners at the prison commissary or other similarly neutral place.

VI. ILLINOIS

Our investigation[1] revealed a serious problem with sexual misconduct in the Illinois correctional facilities for women, including frequent privacy violations and sexually explicit verbal degradation of female prisoners, inappropriate sexual contact and, at times, rape and sexual assault and abuse. Neither Illinois prison rules nor criminal law expressly prohibits such abuse. When female prisoners have attempted to report sexual misconduct, they have faced a biased grievance and investigatory procedure and often have suffered retaliation or even punishment by prison staff. This system for addressing sexual misconduct significantly deters women from lodging complaints of such abuse. Given that the Illinois Department of Corrections is the only governmental body that may initiate investigations into such complaints, incidents of sexual misconduct may be significantly underreported.

The Illinois Department of Corrections (IDOC) acknowledges that sexual misconduct has occurred in its facilities but strongly takes issue with any implication that the agency tolerates or condones sexual misconduct between prisoners and correctional staff. In an unpublished July 1996 letter to the *Chicago Sun-Times,* IDOC Director Odie Washington,[2] stated that the department "has a strict policy of zero tolerance regarding both consensual sex and nonconsensual sex

---

[1] Our conclusions in this chapter are based on interviews conducted in 1994, 1995 and 1996 with thirteen current and former female prisoners each of whom had been incarcerated in at least one of the three Illinois maximum-security prisons for women: Dixon Correctional Center, Dwight Correctional Center and Logan Correctional Center. In addition, we spoke to attorneys and prisoner rights advocates in Illinois who monitor prison conditions generally and who, in some cases, follow particular complaints of sexual misconduct with the Illinois Department of Corrections.

Most of the women we interviewed had previously complained of sexual misconduct by correctional staff. In several cases, their allegations had already been investigated and the complaints monitored by attorneys or advocates working on their behalf. In each instance, we attempted to corroborate prisoner statements with written documentation, such as grievances or prior written statements, and with the testimony of a second person, including other prisoners. None of the women with whom we spoke had been incarcerated at Kankakee, Illinois's only minimum security prison for women.

[2] Since our original investigation, the director of the Illinois Department of Corrections, Howard Peters, became a deputy to the governor of Illinois and was replaced by Odie Washington, who was formerly the warden at Dixon Correctional Center, a women's prison.

between inmates and staff."[3] However, our investigation reveals a gap between the department's stated policy and actual practice. One attorney who represents women prisoners told us, "If [IDOC] really wanted to stop this behavior, they would go about it in a different way." We strongly urge Illinois to reform its prison rules and criminal laws expressly to ban sexual misconduct in prisons, to enforce better those disciplinary measures that already exist to protect prisoners against sexual misconduct, and to uphold the right to an effective remedy of women who file complaints of custodial sexual misconduct.

CONTEXT

Custodial Environment

The number of incarcerated women in Illinois has risen dramatically in the last ten years. As of February 1996, there were over 2,200 women in prison, a number over four times greater than that in 1986.[4] Approximately 60 percent of these women are incarcerated for nonviolent offenses.[5] The majority of incarcerated women are of color, with African American women comprising 68 percent of the female prison population.[6] Male correctional officers outnumber female officers by over two to one,[7] and few written restrictions delineate male officers' responsibilities in overseeing female prisoners.

Although nearly 60 percent of women incarcerated in Illinois are from Cook County, the area around and including Chicago, Illinois women's prisons are

---

[3] Unpublished letter from Odie Washington, director, Illinois Department of Corrections, to *Chicago Sun-Times*, July 22, 1996 (on file with Human Rights Watch).

[4] Chicago Legal Aid to Incarcerated Mothers, "Women in Prison: Fact Sheet," 1996. In 1983 there were only 486 women in prison in the state.

[5] Ibid.

[6] Ibid.

[7] *Corrections Compendium* (Nebraska), October 1992. There were approximately 1,688 male corrections officers working in the women's prisons but less than 700 women officers.

all located at a considerable distance from the metropolitan area.[8] The only prison for women until the 1980s was Dwight Correctional Center, located approximately two hours southwest of Chicago.[9] In response to overcrowding and the expansion of its female prison population, IDOC eventually converted two of its all-male facilities—Logan Correctional Center and Dixon Correctional Center—into prisons for both sexes. Like Dwight, Dixon is located in rural Illinois, almost three hours west of Chicago. In 1995 IDOC began to increase the number of women prisoners at Logan, which, at a distance of nearly four hours from Chicago, is the furthest away of the three prisons. At present, IDOC is planning to make a minimum security prison for 300 women out of a mental health center in Decatur.[10] Decatur is even more isolated than Logan; trips from Chicago to Decatur typically would require an overnight stay.[11] The time and expense of travel to and from the women's prisons make it difficult for advocates and prisoners' families to visit and monitor the treatment of the prisoners.

Another concern is availability of basic services. The female prison population is growing at an accelerating pace, which has led to corresponding decreases in female prisoners' access to educational and other rehabilitative programs and medical care.[12] Such access is provided for in the U.N. Standard

---

[8] This information is based on materials provided to Mary Flowers, Illinois state representative, by Howard A. Peters, then the director of the Illinois Department of Corrections [hereinafter "IDOC Statistical Information"]. We contacted Flowers's office for information regarding proposed sentencing reform for incarcerated mothers. The statistical information was included in the packet of information we received.

[9] For several years, as the number of women rose and Dwight became unable to house them, women were held in county jails.

[10] Anthony Man, "Report: Women's Prison Would Replace Meyer," *Decatur Herald & Review*, April 22, 1995.

[11] Telephone interview, Gail Smith, executive director, Chicago Legal Aid to Incarcerated Mothers, February 29, 1996.

[12] According to the Prison Action Committee (PAC), an Illinois prison monitoring organization staffed by former prisoners, gynecological services are available only three to four hours a week at Dwight for a population of nearly 800 women. (Interview, Barbara Echols, executive director, Prison Action Committee, Chicago, May 9, 1994.) Women housed at Logan do not have access to an infirmary and must be transferred to Dwight for major medical treatment. ("IDOC Statistical Information.") Female prisoners sued the

Minimum Rules.[13] Nonetheless, each of the women's facilities, with the exception of Kankakee, the state's only minimum security prison for women, is operating from 20 to 40 percent over its rated capacity.[14]

State Legal and Regulatory Framework

Neither sexual relations nor sexual contact with prisoners by corrections staff are expressly prohibited under Illinois's rape and sexual assault laws. With respect to prison rules, the prohibition on sexual contact must be read into a broad provision of the Illinois Administrative Code that prohibits employees from "socializing with committed persons."[15] The administrative code also provides that prisoners may be punished with one year in segregation for sexual misconduct, which could cover sexual behavior between prisoners as well as sexual behavior

---

department alleging they were provided substantially inferior educational and vocational programming, compared with those provided to male prisoners, and were being paid lower wages for similar work. (*Moorehead v. McGinnis*, Civil Action No. 86-2020, Complaint, January 21, 1986 (Central District of Illinois).) In addition, the women alleged they were disparately impacted by the absence of a minimum security facility. Women incarcerated in Illinois have historically been allocated fewer resources, educational services and been provided with vocational training for the low-paying jobs traditionally held by women. For example, college courses for women leading to a bachelor's degree were not offered until 1985, more than a decade after similar programs were instituted for men. (Jean Davidson, "Seeking Rights in Prison: Women Inmate's Suit Charges Sexual Bias," *Chicago Tribune*, April 3, 1988.) In 1991 IDOC entered into a consent decree with the attorneys representing the incarcerated women. (*Moorehead v. McGinnis*, Civil Action No. 86-2020, Consent Decree, May 1, 1991.) Pursuant to the 1991 consent decree, the IDOC conducted a survey of educational and vocational needs of incarcerated women, which resulted in the creation of prison programs for women in business occupations and computer operations. ("IDOC Statistical Information.")

[13] Standard Minimum Rules for the Treatment of Prisoners, Rules 22-26 (medical care) and Rules 65 and 77-78 (education and recreation).

[14] "IDOC Statistical Information."

[15] Under the Illinois Administrative Code, "Individuals shall not knowingly socialize with or engage in business transactions with any committed person." 20 Illinois Administrative Code, Section 120.50, "Socializing with Committed Persons."

between a corrections employee and a prisoner.[16] IDOC has used this policy to punish female prisoners who reported sexual misconduct, a practice that Human Rights Watch opposes on the grounds that the deterrent effect on the reporting of sexual misconduct is more damaging than can be justified by any penological purpose served by such punishments.

National and International Law Protections

As discussed in the legal background section of this report, sexual misconduct is clearly prohibited under both U.S. constitutional law and international treaty and customary law that is binding on the U.S. federal government as well as its constituent states.[17] The eighth amendment to the Constitution, which bars cruel and unusual punishment, has been interpreted by U.S. courts to protect prisoners against rape and sexual assault. This constitutional shield is augmented by the Fourth Amendment's guarantee of the right to privacy and personal integrity, which, in a series of lower court cases, has been interpreted to prohibit male guards from inappropriately viewing or strip searching female prisoners or conducting intrusive pat-frisks on female prisoners.

Constitutional protections for prisoners' rights are enforceable via lawsuits filed by or on behalf of prisoners, or by the U.S. Department of Justice (DOJ). Historically, U.S. prisoners have achieved most of their landmark victories through private litigation, particularly suits litigated by prisoners' rights groups such as the National Prison Project of the American Civil Liberties Union. However, if certain stringent intent requirements are met, the DOJ may criminally prosecute abusive prison officials under federal civil rights provisions. In addition, the DOJ has the statutory right to investigate and institute civil actions under the Civil Rights of Institutionalized Persons Act (CRIPA) whenever it finds that a state facility engages in a pattern or practice of subjecting prisoners to "egregious or flagrant conditions" in violation of the constitution.

In addition to constitutional protections, prisoners' rights are protected under international human rights treaties that are legally binding on the United States. The primary international legal instruments protecting the rights of U.S.

---

[16] The Illinois Administrative Code defines sexual misconduct as "engaging in sexual intercourse, deviate sexual conduct or fondling or touching done to sexually arouse either or both persons." Ibid., Section 504, Table A.

[17] For a detailed discussion of United States obligations under U.S. constitutional law and international law pertaining to the treatment of prisoners, see the legal background chapter of this report.

prisoners are the International Covenant on Civil and Political Rights (ICCPR), ratified by the United States in 1993, and the Convention Against Torture and Other Cruel, Inhuman or Degrading Treatment or Punishment, ratified in 1994. The ICCPR guarantees prisoners' right to privacy, except when limitations on this right are demonstrably necessary to maintain prison security. Both treaties bar torture and cruel, inhuman or degrading treatment or punishment, which authoritative international bodies have interpreted as including sexual abuse. To constitute torture, an act must cause severe physical or mental suffering and must be committed for a purpose such as obtaining information from a victim, punishing her or intimidating or coercing her or for any reason based on discrimination of any kind. Cruel, inhuman or degrading treatment or punishment includes acts causing a lesser degree of suffering that need not be committed for a particular purpose.

When prison staff members use force, the threat of force, or other means of coercion to compel a prisoner to engage in sexual intercourse, their acts constitute rape and, therefore, torture. Torture also occurs when prison staff use force or coercion to engage in sexual touching of prisoners where such acts cause serious physical or mental suffering. Instances of sexual touching or of sexual intercourse that does not amount to rape may constitute torture or cruel or inhuman treatment, depending on the level of physical or mental suffering involved. Other forms of sexual misconduct, such as inappropriate pat or strip searches or verbal harassment, that do not rise to the level of torture or of cruel or inhuman treatment, may be condemned as degrading treatment.[18]

---

[18] For a detailed discussion of the prohibition against torture, and other cruel, inhuman or degrading treatment or punishment under international law and its applicability to custodial sexual misconduct, see the legal background chapter of this report.

ABUSES[19]

Custodial sexual misconduct in Illinois's women's prisons includes sexual intercourse, sexual assault and inappropriate sexual contact. It also includes constant and highly sexualized verbal degradation of prisoners and unwarranted visual surveillance. Unless indicated by the use of a full name, the names of the prisoners have been changed to protect their anonymity. In some cases, the location and exact date of prisoner interviews have also been withheld.

Rape, Sexual Assault or Abuse, and Criminal Sexual Contact

Our investigation found that sexual misconduct is not a new problem in the women's prisons in Illinois. In the early 1980s, it came to light that certain corrections employees were involved in the sexual abuse of women incarcerated at Dwight. Press reports revealed that the chief internal affairs officer of IDOC forced at least one prisoner to "commit deviate sexual acts" on him and "to commit lesbian acts upon other female prisoners."[20] Upon learning of this misconduct, the acting warden placed the prisoner in administrative segregation involuntarily for eleven months, ostensibly for her own protection.[21] According to Charles Fasano, who works with the John Howard Association, an Illinois prison monitoring organization, the revelation of these abuses led directly to the resignation of the

---

[19] By rape, we mean sexual intercourse between a prison employee and a prisoner that is accompanied by the use or threat of force or coercion which, under certain circumstances, can take the form of the provision or denial of privileges, money, or goods. Sexual assault is sexual touching, short of intercourse, involving the same coercive influences. Sexual abuse is sexual intercourse or touching involving the offer of goods or privileges absent any actual or perceived threat to the prisoner. Criminal sexual contact refers to sexual intercourse or sexual touching that cannot be shown to involve any of the above elements but which nonetheless constitutes a gross breach of official duty. Rape, sexual assault or abuse, and criminal sexual contact should all be prosecuted as felonies. For a more detailed discussion, see the legal background chapter.

[20] "Prison chief Lane testifies about sex scandal probe," United Press International, May 25, 1983, AM cycle.

[21] "Testimony wrapped up in prison sex lawsuit," United Press International, May 26, 1983, AM cycle.

then warden and the installation of a new warden, Jane Higgins.[22] According to prison advocates, Warden Higgins brought strong leadership skills and implemented programs designed to eliminate sexual misconduct. However, in 1989 Warden Higgins resigned and Gwendolyn Thornton was installed as warden.

Advocates we interviewed noted that following this change in wardens, the efforts of Warden Higgins to reduce sexual misconduct have ceased and allegations of sexual misconduct at Dwight have increased. The John Howard Association has received letters from prisoners raising complaints of sexual misconduct within the women's prisons. According to Fasano:

> I wasn't hearing these things. Jane would never put up with that.
> If she heard about it, she would be on the case. She wouldn't
> put up with it. . . . I've seen a big change and sadly, not for the
> better [in recent years].[23]

Private attorneys and the Prison Action Committee (PAC) similarly reported receiving an increased number of letters alleging such misconduct after Thornton took over.

Another attorney who has worked with female prisoners in Illinois, Ruthanne DeWolfe, noted a steady deterioration in the conditions at Dwight since Warden Higgins's departure. She told us, "There [is] a lack of leadership."[24] According to DeWolfe, Warden Higgins brought to the position strong management skills and a sensitivity to the many gender-related needs of women prisoners. Since her departure, many of the model programs she initiated have been stopped. DeWolfe asserted that at an institution like Dwight, one needs to take a firm line with officers in order to combat problems like sexual misconduct. This, she said, is now missing under Thornton. According to Gail Smith, an attorney who heads Chicago Legal Aid to Incarcerated Mothers (CLAIM), "You

---

[22] Interview, Charles Fasano, John Howard Association, Chicago, May 13, 1994. This branch of the John Howard Association monitors prison and jail conditions in Illinois.

[23] Ibid.

[24] Interview, Ruthanne DeWolfe, attorney, Chicago, May 9, 1994.

were not hearing complaints until just a few years ago, since the switch in wardens."[25]

Allegations of sexual misconduct have continued in the 1990s. Our interviews, conducted in 1994, 1995, and 1996 revealed that corrections officers at Dwight have used physical force or compulsion to have sexual intercourse—vaginally, orally, and anally—or assault sexually incarcerated women. These acts have been used to retaliate against women who have spoken out about conditions in the prison; have self-identified or are viewed as gay; or have resisted engaging in sexual relationships with officers on other occasions. We also found that officers provided goods to women prisoners either to compel them to have anal, oral, and vaginal intercourse and other forms of sexual contact or to reward them for having done so.

Florence R. told Human Rights Watch that in 1992 she was forced to perform oral sex on an officer who targeted her, in her view, because she identified herself as gay.[26] She told us that a number of officers appeared to take her homosexuality as a challenge; they bombarded her with sexual innuendo and advances. One officer who worked nights on her unit, Officer Z, gave her particular problems. He once told her, "Damn, you need a good man. I wish it was me." One night, Florence R. woke up to find Officer Z in her cell. She told us, "He was in there feeling on me. I jumped up and he said, 'I'm going have you!'" Officer Z left when another officer paged him. Several nights later, as Florence R. walked from her work assignment to the medical clinic, Officer Z pulled up in a car and ordered her to get in. He told her he would report her for trying to escape if she refused. Once she was in the car, he drove past the clinic and parked behind another building. He then unzipped his pants, grabbed her by the back of her neck and forced her to perform oral sex on him. According to Florence R., Officer Z was interrupted when others happened upon the car, and he ordered her to move to the backseat. The clinic apparently had contacted Florence R.'s unit when she failed to appear, and a search had been initiated.

Approximately nine months after the assault on Florence R. in early 1993, the same officer reportedly entered Holly L.'s cell one night and raped her.[27] Officer Z worked the overnight shift in Holly L.'s unit and, according to Holly L.,

---

[25] Interview, Gail Smith, Chicago Legal Aid to Incarcerated Mothers, Chicago, May 10, 1994.

[26] Interview, Illinois, May 1994.

[27] Interview, Illinois, May 1994.

had been making sexually aggressive comments to her for weeks. When he was on her unit, he would come to her cell and tell her, "You pretty," or "I wanna make love to you," or "I wanna get up with you when you out." Then, when she was transferred to another unit, the officer was reportedly assigned there. Officer Z continued to harass her and according to Holly L., "started to get more forward every time." Holly L. told us that one evening he entered her cell around 4:00 a.m., ordered her to get off her bed and directed her to open her robe. Then, in her words, he started to "get rough" and told her "Do it . . . you know nobody's gonna believe you." Holly L. submitted to sexual relations with the officer on the floor of her cell.

Florence R. was prescribed sedatives or psychotropic medication by prison doctors after they came forward with their allegations of sexual misconduct. She was reportedly placed on psychotropic medications by prison doctors after she reported being raped.[28] According to Holly L.'s mother, Holly L. was extremely upset after the alleged rape—crying and unable to sleep. The institution, she told us, "suggested" that Holly L. take psychotropic medication.[29]

In addition to these violent attacks, some members of the male corrections staff made physically aggressive sexual advances toward women prisoners. In some instances, these initial advances were accompanied by threats of retaliation against the woman, her family and children if she rejected the sexual advances or informed others about them. In 1993, for example, Brenda N. was ordered by an officer to follow him to the receiving area outside the dining room. "He pushed me against the wall and tried to kiss me."[30] As she turned to leave, the officer grew angry with her, ordered her to "come back here," and said, "Don't you ever pull away from me again." According to Brenda N., "He said he would harm my son if I tell. He named the town where [my son] lives and who he is living with." Over the next few months, the officer repeatedly entered her cell. On her birthday, he reportedly came in, sat on her bed and demanded a kiss. He was interrupted when another prisoner came in. Six weeks later, he reportedly came into an area where Brenda N. was working, pushed her against a wall, grabbed her around her neck and told her, "You have been running your mouth. I will make good on my

---

[28] Interview, Gail Smith, Chicago Legal Aid to Incarcerated Mothers, May 10, 1994.

[29] Interview, Elizabeth Carter (not her real name), June 22, 1994. Carter did not request anonymity in this report. However, since we would necessarily reveal her daughter's identity by referring to her by name, we chose to use a pseudonym.

[30] Interview, Illinois, May 1994.

threat." As Brenda N. told us, "It scares me when he can give me the name of the town. . . . It scares me because I don't know what he can do. It's hard to avoid [an officer] around here." On the day of our interview, she said that this officer called her to the visiting area over an hour before our scheduled meeting time, and while she was waiting, repeatedly approached her and said, "You're looking nice today."

Other women we interviewed reported they too had been propositioned or sexually assaulted by male officers. Yolanda M. told us that she was accosted by an officer on her work detail in July 1993.[31] As she described it, the officer called her into the central dining room, pinned her against the wall and tried to kiss her. Yolanda M. pulled away and threatened to tell his wife, who was also a corrections officer. He reportedly replied, "Go ahead, no one is going to believe you." In the ensuing weeks, the officer not only continued to make sexual advances to Yolanda M., but also threatened her, telling her, "If you ever tell anyone, it'll get worse. See how quick you're in seg[regation]." The harassment, according to Yolanda M., continued through the winter of that year.

Yolanda M. told us that another prisoner had warned her about problems with this same officer before she left prison, but Yolanda M. had not believed her. Yolanda M. told us, "People are always saying they were felt on, groped on or thrown in a corner. I've heard zillions of stories, but I don't always believe it."[32] Now, she said, she understands that such assaults do occur. In May 1994 the officer renewed his sexual advances and reportedly told Yolanda M., "I will get you alone this summer."

Cindy K. also told us that she had two "run-ins sexually" with male officers. On the first occasion, an officer asked her to clean the women's restroom in the visiting area. She told us, "He came in and told me all what he could do to me. He pushed me into a corner. Wherever I was at, he would always come."[33] After she reported the harassment, the officer left her alone.

Gigi H. was reportedly accosted in May 1992 by a roving officer who came onto her unit.[34] According to Gigi H., she was relaxing one night in the common area when an officer called her outside; she followed him downstairs to the basement. The officer then pushed her pants down from behind. Gigi H. said

---

[31] Interview, Illinois, May 1994.

[32] Ibid.

[33] Interview, Illinois, May 1994.

[34] Interview, Illinois, May 1994.

she broke away and ran back upstairs. The officer returned to the unit and confronted Gigi H. In her words, he "started going through that dehumanizing thing" and told her, "Don't nobody care about you being here. Don't nobody care."

Sexual misconduct in Illinois prisons, as elsewhere, often becomes entangled with and is perceived as part of an underground prison economy, where officers provide goods to women in exchange for sexual intercourse or other inappropriate contact. Several female prisoners told us of this exchange. Yolanda M. and Cindy K., for example, reportedly witnessed other prisoners submitting to sexual relations with male officers. According to Yolanda M.:

> I know it went on, I saw it. [Officers] with prisoners in the laundry room and women talk . . . At Logan, I literally saw [officers] getting sex in the laundry room or sex in the hallway.[35]

She said it was also obvious that other prisoners were involved with staff because the officers brought them things such as gum and shampoo. Cindy K. agreed, stating:

> I have seen white shirts [lieutenants] down there go into the girls' rooms. I seen the girls giving them head. . . I guess some of these girls were willing to do it. I was not.[36]

Alice C. told us that in 1993 she used to leave her cell so that a lieutenant could be alone with her cellmate.[37] According to Alice C., the lieutenant would come to her cell at night and Alice C. would leave. While she never actually saw her cellmate have sex with the officer, he was alone with her cellmate for approximately forty-five minutes on each occasion. Another woman at the prison, Alice C. told us, used to undress for the same lieutenant while he stood outside her window. This lieutenant also reportedly made sexual advances to Alice C. According to Alice C., she approached him about a disciplinary ticket because she was worried that it would result in her transfer to another facility. The lieutenant told her that he would take care of it. She told us that the following week the

---

[35] Interview, Illinois, May 1994.

[36] Interview, Illinois, May 1994.

[37] Interview, Illinois, May 1994.

lieutenant came into her cell, "put his hands around my waist and moved his hands up near my bust." He said "now that he did me a favor it was time I did him one."

In mid-1996 we received information about ongoing sexual misconduct at the Dwight Correctional Facility. Reportedly, Anna P., a prisoner at Dwight, was approached by another prisoner in 1995 and told that a guard was interested in having an intimate relationship with her.[38] This prisoner reportedly told Anna P. that "if she was nice to [the guard], he would be nice to her." In exchange for the sexual relationship, the guard provided Anna P. with extra food, candy bars and perfume. The same prisoner facilitated several other similar exchanges. At first Anna P. believed that the guard was in love with her, but when Anna P. later learned that the guard was involved in a sexual relationship with another prisoner, she reportedly decided to end the relationship. However, Anna P. was afraid that if she attempted to do so she would lose her prison job and privileges. In addition, other guards had begun to approach her, saying "you did it with him, why don't you do me too."

In March 1996 Anna P. told Internal Affairs at IDOC about her sexual relationship with the guard and other intimate relations between officers and prisoners that were occurring at Dwight.[39] Two other prisoners, who were not involved with officers, came forward to confirm her story. The prisoners named at least six corrections officers who had engaged in sexual misconduct. As a result of these allegations, three officers resigned and three are on administrative leave with pay pending investigation. One of the later group of officers resigned shortly after being placed on administrative leave. In addition, another employee resigned after an individual sent officials letters the employee had received from a prisoner.[40]

Mistreatment of Prisoners Impregnated by Guards

We have also received reports that some women have become pregnant by corrections staff. Three women—all of whom were interviewed separately—told us about a fourth prisoner, Lucinda F., who was reportedly

---

[38] Telephone interview, Barbara Echols, Prison Action Committee, April 12, 1996.

[39] Telephone interview, Barbara Echols, Prison Action Committee, June 27, 1996.

[40] Tony Parker, "Prison Officer Put on Leave," *The Pantagraph* (Illinois), June 1, 1996.

impregnated by an officer on her unit.[41]   According to the prisoners' reports, Lucinda F. was impregnated by an officer working in the Mental Health Unit (MHU). Evelyn V., who lives on the unit, told us that Officer S was "constantly" going into women's rooms and that she had seen him having sex with prisoners.[42] Officer S's name was repeatedly mentioned by other women as one of the officers who regularly made sexual advances. When the institution discovered Lucinda F. was pregnant, she reportedly was sent to segregation, ostensibly for her own protection. We were told that Lucinda F. received an abortion prior to her transfer to another facility on or around May 10, 1994. According to Brenda N., who spoke with Lucinda F. before the transfer:

> They took her from MHU and locked her in segregation until she
> left. They said it was for her own protection. When she got
> back from the hospital, she spent two weeks in segregation.[43]

We confirmed that Lucinda F. was transferred from Dwight to another facility the week of May 10, 1994. When her pregnancy came to light, the implicated officer reportedly was either suspended or placed in a noncontact position. We have no information that the prison administration has taken any further steps in his case.

Abusive and Degrading Language
To our knowledge, there is no provision within the Illinois Administrative Code that specifically requires the humane treatment of incarcerated persons or restricts the use of vulgar, demeaning or sexualized language by prison staff.[44] The only arguably applicable provision is Section 120.30 of the administrative code

---

[41] We were unable, however, directly to confirm their account. In an unpublished letter to *Chicago Sun Times*, IDOC Director Odie Washington said that IDOC "has no documentation to support a claim that a single inmate was impregnated by a correctional officer in over five years." Unpublished letter from Odie Washington, director, Illinois Department of Corrections, to *Chicago Sun Times*, July 22, 1996.

[42] Interview, Illinois, May 1994.

[43] Interview, Illinois, May 1994.

[44] Provisions of the Illinois Administrative Code cited in this chapter were located with the assistance of the Citizens Assembly, which serves the Illinois General Assembly. We requested provisions within the code that address humane treatment or the use of degrading language.

which provides: "Individuals shall conduct themselves in a manner which will not reflect unfavorably on the department and shall not engage in conduct which is unbecoming or impairs the operations of the department."[45]

Degrading language and treatment appear to pervade the environment at Dwight, although that is less true for Dixon and Logan. Male officers at Dwight reportedly freely make comments about the women's bodies and demand sexual favors. In the officers' station on one maximum security unit at Dwight, male corrections officers reportedly hung a pair of women's underpants on the window and posted on the fan the words "ho [whore] patrol."[46]

Denise S. told us in 1994 of being verbally harassed during class by her high school equivalency diploma instructor.[47] According to Denise S., the instructor asked her sexually graphic and degrading questions, such as "How wide is your anus?" and "How deep is your vagina?" He then followed these questions with comments like "No dick be able to get down in there." When she complained about his conduct in January 1994, the warden responded that the staff person in question was a good teacher and that she should just continue her classes. Denise S. also reported the comments to a lieutenant at the prison who conducts investigations; she believes the investigator then spoke with the instructor. After this, according to Denise S., the instructor "came into the class and said there was a stool pigeon, and you know what happens to stool pigeons."

Other women also reported problems with prison staff engaging in degrading and sexual banter. According to Yolanda M., some officers have made comments to her, such as "Oh, I know you need it," or "You look good today."[48] She told us, "The [officers] are always saying, 'Ah, you're too pretty to be locked up,' or . . . 'I can bring you this or I can bring you that.'" In the summer, she said, officers have told her "That tan looks so good" and "Wear your shorts shorter."

---

[45] We requested a copy of the IDOC policy on sexual harassment from Susan O'Leary, deputy legal counsel for IDOC, but never received it. O'Leary informed us that it was her belief that this policy governed conduct and relations among employees and did not cover the behavior of correctional officers vis-à-vis prisoners. Telephone interview, Susan O'Leary, deputy chief legal counsel, Illinois Department of Corrections, September 27, 1994.

[46] Interview, Illinois, May 1994.

[47] Interview, Illinois, May 1994.

[48] Interview, Illinois, May 1994.

The women felt that the degrading treatment and language was something they could not escape and that they were powerless to confront. They also believed that if they did come forward, they, rather than the officer, would be punished. In Cindy K.'s words, "There's not much I can do about it. . . If I write it up, first thing they are going to do is not believe me, then it's PCU [Protective Custody Unit] and then a transfer. That's how it goes with sexual misconduct."[49] Women we interviewed were even hesitant to discuss the abuse with each other. According to Cindy K., "There are so many females back there that this happens to and they don't tell. They do not want to speak. . .It's the fear. . . they're scared. . . I'm tired of being scared. I'm tired of things not being done."

Privacy Violations

As discussed in more detail in the legal background chapter of this report, prisoners retain an internationally protected right to privacy except when limitations on this right are demonstrably required to maintain prison security. In addition, several U.S. courts have recognized that prisoners have a limited right to bodily privacy. In particular, they have a right to be protected from routine inappropriate visual surveillance and not to be strip searched by officers of the opposite sex, except in cases of emergency.

Illinois only partially complies with these constitutional and international standards protecting privacy. Under the Illinois Administrative Code, male corrections officers may conduct pat-searches on female prisoners and routine searches of the prisoner's housing areas, including the bathrooms and showers. The code provides that "all committed persons and their clothing, property, housing and work assignments are subject to search at any time."[50] While the Illinois Administrative Code does not restrict the scope of pat searches conducted by male officers on female prisoners, it does place some restrictions on the cross-gender strip searches and on cross-gender guarding of prisoners outside the correctional facilities. Under Illinois law, strip searches may be conducted only by employees of the same sex as the prisoner and in a place where the search cannot be observed

---

[49] Interview, Illinois, May 1994.

[50] 20 Illinois Administrative Code, Section 501.220 (b)(1). According to a 1983 Seventh Circuit decision, at that time Illinois did not permit male guards to frisk female prisoners while allowing female guards to frisk male prisoners. *Madyun v. Franzen*, 704 F.2d 954 (7th Cir. 1983).

by others, except in cases of emergency.[51] In addition, "to the extent possible," prisoners moved outside of a facility must be accompanied by a corrections employee of the same sex.[52]

Male officers in the Illinois prison system work in the women's housing units, patrol the women's facilities and supervise women on their work assignments. The Seventh Circuit, which includes Illinois, has ruled on cross-gender guarding in both men's and women's prisons. In 1994 the Seventh Circuit Court of Appeals concluded that prisons must adopt measures to protect prisoners' privacy from viewing by officers of the opposite sex.[53] The circuit court held that prisoners retain a constitutional right to bodily privacy and as a result are entitled to reasonable accommodations to prevent unnecessary observation of their naked bodies by officers of the opposite sex during strip searches or in the housing units.[54] At the same time, the court ruled that occasional or inadvertent sightings of unclothed prisoners, or pat searches limited in nature and scope, were permissible.[55]

---

[51] Ibid., Section 501.220 (b)(2).

[52] Ibid., Section 501.110(c), "Movement of Committed Persons."

[53] *Canedy v. Boardman*, 16 F.3d 183, p. 185 (7th Cir. 1994). The Seventh Circuit stated: "[T]hose who are convicted of criminal offenses do not surrender all of their constitutional rights . . . [T]hough his rights may be diminished by the needs and exigencies of the institutional environment, a prisoner is not wholly stripped of constitutional protection when he is imprisoned for a crime. There is no iron curtain between the Constitution and the prisons of this country. Ibid., p. 186."

[54] Ibid., p. 187.

[55] Ibid. The Seventh Circuit had previously ruled that a prisoner's right to privacy was sufficiently protected by a policy that permitted female guards to conduct pat frisks but limited their scope—female guards were instructed to exclude the genital area. *Smith v. Fairman*, 678 F.2d 52 (7th Cir. 1982). In another decision, *Torres v. Wisconsin Department of Health and Social Services*, the Seventh Circuit permitted the prison administration of a women's prison in Wisconsin to restrict the role of male guards in certain respects. 859 F.2d 1523 (7th Cir. 1988). The administration of Wisconsin's only maximum security prison for women employed only women in supervisory positions on certain housing units. This policy was enacted, according to the prison administrator, for "rehabilitation purposes." The prison already had in place measures to protect the privacy of female prisoners—male guards did not conduct pat-frisks; prisoners were permitted to hang privacy curtains while changing or using the toilet; and corrections officers did not observe prisoners while showering. 639 F. Supp. 271, p. 275 (E.D. Wisc. 1986) (lower

However, in a 1995 case, the Seventh Circuit held that while cross-gender body searches were impermissible, the regular monitoring of housing units by guards of the opposite sex was allowed.[56]

We are not aware of any limitations on male officers' duties at the Logan Correctional Center, and women who have been incarcerated there reported having had, on occasion, only male officers working on the night shifts. Women who have been incarcerated at Logan also report that male guards do not announce themselves when coming on the units and that they occasionally enter shower areas when women are undressed.[57] They told us that the majority of officers at Logan, even on the night shifts, are men. At the Dwight facility, there appear to be fewer violations of privacy than in the other two Illinois women's prisons we investigated, although male officers do work most housing units at Dwight. According to some prisoners, male officers are not assigned to the overnight shift on the lower security units, but they may substitute for the regular female officer on these shifts.[58]

THE SYSTEM'S RESPONSE

IDOC has acknowledged that sexual misconduct between staff and prisoners has occurred,[59] but strongly denies that it tolerates or condones such abuse.[60] In materials provided to Human Rights Watch, IDOC noted that "all cases [of employee misconduct] are investigated. Where substantiated, the employee is referred for discipline, including discharge, pursuant to applicable prison rules and

---

court decision).

[56] *Johnson v. Phelan*, 69 F.3d 144 (7th Cir. 1995).

[57] Interviews, Illinois, May 1994.

[58] Ibid.

[59] Unpublished letter from Odie Washington, director, Illinois Department of Corrections, to *Chicago Sun Times*, July 22, 1996.

[60] Letter from Susan O'Leary, deputy chief legal counsel, Illinois Department of Corrections, to Human Rights Watch, August 13, 1996.

terms of the union contract."[61] IDOC went on to state that incidents are referred for prosecution, as provided by department rules, "where reasonable grounds exist to suspect that an individual has committed a violation of criminal law."[62]

Our own investigation reveals a gap between IDOC's stated policy and its actual practice. While IDOC acknowledges that sexual misconduct occurs, it has at times blamed prisoners for such abuse. In response to the 1996 reports of sexual misconduct at Dwight, for example, IDOC director Odie Washington told a reporter, "this was a typical case of guards being manipulated and, for whatever reason, developing a personal relationship with inmates."[63] In addition, while internal complaints and investigatory procedures exist, they are often biased against the prisoners, exhibit conflicts of interest, and have exposed complainants to retaliation and even punishment. The combined effect of these problems is to render criminal sexual misconduct not only hard to monitor accurately, but difficult to substantiate. Thus for example, of the twenty-nine report complaints of sexual misconduct that IDOC received in 1994-95 in all three facilities for women, only eight were substantiated.[64] Finally, referrals for prosecution do occur, but they are at IDOC's discretion and may come significantly later than the department's own internal investigations. The multiple problems with these procedures have led us to the conclusion that while women complain of sexual misconduct,[65] such abuse may be significantly underreported and underaddressed.

---

[61] Ibid.

[62] Ibid.

[63] Christi Parsons, "Interview with Odie Washington, Director of the Illinois Department of Corrections," *Chicago Tribune,* May 19, 1996.

[64] Letter from Susan O'Leary, deputy chief legal counsel, Illinois Department of Corrections, to Human Rights Watch, August 13, 1996.

[65] According to IDOC, in 1994-95 they received fourteen complaints of sexual misconduct at Dwight, fourteen complaints at Logan and one complaint at Dixon. Out of these complaints, three officers were discharged, two resigned, and three were suspended for periods from two to ten days. The other twenty-one complaints were found to be unsubstantiated. Letter from Susan O'Leary, deputy chief legal counsel, Illinois Department of Corrections, to Human Rights Watch, August 13, 1996.

Right to an Effective Remedy

International human rights law requires national governments not only to prohibit torture, cruel, inhuman or degrading treatment or punishment and unwarranted privacy invasions, but also to ensure that when such abuses occur they can be reported and fully and fairly investigated without the complainant fearing undue punishment or retaliation from the authorities. Similarly, under the U.S. Constitution, prisoners are guaranteed access to the courts to challenge abusive prison conditions or other prison problems.[66] Our investigation revealed that Illinois falls far short of compliance with these standards.

Grievances

Illinois provides a grievance mechanism for prisoners to report abusive incidents to prison officials.[67] Illinois stipulates that, before filing a formal grievance, prisoners must attempt informally to resolve the grievance through an institutional counselor.[68] If not resolved at this informal stage, the grievance may subsequently be filed with and reviewed by a grievance officer. A "committed person" may bypass the first stage of the procedure and file her grievance directly with the warden if there is a "substantial risk of imminent personal injury or other serious or irreparable harm to the committed person."[69] The provision does not make clear whether sexual assaults, sexual advances, or degrading language from prison staff fall under this exception. The administrative code prohibits disciplinary action or reprisal against prisoners for using the grievance mechanism.[70]

---

[66] For a more detailed discussion of the due process rights accorded prisoners under international and U.S. law, see the legal background chapter.

[67] In an unpublished letter to the *Chicago Sun Times*, IDOC director, Odie Washington, stated that "In a three year period, Dwight inmates filed over 1,500 grievances at the institutional level and 270 at the departmental level." Unpublished letter from Odie Washington, director, Illinois Department of Corrections, to *Chicago Sun Times*, July 22, 1996. IDOC did not indicate how many grievances were lodged at the informal level, nor did they classify the grievances by type.

[68] 20 Illinois Administrative Code, Section 504.810 (a).

[69] Ibid., Section 504.840 (a), "Emergency Procedures."

[70] Ibid., Section 504.810(e).

Our interviews indicate that the counselor may actually deter the filing of legitimate grievances. According to Barbara Echols, a former prisoner at Dwight and member of the prison watchdog group PAC, grievances rarely proceed beyond the counselor's initial, informal review. Even if a grievance goes to a grievance officer, the second stage of the process, Echols told us:

> Sometimes the [grievance officer] comments on the grievance but usually [he or she] upholds what the counselor recommends. . . . Many times they will just ignore the grievances. . .You usually hear at a whim, when they want to respond. There are a lot of irregularities in the process. There is a lack of concern in the institution. . . about the nature of the grievance submitted.[71]

We reviewed several grievances filed by the women whom we interviewed that were denied or found meritless by the counselor. None had ever been reviewed formally by a grievance officer. Although it is the prisoner's responsibility to pursue a complaint, the institution bears responsibility for ensuring that the process is open and responsive to prisoners' complaints and concerns. Without such assurance, the prisoners' right to complain is effectively denied.

Internal Investigations

Although the Illinois Administrative Code provides regulations for internal investigations that require employees to document any unusual incidents, including sexual assault, they do not contain specifics on how investigations should be handled.[72] Guidelines for conducting internal investigations into claims of rape, sexual assault or abuse, or other sexual misconduct by correctional employees are not publicly available. We were informed that a directive governing investigations into sexual misconduct does exist, but it is internal and could not be released.[73]

---

[71] Interview, Barbara Echols, Prison Action Committee, Chicago, May 13, 1994.

[72] 20 Illinois Administrative Code, Section 112. This provision was sent to Human Rights Watch in response to our request for IDOC's administrative rules and regulations for investigating cases of alleged sexual misconduct.

[73] Telephone interview, Susan O'Leary, deputy chief legal counsel, Illinois Department of Corrections, September 27, 1994.

Given this restriction, we were unable to determine exactly what procedure the IDOC follows.

Based on our interviews, however, it appears that after a woman comes forward with a complaint of sexual misconduct, she is interviewed by a senior individual within the institution, such as a deputy warden or shift commander, and asked to prepare a written statement. The complaint may then be referred to the Internal Affairs Department of IDOC and/or to an investigator based outside the prison. We were unable to ascertain exactly what proportion of complaints of sexual misconduct are so referred.

During the course of an investigation into sexual misconduct, implicated officers may or may not be reassigned. In one case we reviewed, in the case of Florence R., who was forced to perform oral sex on an officer, the officer was reassigned within the same prison. But the officer continued to have access to Florence R. and made repeated threats against her during the investigation.[74] Other prisoners told us that certain officers had been suspended or assigned to noncontact positions while an investigation was pending.[75] IDOC confirmed that it may place an officer in a noncontact position during an investigation but only in rare cases will authorities temporarily suspend an employee.[76]

Investigations are also flawed by conflicts of interest. In one case we reviewed, for example, a prisoner at Dwight received a disciplinary citation for having sexual contact with guards. According to two corrections employees, the panel created to review the prisoner's citation and determine her punishment included the wife of a guard whom the prisoner had accused of having sexual contact with prisoners.[77]

Bias Against Prisoner Testimony

Our interviews suggest that IDOC does not take allegations of sexual misconduct as seriously as officials contend, and that the department may dismiss

---

[74] Telephone interview, Gail Smith, Chicago Legal Aid to Incarcerated Women, February 29, 1996.

[75] Interviews, Illinois, May 1994.

[76] Telephone interview, Susan O'Leary, deputy chief legal counsel, Illinois Department of Corrections, September 27, 1994.

[77] Tony Parker, "Inmate has Expected Sex Charges," *The Pantagraph* (Illinois), May 1, 1996.

claims of such abuse as unsubstantiated even where some credible evidence of sexual misconduct exists. An example of this is Zelda D., who alleged that she was raped three times by a guard between November 1993 and January 1994. Zelda D. was taken to an outside hospital the evening after the first incident. The examining doctor completed a rape kit[78] and wrote "sexual assault" on her medical record in the box marked "Diagnosis."[79] Despite this finding, prison officials sent another female prisoner to segregation for possible sexual misconduct with Zelda D.[80] Prison officials also placed Zelda D. in temporary custody status in a segregation cell for possible sexual misconduct. Zelda D. was cleared of the sexual misconduct charges days later. After the second incident and despite repeated requests for medical evidence from Zelda D.'s attorney, prison staff denied her medical attention until eight days later. When medical care providers finally examined Zelda D., they noted bruising on her body. [81]

In addition, IDOC's investigation into Zelda D.'s allegations did not provide allowances for the potential retaliation a prisoner may face in identifying correctional staff. Zelda D. recanted her first identification of her rapist within two weeks of the first incident. Her attorney, Margaret Byrne, informed the warden that Zelda D. did not correctly identify the assaulting officer because he had threatened to kill her. By the time Byrne learned of and gave the warden what she believed to be the alleged rapist's last name, however, IDOC informed her that it

---

[78] Rape kits are designed to collect evidence of rape and sexual assault from the victim's body and contain items such as separate evidence bags for vaginal swabs, rectal swabs, pulled head hairs, pulled pubic hairs, saliva samples, pubic hair combings, outer clothing, foreign materials, and underwear.

[79] Emergency and Outpatient Record, November 1993 (on file with Human Rights Watch). IDOC maintains that "no physical signs of sexual assault were identified by health care staff." Unpublished letter from Odie Washington, director, Illinois Department of Corrections, to *Chicago Sun Times*, July 22, 1996.

[80] Interview, Margaret Byrne, attorney, Chicago, May 12, 1994.

[81] Byrne visited Zelda D. four days after the second alleged incident and described her injuries as follows: "She had bruises up her arms, inside her thighs, on her shins, her ribs, the side of her face; one of her eyes was purple." Ibid. Zelda D. did receive medical care for her physical injuries after the third incident. At that time, nursing staff noted in Zelda D.'s medical records bruises along Zelda D.'s right side. In addition, they found scratches and bruises below both of her breasts, bruises down her left arm and her outer left thigh

already had closed their investigation into Zelda D.'s allegations.[82]   Susan
O'Leary, IDOC's deputy counsel, confirmed in September 1994 that the
investigation was closed and gave no indication that IDOC intended to reopen it.[83]

In describing IDOC's approach to investigating sexual misconduct,
O'Leary told Human Rights Watch that in incidents where the evidence consisted
only of the prisoner's word against the officer's, the officer would not be
discharged. Where more than one prisoner comes forward, she told us, "That
makes a more compelling case."[84] But, she still noted that without additional
evidence, "There's not much to be done. The warden would just monitor that
person closely." O'Leary said corroborating evidence was needed and that hearing
officers, who review disciplinary sanctions pursuant to civil service contracts, are
sympathetic to prison guards and will "not take a job away without evidence."
Prisoner testimony alone will not serve as evidence. O'Leary's told us that
prisoners make "spurious complaints of sexual misconduct . . . for a variety of
reasons, including for personal gain or attention, to manipulate a transfer to a more

---

[82] In contrast to Byrne's version, IDOC asserts that Zelda D. gave them the names of two
additional officers prior to naming the officer whom Zelda D. now asserts raped her.
Unpublished letter from Odie Washington, director, Illinois Department of Corrections, to
Chicago Sun Times, July 22, 1996. At a deposition in September 4, 1996 for her civil trial,
Zelda D. was unable to identify a photograph of her alleged assailant. Subsequent to the
deposition, the attorney agreed to drop the case.

[83] Telephone interview, Susan O'Leary, deputy chief legal counsel, Illinois Department of
Corrections, September 27, 1994. IDOC also asserts that Zelda D. was provided a photo
lineup of all white male corrections officers employed at Dwight, but was unable to identify
her alleged attacker from among them. The man who allegedly raped Zelda D. was bearded
and attorney Byrne questions whether the institution either showed Zelda D. a picture of him
bearded or informed her that he might appear clean shaven. She has asked the institution
to provide Zelda D. with a second photo lineup so that Zelda D. could review the pictures
with this possibility in mind; IDOC declined to do so. Zelda D. subsequently drew a picture
of her alleged attacker. IDOC dismissed it as a "crude drawing" that "will do nothing to
assist in the identification of the alleged assailant." Interview, Margaret Byrne, attorney,
Chicago, May 9, 1994. According to IDOC, Zelda D. was permitted to view a second photo
lineup. Letter from Susan O'Leary, deputy chief legal counsel, Illinois Department of
Corrections, to Human Rights Watch, August 13, 1996.

[84] Telephone interview, Susan O'Leary, deputy chief legal counsel, Illinois Department of
Corrections, September 27, 1994.

preferred housing unit or prison, or because they are upset with an employee for doing his or her job."[85]

Lack of Confidentiality

Several additional factors also undermine IDOC's grievance and investigative procedures and significantly deter prisoners from reporting such abuse. The first of these is a lack of confidentiality in the grievance and investigatory procedures. Despite rules requiring that prison officials take steps to protect prisoners' identities during the grievance process,[86] there appears to be little confidentiality for prisoners who raise allegations of sexual misconduct by correctional staff through either the grievance or the investigation procedure. According to Barbara Echols, while she was incarcerated at Dwight, "it was a known fact that if you [filed a grievance] about sexual harassment or sexual assault by an officer, the whole institution [would] know about it."[87] Similarly, the first statement Florence R. wrote was reportedly provided to the implicated officer. Subsequently, according to Florence R., the officer and his colleagues harassed her for submitting the statement.[88]

By contrast, the IDOC appears quite protective of employee confidentiality during investigations. As noted above, our interviews revealed that incarcerated women are not necessarily kept apprised of the progress of an investigation. They submit statements and undergo polygraph exams, but, despite clear prison rules to the contrary, are provided with little additional information afterwards. Corrections employees, meanwhile, are apparently kept fully informed. O'Leary, IDOC's deputy legal counsel, told us that the women are not kept

---

[85] Letter from Susan O'Leary, deputy chief legal counsel, Illinois Department of Corrections, to Human Rights Watch, August 13, 1996.

[86] 20 Illinois Administrative Code, Section 504.860(b) provides that "records regarding the participation of a committed person during the grievance process shall be handled in a manner designed to protect confidentiality as determined by the Chief Administrative Officer."

[87] Interview, Barbara Echols, Prison Action Committee, Chicago, May 13, 1994.

[88] Interview, Illinois, May 1994.

informed for reasons of "confidentiality" for the staff member.[89] This creates a situation in which prisoners may be further harassed or mistreated by officers who have information about an investigation that is not known to the prisoner.

The confidentiality of legal materials also appears to be violated for women who have experienced abuse. Women we interviewed who had their legal materials confiscated subsequent to raising a complaint of sexual misconduct, found that when the legal materials were returned, copies of certain documents, such as their grievances alleging abuse or retaliation against them, had disappeared.[90] In Florence R.'s case, all of her correspondence from CLAIM, as well as her written records concerning the rape, vanished.[91]

According to some of the prisoners we interviewed, the confidentiality of legal mail is similarly not respected. Under procedures governing such correspondence, it should be opened only in the presence of the prisoner and the contents checked for contraband. However, according to some women, the letters we sent, which were clearly marked as "Attorney Mail," were opened before being given to them.[92]

Use of Polygraph Tests and Administrative Segregation

In addition to the lack of confidentiality of investigative procedures, prisoners also are deterred from reporting sexual misconduct by the likelihood that the authorities will subject them to polygraph exams and administrative segregation. While Human Rights Watch takes no position on the use of polygraph examinations *per se* and acknowledges the legitimate penological uses for administrative segregation, we are concerned about the selective use of such procedures to intimidate or, at times, punish female prisoners who come forward with allegations of sexual abuse.

---

[89] Telephone interview, Susan O'Leary, deputy chief legal counsel, Illinois Department of Corrections, September 27, 1994.

[90] Interviews, Illinois, May 1994.

[91] Interview, Gail Smith, Chicago Legal Aid to Incarcerated Women, Chicago, May 10, 1994.

[92] Interviews, Illinois, May 1994. These letters were sent by attorneys employed at Human Rights Watch and involved confidential information pursuant to researching this report.

Under the Illinois Administrative Code, both employees and prisoners may be asked to take polygraph exams.[93] According to IDOC, polygraphs are employed as an investigative tool to question prisoners.[94] The facility is obligated under the administrative code to inform the employee and the prisoner of their own examinations' results, a copy of which they may request in writing.[95] However, one attorney who represents women prisoners told us that women rarely receive the results of their lie detector tests.[96]   O'Leary asserted that prisoners were not required to take such exams. In addition, the administrative code states that prisoners may not be required to take polygraph exams.[97] Some of the women we interviewed, however, said they were consistently pressed to take a polygraph exam, whether or not they so chose. If they refused, their allegation of misconduct by staff was not likely to be pursued. It also appears that exam results have been used to punish prisoners without independent evidence that their allegation is false. Consequently, women often are reluctant to take polygraph exams because they fear they will be used as a tool for punishment and not to further an investigation.

In one example, Florence R. was sentenced to ninety days in segregation after she reportedly failed her polygraph.[98] Further, because Florence R.'s allegations were not substantiated by the institution she received a number of disciplinary tickets for providing what the institution determined to be "false information." According to Florence R., she was ticketed for lying in her initial report, for lying to the investigator, and for reportedly failing her polygraph.[99] In

---

[93] 20 Illinois Administrative Code, Section 112.40, "Polygraph Examinations."

[94] Telephone interview, Susan O'Leary, deputy chief legal counsel, Illinois Department of Corrections, September 27, 1994.

[95] 20 Illinois Administrative Code, Section 112.40.

[96] Telephone interview, Margaret Byrne, attorney, October 16, 1996.

[97] Ibid.

[98] Interview, Gail Smith, Chicago Legal Aid to Incarcerated Mothers, Chicago, May 10, 1994. Florence R. reported that just before her test, the test administrator told her a story about two male prisoners who were having sex—one later lied about it because he did not want others to know he was gay, so he said he had been raped. He then reportedly asked Florence R. if this is what happened to her.

[99] Interview, Illinois, May 1994.

another case, Zelda D. was punished for her initial false identification in what attorney Margaret Byrne described as an unduly harsh manner, relative to other prisoners she has represented.[100] Zelda D. was issued a disciplinary ticket and sentenced to one year in segregation—the maximum punishment—for falsely accusing Officer B.

Human Rights Watch does not oppose punishing prisoners for making false accusations where the prison authorities have evidence beyond the allegations of the implicated guard or staff member to support the conclusion that the prisoner is lying and acted maliciously or in manifestly bad faith. However, such punishment should be used infrequently, because it could discourage prisoners from coming forward with allegations of sexual misconduct. Polygraphs examinations are notoriously unreliable for verifying the veracity of a person's statements. We encourage IDOC to review the use of these exams to ensure their impartiality. In instances where prisoner allegations of sexual misconduct are contradicted only by the testimony of the accused officer or only by a failed polygraph examination, the prisoner should not be punished for false accusation.

In addition to being asked to take polygraph exams, women have been sent to segregation on disciplinary grounds as a result of raising allegations of sexual misconduct. Women we interviewed uniformly feared coming forward to report abuse because of a real or perceived threat that, in the course of the investigation, they would end up in segregation. According to Gigi H., "You are going to do seg time for sexual misconduct, but the officer will be protected through transfers."[101] Brenda N. resisted informing a lieutenant at Dwight about her sexual assault because she knew he would report it and she feared she would then experience problems. The lieutenant, whom she described as friendly and supportive, noticed the bruises on Brenda's neck and pressed her for an explanation. She said, "I told him not to take it on a professional basis because I'd be the one getting into trouble if he handled it on a professional basis. . . .They would have put me in seg."[102]

The Illinois Administrative Code provides that prisoners may be placed in "temporary confinement" or segregation pending an investigation if it is determined that a need exists "to restrict the committed person's access to the

---

[100] Interview, Margaret Byrne, attorney, Chicago, May 9, 1994.

[101] Interview, Illinois, May 1994.

[102] Interview, Illinois, May 1994.

general population to protect him from injury or to conduct the investigation."[103] The employment of such a provision in cases where women are involved in investigations is not only perceived as punitive, but often functions as punishment. Women placed in segregated status are removed from the general population and treated as though they had committed a disciplinary offense.[104]

Illinois further provides that prisoners may be punished with one year in segregation for sexual misconduct.[105] The Illinois regulation does not distinguish sexual contact between prisoners from sexual contact between a corrections employee and a prisoner. According to Odie Washington, director of IDOC, women prisoners involved with guards are also potentially subject to administrative and criminal penalties. Washington stated, "We will take whatever means appropriate to discipline staff and inmates who engage in [sexual] activities."[106] When prison officials at Dwight learned in March 1996 that guards were having sexual relations with prisoners, three prisoners who were involved were placed in segregation and lost a year of good-time credit.[107] Although of the six implicated guards three are on administrative leave with pay pending investigation (the other three resigned), that does not justify additionally punishing the prisoners.

As discussed in the legal background section of this report, Human Rights Watch opposes any punishment of a prisoner who was forced to engage in sexual contact with an officer or who was rewarded for sex with some material or non-material benefit. As a matter of policy, we also oppose the punishment of prisoners whose participation in sexual contact does not appear to result from force or any form of exchange by the officer and thus whose own conduct might constitute a violation of prison rules. In these cases, we strongly believe that any state interests

---

[103] 20 Illinois Administrative Code, Section 504.40(3).

[104] Ibid., Section 504.630 provides that committed persons in temporary confinement pursuant to an investigation be treated the same as those segregated for disciplinary offenses.

[105] The Illinois Administrative Code defines sexual misconduct as "engaging in sexual intercourse, deviate sexual conduct or fondling or touching done to sexually arouse either or both persons." Ibid., Section 504, Table A.

[106] Emily Wilkerson, "Three Dwight guards suspended in sex probe," *State Journal-Register* (Illinois), May 1, 1996.

[107] Ibid.

served by such punishment are vastly outweighed by their deterrent effect on the reporting of sexual abuse.

Inappropriate Confiscation of Property

A number of women we interviewed reported that the institution confiscated their property after they reported an allegation of sexual misconduct. The women's property often either was not given back or was returned with items missing. The day after Anna P. spoke to Internal Affairs, one of the prisoners, who confirmed Anna P.'s story but who had not been involved with an officer, had her room searched and several items of her legal and personal materials were taken.[108] When Zelda D. returned from the hospital after the first alleged rape, all of her clothing and personal items were confiscated, reportedly as part of the IDOC's investigation.[109] They were not returned for over two months. As noted above, Florence R.'s property, including her legal correspondence, was taken after she was hospitalized. Some of her legal papers were never returned.

Attorneys working with prisoners had to write repeatedly to the warden at Dwight to demand the return of the confiscated property. In each case, the warden replied that all of the property had been given back. Byrne noted:

> That always happens. Whenever someone goes into segregation, they take their property away and hold it for an unspecified period of time. Then they get only some of it back. I see no reason why it happens. They get it back without things in it. I understand when they go into segregation there is some property they take for punishment purposes, like audiovisual. [Zelda D.] had nothing for two to three months. There was no explanation. It took forever for them to get it back to her.[110]

One year after Zelda D. was first sent to segregation, prison officials had still had not returned all of her property.[111]

---

[108] Telephone interview, Barbara Echols, Prison Action Committee, April 12, 1996.

[109] Interview, Margaret Byrne, attorney, Chicago, May 9, 1994.

[110] Ibid.

[111] Telephone interview, Margaret Byrne, attorney, January 9, 1995.

Retaliation and Harassment by Officers

Women who have come forward with allegations of sexual misconduct against corrections officers report that harassment and retaliation by corrections officers often occur during the course of the investigation. The women are harassed and repeatedly degraded by officers who exploit the women's perceived lack of credibility. Corrections officers may be reassigned during investigations, but this has not stopped them from moving freely within the prison and intimidating complainants. This harassment not only further abuses the women, it works to discourage other prisoners from coming forward either as witnesses or victims. According to Florence R.:

> The corrections officers were saying, "You're fucked. You ain't got a GED [high school diploma], you flunked your lie detector test." Everyone on the shift swings together. If you get it from one, you get it from all. You feel powerless. They provoke you—say things like 'you're dumb'."[112]

One officer, in particular, used to tell her, "Who's going to believe you? You a fruit loop." Florence R. told us, "They made me feel so small that I was beneath them. They'd say, 'Who you think gonna' stand behind you?'"

According to CLAIM director Gail Smith, Florence R. suffered repeated incidents of harassment and retaliation.[113] The night Florence R. was discovered with the officer, she was asked to prepare a written statement by the shift supervisor. She was then visited by a representative of Internal Affairs and asked to prepare a second statement in front of investigators. She was also required to take a polygraph exam. Over the ensuing months, she repeatedly was harassed by the officer and his colleagues, which led her to become increasingly despondent and suicidal.[114] In Florence R.'s case, the officer was reassigned but continued to reappear on her unit to harass her. According to Smith, the officer showed up outside Florence's door in the middle of the night. On one occasion, shortly after

---

[112] Interview, Illinois, May 1994.

[113] Interview, Gail Smith, Chicago Legal Aid to Incarcerated Mothers, Chicago, May 10, 1994.

[114] Within three weeks of being assaulted, Florence R. cut her wrists. She told us that guards and other prisoners were harassing her for pursuing charges against the guard and that she became upset and depressed.

Florence R. attempted to commit suicide, this officer's colleague called him into the unit where Florence R. was living, and the two stood over her and made harassing comments about the bandages on her wrists.

Alice C. also reportedly was harassed after she agreed to assist in a departmental investigation of a lieutenant charged with sexual misconduct. The lieutenant apparently learned that Alice C. had spoken with an investigator. According to Alice C., he came into her cell and told her "if I knew what was good for me, I'd better keep my mouth shut."[115] Alice C., nonetheless, agreed to participate in the investigation and, on one occasion, an excuse was created for her to leave the institution to take a polygraph test. On the day before the appointment, the lieutenant reportedly returned to Alice C.'s room and told her he knew that the excuse was a ruse and that she should fail her polygraph.

Based on our interviews, harassment comes not only from officers but also from higher levels, at least at Dwight. A number of women we interviewed reported incidents of harassment from a male assistant warden regarding their investigation. According to Florence R., the assistant warden reportedly called her into his office and asked, "Why don't you stop this investigation? I get more paper from your people than from Legal Affairs."[116] In addition, female prisoners who reported sexual misconduct by guards and cooperated fully with the investigation reportedly have been transferred to different prisons.[117] This practice, allegedly done to protect prisoners from guards they have implicated, can function as punishment for prisoners who often develop supportive relationships in prison. The transfer also can take prisoners away from classes they are attending. Such classes provide prisoners with additional good time that will be lost if they do not complete the course. Consequently, the possibility of being transferred operates as a strong disincentive to reporting sexual misconduct. While it is critical to protect the prisoner from retaliation, other methods, including transferring the guard could achieve the same end.

Impunity

According to IDOC, as noted above, prisoners filed twenty-nine complaints of sexual misconduct in 1994-95 at Dwight, Dixon, and Logan of which only eight complaints were substantiated. Those eight complaints resulted in three

---

[115] Interview, Illinois, May 1994.

[116] Interview, Illinois, May 1994.

[117] Telephone interview, Margaret Byrne, attorney, October 16, 1996.

discharges, two resignations and three brief, temporary suspensions.[118] Only one was referred for prosecution.

Our interviews indicate that officers may be temporarily reassigned, and may even be temporarily suspended, but few officers are ever actually dismissed for their actions. Consequently, women we interviewed consistently raised the same names of officers who were known to be physically aggressive and abusive. For example, the officer who allegedly assaulted Florence R. also later reportedly raped Holly L. It appears that IDOC and employees at Dwight knew this officer had a history of sexually abusing prisoners. The day Elizabeth Carter visited her daughter at Dwight, she told us that a female corrections officer approached her and, while pretending to play with Carter's granddaughter, stated that the officer in question was "nuts" and that he had a reputation for sexually assaulting prisoners. The female officer's comments were supported, according to Carter, by comments made to her by IDOC's investigator, whom she contacted regarding Holly L.'s situation. The investigator told Carter that he believed Holly because "this guard had a history." He reportedly stated that "he would do what he could" but that there were labor issues involved.[119] Barbara Echols of PAC stated that while she was incarcerated at Dwight, this same officer was notorious for sexual misconduct among both prisoners and officers.[120]

The system's inadequate response feeds into a continued cycle of sexual misconduct, further entrenching the problem. When women see that officers are allowed to remain in or return to the same or another prison, they are less inclined to report abuse. As Gigi H. stated, "Seeing him here everyday showed me what they thought about it."[121] Attorney Byrne said, "The atmosphere is that it won't do any good to report these acts. Women are terrified, they are afraid to come forward."[122]

Our interviews further indicate that IDOC rarely refers women prisoners' complaints of sexual misconduct to law enforcement authorities for investigation.

---

[118]   Letter from Susan O' Leary, deputy chief legal counsel, Illinois Department of Corrections, to Human Rights Watch, August 13, 1996.

[119]   Telephone interview, Elizabeth Carter, June 22, 1994.

[120]   Interview, Barbara Echols, Prison Action Committee, Chicago, May 13, 1994.

[121]   Interview, Illinois, May 1994.

[122]   Telephone interview, Margaret Byrne, attorney, October 16, 1996.

The initial investigation of complaints and the decision to refer them to local law enforcement appear to rest entirely with IDOC. In a conversation with Human Rights Watch, O'Leary did state that if the department receives an allegation of criminal conduct it would involve the state police. However, according to O'Leary, the department would not "typically [involve the police] in sex cases because the evidence is medical."[123] She told us, "In a rape case, there's probably nothing the state police can do that we wouldn't be doing." Where a prisoner alleged rape, O'Leary stated that a rape kit would be performed at the institution and this would be analyzed by the prison doctor. The results would be given to the warden and the investigator, but there are "no hard and fast rules."[124]

O'Leary did assert that prisoners were still free to call or write to the police.[125] But, our interviews indicate that, despite O'Leary's assertion, actual procedures do not permit incarcerated women to bypass the institution to seek police investigations into alleged rapes. When Byrne contacted the state's attorney, Thomas Brown, to inquire how to file a criminal complaint, she was informed that his office did not have jurisdiction—it had to be referred from IDOC.[126] Byrne's experience was confirmed by two other prison monitors, Ruthanne DeWolfe and Gail Smith. DeWolfe stated that the Will County district attorney took the position that any referrals for criminal prosecution of corrections officers must come from IDOC itself.[127] According to Smith, a former CLAIM employee was similarly informed by the Livingston County state attorney's office that a criminal referral

---

[123] Telephone interview, Susan O'Leary, chief deputy legal counsel, Illinois Department of Corrections, September 27, 1994. It demonstrates an exceedingly narrow view of rape to assert that evidence of the attack can be limited to medical evidence obtained through a rape kit.

[124] Ibid.

[125] This assertion was repeated in O'Leary's letter to Human Rights Watch. Letter from Susan O'Leary, deputy chief legal counsel, Illinois Department of Corrections, to Human Rights Watch, August 13, 1996.

[126] Interview, Margaret Byrne, attorney, Chicago, May 9, 1994. Attorney Byrne wrote to State Attorney Brown in February, after the third rape. At this time, the IDOC had all but informed her that they had ceased the investigation into Zelda D.'s allegations.

[127] Interview, Ruthanne DeWolfe, attorney, Chicago, May 9, 1994.

to either the police or prosecutor must come directly from the Dwight administration after an internal investigation.[128]

In the case of Anna P.'s allegations that guards at Dwight were giving prisoners goods in exchange for sex, three officers reportedly resigned and the others were suspended with pay pending the completion of the internal investigation.[129] Susan O'Leary, IDOC deputy chief legal counsel, told Human Rights Watch that when IDOC forwarded their information on the Dwight allegations to the Livingston County state attorney's office no one at IDOC contemplated the possibility that the female prisoners might be criminally charged.[130] Nonetheless, according to press reports, IDOC spokesperson Nic Howell indicated that charges would be considered against the prisoners, as well as the guards.[131]

IDOC's seeming assumption of jurisdiction over criminal acts occurring in prison is inherently problematic. To be fully transparent and neutral, two simultaneous investigations need to be conducted—a departmental investigation for possible employee misconduct, and a separate, independent investigation into the allegation of criminal conduct. By initially assuming exclusive jurisdiction over criminal acts, such as rape, the department, in effect, is permitted to investigate itself.

Lack of Accountability to External Monitors

Based on our interviews and experience trying to interview women in Illinois, there appears to be an overall lack of accountability in IDOC to outside persons assisting women prisoners, particularly during an investigation of sexual misconduct by prison staff.[132] Family members, attorneys and even a member of

---

[128] Telephone interview, Gail Smith, Chicago Legal Aid to Incarcerated Mothers, March 29, 1995.

[129] Wilkerson, "Three Dwight guards suspended . . ." *State Journal-Register.*

[130] Telephone interview, Susan O'Leary, deputy chief legal counsel, Illinois Department of Corrections, July 1, 1996.

[131] Wilkerson, "Three Dwight guards suspended . . ." *State Journal-Register* ; Tony Parker, "Dwight Prison Investigation Ends," *The Pantagraph* (Illinois), May 1, 1996.

[132] We are only able to comment on Dwight's accountability to outside monitors for abuses. The monitors we interviewed were not following allegations at any other facilities.

Congress who have attempted to monitor investigations into such conduct have either not been fully apprised of the investigation's progress or have been flatly denied access to information. Attorneys report the destruction of documents by IDOC staff, slow response to queries, and daunting procedural irregularities.

Gail Smith, who has worked with women at Dwight since the mid-1980s as the director of CLAIM, told us that she has heard of only one successful investigation into an allegation of sexual misconduct.[133] She monitored Florence R.'s complaint and remains convinced not only that Florence R. was forced to perform oral sex, but also that the institution did nothing to address her complaint or to protect Florence R. from her alleged attacker. During this time, Smith told us, "we were not getting attention or cooperation from the institution."[134] According to Smith, the investigation languished for over five months, and CLAIM was not kept informed of its progress. Legal documents taken from Florence R.'s cell by prison staff disappeared.[135] Moreover, Smith told us, little was done to protect Florence R. from harassment by the implicated officer.

CLAIM's involvement in Florence R.'s case apparently damaged its previously productive relationship with Dwight, where they had worked to provide family law services for incarcerated mothers. According to Smith, "Once we got involved . . . this affected the relationship with [the institution]. . . . If they get an

---

[133] Interview, Gail Smith, Chicago Legal Aid to Incarcerated Mothers, Chicago, May 10, 1994. According to Smith, the institution failed to prevent the officer and his friends from continuing to harass Florence R. This ongoing harassment combined with the isolation and increased vulnerability to attack that Florence R. experienced while in segregation for making a supposedly false report, caused a deterioration in Florence R.'s mental state such that her credibility as a witness became substantially reduced.

[134] Ibid.

[135] CLAIM contacted Warden Thornton on September 2, 1992, and explicitly informed her that documents they knew to exist were not among the items returned to Florence R. Warden Thornton ignored this correspondence for over two months. When she did respond, she merely reiterated to CLAIM that Florence R. received all of her personal property in August 1992. It was precisely this return of property in August 1992 that CLAIM was challenging as incomplete. In other words, the warden completely disregarded the entire purpose of CLAIM's complaint—that while some possessions were returned to Florence R. in August, her legal materials were not.

inkling you are looking into something, then they put the brakes on and it becomes a little harder."[136]

Others who have attempted to press for information or to monitor cases have been stonewalled or mistreated by the IDOC. Holly L.'s mother, Elizabeth Carter, tried to pursue Holly L.'s allegation of rape with both the warden and an IDOC investigator. Despite her efforts, the implicated officer remained on Holly L.'s unit for several weeks after the attack. According to Carter, when she visited her daughter after the alleged rape, Holly L. was "beside herself."[137] She requested to speak with the warden that day and called her again several days later. According to Carter, the warden did not return her phone calls until she contacted an attorney and called other people at IDOC. When the warden finally returned Carter's call, she reportedly told Carter that she would "do what she could to facilitate" and said whoever was guilty, "on either side," would be punished. Carter was never notified about the outcome of the investigation.

It appears that corrections officials have even misled a representative in the U.S. Congress who sought information about an investigation. Soon after Alice C. took a polygraph to assist in an investigation of sexual misconduct by a corrections employee, she says IDOC officials transferred her involuntarily to another facility, further away from her family and children. "I returned to [the prison] that afternoon and the next thing I knew they said I had thirty minutes. They were transferring me."[138]

After her transfer, Alice C.'s family contacted their U.S. congressman, Representative Bob Michels. Rep. Michels then communicated his concerns about Alice C.'s transfer to IDOC, and in September 1993 Howard Peters, then director of IDOC, wrote to him saying he would look into the situation.[139] In November 1993, two months after Alice C. was transferred, Director Peters informed Representative Michels that the investigation had just concluded. He wrote that once the appropriate paperwork was processed "we will have no objections in

---

[136] Interview, Gail Smith, Chicago Legal Aid to Incarcerated Mothers, Chicago, May 10, 1994.

[137] Telephone interview, Elizabeth Carter, June 22, 1994.

[138] Interview, Illinois, May 1994.

[139] During our interview with Alice C., we reviewed a series of correspondence between her family and Representative Michels as well as his correspondence with her, which included copies of letters received from the IDOC.

reconsidering [Alice C.'s request] to return to _____ ."[140]   In fact, the IDOC Administrative Review Board had decided in November to deny Alice C.'s request to return to the other prison.

RECOMMENDATIONS

I.   Prohibiting Sex in Custody

A.   The Illinois Legislature should amend the Illinois Penal Code to recognize that all instances of sexual intercourse or sexual touching between prison staff and prisoners constitute felonious criminal conduct on the part of the prison staff member. Where such intercourse or touching is accompanied by the overt use or threat of force, including through the provision or denial of privileges, money, or goods, it should be prohibited as felony rape and sexual assault. Given the fact that prisoners have limited resources and privileges and the promise of rewards always carries special weight, cases where correctional officers offer goods or privileges without any actual or perceived threat to the prisoner should be prosecuted as felonious sexual abuse. In instances where it can be shown that no coercion occurred, sexual intercourse and sexual contact between corrections employees and prisoners is, at a minimum, an infraction of staff professional duty and should be punished as criminal sexual contact, also a felony. Such a provision should be integrated into already existing laws that criminalize rape and sexual assault. Prisoners should not be criminally sanctioned for misconduct.

B.   IDOC should amend the Illinois Administrative Code to explicitly prohibit corrections employees from engaging in sexual intercourse or any other form of sexual contact with prisoners.

C.   IDOC should cease punishing women prisoners and/or pursuing criminal charges against women prisoners for sexual relations with corrections employees under any circumstances. The Illinois Administrative Code, Section 504 should be revised to prohibit the punishment of prisoners for sexual contact with corrections staff. Even in those instances where evidence overcomes the presumption of some coercive influence on the prisoner and no goods or privileges were exchanged, prison authorities

---

[140] Ibid.

should refrain from punishing her. Whatever penological interest might be served by such sanctions is outweighed by the deterrent effect that such punishments would have on prisoners' willingness to report custodial sexual abuse.

II.   Safeguarding Prisoners Impregnated by Guards

A.   IDOC should refrain from administratively segregating prisoners impregnated by corrections staff unless the prisoner expressly requests it.

B.   IDOC should ensure that pregnant women receive timely and adequate medical care, and that medical treatment recommended by physicians is provided as prescribed.   Medical care should include professional psychiatric counseling for prisoners who are impregnated as a consequence of rape or sexual abuse. Administrative segregation should not preclude the provision of adequate medical and hygienic requirements for a safe pregnancy.[141] Prisoners also should receive neutral counseling on the options available to them.

III.   Prohibiting Abusive and Degrading Language

IDOC should revise the administrative code to prohibit the use of abusive and degrading language toward prisoners. Corrections staff must be made aware, through enforcement, that they are obligated to comply with such provision or be subjected to disciplinary sanctions.

IV.   Protecting Privacy: The Need for a Policy

A.   IDOC should institute a policy to protect the privacy of women prisoners consistent with international human rights law and with several federal court decisions holding that prisoners have a constitutionally protected right to privacy. Corrections employees should be fully trained in this policy and it should be strictly enforced. Such a policy should include, among other things:

1.   a requirement that male officers announce their presence before entering a women's housing unit;

2.   permission for prisoners to cover windows in their cells for limited intervals while changing or using the toilet;

---

[141] Although we did not document allegations of coerced abortions or inadequate medical and hygienic requirements, we found sufficient evidence in other states to be concerned that it needs to be addressed.

3.   a restriction that showers and toilets be searched by female officers only and should not be excessively intrusive.

B.   IDOC should enforce the administrative code provision requiring strip searches to be conducted by corrections officers of the same sex as the prisoner, and in a place where the search cannot be observed by others. Even in emergencies, IDOC should strive to follow this provision.

C.   IDOC should amend its policy on pat searches to stipulate that female officers should conduct such searches whenever possible. Prisoners who either pull away during offensive pat searches or request that the search be conducted by a female officer should not be subjected automatically to disciplinary action.

V.   Ensuring an Effective Remedy
Grievances

A.   IDOC should require counselors to report all incidents of sexual misconduct raised through prisoners' grievances or through their conversations with prisoners to the prison superintendent or another designated supervisor within the facility. Such allegations, including rumors, should be promptly and impartially investigated.

B.   IDOC should make grievance forms readily available in the prison library or other neutral place, and prisoners should be able to seek the assistance of other prisoners to prepare and file grievances.

Investigative Procedures

A.   IDOC should promulgate a written, public procedure for conducting investigations into sexual misconduct between corrections staff and prisoners. The investigative procedure should, at a minimum:
   1.   specify the circumstances necessary to initiate an investigation, either by the Internal Affairs Department or by an investigator at the prison;
   2.   establish a clear structure and time frame for conducting investigations;
   3.   protect as much as possible the confidentiality of the complainant, in particular during any period that the employee retains a contact position over her;
   4.   guard complainants from retaliation and harassment; and

5.   guarantee accountability to outside monitors.

B.   IDOC should enforce provisions in the Illinois Administrative Code that require corrections employees promptly to report unusual incidents, which should include allegations as well as rumors of sexual or other overfamiliar conduct to the prison warden or investigator. Failure to do so should constitute a disciplinary offense.

C.   IDOC should refer promptly all allegations of rape, sexual assault, and criminal sexual contact to the state police for criminal investigation. Apart from possible criminal wrongdoing, IDOC should also look into such allegations for possible violations of prison rules.

Eliminating Bias Against Prisoners

A.   IDOC should cease its practice of discounting, as a matter of course, the testimony of prisoners who alleged ill-treatment, particularly sexual misconduct, by corrections staff without a thorough and impartial investigation.

B.   IDOC should reexamine its policy on the use of polygraph examinations during investigations into employee misconduct. Results of a polygraph examination should not, without other credible evidence, be sufficient to establish that a prisoner has made a false accusation.

VI.   Preventing Retaliation Against Complainants

A.   Officers alleged to have committed rape and sexual abuse should be assigned to a noncontact position or suspended until the circumstances are clarified and the investigation is complete. Any violation of such restrictions should constitute grounds for disciplinary action and/or for immediate suspension.

B.   IDOC should ensure, as much as possible, the confidentiality of prisoners alleging sexual misconduct by prison staff and their witnesses. Their names should not be given to the accused officers while the officers remain in contact positions with the complainants or are assigned to the facility where a complainant resides. IDOC also should prevent the prisoner's name from being revealed generally within the facility.

C.   IDOC should investigate promptly and vigorously all reports of harassment or retaliation against complainants. Employees who are found guilty should be disciplined appropriately.

D.   IDOC should reexamine and monitor the policy of impounding prisoners' property to ensure that prison administrators and other corrections officials do not abuse this power as a way to punish or harass prisoners, or deprive prisoners of materials that are crucial to their allegations.

VII.   Curtailing the Use of Administrative Segregation

IDOC should strictly prohibit the use of administrative segregation to punish complainants. IDOC should authorize the use of administrative segregation during an investigation only at the complainant's explicit request. Since a prisoner placed in administrative segregation for her own protection has not committed a disciplinary offense, she should retain the rights of the general population (e.g., telephone calls, visits, access to recreation, etc.). She should be returned to the general population when she wishes. IDOC should train employees assigned to segregated housing units regarding these provisions.

VIII.   Ensuring Discipline

A.   IDOC should promulgate and enforce clear, public guidelines governing disciplinary action against abusive corrections employees. These guidelines should expressly state that employees found to have engaged in sexual intercourse, sexual contact, or any other sexual misconduct will be punished, including by dismissal. Transfer of employees found to have engaged in sexual contact with prisoners to other positions or facilities does not constitute appropriate punishment.

B.   IDOC should publish, at least quarterly, a summary of reports of and disciplinary actions taken against corrections employees responsible for sexual misconduct or abuse to allow the federal government and nongovernmental organizations to monitor IDOC's efforts to prevent sexual misconduct. The reports should omit the names of prisoners and, if necessary, of employees. But they should include dates, locations, and other relevant details about the reported incidents, and the types of punishment applied.

IX.   Hiring and Training Corrections Employees

A.   IDOC should improve its screening procedures for applicants for corrections positions. Background checks should be completed before new employees are sent into women's correctional facilities. In no case should an employee who has been convicted of an offense related to sexual misconduct in custody be rehired.

B.   IDOC should ensure that comprehensive and mandatory training is provided to current and future corrections employees on particular aspects of working with incarcerated women, prior to their assignments in women's prisons. The training should include, among other things:

1.   a general discussion of profile of female prisoners and their potential vulnerability to sexual misconduct;

2.   IDOC policies on privacy and the prohibition on sexual relations, degrading language, and other sexually oriented or degrading behavior toward incarcerated women and the disciplinary sanctions associated with this behavior; and

3.   appropriate methods for conducting pat searches, strip searches and searches of women's cells, toilets, and showers. The IDOC should collaborate with local nongovernmental organizations experienced in working on issues such as rape and sexual assault.

X.   Educating Prisoners

A.   IDOC should advise incarcerated women, as part of their orientation to the corrections system, as well as prisoners already serving their sentences, of the following:

1.   Corrections officers are strictly prohibited from engaging in sexual contact with prisoners under any circumstances.

2.   Grievances may be filed directly and confidentially with the prison superintendent or prison investigator. Prisoners should be informed about: the issues that may be dealt with through the grievance procedure, with particular emphasis on instances of sexual misconduct; the location of grievance forms in the prison library or other neutral place; bypass mechanisms available for reporting sexual misconduct; the recourse available when corrections officers fail to respond; and the potential to resolve complaints through the investigation procedure and/or the independent review board.

3.   IDOC should also acquaint prisoners with their rights under international human rights treaties ratified by the United States as well as under U.S. constitutional law.

B.   The above information should be included in the prisoner handbook.

XI.   Ensuring Accountability to Outside Monitors

A.   IDOC should provide timely and full written information about a grievance or investigation to the prisoner and the people she designates, such as her attorney and her family, upon their request.

B.   The Illinois Legislature should create a fully empowered and independent review board to investigate, among other things, complaints of sexual misconduct that are not satisfactorily resolved by the grievance or investigative mechanisms. The review board should have the authority to turn over evidence of possible criminal wrongdoing to prosecutorial authorities. The board should also be able to recommend remedial action to stop abuses or other problems uncovered during an investigation.

C.   The review board should develop a system whereby the records of corrections employees who have been the subject of repeated complaints are reviewed by the appropriate authorities.

D.   The review board should provide a toll-free telephone number that prisoners can use to contact investigators or to file anonymous complaints of employee misconduct, including retaliation against complainants.

VII. MICHIGAN

The Michigan Department of Corrections (MDOC) is currently being sued by seven female prisoners on behalf of all others similarly situated for sexual assault, sexual abuse, sexual harassment, and inappropriate visual surveillance within its correctional facilities for women. The suit comes on the heels of a U.S. Department of Justice (DOJ) finding in 1995 that sexual misconduct pervades Michigan's women's prisons, including rape, sexual abuse, sexually aggressive acts by guards, and violations of the female prisoners' legitimate privacy interests. Our own investigation, conducted from 1994 through 1996, and based on interviews with current and former female prisoners as well as attorneys, prisoner rights advocates, and MDOC, revealed that rape, sexual assault or abuse, criminal sexual contact, and other misconduct by corrections staff are continuing and serious problems within the women's prisons in Michigan have been tolerated over the years at both the institutional and departmental levels.

Rather than seeking to end such abuse, the Michigan Department of Corrections has consistently refused to acknowledge that there is a problem of sexual misconduct in its women's prisons. As noted below, MDOC dismissed the female prisoners' class action suit as "erroneous" and issued a written statement characterizing the DOJ's findings as "vindictive and distorted" and "full of half truths, innuendo, distortion and lies."[1] The state has taken the positive steps of establishing minimal grievance and investigatory procedures as well as disciplinary and criminal sanctions for custodial sexual contact; however, its stated policy of "zero tolerance" for such abuse is belied by a pervasive bias against prisoner testimony, a high incidence of retaliation against complainants, and a consistent problem with the enforcement of appropriate penalties.

MDOC cooperated with Human Rights Watch's on-site investigations at its women's facilities and was prompt in its reply to our requests for additional information. Moreover, we commend the state for expressly criminalizing custodial sexual touching and for establishing clear disciplinary penalties for this crime. However, a significant gap exists between MDOC policy and its practice with respect to sexual misconduct. We strongly urge MDOC to enforce its criminal and administrative prohibitions against sexual misconduct, including rape, sexual abuse, and assault, criminal sexual contact, verbal degradation, and privacy violations; to protect prisoners' right to an effective remedy in cases of sexual misconduct by prison staff; and to end impunity for abusive employees. Moreover,

---

[1] Valerie Basheda, "U.S.: Women's Prisons a Disaster," *Detroit News*, March 30, 1995.

we urge the department to publish regular reports of the nature and results of its sexual misconduct investigations to cooperate fully with the Department of Justice and other independent monitors in their efforts to uncover and remedy on-going custodial sexual misconduct in Michigan's prisons for women.

CONTEXT

Custodial Environment

Female prisoners in Michigan, held in increasingly overcrowded facilities, are guarded by a largely male staff. According to recent figures, men constituted from nearly one-half to over two-thirds of the corrections staff in the state's two largest prisons for women, the Florence Crane Women's Facility (Crane) and the Scott Correctional Facility (Scott).[2]

As noted in the legal background chapter of this report, Human Rights Watch does not oppose the presence of male officers in contact positions in female prisons *per se*. Nor do we believe that all male staff abuse prisoners or that custodial abuse is carried out only by males. However, we are concerned that Michigan has not taken adequate steps to protect against the potential for custodial sexual misconduct that arises out of this cross-gender guarding situation. Although Michigan does expressly prohibit sexual misconduct in both prison rules and criminal law, it fails to train male staff adequately to uphold these prohibitions and does not consistently investigate and discipline those employees found to violate them.

Corrections officials have also failed to inform female prisoners adequately regarding the nature of custodial sexual misconduct and the mechanisms available to seek redress. Christina Kampfner, a clinical psychologist who had worked extensively with women in Michigan's prisons, told us that in these relationships, officers often target "like a radar" women with histories of sexual or physical abuse or prisoners in emotionally vulnerable positions, such as those who lack support from family or friends, who are alienated or isolated by other prisoners or staff, and younger women who are incarcerated for the first

---

[2] According to MDOC's 1995 Information Kit, out of 222 corrections officers at Scott, 118 were women. Of 125 corrections officers at Crane, thirty-nine were women. These figures include corrections medical aides, resident unit officers, and work camp supervisors.

time.[3] According to Kampfner, many of these prisoners are so in need of attention that they are easily exploited by the officers.

The gap between policy and practice in Michigan with respect to sexual misconduct is occurring at a time when the women's prisons are increasingly crowded. According to the most recent figures available from MDOC, there are a total of 1,616 prisoners in its women's facilities.[4] The majority of women are held in the Scott Correctional Facility, located in Plymouth, and the Florence Crane Women's Facility,[5] located in Coldwater, which house 771 and 447 women respectively.[6] MDOC also operates Camp Branch, a female camp in Coldwater that holds approximately 400 women. MDOC currently operates both women's prisons in overcrowded conditions—prisoners are double- and triple-bunked—and areas once used for recreational space are being used to house prisoners.[7]

---

[3] Interview, Christina Kampfner, clinical psychologist, Ann Arbor, Michigan, May 17, 1994.

[4] Letter from Nancy Zang, special administrator, Female Offenders Program Michigan Department of Corrections, to Human Rights Watch, October 8, 1996 (on file with Human Rights Watch).

[5] Since we conducted our interviews in 1994, there has been a change of wardens at the Florence Crane Women's Facility. Warden Carol Howes was replaced by Warden Sally Langley.

[6] MDOC Information Kit, 1995.

[7] According to the most recent figures from MDOC, neither Scott nor Crane are technically exceeding their operating capacity, which, according to 1995 figures, is 860 and 460 respectively (MDOC Information Kit, 1995). However, based on a review of the prisons' capacity figures from previous years, it appears that these numbers are fairly malleable. For example, according to April 1994 figures for the Scott Correctional Facility, the prison's operating capacity is 638 (MDOC Client Census Summary, April 1, 1994), 222 prisoners less that it is now estimated to be. To our knowledge, no construction has occurred to account for this increased capacity. One explanation may be that via double- or triple-bunking, more prisoners can be accommodated in the same space, and a prison's capacity can thereby increase.

At the Florence Crane Women's Facility, the crowded conditions are exacerbated by the dilapidated condition of the prison itself. The American Correctional Association audit at the Crane facility in November 1992 found that: "There was a considerable need for improvement. . . . The bathrooms, showers and toilets were in need of replacement and repair. Peeling paint, broken window panes and problems associated with heating and

State Legal and Regulatory Framework

Under Michigan's criminal code, any sexual touching with a prisoner by an employee of or a volunteer with MDOC constitutes fourth-degree "criminal sexual conduct," a misdemeanor.[8] The provision was added in 1988 to a pre-existing section of the criminal code that outlawed sexual touching with someone between the ages of thirteen and sixteen who is physically or mentally incapacitated or that is accompanied by force or coercion. The law applies to sexual contact irrespective of a prisoner's alleged consent.[9] Given the position of authority held by a corrections employee over a prisoner, the Michigan legislature found "the usual notions of consent do not apply."[10] The MDOC employee manual reiterates the prohibition on sexual contact with a prisoner and informs employees that such conduct constitutes a crime under Michigan law.[11] Under certain

---

plumbing definitely indicated a need for an improved, ongoing maintenance." (American Correctional Association, Commission for Accreditation for Corrections Standard Compliance Audit, Florence Crane Women's Facility, November 1992, p. 4.)

[8] Michigan Comparative Law Annotated §750-520(e)(d). Fourth degree criminal sexual conduct is a two-year offense.

[9] According to Deborah LaBelle, an attorney who represents women prisoners in Michigan, the law criminalizing sexual contact in prison was introduced in the state legislature following an alleged rape at Huron Valley Women's Prison, in which an issue was made of the woman's consent. The corrections officer, Alfred Beaster, whose case is discussed in more detail below, admitted to sexual intercourse with the woman but alleged the liaison was consensual. The woman asserted that she was raped. The officer's claims so outraged two female legislators that the legislation was proposed. Telephone interview, Deborah LaBelle, attorney, February 27, 1995.

[10] Michigan House Legislative Analysis Section, "Criminal Sexual Conduct with Prisoner," House Bill 4386 as enrolled Second Analysis (6-29-88). The analysis compared the situation of a prisoner to that of a patient or resident in a mental health facility.

[11] MDOC also has a policy on humane treatment of prisoners that appears to prohibit both degrading treatment of prisoners, although provisions we reviewed seem to apply only to the conduct of other prisoners rather than that of employees. The policy provides that "staff shall discourage, with all appropriate means, any person's use of derogatory, demeaning, humiliating, or degrading actions or language toward others." "Right of Clients to Humane Treatment and Living Conditions," MDOC Policy Directive, No. 03.03.130, June 7, 1982 (supersedes No. PD-DWA-64.02). The provision falls under a section addressing abuse by "a minority of other prisoners." A later clause stipulates that "corrections clients shall not

circumstances, corrections officers who engage in sexual intercourse with prisoners may be charged with third or first degree criminal sexual conduct. Third degree criminal sexual conduct occurs when an individual uses force or coercion to have sex. First degree sexual conduct applies to intercourse that occurs under specified aggravating circumstances.[12]

At present, MDOC operates both of its women's prisons and Camp Branch under a court order issued in 1981, in *Glover v. Johnson*.[13] While the issues raised in *Glover* are outside the scope of this report, the authorities' persistent defiance of both the judicial authorities and the other external monitors involved in *Glover* are indicative of similar problems in MDOC's approach to addressing sexual misconduct in its women's prisons.

At the time *Glover* was decided, it was a landmark decision for incarcerated women regarding their rights and an influential precedent for female prisoners in other states to seek more equal programming. Despite its precedential value, however, women incarcerated in Michigan continue to be denied the full

---

be subjected to personal abuse from corrections staff," but it does not define personal abuse. The same language is also included, without clarification, in a 1991 prisoner guidebook with regard to sexual harassment. "Sexual Harassment Reporting and Prevention," MDOC Policy Directive, No. 02.02.108, August 24, 1992 (supersedes No. PD-DWA-05.02).

[12] There are nine sets of circumstances under which sexual penetration (vaginal, anal, or oral) constitutes a first degree offense, including (a) where a complainant suffers personal injury and the defendant used force or coercion; (b) where the defendant is aided by another in using force or coercion to secure sex; and (c) where the defendant is armed at the time of the offense.

[13] *Glover v. Johnson*, 478 F. Supp. 1075 (1979); *Glover v. Johnson*, 510 F. Supp. 1019 (C.D. Mich. 1981). The 1981 court order, issued after a 1979 opinion finding that Michigan had violated the women's equal protection rights, required MDOC to: provide educational, vocational, apprenticeship and work opportunities, comparable to those available to male prisoners; establish a prison industry at the women's prison; rectify the inferiority of rehabilitation opportunities available to women; update and maintain the law library and provide paralegal training to incarcerated women; and reassess the departmental wage policy to ensure it is fairly applied to female prisoners. The court also ordered the department to pay back wages to a trust fund that was established for the benefit of the women prisoners. The trust was later named the Judith Magid Trust in memory of one of the original attorneys who filed *Glover*.

implementation of the judge's order.[14] Attorneys representing female prisoners have been forced to file repeated contempt motions seeking compliance with *Glover* orders. The district court has found that the state disobeyed the 1981 order in two major contempt rulings.[15]

MDOC's continued noncompliance led the Sixth Circuit Court of Appeals, in 1991, to issue a stern rebuke to the department and to uphold the appointment of a special administrator, a remedy the Circuit Court once found overly intrusive. The Sixth Circuit concluded:

> [The] history of this case shows a *consistent and persistent pattern* of obfuscation, hyper-technical objections, delay, and litigation by exhaustion on the part of the defendants *to avoid compliance with the letter and spirit of the district court's orders.* The plaintiff class has struggled for eleven years to achieve the simple objectives of equal protection under the law generally, and equality of opportunity specifically.[16]

---

[14] In the mid-1980s, when the Florence Crane Women's Facility was opened for women, MDOC refused to extend *Glover's* order to the facility despite the judge's ruling that all women present and future were covered by the case. While the circuit court reaffirmed that indeed *all* women incarcerated by MDOC were covered by the order, MDOC one year later again contended before the district court that the Florence Crane Women's Facility was *not* covered.

[15] Specifically, the court found that Michigan failed to comply with the order concerning: access to the courts; educational programming; vocational programming; apprenticeship opportunities; prison industry, trust fund payments and prisoner wages; and off-ground privileges and work pass programs. *Glover v. Johnson*, 721 F. Supp. 808 (E. D. Mich. 1979) affirmed in part, reversed in part, 934 F. 2d, pp. 706-707 (6th Cir. 1991); *Glover v. Johnson*, 850 F. Supp. 592 (E. D. Mich. 1994).

According to Deborah LaBelle, the lead attorney on *Glover*, between 1979 and 1989, no female prisoner could get an associate's degree through the courses provided at the women's prisons despite the 1979 order requiring that a coherent program with courses leading to such a degree be provided. Meanwhile, male prisoners were obtaining between thirty and fifty such degrees per semester at one male facility. Telephone interview, Michigan, Deborah LaBelle, attorney, February 27, 1995.

[16] *Glover*, 934 F.2d, p. 716. Emphasis added.

While the court upheld the creation of a special administrator, MDOC was permitted to designate who would serve in that position. The director of MDOC, Kenneth McGinnis, appointed Nancy Zang, a former parole officer in Illinois as special administrator of the Female Offenders Program. Zang is based in the director's office and reports directly to him.

The Sixth Circuit's rebuke did not appreciably affect MDOC's recalcitrance, and women have continued to face difficulties gaining the remedies ordered by the court. Deborah LaBelle told us there have been more than eight contempt motions filed against MDOC since 1991.[17] The court has issued nine orders to force compliance since 1991, and in March 1995 issued an opinion finding that MDOC had still not obtained compliance, despite MDOC's insistence that they were fully compliant in all areas.[18] On July 19, 1996, the court again issued an opinion and orders to compel compliance. United States District Judge John Feiken concluded: ". . . Defendants [MDOC *et al.*] have clearly, positively, and repeatedly violated orders of this court. . . .In fact, in the nineteen years of this case, Defendants have demonstrated a galling pattern of disrespect for the inmates they hold, the taxpayers of the State of Michigan, and the dignity of this court."[19]

National and International Law Protections

As discussed in the legal background chapter of this report, sexual misconduct is clearly prohibited under both U.S. constitutional law and international treaty law that is binding on the the U.S. federal government and its constituent states.[20] The eighth amendment to the U.S. Constitution, which bars cruel and unusual punishment, has been interpreted by U.S. courts to protect prisoners against rape and sexual assault. This constitutional shield is further augmented by the Fourth Amendment's guarantee of the rights to privacy and personal integrity, which, in a series of lower court cases, has been interpreted to prohibit male guards from strip searching female prisoners, conducting intrusive pat-frisks, or engaging in inappropriate visual surveillance.

---

[17] Telephone interview, Deborah LaBelle, attorney, February 27, 1995.

[18] Ibid.

[19] *Glover v. Johnson*, 931 F. Supp. 1360, p. 1383 (E.D. Mich. 1996).

[20] For a detailed discussion of United States obligations under U.S. constitutional law and international law pertaining to the treatment of prisoners, see the legal background chapter of this report.

Constitutional protections on prisoners' rights are enforceable via lawsuits filed by or on behalf of prisoners, or by the U.S. Department of Justice (DOJ). Historically, U.S. prisoners have achieved most of their landmark prison victories through private litigation, particularly by suits litigated by prisoners' rights groups such as the National Prison Project of the American Civil Liberties Union or the National Prison Project of the National Women's Law Center. However, if certain stringent intent requirements are met, the DOJ may criminally prosecute abusive prison officials under federal civil rights provisions. In addition, the DOJ has the statutory right to investigate and institute civil actions under the Civil Rights of Institutionalized Persons Act (CRIPA) whenever it finds that a state facility engages in a pattern or practice of subjecting prisoners to "egregious or flagrant conditions" in violation of the constitution.

In addition to constitutional protections, prisoners' rights are also protected under international and human rights treaties that are legally binding on the United States. The primary international legal instruments protecting the rights of U.S. prisoners are the International Covenant on Civil and Political Rights (ICCPR), ratified by the United States in 1993, and the Convention Against Torture and Other Cruel, Inhuman or Degrading Treatment of Punishment, ratified in 1994. Both treaties bar torture and cruel, inhuman or degrading treatment or punishment, which authoritative institutional fora have interpreted as including sexual abuse. To constitute torture, an act must cause severe physical or mental suffering and must be committed for a purpose such as obtaining information from the victim, punishing her, intimidating her, coercing her, or for any reason based on discrimination of any kind. Cruel, inhuman or degrading treatment or punishment includes acts causing a lesser degree of suffering that need not be committed for a particular purpose. The ICCPR guarantees the prisoners' right to privacy, except when limitations on this right are demonstrably necessary to maintain prison security.

When prison staff members use force, the threat of force, or other means of coercion to compel a prisoner to engage in sexual intercourse, their acts constitute rape and, therefore, torture. Torture also occurs when prison staff use force or coercion to engage in sexual touching of prisoners where such acts cause serious physical or mental suffering. Instances of sexual touching or of sexual intercourse that does not amount to rape may constitute torture or cruel or inhuman treatment, depending on the level of physical or mental suffering involved. Other forms of sexual misconduct, such as inappropriate pat or strip searches or verbal harassment, that do not rise to the level of torture or of cruel or inhuman treatment, may be condemned as degrading treatment. [21]

ABUSES[22]

The abuses discussed in this section occurred over a ten-year period from 1986 to 1996. Our own investigation took place from March 1994 through November 1996. We found a serious problem of sexual misconduct in Michigan women's prisons, including rape, sexual assault and abuse, criminal sexual contact, inappropriate visual surveillance, and verbal degradation. Unless indicated by the use of a full name, the names of the prisoners have been changed to protect their anonymity. In some cases, the location and exact date of prisoner interviews have also been withheld.

Rape, Sexual Assault or Abuse, and Criminal Sexual Contact

On March 27, 1996, prisoners' rights attorney Deborah Labelle filed a class action suit, *Neal/Nunn*, on behalf of seven female prisoners and all other females incarcerated in Michigan charging MDOC and several other named defendants with various degrees of sexual assault, sexual harassment, violations of privacy, and physical threats and assaults.[23] Two of the plaintiffs, Tracy Neal and Ikemia Russell, allege sexual assault by male officers at the Scott Correctional

---

[21] For a detailed discussion of the prohibition against torture, and other cruel, inhuman or degrading treatment or punishment under international law and its applicability to custodial sexual misconduct, see the legal background chapter of this report.

[22] By rape, we mean sexual intercourse between a prison employee and a prisoner that is accompanied by the use or threat of force or coercion which, under certain circumstances, can take the form of the provision or denial of privileges, money, or goods. Sexual assault is sexual touching, short of intercourse, involving the same coercive influences. Sexual abuse is sexual intercourse or touching involving the offer of goods or privileges absent any actual or perceived threat to the prisoner. Criminal sexual contact refers to sexual intercourse or sexual touching that cannot be shown to involve any of the above elements but which nonetheless constitutes a gross breach of official duty. Rape, sexual assault or abuse, and criminal sexual contact should all be prosecuted as felonies. For a more detailed discussion, see the legal background chapter.

[23] *Neal v. Michigan Department of Corrections,* Civil Action File No. 96-6986, Circuit Court for the County of Washtenaw, March 27, 1996.

Facility in 1994. A third, Helen Gibbs, alleges that she was sexually assaulted by a male officer at the Florence Crane Women's Facility in 1994. Bertha Clark alleges that a male officer at Scott squeezed her breasts and grabbed her crotch during pat-frisks, and Linda Nunn alleges sex-based, derogatory and abusive name calling and sexually threatening comments by a male officer at Scott. Stacy Barker, whose case is described in more detail below, alleges constant harassment and retaliation at Scott for reporting sexual misconduct by staff members, and "Jane Doe" alleges that male officers at Crane subjected her to constant viewing while dressing and undressing, showering, and using the toilet facilities. All seven women report experiencing sex-based insults, sexual harassment, excessively intrusive cross-gender body searches, constant viewing by male staff and threats of retaliation for reporting staff misconduct.

Such allegations of sexual misconduct are not new to Michigan's women's prisons. Documentation we obtained indicates that these charges are consistent with a pattern and practice of conduct in the women's prisons since, at least, the mid-1980s. In 1984 a prisoner accused a resident unit officer, Alfred Beaster, at Huron Valley Women's Facility,[24] of rape. He ultimately confessed to having sexual relations with a prisoner, but asserted the prisoner was the aggressor. He told the prison investigator that:

> The prisoner dropped her pants, he took his penis out, but she did all of the manipulation. That is, she backed onto his erection. Officer Beaster maintained he didn't lay a hand on her. Beaster told the officers that he wasn't sure if he was inside of her or not as she was backing up on him. He did tell the officers that he ejaculated and that she asked him if he squirted inside of her.[25]

Then, in 1986, a corrections officer at Crane, Raymond Raby, was dismissed after admitting during a police interview that he had sexual relations on a nightly basis with different women incarcerated at Crane. Raby's exploits came to light after a prisoner, Jackie K., reported that Raby molested her. According to Jackie K.'s statement, Raby entered her cell at night and woke her up. He took her into a visiting room where he grabbed her and kissed her, then fondled her breasts

---

[24] This facility has since been closed.

[25] Memorandum from Rider, assistant deputy, Michigan Department of Corrections, to D. Quarles, Michigan Department of Corrections, November 28, 1984.

and put his finger in her vagina.[26] Shortly after Jackie K. complained about him, another prisoner reported seeing an officer fitting Raby's description having oral intercourse with a third prisoner.[27]

In 1988 another woman incarcerated at Crane, Kim J., alleged that she was raped by an officer during the night shift. Kim J. reported the incident to the prison psychologist, who then informed other officials in the prison.[28] According to a statement Kim J. made, the officer raped her in the laundry room after she submitted to a "shakedown" (pat-frisk). The next morning, she awakened to find the officer in her cubicle with his hand between her legs. The authorities took no action against the officer because the only evidence was her accusation.

In another incident, Officer Bernard Rivers in 1990 admitted entering a prisoner's segregation cell and sexually assaulting her. According to the prisoner, Lisa G., Rivers entered her cell in April 1988 and told her he could positively or negatively affect her parole, depending on how she responded to his sexual advances.[29] She involuntarily submitted to sexual relations with him. Lisa G. came forward eighteen months later, after Rivers was again assigned to her housing unit, out of fear that he would force her to have sexual relations with him again. MDOC largely ignored Lisa G.'s allegations for four months until she, with the help of her attorney Deborah LaBelle, obtained a court order and wore a wire inside the prison.[30] She successfully taped a conversation with Rivers. His statements acknowledged the sexual assault and resulted in the sheriff's office recommending prosecution. He committed suicide before trial.

In 1992 the Michigan Women's Commission, a governor-appointed body, launched an investigation into the problems facing incarcerated women, focusing

---

[26] Report from Charles Allen, sergeant, Michigan State Police, October 1985.

[27] Letter from Richardson, Michigan Department of Corrections, from a prisoner, October 1985.

[28] Memorandum from R. Joseph, psychologist, Michigan Department of Corrections, to C. Paradine, hearing officer, Michigan Department of Corrections, September 20, 1988.

[29] Written statement by Lisa G. (on file with Human Rights Watch).

[30] Telephone interview, Deborah LaBelle, attorney, February 27, 1995.

in particular on women incarcerated in county jails.[31] The commission interviewed fifty-nine women who were formerly held in jail and were either released or transferred to Michigan's prisons or community-based programs.[32] In each interview, a pre-established series of questions was asked regarding jail conditions including a final, open question, "Are there any concerns you would like to share about conditions here at the prison?"[33]

The prisoners raised a number of concerns in response to the final question, including incidences of rape, sexual assault, and sexual harassment committed by corrections officers. A majority of the women reported sexual harassment and sexual abuse by the guards, ranging from corrections staff demanding sex or sexual favors, often in exchange for certain items, to intrusive pat-downs, to male guards walking through the showers and rooms while the women were undressed.[34] The women's responses to the last question were used to create a final chapter, "Special Report: Women in Prison," of the Women's Commission's Report. At MDOC Director McGinnis's insistence, the section was

---

[31] Michigan Women's Commission, "Unheard Voices: A Report on Women in Michigan County Jails," July 1993, p. 7. The report was commissioned under the previous governor's administration and carried out by members of the Women's Commission who were appointed by the new governor.

[32] Ibid. Of the fifty-nine women, thirty-three were incarcerated in prison at the time of the interview. Prison personnel selected the women who were interviewed. Letter from the Michigan Women's Commission to Kenneth McGinnis, director, Michigan Department of Corrections, May 13, 1993. Interviews conducted with women who had been transferred to prison were done with the knowledge and permission of MDOC. The prison interviews took place in the open visiting rooms of the Crane and Scott women's facilities, where corrections officers could monitor the conversations, if they chose to do so. Interview, Jenny Elder, former intern, Michigan Women's Commission, Detroit, March 28, 1994. As an intern for the Michigan Women's Commission, Elder conducted a large majority of the interviews.

[33] "Special Report: Women in Prison," deleted from the Michigan Women's Commission's final report "Unheard Voices . . ."

[34] Letter from Marjie Gaynor, Michigan Women's Commission, to Kenneth McGinnis, director, Michigan Department of Corrections, February 3, 1993.

ultimately deleted from the published report, released in July 1993; the chapter has never been made public in any form.[35]

In February 1993 the Office of the Legislative Corrections Ombudsman, a post attached to the state legislature, conducted a second investigation of sexual misconduct at both Scott and Crane.[36] McGinnis asserts that the ombudsman's findings refuted the information compiled by the Women's Commission, even though a significant percentage of the women surveyed reported that sexual harassment and sexual misconduct were problems in the prison.[37]

In June 1994 the U.S. Department of Justice launched an investigation into prison conditions for women incarcerated at the Scott and Crane facilities pursuant to the Civil Rights of Institutionalized Persons Act (CRIPA). The purpose of the investigation was to determine whether there were any violations of the prisoners' constitutional rights. On March 27, 1995, U.S. Assistant Attorney General Deval

---

[35] Interview, Jenny Elder, former intern, Michigan's Women's Commission, Detroit, March 28, 1994.

[36] The Office of the Legislative Corrections Ombudsman was created by the Michigan state legislature to provide an independent and outside means to investigate allegations of wrongdoing within the MDOC. Its role and performance are discussed more fully below under the section on investigations. The ombudsman's survey was prompted by a request from State Representative Jan Dolan.

[37] Letter from Charlene Lowrie, chief investigator, Office of the Legislative Corrections Ombudsman, to Carol Howes, warden, Florence Crane Women's Facility, April 26, 1993. Twenty-four prisoners were reportedly selected at random from the general population at Scott; of these, six, or 25 percent, refused to participate. Nineteen women, of whom one refused to participate, were chosen at Crane. The participating prisoners were asked sixteen questions that required a simple "yes or no" answer. At Scott, three women reported a problem with officers watching prisoners shower. Three witnessed staff sexually harass other prisoners and personally experienced unwanted sexually suggestive remarks or gestures from staff. A substantial majority of those interviewed, 67 percent, reported feeling uncomfortable during shakedowns. Of these, one-third reported being groped, fondled or inappropriately touched at one time or another during a shakedown by staff. At Crane, the ombudsman's investigation revealed the following: 35 percent of the women felt there was a problem with staff watching prisoners shower; 18 percent had experienced some degree of unwanted sexually suggestive remarks; 18 percent had, at one time or another, seen staff engage in a sexual encounter with a prisoner; 29 percent reported seeing staff sexually harass other prisoners; 65 percent felt uncomfortable during shakedowns; and 35 percent were aware of situations involving the exchange of sex for favorable treatment.

Patrick wrote a twelve-page letter to Michigan Governor John Engler that detailed the DOJ's findings. The DOJ concluded:

> [T]he sexual abuse of women prisoners by guards, including rapes, the lack of adequate medical care, including mental health services, grossly deficient sanitation, crowding and other threats to the physical safety and well-being of prisoners, violates their constitutional rights.[38]

According to the DOJ letter, "nearly every woman . . . interviewed reported various sexually aggressive acts of guards."[39] The DOJ found that prisoners at Scott and Crane had been raped, sexually assaulted, and subjected to groping and fondling during pat-frisks. Additionally, they were subjected to "improper visual surveillance by guards" who:

> routinely stand outside the cells of individual prisoners and watch them dress or undress, stand in the shower areas and observe showers and use of toilet facilities. Male maintenance workers stand and watch women inmates who are naked or in various states of undress as well—all on a regular basis without legitimate need. . . . We are unaware of any effort to accommodate the legitimate privacy interests of prisoners.[40]

The status of the DOJ's investigation is discussed in more detail below.

In 1994 we interviewed two women—Stacy Barker and Charlene Billups-Hein—who both sued MDOC for repeated sexual abuse by male corrections officers that they endured at the Huron Valley Women's Prison, now closed, and Scott. Barker was raped and sexually assaulted by the same officer, Craig Keahy, over a period of nearly a year and a half, beginning in October 1989.[41] She told us, "He would come to my room or detail [once or twice a week] and force me to

---

[38] Letter from Deval Patrick, assistant attorney general, U.S. Department of Justice, to John Engler, governor, Michigan, March 27, 1995.

[39] Ibid.

[40] Ibid., p. 4.

[41] Interview, Stacy Barker, Michigan, March 1994.

perform different sexual acts on him. He would threaten or harass me, like 'I'll make your time hard for you . . . I have the keys.'"[42] He was discovered by other officers on various occasions leaving Barker's room off-duty but was always allowed to return to her unit and never reprimanded for violation of rules. After a while, his attacks became more violent. She told us, "He'd say things like, 'Come on and suck my dick'. . . . He'd pull my hair, unzip his pants and force himself in my mouth." Keahy was subsequently discovered by other prison officers, in August 1991, leaving the room of a second woman prisoner. They looked into the prisoner's room and saw that she was naked. While the prisoner initially denied anything had occurred, she was taken to the hospital and an examination was performed which detected the presence of semen. Keahy was convicted in December 1991 on two counts of fourth-degree sexual conduct with a prisoner, a misdemeanor.[43] He was sentenced to community service.

Charlene Billups-Hein was housed in segregation when a male corrections officer, David Rose, started coming to her cell in the early mornings in June and July 1992.[44] According to Billups-Hein, Rose came and spoke with her one night when she was crying and upset. Rose told her he had been having sexual relations with other prisoners and asked her to have sexual intercourse with him. He listed the names and identification numbers of the women with whom he was having sex, many of whom were housed in the segregation unit. According to Billups-Hein, he stated that he had been watching her for a long time and that she would be his fourteenth resident. He had not approached her earlier, Rose said, because she was "with women," implying that she was a lesbian. She told us that she submitted to sexual relations with the officer because she felt that she did not have any choice. When he approached her on subsequent occasions, the officer allegedly brought her various things, such as cigarettes, makeup, perfume, candy, and cookies. She said they had sexual intercourse and that she performed oral sex on him a number of times. Officer Rose was charged with criminal sexual conduct third degree and acquitted. He was returned to Scott where he is currently employed and is reportedly under investigation for renewed charges of sexual misconduct with a different prisoner.

---

[42] Ibid.

[43] Keahy was convicted on December 18, 1991, for sexual contact with the second prisoner and pled no contest to charges of sexual contact with Barker on December 21, 1991. He was sentenced on February 11, 1992.

[44] Interview, Charlene Billups-Hein, Michigan, March 1994.

Other women we interviewed in 1994 reported similar assaults by male officers and staff. In late 1993, Anne B. was taking a break from her work assignment in a back room when her supervisor came in.[45] He approached her from behind and started kissing her. He then pulled her to the ground and had sexual relations with her. She told us, "I felt uncomfortable. It wasn't something I wanted. . . . After that, he acted as if nothing happened. He did his job, I did mine." Anne B. discussed the rape with other women on her work assignment, who described similar encounters with the same employee, although none of them admitted actually submitting to sexual intercourse.

Another incarcerated woman we interviewed, Gloria P., told us that Officer A was assigned to guard her room when she was admitted to a hospital outside the prison for medical treatment.[46] During her stay in the hospital, he became increasingly assertive, touching her, making comments like, "You need a man like me," or suggesting she take a shower and helping her undress. He once turned on a nude dance show on the television in the hospital room and made comments such as, "I like women with a lot of butt" or made reference to their breasts. One day, he sat on the edge of her bed and kissed her. On another occasion, she told us, he kissed her breasts and she performed oral sex on him.

According to Gloria P., "It went on from there, and we had a relationship in the sexual sense" in the hospital and once she returned to the prison. Everyone, including staff, she said, knew about the relationship. She explained, "That person never gets tickets [disciplinary write-up], never needs a pass, could go wherever they wanted and, if anybody ever had a problem with her, he'd [take care of it]."[47] During this time, he brought her various things, such as nail polish, money, a ring, and candy. One night, she stated, the relationship "got really intense"—he started rubbing her hair while other prisoners were watching, and they went into a nearby closet to kiss. Within days, Gloria P. was moved to another unit but continued to see Officer A in the yard, or he would switch shifts with officers on either her unit or a neighboring unit in order to see her.

On February 22, 1996, we interviewed an attorney representing a female prisoner who was charging a male officer at Scott with sexual assault.[48] The assault

---

[45] Interview, Michigan, March 1994.

[46] Interview, Michigan, May 1994.

[47] Interview, Michigan, May 1994.

[48] Interview, Ada Montgomery, attorney, Michigan, February 22, 1996.

occurred during the midnight shift on July 31, 1995. The prisoner was asleep in her cell when the officer entered, tied her down to her bunk, sexually abused her, and hit her repeatedly. The officer eventually left and during the early hours of the morning, another officer found the prisoner tied to her bed and badly beaten. The prisoner was taken to the hospital and then returned to Scott. The officer was placed on leave immediately and eventually charged with first-degree criminal sexual conduct. He pled guilty to assault with intent to commit criminal sexual contact and received four years probation, one of which he must serve in jail.[49]

In mid-1996, we obtained information about a December 26, 1995, sexual assault by a male officer on a female prisoner at Scott. The assault allegedly occurred during the midnight shift when the officer on duty came into the prisoner's cell, unzipped his pants, and raped her. After hearing a noise outside her cell, he told her to meet him in the bathroom area, where he raped her again. After coming into her cell later in the night and raping her another time, he told her the rapes would be "our little secret." The prisoner reported the rapes on January 9, 1996. She was visited by an inspector at the facility that same day and by a state police officer the following day. At this writing, the prisoner is still incarcerated at Scott and has no knowledge about the progress of the investigation. The officer has not been assigned to her unit but is still working at the facility.

On November 4, 1996, we received reports of an alleged sexual assault at the Camp Branch facility. The assault occurred on October 29, 1996 and was allegedly committed by a civilian food service employee. State troopers were contacted and are investigating the case. To date, no warrant has been issued.

Prisoners who are not involved with officers often witness their sexual activities with other prisoners. According to Frances U., when she worked nights in the school building, she often saw officers in the library with their pants down with a prisoner. She told us, "We would watch officers taking women to the basement. If you couldn't find an officer, you would wait to see which room he came out of. It runs rampant."[50]

Mistreatment of Prisoners Impregnated by Guards

As a result of custodial sexual misconduct, some prisoners have been impregnated by corrections staff. These women are particularly vulnerable to harassment by staff and to the punitive investigatory measures at times employed by MDOC. The experience of one woman, Anne B., whom we interviewed in

---

[49] Interview, Ada Montgomery, attorney, Michigan, November 4, 1996.

[50] Telephone interview, Michigan, May 1994.

1994, is particularly telling. In 1993 Anne B. reported that she had been sexually assaulted by a corrections employee and requested a pregnancy test. Almost immediately after the test results returned positive, the authorities removed her from the prison where the assault occurred and placed her in a segregated cell at Huron Valley Men's Prison (HVM) infirmary.

While at HVM, Anne B. was locked in for nearly twenty-four hours a day and denied access to a phone. Attorney Deborah LaBelle told us that she learned of Anne B.'s predicament only through another prisoner at HVM who contacted LaBelle.[51] Anne B. was removed from her cell only for meetings with MDOC staff investigating her pregnancy. According to Anne B., these investigators repeatedly interrogated her about the circumstances of her pregnancy. One investigator threatened to keep her in segregation throughout her pregnancy, take away her accrued good time, and return her to the facility where she was assaulted unless she assisted with the investigation. Anne B. also told us that this investigator pressed her to have an abortion, repeatedly asking her, "Don't you think it'd just be better for you and the child to just have an abortion?"[52] She resisted this pressure and carried her pregnancy to term.

Anne B. was released from segregation after nearly three months and placed in the general population at another women's prison in the state. She told us that in this new facility she had been continuously harassed by prison staff about what she had told investigators and whether she reported who impregnated her. The doctor at this prison reportedly refused to treat Anne B. during her pregnancy, and she had to receive prenatal care from a doctor in a nearby town.

In February, 1996, we learned of another female prisoner who had been sexually assaulted by a male officer during an August 1995 stay in a hospital at the Huron Valley Men's Prison, where she had been sent for treatment for an ongoing medical problem. The prisoner had taken a shower and was toweling off in the bathroom when the officer, an employee of the HVM who had been guarding her, entered the room and had sexual relations with her. Subsequent to the incident, she requested a pregnancy test and was found to be pregnant. The baby was determined by a paternity test to be his, and he was charged with fourth degree

---

[51] Telephone interview, Deborah LaBelle, February 27, 1995. LaBelle had another experience of being unable to locate a client within the correctional system in December 1994. The prisoner was transferred to HVM from another facility, but no one had been notified.

[52] Interview, Michigan, March 1994.

criminal sexual misconduct, to which he pled no contest.[53] A person familiar with the case told us that after the prisoner decided to report the officer, she was harassed by other officers at Scott. One officer reportedly told her that it might make her time easier if she did not pursue the case.

Privacy Violations

Despite clear decisions in U.S. courts and relevant international law, Michigan has no policy in place to ensure the privacy of incarcerated women. MDOC makes no distinction between male and female corrections officers in conducting pat-frisks or searches of a prisoner's cell or the shower and toilet areas.[54] In practice, male corrections officers patrol these areas and are in a position to view incarcerated women in a state of undress or while using the shower or toilet facilities.

MDOC's use of male corrections staff in the housing units of the women's prisons and the dearth of restrictions on their job assignments appear to be rooted in a 1982 federal court decision, *Griffin v. Michigan Dept. of Corrections.*[55] *Griffin* was a class action lawsuit filed by female corrections officers who alleged that they were unfairly discriminated against, in violation of Title VII of the Civil Rights Act banning sex discrimination, because MDOC limited their job assignments to female facilities and they were denied positions in the over twenty men's prisons. These assignments, in turn, adversely affected their professional advancement. At the time, the MDOC restricted female corrections officers from working on the housing units in the men's prisons for the security and safety of the female officers and for reasons of prisoner privacy and rehabilitation.[56]

The judge in *Griffin* flatly dismissed the contention that prisoners had a constitutionally protected right to privacy. He found that:

> Any contention by [MDOC] that they are entitled to the Title VII
> [bona fide occupational qualification] exception on the basis of

---

[53] Interview, Bob Greenstein, attorney who assisted in the representation of the prisoner, November 5, 1996.

[54] "Search and Arrest of Prisoners, Employees and Visitors," MDOC Policy Directive, No. PD-DWA-30.05, April 27, 1989.

[55] *Griffin v. Michigan Dept. of Corrections*, 654 F. Supp. 690 (E. D. Mich. 1982).

[56] Ibid., pp. 698-699.

> the prisoner's right to privacy . . . is without merit. Prisoners do not possess any protected right under the Constitution against being viewed while naked by corrections officers of the opposite sex.[57]

The judge's blunt denial to prisoners of a constitutionally protected right to privacy was made without reference to or consideration of any legal precedent and was strikingly inconsistent with similar decisions from other jurisdictions that predated *Griffin.* Prior to 1982, other courts repeatedly recognized that prisoners had a constitutionally protected right of privacy, including the right to be protected from being unduly observed while naked or while using the toilet.[58] Where the employment rights of corrections officers were at issue, the courts directed the state to balance the equal employment opportunities of the corrections officers with the need to protect the prisoners' right to privacy. *Griffin,* however, decided otherwise.

MDOC has chosen to rely on *Griffin* rather than on other federal court decisions since *Griffin* that ordered or allowed prison officials to protect prisoners from unwanted and unwarranted intrusions on their privacy by guards of the opposite sex.[59] The court did not address the privacy rights of female prisoners which subsequent courts have acknowledged are entitled to a different analysis. A number of decisions have specifically dealt with the role of male corrections officers, upholding or directing limitations on cross-gender pat-downs or frisks by corrections officers of the opposite sex,[60] and permitting the removal of male officers from the housing units.[61] In some of these decisions, the court has

---

[57] Ibid., p. 703.

[58] See, for example, *Lee v. Downs,* 641 F. 2d 1117 (4th Cir. 1981); *Harden v. Dayton Human Rehabilitation,* 520 F. Supp. 769 (S.D. Ohio 1981); *Bowling v. Enomoto,* 514 F. Supp. 201 (N.D. Cal. 1981); *Forts v. Ward,* 621 F. 2d 1210 (2d Cir. 1980).

[59] See *Canedy v. Boardman,* 16 F. 3d 183 (7th Cir. 1994); *Jordan v. Gardner,* 986 F. 2d 1521 (9th Cir. 1993); *Grummet v. Rushen,* 779 F. 2d. 491 (9th Cir. 1985); *Hardin v. Stynchcomb,* 691 F. 2d 1364 (11th Cir. 1982), rehearing denied, 696 F. 2d 1007 (11th Cir. 1983).

[60] *Jordan,* p.1521; *Smith v. Fairman,* 678 F.2d 52 (7th Cir. 1982). See also *Madyun v. Franzen,* 704 F.2d 954 (7th Cir. 1983), cert. denied, 464 U.S. 996 (1983).

[61] *Torres v. Wisconsin Department of Health and Social Services,* 859 F. 2d 1523 (7th Cir. 1988), cert. denied, 489 U.S. 1017 (1989), and cert. denied, 489 U.S. 1092 (1989).

explicitly stated that *Griffin* is the exception rather than the rule.[62] Strikingly, in contrast MDOC's combative approach to *Glover* and its tendency to appeal virtually every adverse district court ruling, it did not appeal *Griffin*.

Abusive Pat-Frisks

MDOC does train corrections officers in the proper procedure for conducting pat-frisks: they should use the back of their hand, rather than the palm, when searching the chest and genital areas.[63] MDOC policy requires each nonhousing corrections officer to search at least five "randomly selected" prisoners per shift. These searches are intended to prevent prisoners from possessing contraband; under departmental policy "no search shall be conducted for the purpose of harassing or humiliating a prisoner."[64]

Nonetheless, male corrections officers frequently abuse their power to conduct random pat-frisks in a degrading and sexually hostile manner. During pat-frisks and pat-searches, male officers often use their open hands and fingers to grope or grip a women's breasts and nipples, vagina, buttocks, anus, and thighs. They reportedly target certain women, usually the younger ones, while older, long-term prisoners are rarely frisked. Joann F. told us:

> The male officers sit by the door to the kitchen and shake the women down as they leave. We watch the way they do it and who they pick. I watched one who felt a woman down in front of everyone else as she left. It's always male officers at the door in the kitchen who do the shakedowns.[65]

---

[62] See, for example, *Canedy*, p. 183.

[63] Human Rights Watch researchers who visited Scott and Crane were pat-searched by female corrections officers who used the back of their hand when searching the chest and groin.

[64] "Search and Arrest of Prisoners, Employees and Visitors," MDOC Policy Directive, PD-DWA-30.05, April 27, 1989, p. 4.

[65] Interview, Michigan, March 1994.

Carol H. noted, "The [women] look ashamed because they have the officer pawing at their body. It depends on what you look like, what you have on. You can guess who and when they are going to shake a [woman] down."[66]

Corrections officers have used the frisks and pat-searches to exercise undue power and control over incarcerated women. When ordered to submit to a frisk or pat-search, a woman must comply or risk disciplinary action. In some instances, women who have requested that a female corrections officer conduct the frisk or who have pulled away during an offensive frisk have received major misconduct tickets for disobeying a direct order. Such tickets have resulted in administrative segregation and loss of good time and disciplinary credits. According to one grievance we reviewed, prisoner Maxine Q. was being pat-frisked by Officer W when, she alleged, he cupped her breasts and then groped her vagina as he ran his hands between her legs. Maxine Q. pulled away and requested the presence of a female officer. A second prisoner who witnessed the frisk contacted a female officer. Maxine Q. then agreed to continue the frisk. The male officer wrote two misconduct tickets against her for disobeying a direct order to submit to a frisk and for creating a disturbance, both of which constitute a serious disciplinary offense. In another incident, a prisoner was found guilty of assaulting a resident unit officer (RUO) and placed in segregation after she pushed the male officer's hands off her breasts during a pat-frisk. Another prisoner had previously filed a grievance against the same RUO for fondling her breasts and groping her during a pat-frisk.

On June 15, 1995, MDOC introduced a housing unit policy requiring female prisoners to wear bras.[67] In some instances, officers have required female prisoners to lift their shirts in order to ascertain whether or not they are complying with that policy.

While the policy stipulates that a strip search should be performed by employees of the same sex as the prisoner, it creates several broad exceptions. A male staff member may strip search a female prisoner he is assigned to transport outside the facility or in case of emergency. A male supervisor may be present during a strip search if his presence is "required by policy."[68]

---

[66] Interview, Michigan, March 1994.

[67] Housing Unit Rules, Crane Correctional Facility, effective June 6, 1995.

[68] Ibid.

Inappropriate Visual Surveillance
Housing Units

Crane currently houses 447 women in an open dormitory setting.[69] Initially, there were four units per building, with each unit separated into a cubicle with two or four women per cubicle. The cubicles were placed against the walls with six- to eight-foot partitions on the sides and front providing privacy. MDOC has now begun to eliminate the partitions in front of and between the cubicles, thereby eliminating all privacy. A woman prisoner reported being called on by MDOC to assist in the removal of the partitions. Moreover, as of early 1996, the majority of the housing units at Crane have all male officers. All the assistant unit managers are male. Female prisoners report being forced to dress and undress under the direct supervision of officers and staff of the opposite gender.

On January 8, 1996 Michigan prisoners' rights attorney Deborah LaBelle filed a motion in federal district court, as part of the ongoing *Glover* litigation, protesting the removal of privacy partitions in the women's housing units at Crane.[70] To date, attorneys pursuing the motion have received over 200 letters from women incarcerated at Crane noting that the loss of privacy has caused "the loss of their last vestiges of dignity." Prisoners report in these letters that:

- officers come and go without announcing themselves;

- it is extremely hard to dress without being in full view of the other inmates, along with many male officers;

- it is not right that they have to be subjected to this open dorm atmosphere with the majority of officers being male;

- they live in an open dorm and are subject to constant viewing from any individual passing their unit. They do not even have space to get dressed

---

[69] The housing of prisoners in an open dormitory setting is a direct result of overcrowding in the Crane facility. This overcrowding began in early 1994, after MDOC closed the Annex at Crane and moved all the prisoners into the prison's main building. In order to accommodate the new prisoners, MDOC housed them in what was formerly an open recreation area. MDOC argued in court that this was a temporary measure. However, it has continued the practice to date.

[70] *Glover v. Johnson,* Civil Action File No. 77-71229, January 8, 1996.

in the living area, and if they reach out their hands while dressing and so
does their neighbor, they can touch one another; and

the officers walk in at every opportunity without prior notice, sometimes
catching them nude or in various other stages of undress.

In mid-1996, the court ruled that the January 8 motion was within its
jurisdiction pursuant to *Glover*, and the judge stated his intent to visit the facility.
The visit has not yet occurred. However, during a recent visit to Crane pursuant
to the *Neal/Nunn* class action suit, a visit which was discontinued in the middle
because of a temporary stay of the suit granted to MDOC by the district court of
appeals, attorneys acting for the women prisoners reported that in one of the units,
partitions have been reinstalled. This is a positive step. However, the new
partitions are only four feet in height, and as the cubicle areas are double-bunked,
the women on the top bunk in particular will still be vulnerable to constant viewing
by male officers.

Searches of the Showers and Toilets

Prisoners we interviewed stated that some male corrections officers
routinely patrol the showers and toilet areas while the women are using these
facilities. Such checks, ostensibly a means to insure that no sexual misconduct is
occurring between prisoners, are entirely unwarranted, since the facilities are
designed particularly to allow for proper monitoring.[71] In practice, however, male
corrections officers appear to abuse their authority freely to conduct "searches";
they fail to announce their presence in the area and pull back shower curtains on
prisoners to comment or stare. At times, this occurs even after a prisoner has been
asked to identify herself and show her face. Carol H. told us that officers come into
the bathrooms while they are in use to "chitchat" or get water. As she put it:

The women can complain and bitch, but it doesn't do any good.
The [officers] pull the curtains back and look. There is an
agreement that male [officers] could look under the curtain, and
as long as the feet were in the right position, they would not pull
back the curtain. But, they do it anyway. . . . If we complain, the

---

[71] The shower curtains do not extend to the floor but expose part of the prisoner's legs to
enable corrections staff to determine how many people are in the shower and whether there
is any misconduct. Similarly, toilet doors do not fully cover a woman when standing up,
and conceal only her shoulders and below when sitting down.

> male guards respond, "I can do what I damn well please" or,
> "Well, we've got to have shower checks."[72]

When Carol H. objected to the officer's conduct, he responded, "You don't have anything I haven't seen before." She filed a grievance that was denied, she was told, because officers are permitted to conduct shower checks.

Medical Appointments

Male corrections officers have also accompanied women on gynecological visits and while female prisoners are giving birth, and remained in the examination or delivery room. One prisoner, Nina L., filed a grievance over the lack of privacy during gynecological exams, stating that she felt uncomfortable discussing her medical condition or undressing in front of the male officer. She asked the officer if he would step outside while she was examined, but he refused. Nina L. pursued the grievance until it was reviewed by the warden, who told her that it was prison policy for the officer to keep the prisoner in his sight, and that the prisoner could have refused the outside medical visit.[73] In other words, the prisoner was expected to choose between foregoing medical treatment or undressing in front of a male officer.

Male officers have also reportedly watched prisoners giving birth. Michelle T., a former prisoner, told us that she was accompanied by two male officers in the delivery room while she was giving birth. According to Michelle T., the officers handcuffed her to the bed while she was in labor and positioned

---

[72] Interview, Michigan, March 1994.

[73] A privacy screen is reportedly provided during gynecological exams to shield parts of the prisoner's body, but the officer may still hear her conversation with the doctor. Nina L. asserted that she would have to undress in front of the male officer. The investigation into her complaint never established that a privacy screen was indeed provided.

themselves where they could view her genital area while giving birth.[74] She told us they made derogatory comments about her throughout the delivery.[75]

THE SYSTEM'S RESPONSE

MDOC Director Kenneth L. McGinnis has acknowledged that sexual misconduct does occur within Michigan's prisons.[76] However, he has repeatedly contended that the department has "zero tolerance for such behavior,"[77] despite the contrary findings of the Women's Commission, the Legislative Correction's Ombudsman, and the U.S. Department of Justice. Unsurprisingly, in light of its failure to recognize the problem of sexual misconduct, MDOC has also failed to take adequate steps to respond to this abuse. In particular, the department's grievance, investigatory, and disciplinary procedures and practices and its manner of treating prisoners who have complained of sexual misconduct are in urgent need of reform. Moreover, the role of the state criminal justice system in investigating

---

[74] In Britain, revelations about the similar treatment of pregnant inmates recently erupted into a public scandal, which led the British prison authorities to modify their policies. In January 1996, a British television news show aired the story of a pregnant prisoner who was chained and handcuffed at times during her twelve-hour labor. The public outcry over the practice caused the British Prison Service not only to bar the chaining and handcuffing of pregnant prisoners once they have entered the maternity unit, but also to require officers to keep guard outside of the ward instead of within the room behind a screen. "Prisons modify maternity rule," *The Guardian*, January 16, 1996; George Jones, Minister defends handcuffing," *The Telegraph*, January 10, 1996. As one commentator noted with regard to the practice, "To most people, the chaining of women prisoners up to the point of giving birth will seem a monstrosity. It has occurred because the interests of women have been ignored in an orgy of security resulting from the misdeeds of men." Stephen Shaw, letter to the editor, *The Independent*, December 12, 1996.

[75] Interview, Ann Arbor, March 28, 1994. Michelle T. also reported that when she went into labor, she was placed in leg irons and belly chains to go to the hospital. Once at the hospital, the doctor told her to walk to assist her labor. She was required to do so by the guards while still in leg irons.

[76] Deposition of Kenneth McGinnis, Circuit Court for the County of Wayne, May 1, 1995, p. 83 [hereinafter McGinnis Deposition].

[77] Press Release, Michigan Department of Corrections, January 7, 1993.

and prosecuting criminal sexual misconduct needs to be enhanced and its record improved.

The Right to an Effective Remedy

As discussed in the legal background chapter of this report, international human rights law obligates national governments not only to prohibit torture and cruel, inhuman, or degrading treatment, but also to ensure that when such abuses occur, they can be reported and fully and fairly investigated without the complainant fearing punishment or retaliation from the authorities.[78] In addition, under U.S. law, prisoners are also guaranteed access to the courts to challenge prison conditions or other prison problems.

Flawed Grievance and Investigatory Procedures

Michigan has both general grievance and investigatory procedures that can be applied to sexual misconduct. The state's grievance procedure, in principle, allows prisoners to challenge "alleged violations of policy and procedure, unsatisfactory conditions of confinement, official acts, or denial of rights which directly affect them." It is a three-stage process which allows for a first-stage internal complaint to a grievance coordinator, a second stage appeal to the warden, and a third stage appeal to the director of MDOC itself. At each stage, both prisoners and staff are required to respond to and/or appeal grievances within proscribed time periods. As with grievance procedures in other states, Michigan requires the prisoner to consult informally with the staff person involved before filing a formal grievance. The only exceptions to this process are grievances regarding racial discrimination or staff corruption, which may be submitted directly to the director. Whether sexual misconduct is considered a form of staff corruption is not expressly indicated.

According to MDOC, three potential mechanisms may be employed to investigate charges of sexual misconduct raised by prisoners: institutional investigations, internal affairs investigations, and referrals to the state police. Which mechanism is used depends on the nature and seriousness of the allegation and the individual involved.[79]

---

[78] For a detailed discussion of international law and due process standards, see the legal background chapter of this report.

[79] Written response from Michigan Department of Corrections to written questions posed by Human Rights Watch, June 1994 (on file with Human Rights Watch).

Inspectors operating within the prisons commonly endeavor to substantiate the prisoner's claim through conversations with the officer, the prisoner and any witnesses or other relevant parties. The results of this investigation are then shared with a supervisor who makes a recommendation to the warden, usually orally, about what additional steps, if any, should occur. According to an April 1994 MDOC policy directive, whenever investigations conducted at this level indicate that an employee is "alleged to have committed criminal activity of a major magnitude,"[80] including sexual assault, prison officials must "immediately notify" the department's internal affairs section.

While these procedures exist, there appears to be no clear guidelines to determine when a particular mechanism, alone or in conjunction with another, will be used, and prison officials retain a considerable amount of discretion in determining whether or not an investigation of whatever sort should be initiated.[81] Moreover, in practice they have often effectively denied women the right to complain of such abuse and are fraught at all levels of the process with a bias against prisoner testimony and conflicts of interest. Finally, the process of filing a complaint of sexual misconduct or having it investigated routinely subjects complainants to retaliation and punishment.

Effective Denial of the Right to Complain

While Michigan's grievance procedure may not be flawed on its face and has been certified under the CRIPA process described in the legal background chapter of this report, it is highly ineffective for reporting and addressing sexual misconduct. Problems begin at the initial, informal step in the process requiring prisoners to confront the officer against whom they are filing a grievance. Where prisoners fail to take this step, their grievances have been rejected.[82] Yet, the fact

---

[80] MDOC policy directive, No. 01.01.140, section H(1), April 4, 1994.

[81] In his May 1995 deposition, Director McGinnis stated that "in all probability" an allegation of a prisoner having sexual relations with an officer would be reported to internal affairs, but that it would depend "on the circumstances and the level of information available." He went on to note that an allegation of sexual harassment would "probably not" be referred to internal affairs, but would "probably be done locally."

[82] In one case that we investigated, a prisoner complained against an officer in 1988 for staring at her while she was partially undressed. According to her grievance, the prisoner was dressing when she heard the officer's radio and tried to conceal herself by turning her back to the door. When she turned around, the officer was standing in the door and had turned his radio off, apparently so that she would not hear him. The reviewing captain

that they will have to confront their abuser often deters women from reporting sexual abuse for fear of the retribution discussed in more detail below. In reviewing MDOC's grievance procedure, the DOJ stated that this requirement has the purpose, intent, or effect of intimidating the inmates and discouraging the filing of grievances.[83]

Moreover, even if the prisoner were to succeed in lodging a complaint without first confronting the officer, her complaint is likely to be made known to him almost immediately. While Human Rights Watch believes that the officer should have the right to confront the complainant, MDOC often allows this to happen when he is still in a contact position over her. This further exposes prisoners to retaliation and so deters them from filing grievances of sexual misconduct that it effectively denies them their right to complain. Moreover, her complaint is often made know to persons not directly related to the incident.

Bias Against Prisoner Testimony

Where women prisoners do decide to lodge a formal grievance of sexual misconduct, they face a review and investigatory procedure that is tainted by a pervasive bias against prisoner testimony. Corrections officers responding to grievances of sexual misconduct generally deny that the incidents ever occurred. In one grievance we reviewed, an officer responded to a prisoner's complaint of an offensive pat-frisk in the following manner, "I shake down [frisk] everybody the same way, no exceptions. . . . The balance of the allegations are *untrue*. At *no* time did these allegations ever happen or occur [emphasis in the original]." In another grievance, the officer responded, "The statement in this grievance is a flat out lie and therefore there is not merit to it." In a third, the officer asserted that the prisoner wrote the grievance as a means to avoid a disciplinary ticket, stating, "This grievance has been filed in an attempt to get out of one misconduct. . . . This grievance has been falsified and is totally untrue." On this basis, the grievance is then denied.

The officers' denials do not, in and of themselves, constitute a violation of the procedure; some grievances may result from misunderstandings or prisoners' mischaracterization of a situation. And prisoners are granted the right, at their own initiative, to lodge an appeal. However, the problem is that reviewing

---

rejected the grievance simply because the prisoner did not attempt to resolve it verbally with the officer before filing a formal grievance. The warden upheld the captain's decision.

[83] Letter from Deval Patrick, assistant attorney general, U.S. Department of Justice, to John Engler, governor, state of Michigan, March 27, 1995.

officers—warden, captains, or sergeants—have often accepted without further inquiry the accused's blunt assertions that the prisoner lied. In one case, a prisoner filed grievances against two officers, one of whom was in training, for standing in the showers and watching the prisoners. The responding officer denied any unprofessional conduct. When the prisoner appealed her grievance to Warden Carol Howes at Crane, Howes responded that action would be taken where there were instances of abuse or where the prisoner's claim could be verified. She deemed the prisoner's own complaint insufficient to support the allegation of abuse and dismissed it.

As with the grievance procedure, the integrity of the investigative process is often compromised by a bias against prisoner testimony. MDOC proceeds on the assumption that any statement made by a prisoner is *per se* not credible and insufficient in and of itself to support a charge against a corrections employee. Documentation we obtained reveals that MDOC has repeatedly stated that it will not uphold an employee's dismissal where the only evidence of inappropriate or illegal conduct is the prisoner's testimony. While prisoners must prove the veracity of their allegations of sexual misconduct by prison staff, their words and the words of other prisoners around them who may have witnessed the incident are deemed insufficient. Meanwhile, a corrections employee's statement is presumed, *prima facie*, to be a true and accurate portrayal of what transpired.[84]

From our interviews and the documentation we obtained, it seems that after a prisoner comes forward to allege sexual misconduct, she is repeatedly interviewed and required to prepare a written statement. The accused employee is also questioned informally or receives a short set of questions designed by the investigator. These questions often require no more than a yes or no response from the officer and can be fairly leading, such as: "Have you today or previously had any contact with ___ that is sexual in nature or that could be considered to be sexual by her?" "Have you ever been alone with ___ for any reason, either today or previously?" "Have you had any contact of any kind with ___ either today or

---

[84] In a June 6, 1995 deposition, Warden Joan Yukins of Scott Correctional Facility stated, "If that was the only information we had, a prisoner's word against a staff member's word, no other substantiating evidence, no other documents, no other witnesses, the staff member's word would take precedence." Deposition of Warden Joan Yukins, in the circuit court for the County of Wayne, June 6, 1995 [hereinafter Yukins Deposition].

previously?"[85]   Their responses in the negative to the questions posed have sometimes proven sufficient to close any further inquiry into a prisoner's charges.

Bias against prisoner testimony exists even in cases where prisoners pass polygraph examinations. Kim J., a prisoner discussed above, passed a polygraph examination regarding her charges that an officer raped her. The accused officer refused to submit to a polygraph exam. MDOC declined to proceed with any disciplinary action because, according to documents we obtained, it "[does] not recognize prisoner testimony, nor [does it] recognize results of polygraph examinations."[86]

This tendency to reject prisoner testimony out of hand has had a chilling effect on the reporting of sexual misconduct and has allowed abusive staff to continue working unchecked, free to abuse other prisoners. In 1986 a prisoner at Crane asserted that she had sexual relations with a corrections officer, Don Davenport, in exchange for favorable treatment. When she stopped meeting him, she allegedly began to receive misconduct tickets from this officer and others on his shift.[87] Three additional prisoners were interviewed who substantiated various

---

[85] In another case, a captain accused of overfamiliarity received the following:

> 1. You are sometimes in a hurry to end roll call because you want to visit a prisoner early in the morning by the name of ___.
> 2. You are seen many days spending a lot of time with ___ on the back yard.
> 3. You have a relationship going on with ___.
> 4. You have sent clothing items to ___ by direct mail, or you had a third part mail the items in.
> Please submit to me in writing as to where and when these overfamiliar actions took place. Please explain fully..."

The captain's "full" responses were a simple "no" to questions two and four, and a sentence statement in one and three that he always conducted himself professionally and according to rules.

[86] Memorandum from Patrick Foltz, acting deputy warden, Florence Crane Women's Facility, to Carol Howes, warden, Florence Crane Women's Facility, October 24, 1988. The warden of Crane wrote to attorney LaBelle and told her "they will *not* uphold an employee's dismissal where the only evidence is the prisoner's word against staff that an inappropriate or illegal action took place" (emphasis in the original). Letter from Carol R. Howes, warden, Florence Crane Women's Facility, to Deborah LaBelle, attorney, October 26, 1988.

[87] Memorandum from Patrick Foltz, acting deputy warden, Florence Crane Women's facility, to investigative file, Michigan Department of Corrections, July 29, 1986.

elements of the prisoner's account.[88] Davenport and a second officer, who was partially implicated, denied the allegations. The institution discontinued its investigation for undisclosed reasons within two weeks, three days after receiving notice from the county prosecutor that he would take no further action.[89] No separate disciplinary inquiry was instituted, and Davenport remained employed at Crane. He was subsequently convicted in 1989 for arranging an attack on a female prisoner after she reported that he was bringing drugs into the facility and sexually harassing prisoners.

Even a series of complaints from prisoners indicating a pattern of abuse by a particular officer sometimes proved inadequate to substantiate charges of sexual abuse where the only victims and witnesses were prisoners. In March 1993 four prisoners at Scott alleged a pattern of sexual harassment by the resident unit officer (RUO) on their unit, ranging from abusive pat-frisks to inappropriate shower checks. One prisoner asserted that the RUO fondled and groped her during a frisk while another complained that he tried to pull the shower curtain back while she was showering. A third prisoner was found guilty of assaulting the officer and put in segregation after she pulled away during a frisk when the RUO fondled her breasts. The women's allegations of mistreatment were supported by letters and statements from other prisoners on the unit.[90] The investigator dismissed the prisoners' allegations as a conspiracy to remove the officer from the unit. In so doing, the investigator cited interviews he had with prisoners who had not raised complaints, but gave no reason why those prisoners were deemed more credible than the ones who reported the abuse and the ones who prepared statements.

In addition to frequently dismissing prisoners' allegations out of hand, MDOC has sometimes also failed to respond to corrections staff's reports of a pattern of sexual misconduct by particular officers. Between January and October 1992, staff and prisoners reported that a food service supervisor at Scott was overfamiliar or sexually involved with various prisoners. In the first incident, in

---

[88] Michigan State Police, Standard Crime Report, No. 43-1352-86, July 1986.

[89] Memorandum from Patrick Foltz, acting deputy warden, Florence Crane Women's Facility, to Carol Howes, warden, Florence Crane Women's Facility, August 11, 1986.

[90] It was also not the first time that a prisoner had alleged that this officer had engaged in sexual misconduct. During our investigation, we reviewed a grievance filed by another prisoner in 1991 alleging similar abuse by the same officer. That prisoner's grievance was also denied and she received a ticket for a major misconduct for "interference with the administration of rules."

January 1992, an officer reported finding a prisoner in this employee's car while the prisoner worked a maintenance detail.[91] The food service director dismissed the officer's report because another employee witnessed the prisoner standing a few cars away, despite the latter having arrived on the scene later.[92] Although the food service supervisor received a written reprimand following the car incident and an oral reprimand subsequent to a separate incident, the prison administrators made no apparent effort to investigate a possible pattern of ongoing misconduct with a series of prisoners.

In Stacy Barker's case, prisoners and staff repeatedly alleged seeing Officer Keahy leaving her cell when he was working the night shift. The institution initiated an investigation but took no action against the officer for over a year and a half, until he was discovered engaging in sex with another prisoner. As noted above, he was later tried and convicted in December 1991. Similarly, no action was taken against Raymond Raby for over a year, despite several reports by sergeants and his supervisor that he was engaged in inappropriate sexual conduct: in one report, his supervisor stated he saw Raby leaving a prisoner's cell with his shirt untucked; in another, Raby was allegedly seen running away from the women's housing area. While Raby was suspended temporarily, he was later reinstated for a year despite these reports. He was finally dismissed after he confessed to the state police that he was having sex with prisoners on a nightly basis.[93] He was never prosecuted.

Conflicts of Interest

The legitimacy of the grievance and investigatory procedures is undermined completely in cases where officers are assigned to investigate themselves. According to Joan Yukins, the warden of Scott Correctional Facility,

---

[91] Memorandum from Emmett R. Baylor, Jr., deputy warden, Scott Correctional Facility, to S. Rizzo, food service director, Scott Correctional Facility, January 6, 1992.

[92] Memorandum from S. Rizzo, food service director, Scott Correctional Facility, to Joan Yukins, warden, Scott Correctional facility, January 16, 1992.

[93] Telephone interview, Deborah LaBelle, attorney, February 27, 1995.

as late as 1995 it was departmental policy to allow an employee to participate in investigating a grievance against him or her.[94]

While the creation of institutional inspectors and an internal affairs section are important steps toward guaranteeing the impartiality of the grievance and investigatory procedures, we found that the credibility of such investigations is still undermined by many of the same procedural irregularities that we discovered with respect to the grievance procedure, including bias against prisoner testimony, conflicts of interest, and fear of retaliation or punishment.

In one 1988 case that we reviewed, a male captain accused of inappropriately strip searching a prisoner was placed in charge of the investigation into his own misconduct. After interviewing the prisoner himself and obtaining exculpatory statements from officers under his supervision, the captain concluded that the prisoner's allegation had no merit. The warden upheld the captain's finding and did not question the inherent conflict of interest in an officer investigating himself.

The prisoner involved subsequently received a ticket for major misconduct for interference with the administration of rules—a ticket that can result in segregation and loss of good time credit—for having made a "false accusation." The hearing officer on the ticket determined that the captain would have to have intentionally engaged in conduct that could affect his rank and continued employment in order for the prisoner's allegation to be true. In other words, in the prison administration's eyes, no corrections staff person would knowingly engage in misconduct that could affect his employment; therefore, the prisoner must have lied.

In August 1992 a deputy warden at Scott headed an investigation in which he and eleven other staff members were implicated in various acts of overfamiliarity with prisoners. The investigation was triggered by an anonymous letter sent to the legislative ombudsman. The deputy warden was put in charge of questioning the staff and reporting back to the warden. Not surprisingly, the deputy warden cleared himself of the allegations, stating in his memorandum to the warden, "This is the most ludicrous, ridiculous, trumped up lie I have ever been

---

[94] In a June 6, 1995 deposition, Joan Yukins, the warden at Scott facility, testified that until June 5, 1995, when a new policy was put into effect, it was usual that the officer cited in the grievance would make the response to the grievance. Under the new policy, another person would be called upon to investigate the grievance. Yukins Deposition.

accused of. I unequivocally deny these charges . . ."[95] To our knowledge, no further review was conducted.

In one case that we investigated, Phyllis W. reported a corrections officer for continuously harassing her and making comments about her buttocks, charges that the officer flatly rejected. Although he was the accused, the officer went on to participate in the "investigation" into Phyllis W.'s grievance, which entailed an interview with her by the officer and his superior. During the interview, Phyllis W. refused to answer several questions and appealed her grievance to the second level of review, wherein she restated her allegations. The appeals officer apparently considered the previous interview to be adequate and rejected her grievance. He wrote:

> Your grievance has been thoroughly investigated. The investigation failed to find conclusive evidence to support your claim. Because your claim has not been substantiated, no further action is recommended.

The Role of the State Police

Not all investigations into alleged sexual misconduct are handled exclusively by the given prison or MDOC. Cases of suspected criminal conduct are at times referred to the state police. MDOC's internal affairs section coordinates these referrals in conjunction with other departmental investigators.[96] According to a summary of sexual misconduct complaints provided to Human Rights Watch by MDOC, of thirty-nine complaints it recorded at the Crane and Scott facilities in 1994 and 1995, twenty-seven were referred to the state police.[97] However, these referrals did not necessarily result in disciplinary action. Only five of the twenty-seven referrals appear to have been sustained.[98] Of particular concern to Human Rights Watch is that in some instances, referrals to the state police have had the effect of discontinuing the departments own investigation. Thus, as in the

---

[95] Memorandum from Emmett R. Baylor, deputy warden, Scott Correctional Facility, to Joan Yukins, warden, Scott Correctional Facility, August 18, 1992.

[96] MDOC Policy Directive, No. 01.01.140, Section IV.A., April 4, 1994.

[97] Written response from Michigan Department of Corrections to written questions posed by Human Rights Watch, June 1994 (on file with Human Rights Watch).

[98] Ibid.

Davenport case mentioned above, an employee that the state decides not to prosecute may, as a result of the department of correction's failure to pursue its own investigation, also escape sanction for a violation of prison rules.

Retaliation and Punishment

Although MDOC clearly prohibits reprisal for the filing of a grievance,[99] the threat of retaliation pervades the prison environment in Michigan. Such retaliation can function as punishment for having reported misconduct[100] or as a means of coercing prisoners to acquiesce to unwanted sexual relations with corrections employees, and acts as a powerful deterrent to the reporting of sexual misconduct by corrections staff.

From the outset, the accused employee is informed of the name and prison identification number of the complainant, even though it is often unnecessary to reveal the identity of the prisoner. While, as noted earlier, Human Rights Watch supports the right of the accused to confront his accuser, we believe that MDOC does not take adequate steps to ensure that this does not result in retaliation against the prisoner. For example, in one April 1992 investigation, the deputy warden for custody requested an employee's phone bills to document allegations that the officer had permitted prisoners to call his home. The request was accompanied by the heading "staff investigation for over familiarization with . . ." and listed the names of several prisoners. The officer was still in a contact position over the prisoners when the request was made, thus unduly exposing them to the possibility of retaliation.

Prisoners who have themselves reported sexual misconduct through the grievance or investigatory process, or those whose abuse was revealed by others, have been subjected repeatedly to room searches, pat-frisks and disciplinary tickets. According to attorney Deborah LaBelle, "harassment is constant and insidious" for

---

[99] The grievance policy provides that prisoners will not be penalized in any way for exercising the right to grieve and staff are to "avoid any action that gives the appearance of reprisal for using the grievance procedure or for assisting other prisoners . . . in its use." MDOC, "Grievance Policy—Prisoner/Parolee," MDOC Policy Directive No. 03.02.130 March 21, 1988.

[100] Such retaliation is not limited to women who come forward to report allegations of sexual abuse; it extends to any prisoner who challenges her treatment by corrections authorities. Women active in the *Glover* lawsuit, both named plaintiffs and those who have attempted to exercise their constitutional right to equal education and vocational opportunities pursuant to *Glover*, have experienced retaliation not only from corrections officers but also from those at higher levels in MDOC.

those who challenge sexual abuse: "They receive misconducts for the most minute infractions of rules that are not generally enforced against anyone else."[101] Barker described her experience after allegations came to light:

> It's normal to do it [frisk] a certain amount of times. But at times I can be shaken down before I leave the unit, when I come in, while I'm in the unit. And when I'm the only one that this is happening to, I feel that's harassment. Certain officers just say certain things. And it's just really hard being in a situation like this and speaking up about something.[102]

Charlene Billups-Hein, for example, was repeatedly ticketed for minor infractions. After she came forward, officers and prisoners treated her, in her words, "like the bubonic plague," making derisive comments and encouraging others to avoid or ignore her.[103] She told us that whenever she walked by one particular officer, he told those around him to shut up, and they stared at her as she walked by.

Gloria P., who was also involved in a different investigation of an officer, has had similar experiences. She told us:

> Officer C would follow me everywhere I went. He was the yard officer. Or, he would stand by another officer and talk about me in a loud voice, but not talking to me. To this day, he says, "I hate you" whenever he sees me.[104]

When her father or brother visit, according to Gloria P., "He would tell other prisoners, 'She don't like p-u-s-s-y-s [sic].'"

---

[101] Telephone interview, Deborah LaBelle, attorney, February 27, 1995.

[102] Deposition of Stacy Barker, January 13, 1994. Barker currently has a suit pending against MDOC for the sexual abuse she has endured while incarcerated. The deposition was taken by MDOC pursuant to this litigation.

[103] Interview, Michigan, March 1994.

[104] Interview, Michigan, May 1994.

In Carol H.'s experience, "To complain, you can file a grievance, but that will bring instant retaliation to you."[105] She observed that when women approach the officer to discuss the grievance informally, as required by departmental policy, the officer will often respond, "Well, if you file that grievance, I will write you up for a misconduct." Carol H. continued, "He's not supposed to do that, it's against policy. The ticket sticks because it's his word against hers." In her experience, prisoners who "want to go home," such as those with short sentences or approaching parole, are less inclined to complain.

People outside the prison who are related to or working with a prisoner have also been forced to endure forms of retaliation ultimately targeted at the prisoners. Christina Kampfner, a clinical psychologist who was permitted under court order to counsel one prisoner who was raped by a corrections officer, reported that she was routinely forced to wait up to two hours before being cleared to enter the prison and repeatedly had to present the court order to gain access.[106] This occurred even though she visited the prison on a regular basis. As a result, she had to leave extended periods of time free and was forced to reduce the number of times she visited the prison. Stacy Barker's family reportedly experienced similar problems. According to Barker, her parents contacted the prison several days prior to a visit to ensure that she had visits available. But when they arrived at the prison they were informed, erroneously, that no visits remained for the month. The visitation date in question happened to be the birthday of Barker's daughter, who had joined her grandparents for the denied visit.

Even if MDOC were to take the welcome step of removing the accused officer from any contact with the complainant, this is no guarantee that the prisoner will escape retaliation. Because complaints are often made known to persons not directly related to the incident, other officers may retaliate against the prisoner on behalf of their colleague. In Joann F.'s experience, a woman can report the misconduct of a corrections officer who consequently may be reprimanded, but the abuses do not necessarily cease because the guilty officer's friends on the force may write misconduct tickets against the complainant.[107] Carol H. has observed a similar pattern of retaliation. As she described it, "If one officer is writing up a prisoner, then it's more apparent what's going on. So they use the good ole boy

---

[105] Interview, Michigan, March 1994.

[106] Interview, Christina Kampfner, clinical psychologist, Ann Arbor, May 17, 1994.

[107] Interview, Michigan, March 1994.

network where others will write her up."[108] Similarly, if an officer said a prisoner did something, other officers would usually vouch for that officer.

Retaliation or the threat or fear of reprisal from corrections staff serves as a very effective way to keep women in sexual relationships with the officers. Within the prisons, some women may enter into seemingly uncoerced sexual relationships with corrections staff. However, women who seek to end these relationships often experience retaliation, hostility and increasingly violent sexual demands. Gloria P. was repeatedly harassed by Officer A. When she learned she was granted parole, she told him she was going home. He reportedly responded, "No you aren't. You are staying with me."[109] She told us she sought to end the relationship with him because he had become ever more hostile and verbally abusive. He began to write her disciplinary tickets and to accost her verbally, often in front of other prisoners and/or officers. The situation worsened until one evening she reportedly cursed at him in front of other officers and received a major misconduct ticket that resulted in the revocation of her parole.

In some cases, prisoners who have accused corrections staff of sexual misconduct have been effectively punished by the institution for coming forward. Often, after alleging sexual misconduct, female prisoners are involuntarily placed in segregation, ostensibly for their own protection, without any charge being filed against them, pending the institution's investigation of their cases. While the prisoner suffers what amounts to punishment for coming forward, often no action is taken against the implicated officer. He generally remains on duty and continues to have responsibilities over and contact with other prisoners. In one case we reviewed from 1990, the institution determined that sufficient evidence existed, including corroborating statements by other staff and prisoners, to refer the case to the Michigan state police. The officer had allegedly cornered and groped a prisoner. While the warden determined that a suspension of the officer was not necessary, she still sent the prisoner to segregation without her consent, supposedly for her own protection. Kim J., mentioned above, was also sent involuntarily to segregation while her charges that an officer raped her were investigated. She was subsequently transferred to a higher-security facility. The officer, to our knowledge, was never disciplined in any way.

The combination of bias against prisoner testimony, conflicts of interest, and fear of retaliation that pervades the MDOC grievance and investigatory procedure makes complaints of sexual misconduct extremely difficult to

---

[108] Interview, Michigan, March 1994.

[109] Interview, Michigan, May 1994.

substantiate. Even if prisoners do decide to complain, their testimony often will not be credited, absent medical evidence or witnesses who are not prisoners. Given the closed nature of the prison environment, such evidence is often very difficult to obtain. Thus, for example, of the thirty-nine reported complaints of sexual misconduct MDOC recorded in 1994 and 1995, only five were sustained.[110]

Inadequate Documentation

One of the biggest obstacles to eradicating sexual misconduct is its invisibility both within and beyond the correctional system. The hidden nature of the problem reflects not only the obstacles to substantiating such complaints, but also MDOC's failure fully to record such complaints and any investigation of them in a consistent and centralized fashion. When allegations of sexual misconduct are not substantiated, no formal record of the complaint is kept with respect to the implicated officer.[111] Thus, an officer may have had several allegations of sexual misconduct lodged against him, but because no complaint was ever substantiated and no disciplinary action was ever taken, the allegations are unlikely to appear in his or her personnel file. Clearly, no officer should be held to account for abuses he or she was not proven to commit. However, the state's failure to keep a formal record of sexual misconduct allegations by the officer named not only renders it unlikely that the future conduct of the officer will be adequately monitored, but also makes it virtually impossible to collect information about a past pattern or practice of alleged sexual misconduct which might prove relevant to substantiating subsequent allegations of abuse.

MDOC officials have noted that any complaints of sexual misconduct, at whatever level, whether substantiated or not, should be referred to a supervisor. However, it is clear that there is no written policy in this regard and no clear department-wide system of keeping track of complaints of or investigations into sexual misconduct. A given correctional facility may or may not be able to report at any specific moment exactly how many complaints of sexual misconduct have been lodged at the facility or in what manner they have been or are being addressed. In addition, no guarantee exists that reports of investigations from within the facility are necessarily contained in monthly reports by the wardens to the director of MDOC. According to Joan Yukins, the warden at Scott, no format exists to report to the central office on a monthly basis regarding investigations of

---

[110] Written response from Michigan Department of Corrections to written questions posed by Human Rights Watch, June 1994.

[111] Yukins Deposition.

overfamiliarity or disciplinary actions, including dismissals taken with respect to them.[112] As a result, legitimate cases of sexual misconduct, valuable evidence in support of complaints of such abuse, the records of known abusers, and the proper oversight of supervisors are falling through the cracks. This not only puts the prisoners at greater risk of sexual misconduct but also makes it more difficult to monitor such abuse effectively. As such, it raises the question of whether MDOC's own figures regarding sexual misconduct, cited above, are reflective of the full scope of the problem.

Impunity
According to MDOC policy, the disciplinary sanction for maintaining an improper relationship with a prisoner, including romantic, sexual or overly familiar relationship, is discharge.[113] While MDOC has actually dismissed staff over the years, we reviewed a significant number of past investigations that reveal that MDOC, instead of dismissing corrections employees found guilty of sexual misconduct, often allowed them to resign or to voluntarily transfer to men's facilities. Director McGinnis has acknowledged that resignation or transfer in lieu of discipline "occurs periodically" in Michigan's facilities,[114] but that such actions usually function as a form of settlement when a dismissal appears unlikely to be upheld during the civil service proceeding or labor relations arbitration that accompanies such sanctions.

Aside from being an inappropriate penalty, the option of resignation in a number of cases has resulted in the rehiring of implicated staff who had never been exonerated of sexual involvement with prisoners. Resignation does not prevent such employees from seeking future employment as corrections officers either with MDOC or elsewhere. Beaster, the residential unit officer who admitted having sexual relations with a prisoner but claimed that she had backed into his erect penis, was permitted to resign. He subsequently worked for the department of corrections in a neighboring state.[115] A second corrections officer was rehired, with back pay, six months after he voluntarily resigned rather than face an investigation into

---

[112] Ibid.

[113] Director's Office Memorandum 1996, Disciplinary Guide and Progressive Penalty Grid, Department of Corrections, State of Michigan (effective September 5, 1996).

[114] McGinnis Deposition.

[115] Telephone interview, Deborah LaBelle, attorney, February 27, 1995.

allegations of sexual misconduct. The institution had collected letters and pictures he sent to the prisoner while she was incarcerated. The officer was suspended three months later for overfamiliarity with another prisoner. A third corrections officer, who resigned from Crane for "romantic involvement" with a prisoner, contacted the institution about future employment. He was informed that he could be reconsidered for employment once the prisoner was no longer at the facility.

While an offer to resign or transfer may occur after an official finding that sexual misconduct took place, it can also be used to sidestep the disciplinary process altogether. In these cases, a employee may resign once faced with the likelihood of a disciplinary hearing before any formal finding of sexual misconduct is made. For example, in one 1992 case we investigated involving a resident unit officer at Scott, the officer denied having sexual relations with the prisoner but then failed a polygraph exam. He was allowed to resign voluntarily in lieu of discipline. Because no disciplinary hearing ever occurred, no record of the employee's suspected activity will be retained by MDOC. The employee may thus seek work elsewhere in the correctional system, and no guarantee exists that his past record of alleged sexual misconduct will be known to his new employers.

Where officers are not offered the option to resign or transfer, they may still be able to escape disciplinary sanction altogether and remain at the facility. Kim J.'s alleged attacker was never investigated thoroughly because the only evidence was her testimony.[116] Another officer who fondled a prisoner's breast while she was asleep was promoted to a RUO position after the investigation closed. He asserted he was merely looking for her identification card. Although she passed a polygraph exam, MDOC decided "from an administrative standpoint there was no evidence of wrongdoing,"[117] while the local prosecutor dropped the case reportedly because the prisoner was the sole witness. In a third case, the department suspended David Rose during his criminal trial for allegedly raping Charlene Billups-Hein, but did not investigate his actions for possible violations of prison rules. In 1993, after his acquittal, MDOC allowed Rose to return to his

---

[116] Memorandum from Patrick Foltz, acting deputy warden, Florence Crane Women's Facility, to Carol Howes, warden, Florence Crane Women's Facility, October 24, 1988. Documentation on the case indicates that Kim J. initially refused to talk to male investigators who questioned her about the allegations and even denied anything occurred. She eventually gave a written statement detailing the incident and submitted to a polygraph exam. It appears the local prosecutor declined to proceed because of Kim J.'s initial denial.

[117] Memorandum from Patrick Foltz, acting deputy warden, Florence Crane Women's Facility, to File, September 21, 1990.

former position at Scott, and even assigned him on occasion to work on the unit where Billups-Hein is incarcerated.[118]   According to a recent deposition of Inspector Howard, at Scott, Rose is once again under "investigation" for sexual misconduct with a prisoner with whom he had been previously reported to be involved, but remains on staff at Scott.[119]

In other cases, where MDOC did take action to dismiss an employee, the dismissal only followed an employee's explicit admission of wrongdoing, even though extensive evidence already existed. Raymond Raby, for example, was repeatedly reprimanded, then suspended, only to return to the institution for a full year before he was finally fired in 1986. He was dismissed only after he admitted to state police that he was sexually involved with prisoners on a nightly basis. In Officer Keahy's case, the institution received numerous reports that he was seen leaving Stacy Barker's room, but failed to take any disciplinary action until he was caught raping another prisoner.[120] As stated earlier, he was subsequently convicted in December 1991 and received two six-month sentences for fourth-degree sexual conduct that he was permitted to serve concurrently.

As noted above, only complaints that exhibit "a reasonable suspicion" of a criminal act will be referred to the Michigan state police.[121] To our knowledge, very few such referrals actually result in prosection. According to MDOC's own figures, of twenty-seven complaints of sexual misconduct referred to the state police in 1994 and 1995, only two were referred for prosecution.[122]

Lack of Independent Oversight

One of the key ways to combat impunity with respect to sexual misconduct in any prison facility is to open the system up to investigation and oversight by outside, independent monitors. Given MDOC's refusal to recognize

---

[118] Telephone interview, Deborah LaBelle, attorney, February 27, 1995.

[119] Deposition of Inspector Howard, Michigan Department of Corrections, April 5, 1995 [hereinafter Howard Deposition].

[120] MDOC did remove the officer from Barker's unit, but put him in a contact position with prisoners in another unit, which simply put those prisoners at risk.

[121] Letter from Nancy Zang, special administrator, Female Offenders Program, Michigan Department of Correction, to Human Rights Watch, October 8, 1996, section 6.

[122] Ibid, section 2.

that it has a problem with such misconduct, it is perhaps not surprising that the Michigan government has been extremely hostile to any sort of independent review of its correctional system. The Michigan Women's Commission, which was appointed by the governor, has its findings of possible sexual misconduct suppressed. The office of the Legislative Corrections Ombudsman, which was established by the state legislature in 1988 to oversee conditions in Michigan's prisons, had its investigatory powers restricted in 1995 and its staff reduced. Moreover, when the Department of Justice, which has the legal authority to investigate constitutional rights violations within state prisons, tried to enter women's prisons in Michigan, the state refused to cooperate with the DOJ's investigation and blocked the DOJ from entering the prisons to conduct interviews.[123] A district court judge rejected the DOJ's effort to obtain a temporary restraining order to enter the prisons. MDOC eventually permitted DOJ attorneys to interview prisoners during regular visiting hours, in the nonconfidential setting of the prison visiting rooms, but denied the DOJ access to the prison more generally.

Michigan Women's Commission

In the months preceding the formal publication of the report of the Women's Commission, both the director and governor went on record to refute allegations of sexual misconduct in the women's prisons. On January 6, 1993, Governor John Engler released a statement asserting that sexual abuse is not a problem in the prison system. He maintained:

> The vast majority of our 14,000 corrections employees perform
> their duties in a manner which is beyond reproach. The few
> which don't are dealt with swiftly and severely. The state of
> Michigan does not tolerate sexual harassment, abuse or
> assaults.[124]

On January 7, 1993, MDOC Director McGinnis released a statement contending that the MDOC has "zero tolerance" for sexual abuse, harassment, or sexual contact between employees and prisoners. He stated further, "Our record of disciplinary

---

[123] In order to gain access to the institution to investigate, the DOJ must file a letter with the state and the institution's directors noting its intention to investigate.

[124] Michigan Department of Corrections, Press Release, January 7, 1993.

actions and dismissals verify this fact."[125]   Responding to McGinnis's statements, the Michigan Women's Commission, its staff, and a former intern, Jenny Elder, met with Director McGinnis in May 1993. Elder had conducted the majority of interviews for the report and had drafted the controversial chapter on women in prison. According to Elder:

> I told him [the director] about the sexual harassment and health care concerns raised in the interviews, such as TB, hepatitis. He was very defensive. McGinnis was not prepared to make any promises to look into these issues. He referred to the grievance procedure as available to the women and that [the MDOC] had not gotten more than one or two letters alleging sexual harassment. He tried to imply the women were lying.[126]

MDOC has since dismissed the information gathered by the Women's Commission about sexual misconduct in the prisons as "unsubstantiated anecdotal information"[127] that was "extremely misleading and written to incite sensationalism rather than fact."[128]   On the other hand, to our knowledge, MDOC has not challenged the commission's findings, based on the same interviews, that sexual harassment was a serious problem in Michigan jails.

Legislative Ombudsman

The Michigan State Legislature created the office of the Legislative Corrections Ombudsman in 1988 to provide an independent and external means to investigate allegations of wrongdoing by MDOC. This was a commendable step, designed to ensure that prisoners alleging abuse by MDOC employees had recourse beyond the department itself. Unfortunately, in late 1995, the Michigan state

---

[125] Interview, Jenny Elder, former intern, Michigan's Women's Commission, March 28, 1994.

[126] Ibid.

[127] Letter from Kenneth McGinnis, director, Michigan Department of Corrections, to Marjie Gaynor, Michigan's Women's Commission, June 22, 1993.

[128] Letter from Nancy Zang, special administrator, Female Offenders Program, Michigan Department of Corrections, June 18, 1993.

legislature voted to amend the ombudsman's position and moved to restrict its independence.

Under the original legislation, the ombudsman, according to MDOC policy, was authorized by law to investigate "any administrative act by [MDOC] or its employees, which is alleged to be contrary to law or department policy," even if the allegation is "unaccompanied by adequate justification or based upon irrelevant, immaterial or erroneous information."[129] Prisoners were authorized to write to the ombudsman directly, and their letters could not be opened or screened by prison officials.[130] While the amended law retains the confidentiality of communications between the ombudsman and prisoners, it now restricts the ombudsman's authority to initiate investigations. Rather than relying on prisoner communications or other sources to prompt an investigation, the ombudsman may now start an investigation only upon receipt of a complaint from a legislator. The only investigations he can undertake on his own initiative relate to significant health and safety issues of prisoners or parolees.[131]

In our view, the Michigan state legislature should act to strengthen rather than reduce the ombudsman's independent investigative authority. Given the myriad problems with the manner in which MDOC monitors, investigates and punishes sexual misconduct within its women's facilities and the real risk of retaliation or punishment faced by women who report such abuse, a strong, independent and confidential investigative authority is crucial to any meaningful effort to eradicate sexual abuse in custody. The new restrictions on the ombudsman's power and resources suggest that neither the state legislature nor MDOC are fully committed to this end.

---

[129] "Legislative Corrections Ombudsman," MDOC Policy Directive No.03.02.135 June 27, 1988.

[130] Ibid., section D.

[131] Enrolled Senate Bill 501, 88th legislature, regular session, 1995, section 4 (1)(a). The amendment also provides in section 4 (1)(b) that the ombudsman may commence an investigation on his own initiative "for significant prisoner health and safety issues and other matters for which there is no effective administrative remedy, all as determined by the council."

Department of Justice

On March 27, 1995, U.S. Assistant Attorney General Deval Patrick wrote a twelve-page letter to Michigan Governor John Engler that detailed the DOJ's findings regarding conditions at Crane and Scott. Specifically, the DOJ concluded:

> that sexual abuse of women prisoners by guards, including rapes, the lack of adequate medical care, including mental health services, grossly deficient sanitation, crowding and other threats to the physical safety and well-being of prisoners violates their constitutional rights.[132]

According to the letter, "nearly every women . . . interviewed reported various sexually aggressive acts of guards."[133] The DOJ found that prisoners at Scott and Crane had been raped, sexually assaulted, and subjected to groping and fondling during pat-frisks. Additionally, they were subjected to "improper visual surveillance by guards."[134]

The MDOC has responded to the DOJ's findings in much the same way it responded to the Michigan Women's Commission report. A MDOC spokesman dismissed the findings as "anecdotal and half-truths."[135] MDOC Director McGinnis characterized the DOJ's findings as "outrageous, unverified claims"[136] and issued a written statement calling the DOJ's letter "'vindictive and distorted' and full of 'half-truths, innuendo, distortion and lies.'"[137]

The DOJ issued the letter as a prerequisite to possibly filing suit against Michigan under CRIPA. The suit could not be filed sooner than forty-nine days

---

[132] Letter from Deval Patrick, assistant attorney general, U.S. Department of Justice, to John Engler, governor, Michigan, March 27, 1995.

[133] Ibid.

[134] Ibid.

[135] Lori Montgomery and Dawson Bell, "Rapes by guards reported: U.S. finds abuse at 2 state women's facilities." *Detroit Free Press*, March 30, 1995.

[136] Jack Kresnak and Dawson Bell, "Prison report hailed, jeered," *Detroit Free Press*, March 31, 1995.

[137] Basheda, "U.S.: Women's prisons a disaster," *Detroit News*.

after the letter was sent to Governor Engler, which would have been mid-May 1995. Today, eighteen months after the requisite forty-nine days expired, the DOJ has yet to file suit. On October 1, 1996, the DOJ described to us its inquiry into prison conditions in Michigan as an "open investigation," but declined to say if or when it may sue MDOC for CRIPA violations.[138]

Lack Of Training

MDOC requires new corrections officers to successfully complete 320 hours of classroom training, which consists of academic, practical, and physical training. Two months of on-the-job training at the officer's assigned facility must also be completed.[139] According to Director McGinnis, no training in cross-gender guarding was provided to MDOC staff prior to 1994.[140] Our interviews indicate that, while MDOC materials describing training now include a reference to "sexual harassment," this training has not been fully carried out and has yet to address in any detail the question of sexual misconduct.

In addition to failing to train officers adequately to refrain from custodial sexual misconduct, MDOC has not yet educated prisoners about the prohibitions on and remedies for such abuse. A 1991 prisoner guidebook, which is provided to all prisoners, does stipulate that "[p]risoners shall not be subjected to personal abuse from Corrections staff," and "[s]taff will discourage, with all appropriate means, any person's use of derogatory, demeaning, humiliating or degrading actions or language toward others."[141] Whether the latter admonition extends to corrections staff is unclear. A revised guidebook[142] issued in 1993 and provided to prisoners at Scott Correctional Facility, fails to mention that sexual abuse by

---

[138] Interview, Department of Justice, October 1, 1996.

[139] Michigan Department of Corrections Information Kit, 1995.

[140] McGinnis Deposition.

[141] Michigan Department of Corrections, Prisoner Guidebook, July 1991, p. 16.

[142] Scott Correctional Facility, Prisoner Guidebook, 1993.

corrections staff is prohibited and, in some cases, criminalized; nor does it indicate how prisoners should proceed in reporting such behavior.[143]

RECOMMENDATIONS

I.   Prohibiting Sex in Custody

A.   The Michigan state district attorney should strictly enforce Michigan's prohibition against criminal sexual conduct and ensure that those correctional employees who violate this law are held fully to account.

B.   MDOC should strengthen its policy directive to explicitly ban sexual intercourse, sexual touching or any other form of sexual contact between corrections employees and prisoners and to require that prisoners are free from torture or cruel, inhuman, or degrading treatment as a matter of compliance with U.S. obligations under international law.

C.   MDOC should remove all administrative provisions that allow for the punishment of prisoners who engage in sexual intercourse, sexual contact or any other form of sexual conduct with corrections staff, and cease punishing prisoners found to have engaged in such behavior. Punishment of prisoners for sexual misconduct has the effect of deterring their reporting of such abuse by corrections staff.

D.   MDOC should cease using administrative segregation as de facto punishment when prisoners report sexual misconduct by guards.

II.   Safeguarding Prisoners Impregnated by Guards

A.   MDOC should stop punishing or harassing in any way prisoners who are impregnated by officers.   MDOC should also refrain from

---

[143] The guidebook was provided to us in response to a number of questions we put to MDOC in writing, in particular: "What is the procedure for female prisoners to raise an allegation of sexual harassment, overfamiliarity or sexual abuse?" and "What is the procedure for investigating allegations of sexual harassment, overfamiliarity or sexual abuse?" We are limited to commenting on the content of the guidebook for Scott since no similar guidebook for Crane was provided. We are unaware whether the guidebook provided to prisoners at Crane informs prisoners how to report sexual misconduct and how such allegations would be investigated.

administratively segregating pregnant prisoners, unless they expressly request it. Such segregation should provide for the provision of adequate medical and hygienic requirements necessary for a safe pregnancy.

B.   MDOC should ensure that women who are impregnated by corrections staff are not pressured in any way to undergo abortions. Prisoners should receive neutral counseling on all options available to them.

C.   MDOC should ensure that pregnant women receive timely and adequate medical care, and that medical treatment recommended by physicians is provided as prescribed. Such medical care should include professional psychiatric counseling for prisoners impregnated as a result of rape or sexual assault or abuse and others victims of sexual misconduct who request it.

III.   Prohibiting Abusive and Degrading Language
MDOC should strengthen its policy directive to mandate humane treatment of prisoners and prohibit derogatory language. Corrections staff must be made aware, through enforcement, that they are obligated to comply with such provisions or be subjected to disciplinary sanctions.

IV.   Protecting Privacy: The Need for a Policy
A.   MDOC should institute a policy to protect the privacy of women prisoners consistent with several federal court decisions recognizing that prisoners have a constitutionally protected right to privacy. Corrections employees should be fully trained in this policy, and it should be enforced strictly. Such a policy should include, among other things:
    1.   a requirement that male officers announce their presence before entering a women's housing unit, toilet, or shower area;
    2.   permission for prisoners to cover their cell windows for limited intervals while undressing or using the toilets in their cells; and
    3.   a rule that only female officers should be present during gynecological examinations.

B.   MDOC should cease "unclothed body searches" of women prisoners either by or in the presence of male employees, or under circumstances where a male employee may be in a position to observe the prisoner while she is undressed. Strip searches should be administered in a location that limits access by other prisoners or employees.

C.   MDOC should use female officers to pat-search female prisoners whenever possible. All officers should be trained in the appropriate conduct of pat-frisks and in the disciplinary sanctions associated with improperly performed searches. Women prisoners who either pull away during offensive pat-searches or request that the search be conducted by a female officer should not be subjected automatically to disciplinary action.

D.   MDOC should rescind immediately the requirement that officers meet quotas for pat-searches per shift. This practice may encourage officers to conduct searches without reasonable cause to believe that a prisoner possesses contraband.

E.   MDOC should rescind the policy requiring female prisoners to wear bras.

V.   **Ensuring the Right to an Effective Remedy**
       Grievances

A.   MDOC should amend its grievance procedure in cases of alleged sexual misconduct by corrections employees, expressly authorizing prisoners to bypass the informal level of review and file their complaints directly with the prison superintendent or investigator.

B.   MDOC should take steps to insure that its grievance procedure includes provisions that *inter alia* protect the confidentiality of the complainant and witnesses during the time in which the officer is still potentially in contact with them; withholds information about complaints from those not directly or by authority involved in the alleged incident; ensures that prisoner testimony is give due weight; and prevents the implicated officer from conducting the investigation.

C.   MDOC should make grievance forms readily available in the prison library or other neutral place.

D.   MDOC should, under all circumstances, refrain from assigning implicated officers to investigate allegations of their own misconduct. Officers alleged to have committed rape, sexual assault or abuse, or criminal sexual contact should be assigned to noncontact positions or suspended until the circumstances are clarified and the investigation completed.

Investigations

A.   MDOC should promulgate a written procedure for conducting investigations into custodial misconduct, with specific reference to sexual misconduct, both at the level of the facility itself or at the level of the internal affairs section or other departmental divisions. The investigative procedure should, at a minimum:

    1.   clarify which investigations should be conducted from within the facility, which by internal affairs, and the relationship between the two entities with respect to any such investigation;

    2.   specify the circumstances necessary to initiate an investigation at either end;

    3.   describe exactly the steps investigators within prison facilities should follow in conducting an investigation;

    4.   set forth the same criteria for investigations by the internal affairs section;

    5.   set forth a clear structure and time frame for conducting investigations; and

    6.   provide for a special investigator in the office of internal affairs section trained to handle sexual misconduct complaints, in particular, with the necessary human and material resources to do so.

B.   In establishing these clear and exhaustive investigatory policies, the MDOC should endeavor to:

    1.   protect as much as possible the anonymity of the complainant;

    2.   guard complainants and witnesses from retaliation and harassment; and

    3.   ensure accountability to outside monitors. For example, the complainant's legal counsel, upon request, should be provided a written record of the investigation, including all statements made by the complainants and witnesses.

C.   MDOC should integrate this expanded investigative procedure into its operations manual and make it available as a public document.

D.   MDOC should require all corrections employees to report promptly any allegations, including rumors, of sexual misconduct or other overfamiliar conduct to the prison warden and should reward those that do while sanctioning those who do not.

E.   MDOC should refer all allegations of rape, sexual assault, and other alleged criminal conduct promptly to the state police for criminal investigation. When a referral is made to the state police, MDOC should continue, not cease, its own internal investigation into possible employee misconduct and proceed with disciplinary action when appropriate.

VI.   Preventing Retaliation Against Complainants

A.   MDOC should ensure, as much as possible, the confidentiality of allegations of sexual misconduct by prison staff and the anonymity of both complainant and witnesses during the period that the accused remains in a contact position with the complainant or is assigned to the facility where the complainant resides. MDOC should also seek to prevent the complainant's name from being revealed generally within the facility.

B.   MDOC should restrict access to prisoner files not already protected and ensure that better protections for the confidentiality of records are provided.

C.   MDOC should suspend any employee accused of sexual misconduct, including overfamiliarity with a prisoner, if such misconduct once proven would result in dismissal.

D.   MDOC should investigate reports of retribution promptly and vigorously and should discipline transgressing employees appropriately.

E.   MDOC should ensure prisoners the right to counsel in cases of sexual assault.

VII.   Curtailing the Use of Administrative Segregation and Other Punishment

A.   MDOC should authorize the use of administrative segregation during an investigation only at the prisoner's explicit request. Since a prisoner placed in administrative segregation for her own protection has not committed a disciplinary offense, she should retain the rights of the general population (e.g., telephone calls, visits, access to recreation, etc.). She should be returned to the general population when she requests to be. MDOC should train employees assigned to segregated housing units regarding such provisions.

B. MDOC should ensure that prisoners who complain of sexual misconduct are not directly or indirectly punished for such complaints through the loss of good time toward early parole or any form of disciplinary segregation.

C. MDOC should ensure that prisoners who file grievances are not wrongfully charged with "interference with the administration of rules" or other disciplinary offenses, such as "false accusation," solely because the accused officer denies any misconduct or because the alleged incident is "unsubstantiated."

VIII. Ensuring Discipline

A. MDOC should create a clear policy on disciplinary action against abusive corrections employees for all forms of sexual misconduct.

B. MDOC should ensure that an employee found to have engaged in sexual relations or sexual contact with prisoners will be dismissed. Transfer of such employees to other positions or facilities does not constitute appropriate punishment.

IX. Ensuring Accountability to Outside Monitors
Michigan Women's Commission

MDOC should publish the full report of the Michigan Women's Commission.

Office of the Legislative Corrections Ombudsman

A. The Michigan Legislature should strengthen the office of the Legislative Corrections Ombudsman to function as a fully empowered and independent review board to investigate, among other things, complaints of sexual misconduct. The review board should have the authority to turn over evidence of possible criminal wrongdoing to prosecutorial authorities. The board should also be able to recommend remedial action to stop abuses or other problems during an investigation.

B. The review board should develop a system whereby the records of any corrections employee who has been the subject of repeated sexual misconduct complaints are reviewed by the appropriate authorities.

C.   The review board should further provide a toll-free telephone number that prisoners can use to contact investigators or to file anonymous complaints of misconduct, including retaliation against complainants.

Department of Justice

As a matter of urgency, the Michigan governor and the MDOC director should cooperate fully with the Department of Justice in its ongoing investigation into abuses in Michigan's women prisons.

Nongovernmental Actors

MDOC should provide timely and written information about an investigation to the complainant and the people she designates, such as her attorney and her family, upon their request.

X.   Hiring, Training, Education, and Information
Correctional Employees

A.   MDOC should improve its screening procedures for applicants for corrections positions. Background checks should be completed before new employees are sent into correctional facilities. In no case should MDOC rehire an employee who has been convicted of an offense related to sexual misconduct in custody or who resigned in order to avoid such investigation.

B.   MDOC should, as soon as possible, implement comprehensive and mandatory training on issues specific to incarcerated women for all current and future corrections employees assigned to women's prisons. This training should include, among other things:

  1.   a general discussion or profile of female prisoners and their potential vulnerability to sexual misconduct;

  2.   MDOC policies prohibiting all sexual contact, degrading language, inappropriate visual surveillance, and other sexually oriented or degrading behavior toward incarcerated women and the disciplinary or criminal sanctions associated with this behavior;

  3.   appropriate methods for conducting pat-searches, strip searches, and searches of women's cells, housing units, and bathroom areas; and

  4.   MDOC should, in developing and implementing this training, collaborate with local nongovernmental organizations

experienced in working on issues affecting incarcerated women, including rape and sexual assault.

Prisoners

A.   MDOC should advise incarcerated women, as part of their orientation to the corrections system, as well as prisoners already serving their sentences, of the following:

1.   Corrections officers are strictly prohibited from having any form of sexual contact with prisoners. The orientation should also include a thorough review of departmental process regarding privacy and humane treatment; the procedures for reporting and investigating sexual misconduct; and the departmental or criminal law sanctions associated with it.

2.   Grievances relating to sexual misconduct may be filed directly and confidentially with the prison investigator. All grievances should be acknowledged and resolved as soon as possible. Prisoners should be informed about the issues that may be dealt with through the grievance procedure, with a particular emphasis on instances of sexual misconduct; the location of grievance forms; any specific procedures for reporting sexual misconduct; the recourse available when corrections officers fail to respond; and the potential to resolve complaints through the internal investigation procedure and the independent review board when one is established.

3.   MDOC should also acquaint prisoners with their rights under international human rights treaties ratified by the U.S., as well as under U.S. constitutional law.

B.   The above information should be included in the prisoner handbook.

Improving Documentation

A.   MDOC should take immediate steps to improve its system for the documentation of custodial misconduct, including sexual misconduct, and make available on a semi-annual basis reliable and accurate public reports of such misconduct arranged by date, location, and type of allegation; rank and function of employee; and specific actions taken by the facility, internal affairs or other departmental division, or state criminal justice authorities.

B.   As a necessary step toward improving its capacity to provide such thorough and timely information, MDOC should:

1.   keep files by name of officer of all allegations of custodial misconduct, including those that were not substantiated;

2.   ensure that each warden or supervisor reports monthly to the director regarding all allegations or findings of misconduct, including sexual misconduct, and the actions taken or recommended with respect to each; and

3.   create a position within MDOC charged primarily with data collection regarding administrative or criminal misconduct by correctional employees, who will review monthly the reports of each facility and provide semi-annual reports to the director.

VIII. NEW YORK

In 1996 the New York state legislature passed legislation criminalizing all sex between prisoners and guards. This step is welcome. However, for the criminalization of custodial sexual misconduct to be effective, it must be accompanied by additional steps to reform the prison environment that has allowed such misconduct to thrive. At present, New York State allows men to work in contact positions in women's prisons but has made little effort to regulate male guards' access to women's housing areas. Moreover, neither the Department of Correctional Services' (DOCS) internal grievance procedure nor its investigatory procedure functions effectively for complaints of sexual misconduct, and both often expose complainants to retaliation.

Women incarcerated in New York have been raped, sexually assaulted or abused, and verbally degraded by male correctional employees and suffer frequent privacy violations, particularly with respect to abusive strip searches. These findings reflect an investigation that took place from 1994 through 1996 and are based on interviews with eleven current and former prisoners who have served time in one or more of New York's four prisons for women:[1] Albion Correctional Facility, Bayview Correctional Facility, Bedford Hills Correctional Facility, and Taconic Correctional Facility.[2] We also interviewed the superintendent of Bedford Hills Correctional, Facility Elaine Lord; a former DOCS employee; and a number of attorneys working with incarcerated women in the state.

We urge Gov. George Pataki and the New York Department of Correctional Services to enforce the new law criminalizing sexual contact between prisoners and correctional employees and to enact legislation prohibiting cross-gender pat-frisks except in emergency situations. We also call on New York State to undertake substantial prison reform to guarantee prisoners' right to privacy and to ensure that abusive employees are disciplined. In addition, guards should be trained and prisoners educated as to the prohibitions against custodial sexual misconduct.

---

[1] These women were identified with the assistance of attorneys who had received allegations from prisoners of sexual misconduct or other abuse by corrections staff.

[2] Some of the women we interviewed also served time in Groveland Correctional Facility, which formerly held both men and women. Bayview also serves as a transitional facility and some prisoners incarcerated there are on work release status.

CONTEXT

Custodial Environment

The population of incarcerated women in New York has increased dramatically in the last ten years. According to statistical information obtained from the New York DOCS, the female prison population increased 230 percent between 1985 and 1992, from 1,061 to 3,500 women.[3] In comparison, the male population in the same time period grew by 74 percent.[4] According to the Correctional Association of New York, a nongovernmental organization, over 90 percent of prisoners in New York prisons are incarcerated pursuant to the "Rockefeller Drug Laws"and the "Second Felony Law," which mandate severe prison terms for possessing relatively small amounts of drugs.[5] While fewer than 25 percent of women are incarcerated in New York State for violent felonies, two out of three women have been committed for a drug-related felony.[6] Over 50 percent of incarcerated women are African American, and approximately 35 percent are Latina. In addition, the majority of incarcerated women are mothers, and many are single caretakers.[7]

This growing population of female prisoners in New York is being guarded largely by male officers, although this was not always the case. Until 1976 only women were permitted to work as corrections officers in the housing units of New York State prisons for women. Male corrections officers were limited to assignments such as the grounds, the school, and the library.[8] In February 1977

---

[3] As of September 19, 1996, 3,710 women were incarcerated in New York State prisons. Correctional Association of New York, "Women in Prison Fact Sheet," New York City, New York, September 1995.

[4] New York Department of Correctional Services, "Characteristics of Inmates under Custody: 1985-1992,"Albany, New York.

[5] For example, a person must receive a term of fifteen years to life if convicted of selling two ounces of a narcotic or possessing four ounces. Correctional Association of New York, "Mandatory Sentencing Laws and Drug Offenders in New York State," New York City, New York, February 1995.

[6] Correctional Association of New York, "Women in Prison Fact Sheet," November 1994.

[7] Correctional Association of New York, Women in Prison Fact Sheet," September 1995.

[8] *Forts v. Ward*, 471 F. **Supp.** 1095, p. 1096 (S.D.N.Y. 1978).

DOCS eliminated the assignment of jobs by sex in an effort to comply with Title VII of the Civil Rights Act on sex discrimination. DOCS began allowing, with limited restrictions, cross-gender guarding in the housing units.[9] Currently, men represent the vast majority of corrections officers in the women's prisons, including the evening and night shifts in the housing units.[10]

As noted in the legal background chapter of this report, Human Rights Watch does not oppose *per se* the presence of male guards in supervisory and/or contact positions in women's prisons. However, we are concerned that in New York, as in other states, DOCS is not taking adequate steps to protect women against custodial sexual misconduct. Corrections authorities do not inform female prisoners about the risk of sexual misconduct or the existence of mechanisms to report and seek remedy for such abuse should it occur. Female prisoners not only lack such guidance but also often enter the correctional system particularly vulnerable to the risks of sexual misconduct they may encounter. Many of them tolerate sexual solicitation and sexual relations because they are, as one former DOCS employee put it, "used to being used."[11] He stated it was common knowledge among the staff that a large number of the women had personal histories of sexual abuse and spoke openly about being molested or raped prior to incarceration. In fact, as he explained, officers often exploit the women's vulnerabilities.

State Legal and Regulatory Framework

Neither prison rules nor the state criminal law in New York adequately defines and prohibits sexual misconduct involving prison employees. The only written prohibition on sexual misconduct in the employee manual is a vague, overly broad provision regarding staff association with prisoners that fails to set forth penalties for violations. The provision, Rule 2.15, states that no employee:

---

[9] Ibid., pp. 1096-97.

[10] According to a 1992 survey, male corrections officers working in women's prisons in New York outnumbered female corrections officers three to one. *Corrections Compendium* (Nebraska), October 1992. Then Acting Commissioner of the Department of Corrections Philip Coombe, Jr. stated at a Coalition for Women Prisoners meeting in December 1995 that women constituted 24 percent of the guards at Albion and 48 percent at Bedford Hills.

[11] Interview, New York, January 17, 1994.

shall knowingly . . . associate or have any dealings with criminals . . . [or] engage in any conversation, communication, dealing, transaction, association or relationship with any inmate.[12]

Currently, as demonstrated below, incarcerated women have been viewed by DOCS as consensual partners in sexual relationships with corrections officers and have been punished for such misconduct.[13] The prisoner handbook, "Standards of Inmate Behavior: All Institutions," prohibits sexual relations or even soliciting or encouraging another to have sexual relations. Rule 101 states: "inmates shall not engage in, encourage, solicit or attempt to force others to engage in sexual acts." The provision does not define "others." In contrast to the employee manual, the prisoner handbook specifies that violation of Rule 101 can result in confinement to the Special Housing Unit (SHU or "the box"), loss of privileges, and a mandatory fine.

A new initiative amending the penal code to criminalize sex in custody was passed by the New York State legislature and signed by Gov. George Pataki on July 2, 1996, going into force thirty days later.[14] Such contact was, at one time, a crime under New York's penal code, which treated sexual encounters with an incarcerated person on the same level as rape.[15] That law was repealed. In the late 1980s, DOCS attempted to change the state law to again criminalize sexual contact with a prisoner if such contact occurred while performing one's duties. However,

---

[12] New York Department of Correctional Services (DOCS) employee manual, Rule 2.15.

[13] Elaine Lord, superintendent, Bedford Hills Correctional Facility, firmly believes that incarcerated women cannot meaningfully consent to sexual relations with staff. She told us: "Where you have power over a person, it cannot be consensual . . . You cannot be in the position of an inmate and make that kind of decision. A staff person is a staff person and that's not what he's being paid to do. Eventually, it makes other people feel unsafe."

[14] The bill passed the Assembly on May 6, 1996 and the Senate on June 14, 1996. Telephone interviews, Michael Avitzur, legislative aide to Sen. Catherine M. Abate, June 21, 1996; August 12, 1996. State Sen. Michael Nozzolio, head of the Senate's Crime and Corrections Committee , and Assembly Member Keith Wright offered the amendment in the Senate and Assembly, respectively. Gary Craig, "Nozzolio bill would outlaw sex between guards, cons," *Rochester Democrat and Chronicle*, February 10, 1996.

[15] Memorandum from Anthony Annucci, counsel, New York Department of Correctional Services, to Elizabeth Moore, counsel to the governor [no date].

according to Superintendent Lord, the proposed legislation never made it past the committee stage because there was no interest in adding a new felony to the criminal code.[16]

The initiative amended New York Penal Law Section 130.05 to criminalize all sexual contact between a corrections employee and a prisoner. Employees who engage in sexual intercourse with a prisoner may be charged with one of three offenses: third degree felony of rape, for sexual intercourse with a prisoner; third degree felony of sodomy, for sodomy with a prisoner;[17] and a misdemeanor offense of sexual misconduct or sexual abuse, for sexual contact with a prisoner.[18] Similar initiatives had been proposed by prisoners' rights advocates in the past.[19]

DOCS indicated its support for the amendment in a written memorandum, and then Acting Commissioner Philip Coombe Jr. stated, "[T]here should never be a sexual relationship between an officer and inmate. It is our position that this should be first-degree rape."[20] DOCS views the provision as additional leverage

---

[16] Interview, Elaine Lord, Superintendent, Bedford Hills Correctional facility, June 22, 1994. Anthony Annucci, DOCS counsel, echoed Lord's observations when we spoke to him on February 7, 1995.

[17] Although Human Rights Watch supports the criminal prosecution of prison staff guilty of sexual contact with prisoners, we believe that the crime is predicated on the abuse of custodial authority, not on the irrelevant distinction between oral, anal, and vaginal sex. We are also sensitive to the abuse of sodomy laws against sexual minorities. For that reason, we believe instances of custodial sexual abuse should not be distinguished and prosecuted under sodomy laws.

[18] Memorandum from Anthony Annucci, counsel, New York Department of Correctional services [no date].

[19] Ruth Cassell, an attorney with Prisoners Legal Services, submitted draft legislation to the New York State Division of Women, an executive body, in 1993 . The proposed legislation, she told us, was "rejected out of hand." Telephone interview, Ruth Cassell, Prisoners Legal Services, November 17, 1994. In 1995 the Coalition for Women Prisoners in New York also submitted a similar proposal. Craig, "Nozzolio bill would outlaw . . .," *Rochester Democrat and Chronicle.*

[20] Linda Stasi, "Hard Cell on Sex: female prisoners see widespread abuse," *New York Daily News*, September 1995.

in disciplining disobedient staff.[21]   However, the guards' union, Council 82, expressed strong opposition to the amendment, stating that criminalization, in addition to internal discipline, of sex between guards and prisoners would be overkill.[22]

National and International Law Protections

As discussed in the legal background section of this report, sexual misconduct is clearly prohibited under both U.S. constitutional law and international treaty law that is binding on the U.S. federal government as well as its constituent states.[23]   The Eighth Amendment to the Constitution, which bars cruel and unusual punishment, has been interpreted by U.S. courts to protect prisoners against rape and sexual assault.   This constitutional shield is augmented by the Fourth Amendment's guarantee of the right to privacy and personal integrity, which, in a series of lower court cases, has been interpreted to prohibit male guards from inappropriately viewing or strip searching female prisoners or conducting intrusive pat-frisks on female prisoners.

Constitutional protections for prisoners' rights are enforceable via lawsuits filed by or on behalf of prisoners, or by the U.S. Department of Justice (DOJ). Historically, U.S. prisoners have achieved most of their landmark victories through private litigation, particularly suits litigated by prisoners' rights groups such as the National Prison Project of the American Civil Liberties Union.   However, if certain stringent intent requirements are met, the DOJ may criminally prosecute abusive prison officials under federal civil rights provisions.   In addition, the DOJ has the statutory right to investigate and institute civil actions under the Civil Rights of Institutionalized Persons Act (CRIPA) whenever it finds that a state facility engages in a pattern or practice of subjecting prisoners to "egregious or flagrant conditions" in violation of the constitution.

In addition to constitutional protections, prisoners' rights are protected under international human rights treaties that are legally binding on the United States.   The primary international legal instruments protecting the rights of U.S.

---

[21] Telephone interview, Anthony Annucci, counsel, New York Department of Correctional Services, February 7, 1995.

[22] Craig, "Nozzolio bill would outlaw . . ." *Rochester Democrat and Chronicle.*

[23] For a detailed discussion of United States obligations under U.S. constitutional law and international law pertaining to the treatment of prisoners, see the legal background chapter of this report.

prisoners are the International Covenant of Civil and Political Rights (ICCPR), ratified by the United States in 1993, and the Convention Against Torture and Other Cruel, Inhuman or Degrading Treatment or Punishment, ratified in 1994. The ICCPR guarantees prisoners' right to privacy, except when limitations on this right are demonstrably necessary to maintain prison security. Both treaties bar torture and cruel, inhuman or degrading treatment or punishment, which authoritative international bodies have interpreted as including sexual abuse. To constitute torture, an act must cause severe physical or mental suffering and must be committed for a purpose such as obtaining information from a victim, punishing her or intimidating her or coercing her or for any reason based on discrimination of any kind. Cruel, inhuman or degrading treatment or punishment includes acts causing a lesser degree of suffering that need not be committed for a particular purpose.

When prison staff members use force, the threat of force, or other means of coercion to compel a prisoner to engage in sexual intercourse, their acts constitute rape and, therefore, torture. Torture also occurs when prison staff use force or coercion to engage in sexual touching of prisoners where such acts cause serious physical or mental suffering. Instances of sexual touching or of sexual intercourse that does not amount to rape may constitute torture or cruel or inhuman treatment, depending on the level of physical or mental suffering involved. Other forms of sexual misconduct, such as inappropriate pat or strip searches or verbal harassment, that do not rise to the level of torture or of cruel or inhuman treatment, may be condemned as degrading treatment. [24]

---

[24] For a detailed discussion of the prohibition against torture, and other cruel, inhuman or degrading treatment or punishment under international law and its applicability to custodial sexual misconduct, see the legal background chapter of this report.

ABUSES[25]

Custodial sexual misconduct in New York includes sexual intercourse and inappropriate sexual touching by prison staff, as well as constant and highly sexualized and degrading language and unwarranted invasions of women prisoners' privacy.   Unless indicated by the use of a full name, the names of the prisoners have been changed to protect their anonymity.   In some cases, the location and exact date of prisoner interviews have also been withheld.

Rape, Sexual Assault or Abuse, and Criminal Sexual Contact

Evidence of sexual misconduct in New York's women's prisons goes back several years.   In 1984, Prisoners Legal Services (PLS)[26] filed a class action lawsuit against DOCS on behalf of women incarcerated at Bayview alleging, among other things, inadequate medical care, unsafe and decrepit conditions, a pattern of sexual harassment of prisoners, and lack of privacy from male guards.[27]   Although the central issue was inadequate medical care, PLS also produced evidence that male corrections staff were engaging in sexual relations with, and sexually and verbally assaulting incarcerated women.   At the time, according to PLS attorney Bill Gibney, PLS had received numerous complaints that male corrections officers were seeking sexual favors from incarcerated women through threat or offer of goods,

---

[25] By rape, we mean sexual intercourse between a prison employee and a prisoner that is accompanied by the use or threat of force or coercion which, under certain circumstances, can take the form of the provision or denial of privileges, money, or goods. Sexual assault is sexual touching, short of intercourse, involving the same coercive influences. Sexual abuse is sexual intercourse or touching involving the offer of goods or privileges absent any actual or perceived threat to the prisoner.   Criminal sexual contact refers to sexual intercourse or sexual touching that cannot be shown to involve any of the above elements but which nonetheless constitutes a gross breach of official duty. Rape, sexual assault or abuse, and criminal sexual contact should all be prosecuted as felonies. For a more detailed discussion, see the legal background chapter.

[26] Prisoners Legal Services provides legal services, primarily in civil matters, to indigent person incarcerated in New York. It is a statewide organization, with seven offices throughout the state. Prisoners Legal Services was not included in the budget New York Gov. George Pataki submitted in 1996; however, it expects that whatever bill is finally passed will contain funding for PLS at the level provided in 1995. Telephone interview, Ruth Cassell, Prisoners Legal Services, June 17, 1996.

[27] *Blackman v. Coughlin*, Civil Action No. 84-5698, Complaint-Class Action, August 1984.

and "trading" prisoners to other officers for sex.[28] If the women did not comply with requests for sexual favors, according to Gibney, the officers threatened to write disciplinary tickets, take away their privileges, and have them transferred upstate. Seven corrections officers allegedly involved in these incidents were removed, but on grounds other than sexual misconduct. To our knowledge, four of these were reassigned rather than terminated.[29] PLS settled the suit with DOCS in 1993. DOCS did not agree to a particular course of conduct to combat sexual misconduct at Bayview but has met with PLS attorneys to shape a remedy.[30]

PLS, meanwhile, has continued to monitor sexual misconduct at Bayview and to pursue allegations with DOCS and Bayview's administration. In 1994 PLS conducted a series of interviews with prisoners and heard continuing allegations of sexual contact. According to PLS attorney Ruth Cassell, the women at Bayview described sexual activity in the prison as pervasive; they told her that "every guard had a girlfriend." PLS raised their concerns with the prison administration with little success. According to Cassell:

> We're not getting very far at Bayview. When we talked to the superintendent and the department, they said they are "doing all they can." It's like hitting your head against a wall. The women tell you sex is rampant, but they are afraid to talk because they fear being sent upstate.[31]

She remains convinced, based on the interviews and her observation of the interaction between guards and prisoners at the facility, that the prisoners are telling

---

[28] Telephone interview, Bill Gibney, Prisoners Legal Services, June 22, 1994.

[29] Interview, Kathryn Schmidt, Prisoners Legal Services, New York, January 14, 1994.

[30] Ibid. A stipulation and order was signed in September 1993. *Blackman v. Coughlin*, Civil Action No. 84-5698 (RO), Stipulation and Order, September 1993. This order addressed only reforms in medical treatment for prisoners. Regarding the charges of sexual harassment and invasion of privacy, the order merely provides "the parties agree that prisoner complaints regarding sexual harassment and invasion of privacy have been reduced since the filing of this complaint."

[31] Telephone interview, Ruth Cassell, Prisoners Legal Services, August 24, 1994.

the truth. According to another PLS attorney Bill Gibney, "[It's] an issue you just have to stay on top of all of the time. You don't just solve it."[32]

We found that rape, sexual assault, and criminal sexual contact have occurred at other women's prisons in New York, besides Bayview. Ruth Cassell has observed a pattern of sexual abuse within the women's prisons over a period of years. She testified before a Governor's Task Force on Sexual Harassment in September 1992 that she had personally advised or represented twenty-five women prisoners who claimed to have been sexually abused by male corrections officers and prison staff.[33] She found:

> Women complain of male corrections officers refusing to leave their cells so they can dress, caressing their breasts and other parts of their bodies, pulling down their pants in front of them, touching themselves, making lewd and offensive comments, following them around the facility, assigning them to their offices as clerks, watching them use the bathroom and shower, coming on to the unit without warning of their presence, and frequently promising them favors and presents for sexual activity.[34]

A client of Ruth Cassell's incarcerated at Bedford Hills told Cassell in 1995 that she had been forced to have oral and anal sex with a guard, Shelbourne Reid, over a period of approximately seven months.[35] Reid reportedly threatened to harm her daughter if she did not have sex with him. According to Cassell, in early August 1995, Reid awakened the prisoner in the early morning hours [approximately 2:00 a.m.] and forced her to perform oral sex on him. The woman preserved the semen in a perfume bottle placed in a fridge. The next morning, Cassell's client gave the bottle to a female guard and told her Reid's name. This guard spoke with the superintendent who, reportedly, ordered Reid escorted off the

---

[32] Telephone interview, Bill Gibney, Prisoners Legal Services, June 22, 1994.

[33] Testimony of Ruth Cassell before the Governor's Task Force on Sexual Harassment, September 24, 1992, reprinted in *Out of Silence*, a newsletter of the Women in Jail and Prison Project, Correctional Association of New York, May 1993.

[34] Ibid.

[35] Interview, Ruth Cassell, Prisoners Legal Services, New York, February 16, 1996.

prison once the material in the bottle was proved to be semen.[36] Reid admitted he raped the female prisoner and was fired. On December 13, 1995, Reid entered a plea of sex abuse in the first degree with a sentence of five years' probation.

Cassell told us of another client, a paraplegic prisoner, who was raped every time she was driven to physical therapy. The driver, employed by the prison, pulled over and forced the prisoner to perform oral sex. He would then provide her with contraband. According to Cassell, the prisoner was later disciplined for the possession of the contraband and sentenced to the Special Housing Unit (SHU) for a period of time. The hearing officer on her disciplinary report did not act on her explanation about the source of the contraband. Following the charges, the prison reportedly stopped taking the woman out for therapy.[37]

Women also reported to PLS a pattern of sexual aggression and sexual intimidation from male corrections officers over the years.[38]

> Sandra F. was repeatedly harassed by Captain W in 1991. When she went into his office, he would reach for her hands and ask for a hug. On one occasion, he pulled down his pants in front of her to reveal his erect penis. On a separate occasion, he tried to kiss her while she was in his office.

According to an affidavit by Wanda A., the same captain repeatedly called Zoe L., Wanda A.'s friend, to his office a few times a week over a four- or five-month period in 1991. Zoe L. told Wanda A. she had had oral sex with Captain W and wanted to end the relationship but did not know how. Terry S. told PLS, in a third affidavit, that Corrections Officer A came into her room and groped her breasts after she asked him for a cigarette. When escorting her later that day to the hospital, he kissed her and put his hands inside her dress.

Michelle C. told us that she was harassed and then sexually assaulted in her cell in August 1993.[39] According to Michelle C., Officer D started to harass her about a week after she arrived, making what she described as "little comments,"

---

[36] Ibid.

[37] Interview, Ruth Cassell, Prisoners Legal Services, New York, April 19, 1994.

[38] The following are summaries of some of the affidavits Cassell has collected. The women's names have been altered to protect their identity.

[39] Interview, New York, April 1994.

such as "I want you to suck my dick." He usually was on the 3:00 p.m. to 11:00 p.m. shift, but on the night of the assault, he worked a double shift and was on the hall all night. She was awakened by Officer D, who had his hands in her underpants.[40] "I was scared. I didn't say nothing." The officer left, she said, after he heard another woman across the hall. Michelle C. stated that she reported the incident to PLS and the DOCS inspector general after the officer started to harass another woman as well.

Iris R. told us that the officer who supervised her work assignment grabbed her and kissed her when she was working alone in a basement area. Iris R. stated that she was "totally surprised" by the officer's sexual advance and felt she had no choice but to submit.[41] He reportedly told her, "I could make this easy for you or I could make this hard for you. It's up to you." Iris R. told us:

> I was scared to death. I had just gotten into the prison system.
> I spent a few weeks at Bedford and just arrived. I didn't know
> how to present myself or carry myself. Plus, I was having
> problems with my daughter's father. He knew about this.[42]

The officer was able to control Iris R.'s schedule and manipulate his work assignments, reportedly with the assistance of another officer, in order to substitute on her housing unit at night. On these occasions, he reportedly directed Iris R. to take a shower or sleep without underwear. While on duty, according to Iris R., he would then watch her shower or "put his hand up my nightgown."

According to Michelle C., women in Taconic Correctional Facility have also been groped and fondled by a prison doctor during examination. The doctor was nicknamed "Dr. Feelgood" because of how he touched the prisoners. A former DOCS employee confirmed Michelle C.'s allegations. During the doctor's employment, two women under his supervision complained that he "was fondling their breasts and sticking his finger where he wasn't supposed to."[43] The doctor

---

[40] At the prison, women are housed in individual cells, to which they have their own keys. The doors are unlocked at night.

[41] Telephone interview, July 12, 1994.

[42] Ibid.

[43] Interview, New York, April 1994.

was removed from the facility in April 1994, reportedly by law enforcement officers, but returned several days later.[44]

Women we interviewed often submitted to sexual relations with a corrections officer or staff member out of fear of retaliation or as a means of exchange, which at times was also accompanied by a sense of compulsion. Women prisoners and a former staff member we interviewed described an environment in the prisons in which prisoners engage in sexual relations with staff in exchange for favorable treatment or for various items, including gum (a coveted item because it is not otherwise available within prison),[45] cigarettes, and drugs. Michelle C. commented, "The women here will suck an officer's dick for gum." While many women appear to engage willingly in such exchanges, others are drawn into the prison's underground economy by threats or coercion from prison staff, who retain virtually complete authority over the prisoner's access to the most basic privileges and goods.

A former employee described the situation in the following way. In his opinion, many female prisoners are drawn into trading sex for favorable treatment in order to get on the officers' good side and to "make their time easier."[46] As he described it, "Give 'em two pieces of gum and a cigarette, and they'll do anything you tell them." According to the former employee, women who did not want to get involved are coerced, upon threats of harassment or retaliation. Male staff, particularly those working on the night shift, came into the women's cells, watched them while they were on the toilet or dressing, and told them to just ask if they needed anything. He was aware of a number of sexual relationships between corrections staff and prisoners. One prisoner, he said, came to him because an officer repeatedly came to her cell at night to solicit sex from her. In another situation, a prisoner told him that she had sex with an officer just to get food the officer brought back from restaurants.

In Iris R.'s experience, sexual relationships between corrections employees and prisoners were common. She both witnessed and heard from other prisoners who were sexually involved with officers. Iris R. was transferred to Bedford Hills after she became pregnant; she told us that an officer used to come into her hallmate's cell at night and they would have oral sex or he would take the

---

[44] Ibid.

[45] Gum is reportedly restricted within prison for security reasons because it may be used to block locks.

[46] Interview, New York, January 17, 1994.

prisoner into the storage closet. On other occasions, "they'd be in the bubble [officers' station] and she'd be rubbing him."[47] Iris R. assumed that the officer's conduct was discovered, because at some point he was moved to another unit.

Pam M. was reportedly involved with two different officers at one prison. The relationship with Officer A began after he made sexual advances toward her. While he was on duty, either he came into her cell or she went to where he worked, and they went into the officers' bathroom. She told us, "The officers swap shifts, work overtime, to be with the women."[48] Pam M. became involved with Officer B after he put money in her account and started writing her letters and sending her packages. Pam M. said that Officer B told her, "I'm going to take you from him [Officer A]." He had her call his unit at night and, according to Pam M., bid to work on her unit. She said, "We were together. Everyone knew."

Rachel H. told us that she felt obliged to allow a corrections officer to kiss and grope her. She said:

> He used to bring me stuff . . . I felt I owed him. He did everything for me. I was away from my family and kid, upstate. I really felt like I owed him. I felt like he deserved it but he did it for a reason . . . He did it because he wanted to get the panties.[49]

Rachel H. also witnessed a woman on her hall having sex with an officer. She said:

> [The woman was] getting it in her room one day so she gets what she needs . . . She was against the wall gettin' it from one of the civilians in her room on the seventh floor.[50]

According to Rachel H., the woman was leaning against a wall while the officer stood behind her, with his pants down, engaging in sexual intercourse.

The superintendent at Bedford Hills, Elaine Lord, acknowledged that incarcerated women may be inclined to submit to sexual relations with prison staff.

---

[47] Telephone interview, July 12, 1994.

[48] Interview, New York, August 1994.

[49] Interview, New York, April 1994.

[50] Ibid.

She told us that she had been approached by women prisoners who viewed sexual relations with male officers as a necessary means to obtain certain things. Lord blamed this on the use of a male model for all prisoners. "The system creates a need to get . . . things. It's part of the problem of using a male model as your basis. There are too many things to be bargained for."[51] She cited the example of shampoo. DOCS provides all prisoners soap, but not shampoo; while soap alone may be sufficient for men, who have shorter hair, it is too dry for women and inappropriate for washing women's hair. In addition, Rhea Schaenman Mallet, formerly of the Correctional Association, informed us that DOCS allocates a set number of sanitary napkins to each prisoner for the year. This leads to a scarce supply of sanitary napkins, and many women are reusing napkins and sharing them.[52]

In some cases, prisoners told us that they engaged in sexual relations with officers for companionship or attention, not because they felt pressured. Such prisoners considered themselves willing participants in sexual relationships with officers. Their descriptions of the experience, however, frequently revealed the inappropriate, often abusive nature of such relationships. Once a sexual relationship with a correction employee has begun, prisoners generally find it difficult to end these sexual encounters. Iris R. told us, "I was really pressured, really trapped. I thought, my God, this person is really in control of me."[53] After she was transferred to a new work assignment, the officer used to corner her in the yard and set times and locations for her to meet him. One of the locations the officer chose was the basement of her work assignment. Three or four times, Iris R. told us, the officer locked her in the basement and left her there because he received a call on his radio. Iris R. allowed herself to believe her relationship with her work supervisor to be meaningful, even though she initially was, in her words, "scared to death." According to Iris R.:

> After awhile, he kind of sucked me in. You do it to make
> yourself feel okay. You have to feel an emotional [bond]. He
> told me lies . . . how much he cared about me, how much he

---

[51] Interview, Elaine Lord, Superintendent, Bedford Hills Corrections Center, June 22, 1994.

[52] Interview, Rhea Schaenman Mallet, Correctional Association of New York, January 30, 1996. A bill was introduced in 1996 by Sen. Catherine Abate requiring that female prisoners be able to receive sanitary napkins as needed.

[53] Telephone interview, July 12, 1994.

wanted to be with me when I got out. It's a hard situation, that's
what keeps you [involved].[54]

In Pam M.'s case, Officer B became increasingly possessive and violent
as the relationship progressed:

Nobody could talk to me. He became violent with his hands. If
I was talking to another man, he would hit me. He had the
impression I was gay. He would ticket another [woman]
whenever I talked to her. . . . [At this prison,] there's no leaving
an officer. You will have problems.[55]

Pam M. was subsequently transferred to another facility, where she became
involved with another officer. While she felt that her relationship was not forcible,
she stated that "basically you're using them, they're using you."[56] She described
the prison as "like a camp where each officer is fucking five to six [women]." Pam
M. stated that her relationship with the officer was well known within the prison.
Both she and the officer were questioned, but both denied any involvement.

Mistreatment of Prisoners Impregnated by Guards
Over the years, a number of women have become pregnant by corrections
staff while in custody and have been punished under Rule 101 of the prisoner rule
book, which forbids sexual relations as well as soliciting or encouraging another
person to engage in sexual relations. In the past, DOCS has penalized prisoners
even when they stated that they were coerced into sexual intercourse with the
guards, and the punishment has often been severe, including prolonged terms in
segregation. As noted in the legal background chapter of this report, Human Rights
Watch believes that under no circumstances should a prisoner who has had sexual
contact with corrections staff be punished. The chilling effect that such punishment
has on reports of sexual misconduct by guards far outweighs any benefit.
Ruth Cassell has represented seven prisoners impregnated by corrections
employees over the last ten years. Cassell told us of a prisoner impregnated by a

---

[54] Ibid.

[55] Interview, New York, August 1994.

[56] Ibid.

guard in Bayview in May 1995.[57]   According to Cassell, when the prisoner became sick, blood tests determined that she was pregnant. Reportedly, the prison doctor began pressuring the prisoner to have an abortion but stopped after her father called the deputy superintendent. The prisoner was immediately transferred to Bedford Hills, where she was placed in segregation and charged with false statements, sexual offenses, and lewd behavior. The last two charges were eventually dropped, but because the prisoner would not reveal the father's name she was found guilty of false statements. The prison authorities confronted a guard that several prisoners previously had stated was having an intimate relationship with the now pregnant prisoner. According to Cassell, the guard then resigned.

Ruth Cassell told us that another young prisoner at Bedford Hills became pregnant in June 1994 after submitting on one occasion to sexual intercourse with her work supervisor. According to Cassell, the work supervisor directed the prisoner to meet him in a particular location, where he demanded sexual relations with her. The prisoner complied. When she missed her period, the work supervisor reportedly brought her pills he said would induce a miscarriage.[58]

According to Cassell, the Office of the Inspector General, which operates out of DOCS and investigates violations of prison rules, brought charges against this young woman for sexual misconduct after determining she was pregnant. At the hearing, she was sentenced to 730 days, or two years, in segregation, with a twenty-four-month loss of good time credit, because the investigators believed the prisoner was lying about who impregnated her. After she had spent two and one-half months in segregation, all charges against her were dismissed, except the Rule 101 violation of engaging in sexual relations, for which she was sentenced to time served. Thus, she was punished under Rule 101 even though she testified that she was coerced into having sex. She had an abortion in August 1994.[59]

Iris R. was charged with sexual intercourse and sentenced to nine months in segregation, after medical examinations showed her to be pregnant. When Iris R. learned of the pregnancy she contacted a lieutenant at the prison and voluntarily provided the details of her situation.[60] The lieutenant assured her there would be

---

[57] Interview, Ruth Cassell, Prisoners Legal Services, New York, February 16, 1996.

[58] Telephone interview, Ruth Cassell, Prisoners Legal Services, January 26, 1995. The pills did not induce a miscarriage, however.

[59] Ibid.

[60] Telephone interview, July 12, 1994.

no negative repercussions for her and the authorities would discipline the officer. She said he told her, "You've got to work with us on this. We have to know who the father is, what happened to you . . . We can make sure you don't go to SHU [segregation]." Within a few hours after they confirmed her pregnancy, she was transferred to Bedford Hills and then placed in segregation.

Iris R.'s punishment, however, was not limited to segregation, but extended to her medical care and treatment by the medical staff at Bedford Hills. After she was transferred to Bedford Hills, Iris R. told us that she was pressured repeatedly by the medical staff to have an abortion. When she first came forward, Iris R. thought that she might have an abortion but later changed her mind. According to Iris R., she was taken from SHU on five occasions to meet with a female doctor in the medical building who reportedly pressured her to abort. The doctor, Iris R. said, repeatedly harangued her by saying "You said you were going to terminate this pregnancy. Now why aren't you going to do it?" She also allegedly told Iris that she was "allowing men to influence her decision" not to abort and that "nobody's going to adopt this baby—it's going to end up in an institution." Iris R. believed that "these meetings were strictly to harass [her]." No prenatal exam was conducted at the time.

Over four months into her pregnancy, Iris R. began bleeding and stopped feeling the fetus move, allegedly after her cell was sprayed with insecticide. Despite her symptoms, Iris R. said the medical staff refused to see her immediately. Once she was examined, they sent her back to her unit. The next day, she was admitted briefly to an outside hospital and returned to Bedford the same day. Upon her return, she was placed in the prison hospital, but subsequent treatment reportedly scheduled by the outside hospital—including a sonogram—was never performed. Iris R. continued to suffer cramping and bleeding over the next two weeks, before she was finally taken a second time to the outside hospital. A sonogram confirmed that the fetus was dead, and an abortion was performed.

Women who are impregnated by prison staff, it appears, may also be refused participation in Bedford's nursery program because of the status of the father. The nursery program allows incarcerated women to keep their babies at the facility for up to one year to allow for mother-child bonding. Women impregnated by corrections officers, however, are sometimes denied this opportunity. After her transfer to Bedford Hills, Iris R. stated that she applied to the nursery program was initially accepted, and received a letter of acceptance. She later received a second letter withdrawing the offer when the institution realized that the father of her child was a corrections officer.[61] A second woman impregnated by a corrections officer,

---

[61] Telephone interview, July 12, 1994.

who gave birth in 1993, was similarly denied entry into the nursery program. According to Superintendent Lord, the decision was made to exclude the prisoner because she has a long sentence and there was little chance of reunification. She said:

> Eighty percent of the women leave here with the baby, or they get an extension for the baby, or leave close to the time the baby leaves. It was decided in her circumstances that it was not appropriate—for bonding, [et. cetera]—for the baby to stay.[62]

The baby's caretakers, she noted, had brought the baby to the facility for visitation. In addition, the female prisoner impregnated in the spring of 1995 was also excluded from the nursery program. In this case, the reported reason for denial was that of her four children, two had been taken away by the state.[63] The exclusion of these women from the nursery program has the effect, intended or not, of penalizing them for engaging in sexual relations with guards.

Abusive and Degrading Language

Sexual misconduct in New York's women's prisons takes place in an environment where some male corrections officers and staff use sexually explicit and derogatory language when communicating with or referring to female prisoners. Such behavior directly breaches regulations set out in the DOCS employee manual, which provides that "an employee shall refrain from the use of indecent, profane or abusive language or gestures while on duty or on State property." DOCS also has a policy on sexual harassment, but it is limited by definition to sexual harassment among employees and does not cover sexual harassment of prisoners.[64]

Women we interviewed testified to a range of degrading language and treatment. Michelle C., whose rape is described above, told us that she was

---

[62] Interview, Elaine Lord, superintendent, Bedford Hills Correctional Facility, June 22, 1994.

[63] Interview, Ruth Cassell, Prisoners Legal Services, New York, February 16, 1996.

[64] State of New York Department of Correctional Services, Directive 2605, "Sexual Harassment in the Work Place," February 13, 1989. Under the directive, sexual harassment constitutes a form of employee misconduct and anyone found guilty is subject to disciplinary action.

repeatedly harassed by a sergeant.[65] On one occasion, he reportedly asked her for a pair of her underpants and asked, "Can I feel you?" Then, on October 30, 1993, he appeared outside her door while working the overnight shift. Michelle C. recounted:

> He worked a double [shift] that night. It was around 12:30 a.m. on a weekend. He came up to the floor. . . .He stood there a minute and felt himself. He left without doing anything else.[66]

At the same prison, Judith D. told us that her unit officer repeatedly used degrading and sexualized language when speaking to prisoners. She stated:

> Last night, a girl was cleaning the showers, and he likes to stand there over top of you while you clean. [He'll say] "Look at all of these pubic hairs," and he'll be pointing to the wall. This is something we are subjected to down there.[67]

At another prison, Kathy T. told us that her problems with Officer T started almost immediately after she moved onto the honor floor.[68] "It started with little comments, like, 'In that position, I could have a wonderful time with you.'"[69] According to Kathy T., he would come into her cell and compliment her clothing or appearance. Or, she said, he would ask her "Can you come and help me in the closet?" She stated that she tried to ignore him but tolerated his behavior while living on the unit— "If he makes a pass at you and you resist, you're going to get dogged [harassed]. Those who don't resist, don't get dogged. I've been getting dogged by him for four years." Nadine P. reported similar problems with Officer

---

[65] Interview, New York, April 1994.

[66] Ibid.

[67] Interview, New York, April 1994.

[68] The honor floor is reserved for prisoners with low security status and good behavior records. It is a coveted unit, because prisoners living there are accorded more privileges than the general population.

[69] Interview, New York, April 1994.

T. According to Nadine P., while she was housed on the unit, Officer T "was telling me how pretty I was, how big my butt was."[70]

Privacy Violations

As discussed in more detail in the legal background chapter of this report, prisoners retain an internationally protected right to privacy except when limitations on this right are demonstrably required by the nature of the prison environment. In addition, several U.S. courts have reached decisions that delineate prisoners' limited right to bodily privacy in cross-gender guarding situations. In particular, U.S. courts have recognized that prisoners have a right not to be strip searched by officers of the opposite sex, except in cases of emergency; to be protected from regular inappropriate visual surveillance by officers of the opposite sex; and in the case of female prisoners, not to be routinely subjected to pat frisks by male officers.[71]

One of these decisions was handed down in 1978 in the case of *Forts v. Ward*, brought by female prisoners incarcerated at Bedford Hills.[72] The women prevailed at the district court level where the judge recognized their constitutional right to privacy and issued a court order preventing male corrections officers from working in the women's housing units at night and in the prison infirmary when they might observe women sleeping naked. Further, the judge directed the prison to install translucent screens to shield the women while showering.[73] At the time, prison rules already permitted prisoners to cover their cell windows for fifteen-minute intervals and prohibited the assignment of guards of the opposite sex to areas where prisoners who were showering were "open to view."[74]

---

[70] Interview, New York, April 1994.

[71] For a detailed discussion of prisoners' privacy rights under the U.S. Constitution, see the legal background chapter of this report.

[72] *Forts v. Ward*, 471 F. Supp. 1095, p. 1097 (S.D.N.Y. 1978) *vacated in part by* 621 F.2d 1210. The lawsuit was initiated following the 1977 DOCS policy change that allowed men to hold contact positions in women's facilities.

[73] Ibid., p. 1102.

[74] Ibid.

While the lower court's ruling was largely upheld on appeal, the circuit court recognized a far narrower right to privacy for incarcerated women.[75] The appellate court determined that while incarcerated women have a constitutional right to privacy, the employment rights of male officers take precedence.[76] It vacated the lower court ruling insofar as that ruling had prohibited the assignment of male guards to the housing units at night. The appeals court stated, "Since appropriate sleepwear can sufficiently protect [a prisoner's privacy] interest, its use should be preferred to any loss of employment opportunities."[77]

Rather than implementing and enforcing policies to balance the employment rights of male guards with female prisoners' right to privacy, it appears that DOCS has failed to protect adequately the latter. For example, in late 1995, one of Ruth Cassell's clients, a pre-operative transsexual who was in the women's prison system, was transferred from Bedford Hills to Bayview.[78] Although her privacy had been protected adequately at Bedford Hills, in Bayview she was forced to shower in an open shower area that only provided cover for three sides of her body. When the prisoner protested that prisoners and guards gathered around her when she showered and made degrading comments, the prison authorities told her that no additional privacy would be provided.[79] In addition, we documented the following cases where women's right to privacy was violated by abusive body searches.

Body Searches

Under DOCS procedures, corrections officers may pat-frisk prisoners of the opposite sex.[80] Pat-frisks may be conducted in a variety of circumstances:

---

[75] 621 F.2d 1210.

[76] The district court, in fact, assumed that male officers viewing incarcerated women naked was a violation of the women's constitutional right to privacy. Ibid., p. 1214.

[77] Ibid., p. 1217.

[78] Although the prisoner looks like a woman and has breasts, she still has a penis.

[79] Interview, Ruth Cassell, Prisoners Legal Services, New York, February 16, 1996.

[80] They make only one exception—for Muslim males—prohibiting female officers from conducting a nonemergency pat-frisk of any Muslim male. New York Department of Corrections Services, "Control and Search for Contraband," Directive No. 4910, February

when entering the visiting room; going or returning to housing areas or outside work details; to and from program and recreation areas, where reasonable grounds exist to believe a prisoner is carrying contraband; and as directed by supervisory staff.   A bill prohibiting male corrections officers from pat-frisking female prisoners was submitted to the New York State Senate in the 1996. The bill would allow cross-gender pat-frisks when the officer has probable cause to believe that a pat-frisk is necessary to protect the immediate safety of other prisoners or prison employees, or to prevent an escape. While then Acting Commissioner Coombe in early 1996 suggested assigning only female guards to certain posts at Albion, the prison with the most reports of abusive pat-frisks, and possibly using hand-held metal detectors there, DOCS reacted to this bill as an unnecessary interference on their duties.[81]

DOCS procedure also provides for both strip searches and "strip frisks" of prisoners, under limited circumstances, to search for and control the possession of contraband.[82] A strip search is a search of a prisoner's clothes once they are

---

1, 1994. A pat-frisk is defined as "a search by hand of an inmate's person and his or her clothes while the inmate is clothed. . . The inmate will be required to run fingers through hair and spread fingers for visual inspection. The search shall include searching into the inmate's clothing. Requiring an inmate to open his or her mouth is not part of a pat-frisk."

[81] Interview, Ruth Cassell, Prisoners Legal Services, New York, January 30, 1996.

[82] Ibid. New York's strip search and strip frisk policy has been shaped through litigation, and DOCS currently operates under a consent order. In 1977 a male prisoner incarcerated by DOCS, Michael Hurley, filed suit challenging the constitutionality of the strip frisk procedure. Under the procedure, prisoners housed in the Special Housing Unit (SHU) were routinely strip frisked whenever they entered or left the correctional facility. *Hurley v. Ward*, 584 F. 2d. 609 (2d Cir., 1978). His suit was later certified as a class action on behalf of all prisoners in DOCS custody. *Hurley v. Coughlin*, Civil Action File No. 77-3847 (RLC),Consent Decree in Full Resolution of Action, July 21, 1983. (*Hurley v. Ward* was subsequently renamed *Hurley v. Coughlin* after DOCS Commissioner Coughlin replaced Commissioner Ward.) In July 1983 both parties reached agreement on a consent decree that altered DOCS strip frisk procedure. Specifically, DOCS agreed to conduct strip frisks only upon a determination of probable cause, by a sergeant or higher ranking officer, and conducted by staff of the same sex as the prisoner. Strip frisks without probable cause were permitted in limited circumstances, such as where a prisoner was transferred, after a contact visit, or upon entry to the Special Housing Unit. The court, in 1993, found DOCS in massive noncompliance with the consent order, and a new order further regulating strip frisks was entered in January 1994. The new order further detailed the conditions under which a strip frisk could be conducted and the procedure to be followed by prison staff.

removed and a visual inspection of the prisoner's body. A strip frisk involves a visual inspection of body cavities, including the mouth. During a strip frisk, all prisoners are required to bend over and spread their buttocks. In addition, incarcerated women must squat and expose their vaginas. By policy, both strip searches and strip frisks may only be conducted where a sergeant or higher ranking official has probable cause that a prisoner has contraband. The procedure provides a number of safeguards to ensure that the search is conducted as humanely as possible: only the officer conducting the search may be present;[83] searches must be conducted by an employee of the same sex as the prisoner; officers are required to "conduct themselves professionally" and "conduct such searches in a manner least degrading to all involved." Further, the search must be conducted in a location where privacy is safeguarded, the room is clean and sufficiently warm, and the prisoner's clothing is not on the floor. DOCS policy provides that during a strip frisk a female prisoner need not remove her bra or panties until after a search of her mouth is made.

We received reports that within Albion, prisoners have been forced to strip in a room with an open door where male correctional staff were present, in violation of DOCS policy, and that such searches were videotaped. Jane N. told us that she was strip searched by two female officers in the presence of two male officers when she entered segregation.[84] The search took place in a small room that had a door with an uncovered window. One of the female officers held the video camera while the other conducted the search. Throughout the search, the door remained open and two male officers stood in the doorway—one leaning against the opposite wall and facing into the room.

Following the search, Jane N. was given a robe and shoes and taken to her cell. She described the robe as "ripped up and dingy," without a string to tie it shut, and small, leaving her partially exposed. Once in the prison cell, she stated, officers provided her with panties and a bra, but no other clothing for several hours.

Hurley v. Ward, Civil Action File No. 77-3847 (RLC), Stipulation and Order, January 3, 1994.

[83] An exception is made if the prisoner has a record of assaults or attempted assaults or there is reason to believe he or she will resist the search. In such cases, a sergeant or higher ranking officer, of the same sex as the prisoner, may be present. Policy Directive No. 4910, Sub-section G.

[84] Interview, New York, March 1995.

Jane N. alleged that an officer later came to her cell and took photos—"two closeups and two far-away shots"—of her wearing only a bra and panties.

Pam M. told us of a similar experience. In June 1994, she was taken to segregation prior to her transfer from Albion. In the presence of a male and a female officer, she was directed to remove all of her clothing while being videotaped. She said they followed the normal procedure for a strip search but that "[I]t was the first time I was stripped in front of a man."[85]

According to Betsy Fuller, an attorney with PLS, the practice of routinely videotaping all strip searches on admission to segregation began in January or February 1994 and continued until July 1994.[86] Fuller estimates that with twenty to twenty-five women entering SHU monthly, approximately one hundred to 120 were searched and videotaped altogether. An unknown number of these tapes were then reviewed by the male deputy of security pursuant to regulations governing the use of videotapes. According to Fuller, the tapes were reviewed to determine if an incident involving the use of force occurred. If not, the tape was recycled.

Fuller watched between six to eight of these tapes, which she described to us as "images I will never forget." In one video that she reviewed, a woman within a week of parole was sent to segregation because contraband was allegedly found in her cell. When asked to strip, according to Fuller, the woman was "completely freaked out" by the camera and hysterical throughout the strip search. She repeatedly asked to speak with a supervisor but was ignored. Her questions regarding the reason for the search were also ignored. Fuller told us that the prisoner's mental pain was hard to watch.

The videos, furthermore, showed that the searches were conducted in a manner that violated DOCS policy, with women being required to undress completely before the examination of their mouth and ears, and to remain undressed during the entire search. Fuller stated that she could hear men's voices clearly outside the door. The presence of men was apparently justified by DOCS regulations requiring a sergeant's presence if a prisoner is agitated or likely to resist. Since male sergeants, under the regulations, are not allowed to be present during the searches, they waited outside the door and the door remained open. This, according to Fuller, violated DOCS policy. In other cases, up to four female officers were present, as opposed to only one as provided under the policy.

The searches did not end there. As in Jane N.'s case, many women were denied adequate clothing and were forced to wear bathrobes for hours. Fuller

---

[85] Interview, New York, August 1994.

[86] Telephone interview, Betsy Fuller, Prisoners Legal Services, October 4, 1994.

stated that DOCS policy requires that prisoners entering segregation be given clothing—pants, shoes, underwear, and a shirt—but at this prison the women were provided with only robes and, in some cases, with only transparent paper bathrobes.[87] The prisoners' humiliation, Fuller stated, was compounded by two factors. Many of the women were aware that the videos would be reviewed by the male deputy of security, and many had a history of sexual abuse.

THE SYSTEM'S RESPONSE

In response to intense pressure by nongovernmental organizations on behalf of women incarcerated in New York, in late 1995 and 1996 the New York department of corrections, under then Acting Commission Coombe and current Acting Commissioner Glenn Goord, has begun to address the problem of sexual misconduct within its women's prisons through its support of legislative reform efforts, public statements, and improved interaction with nongovernmental organizations. Since September 1995, DOCS regularly has sent representatives to meetings of the Coalition for Women Prisoners. In addition, DOCS has formed a task force to examine issues facing incarcerated women. The task force is entirely female and is composed of different DOCS officials, certain wardens, officials from state agencies, superintendents, and others. But in contrast with these recent positive steps, our investigation indicates that DOCS is not consistently responsive to allegations of sexual misconduct, and that its reporting and investigative procedures are seriously flawed. In particular, DOCS does not distinguish between prisoner grievances of sexual misconduct and other allegations of staff misconduct.[88] This policy makes it difficult for DOCS officials to notice a problem of pervasive sexual misconduct. In addition, prior to the passage of the 1996 bill prohibiting all sexual contact between corrections officials and prisoners, no

---

[87] Fuller has been told by DOCS that the practice of videotaping the strip frisks started after PLS wrote to prison administrators at Albion requesting the records and any videotapes for a prisoner who alleged she was beaten up when she was escorted to SHU. This letter followed a general format used by PLS sent to the men's prisons because, Fuller stated, men admitted to SHU are often videotaped because they are more likely to use force.

[88] Letter from James B. Flateau, public information director, New York Department of Correctional Services, to Human Rights Watch, September 25, 1996.

allegations of sexual misconduct were forwarded to either the Inspector General's office or local law enforcement.[89]

Denial of an Effective Remedy

As discussed in the legal background chapter of this report, international human rights law obligates governments not only to prohibit torture and cruel, inhuman or degrading treatment and privacy violations, but also to ensure that when such abuses occur they can be reported and fully and fairly investigated without the complainant fearing punishment or retaliation from the authorities. In addition, under U.S. law, prisoners are also guaranteed access to the courts to challenge prison conditions or other prison problems. Nonetheless, women prisoners in New York prisons have frequently been denied an effective remedy because the grievance and investigative procedures for complaints by prisoners function poorly. Moreover, the lack of confidentiality of such procedures has on a number of occasions exposed prisoners who report custodial sexual misconduct to retaliation and punishment.

Grievances

New York provides a grievance mechanism for prisoners to raise complaints about the content or application of departmental policies, regulations, procedures or rules, or the absence of a policy, regulation or rule.[90] The grievance mechanism should provide redress for sexual misconduct complaints, but rarely does. In fact, as stated above, DOCS makes no distinction between sexual misconduct grievances and other complaints about staff misconduct. Under the procedure, all grievances are reviewed by a five-person committee composed of two voting prisoners, two voting staff members, and one non-voting chairperson,[91]

---

[89] Ibid.

[90] "Inmate Grievance Program," Policy Directive No. 4040, November 27, 1991.

[91] New York is the only state we visited where grievances are reviewed by a committee, rather than an individual grievance officer or coordinator. It is also the only state we visited where prisoners actually participate in the review of grievances.

Statistical information prepared by DOCS indicates that incarcerated women are less likely to file grievances than male prisoners, but they file complaints of staff misconduct significantly more often. According to reports prepared in 1993 and 1994 by DOCS on the nature and type of grievances filed, incarcerated women filed only 4 percent of all grievances in both years, while they accounted for 6 percent of the prison population. Meanwhile, grievances about staff misconduct constituted nearly one-third of the women's

Prisoners may appeal the committee's decision to the prison superintendent and, if dissatisfied with that response, to the Central Office Review Committee (CORC).

One of the principle problems with the grievance procedure is that prisoners are not informed of their right to report abuses, or they do not know with whom to speak or whom they can trust. Months into her incarceration, Iris R. told us, a sergeant called her into his office to discuss comments he overheard officers making about her breasts.[92] He reportedly assured Iris R. that if she was approached, she could seek his help. Her initial thought was that the officer was also "coming on to me." Iris R. also commented to us that by the time this conversation took place:

> It had already happened. I was already approached. They should have said this at the beginning—if it happens, you should come forward and you'll be believed.

Outside monitors consider the grievance mechanism to be ineffective and biased. Based on their experiences, the grievance system proved unable to resolve serious complaints about DOCS policies. When New York sought federal certification of its grievance mechanism from the U.S. Department of Justice in 1992, attorneys with PLS prepared a lengthy packet to oppose certification that highlighted the ineffectiveness of the grievance mechanism.[93] PLS focused in

---

grievances. Overall, only one-fifth of all grievances filed in 1993 and 1994 raised a complaint of staff misconduct. It is impossible, however, to determine what contributes to this difference as staff conduct is presented as a general category, with no distinction as to complaints of sexual misconduct or sexually degrading language. DOCS, "A Compilation of Grievances Filed by Nature and Type, by Facility: January 1 - June 15, 1993;" DOCS, "A Compilation of Grievances Filed by Nature and Type, by Facility: January 1 - June 15, 1994."

[92] Telephone interview, July 12, 1994.

[93] As described in the legal background chapter of this report, states may seek certification of their grievance procedure pursuant to the Civil Rights of Institutionalized Persons Act (CRIPA). Once certified, the grievance mechanism may serve as an initial remedial process which a prisoner must use prior to filing suit and a federal judge may delay a prisoner's lawsuit for a specified period until the prisoner has pursued her complaint through the grievance procedure.

particular on DOCS strip frisk and strip search policies.[94] According to PLS, prior to the original *Hurley v. Ward* lawsuit filed in 1977, thirty-two prisoners had filed grievances challenging the strip frisk and strip search policy. All the grievances were denied. The procedure for strip frisks was subsequently modified once after other prisoners joined *Hurley* in a class action lawsuit against DOCS, then again after another court order was issued.[95] Moreover, PLS pointed out that of seventeen cases where a state-wide policy was directed to change in response to a grievance, not once did the policy change. Despite this demonstrated inability to "provide a meaningful remedy," as required for certification, the U.S. Department of Justice certified the grievance system in late 1992.

Again, in another situation, the grievance mechanism failed to resolve an abusive policy without litigation. It was not until July 1994 that DOCS stopped the routine videotaping of strip searches as described above, after attorneys with PLS repeatedly contacted the institution. As a result of PLS's involvement, DOCS introduced additional protections into the procedure by: requiring strip searches to be approved by a higher ranking officer; agreeing to review the videotapes only if an incident report was filed; and allowing only a female supervisor to review them. According to Fuller, CORC has been investigating complaints of abusive strip frisks and other improper searches more diligently.[96] The lawsuit by the women subjected to the videotaping was settled in January 1996, when DOCS agreed to pay each woman $1,000 for each videotaped search that she had undergone.[97]

---

[94] This is one of numerous problems with the procedure that Prisoners Legal Services raised.

[95] The case is discussed more fully above in the section on body searches. The lawsuit contended that New York's strip search and strip frisk policy was unconstitutional. As a result, New York DOCS in June 1995 entered into a consent decree pursuant to which it has modified its method for conducting such searches.

[96] Telephone interview, Betsy Fuller, Prisoners Legal Services, October 4, 1994.

[97] *Hurley v. Coughlin*, Civil Action No. 77-3847 (RLC), Stipulation and Order, January 3, 1996.

Investigations and the Failure to Report

Investigations are, generally, a necessary step to discipline corrections officers, yet there appears to be no standard DOCS investigatory policy.[98] At Bedford Hills Correctional Facility, there appears to be no written or specific procedure for reporting and investigating allegations of sexual misconduct. Superintendent Lord told us that she turns over complaints "where it is not just an issue of sexual harassment" to the inspector general's office, an investigative unit within DOCS. The inspector general's staff, she said, then takes over the investigation and, upon its conclusion, reports its findings to her.

Our interviews indicated that generally once a complaint is turned over to the inspector general's office, an investigator from that office visits the prison and interviews the complainant, other prisoners who witnessed the situation or have knowledge about it and, presumably, the implicated officer. Many of these investigators, according to Ruth Cassell, are former corrections officers, some of whom have worked with the implicated officer or at the prison where they are conducting the investigation.[99] Once the investigator completes the interviews, he or she prepares and submits a report with his or her findings. According to Superintendent Lord, if the inspector general finds "justification" or substantiates the allegation, the information is then turned over to DOCS Department of Labor Relations. However, Labor Relations is not bound by the inspector general's determination and makes an independent decision as to whether or not to proceed with disciplinary action against the implicated officer.[100] Moreover, DOCS informed Human Rights Watch that in 1994-1995 no allegations of sexual misconduct were forwarded to the Inspector General's office.[101]

There appears to be very little accountability to outside monitors regarding the investigative process; our interviews indicate that prisoners and their attorneys are often frozen out of this process. Kathryn Schmidt, with PLS, commented,

---

[98] Interview, Kathryn Schmidt, Prisoners Legal Services, New York, January 14, 1994.

[99] Telephone interview, Ruth Cassell, Prisoners Legal Services, January 26, 1995.

[100] Interview, Elaine Lord, superintendent, Bedford Hills Correctional Facility, June 22, 1994.

[101] Letter from James B. Flateau, public information director, New York Department of Correctional Services, to Human Rights Watch, September 25, 1996.

"[DOCS] is not very informative about the outcome of investigations."[102] She was monitoring the progress of two inquiries into sexual misconduct at the time of our interview, and her knowledge about their progress was limited to what DOCS officials told her during one meeting. At that meeting, DOCS permitted her to view the papers pertaining to the two pending investigations but refused to provide her with copies of those papers despite PLS's role as class counsel.

Attorneys, too, have difficulty obtaining statements that their clients may have given to prison officials or investigators. In late 1994 Ruth Cassell represented a prisoner who had been impregnated by a corrections employee at Bedford. The woman had been interviewed for several hours by the superintendent and a lieutenant, and a statement had been written. When Cassell requested a copy of this written statement, the DOCS counsel refused to turn it over while the investigation was pending.[103]

Bias Against Prisoner Testimony

The lack of accountability to outside monitors is particularly troublesome since the integrity of the investigative process is compromised by a number of factors. First, a bias against prisoner testimony pervades the system, beginning with the initial investigation and continuing through the disciplinary determination. One investigator reportedly told Kathryn Schmidt that he did not believe the incarcerated women he interviewed and that, in his view, their sole purpose in raising such allegations was to get money.[104]

Our interviews show that the only witness to sexual misconduct is often the victim herself, or another prisoner who witnessed something unusual or who herself experienced problems with the same officer. But, given DOCS's bias against prisoner testimony, the latter's testimony is also deemed insufficient because of her status as a prisoner. One attorney told us that, in his opinion, "No number of inmates stacked on top of each other is enough to sanction a guard. You need some tangible proof."[105] Thus, the only evidence a prisoner may rely on is physical evidence or the testimony of another corrections employee, both of which are difficult to obtain. Given such bias, it is no surprise that prisoners' claims of

---

[102] Interview, Kathryn Schmidt, Prisoners Legal Services, New York, April 19, 1994.

[103] Telephone interview, Ruth Cassell, Prisoners Legal Services, January 26, 1995.

[104] Interview, Kathryn Schmidt, Prisoners Legal Services, New York, January 14, 1994.

[105] Telephone interview, Bill Gibney, Prisoners Legal Services, June 20, 1994.

sexual misconduct by corrections staff are rarely substantiated pursuant to an investigation by prison authorities. For example, when PLS was opposing certification of the New York grievance system, it asked DOCS to provide examples of an instance when in a dispute between a prisoner and a guard, the prisoner was believed over the guard. DOCS was unable to find one.[106]

Conflicts of Interest

The fact that corrections officers, in practice, rarely assist with investigations of their colleagues is a second obstacle to effective investigations. DOCS's policy requires corrections employees to file incident reports for anything unusual or where force is employed. Many corrections employees, however, fail to report unusual incidents because of an unwritten rule among corrections officers that one does not report on a colleague. According to one former employee we interviewed:

> If one officer squeals on another [at one prison], it will be known [at another prison] by the next day. You will be blackballed at every other facility. It's a brotherhood thing. All officers stick together. . . . It's an officer thing—you don't squeal. It's in the police department, it's in corrections. There's nothing to do about it. [If you report], they will treat you like a criminal in the street, [because] you broke the code. They watch out for each other, and that goes with every officer job.[107]

The "code" is reportedly enforced and practiced among higher ranking staff as well, and officers know which supervisors will tolerate misconduct. The former DOCS employee told us that some supervisors may report their subordinates. The offending officers:

> know when, how and with whom to do it. They know not during the day or around civilian staff.[108] Counselors will write them up in a heartbeat. If a counselor eyewitnesses, then

---

[106] Telephone Interview, John Gresham, attorney, February 20, 1996.

[107] Interview, New York, January 17, 1994.

[108] Civilian or nonsecurity staff are employees other than correctional officers.

something will be done. If the counselor just heard about it, then nothing gets done because they do not believe the inmates.[109]

A third problem with the investigative procedure is that many prisoners are unwilling to report sexual misconduct by prison employees for fear of being punished themselves. As stated earlier, Rule 101 of the prisoner handbook proscribes sexual relations, regardless of consent, and a violation of this provision can result in disciplinary action against the prisoner. In Iris's case, the officer told her that if she did come forward, no one would believe her, and she would be "put in the box [SHU] and get in a whole lot of trouble."[110]

Retaliation
Incarcerated women have been harassed by corrections officers to prevent them from reporting sexual misconduct and to retaliate against them for filing complaints or resisting sexual advances. According to Bill Gibney of PLS, women report that corrections authorities threaten to transfer them if they speak out about sexual misconduct.[111] Women incarcerated at Bayview are particularly hesitant to come forward because this facility, located in New York City, the area some 70 percent of the state's female prisoners come from, is particularly desirable. Albion, which houses approximately half of the state's female prisoners, is located about ten hours from New York City. Rachel H. spoke of this threat, saying, "They will threaten you with an administrative move in a minute, especially if you live in the five boroughs."[112] A transfer to other prisons that are located further upstate means that families often lack the resources to visit the prison.

Some prisoners do not report abuses because they fear that to do so would worsen the conditions of their incarceration. Judith D. told us that Officer J, who harasses women on her unit, "has let it be known that if we push it, he'll get us out of work release." She also said that her cellmate was harassed by this officer because she declined his advances. According to Judith D., the officer:

---

[109] Interview, New York, January 17, 1994.

[110] Telephone interview, July 12, 1994.

[111] Telephone interview, Bill Gibney, Prisoners Legal Services, June 20, 1994.

[112] Interview, New York, April 1994.

started harassing her [the cellmate] 'cause he liked her but she
didn't like him. She would get stuff from her boyfriend. She
got packages all the time. He [the officer] would write her
disciplinary tickets. They think they're gods or something.
They have so much power over us. Once they have a crush on
a women, they don't want them to have another man.[113]

A former DOCS employee corroborated that women who reject an
officer's sexual advances are often subjected to harassment and retaliation.
Officers, he said, "can make their lives a living hell—hold their packages, stop
their visits, or they can pull a surprise search and plant something in their cell."[114]
When asked how officers could stop visits, he said this was "the easiest one"—an
officer might deny the visit "because the person is wearing green, [or] they're not
on the visiting list. . . . They can just not find a person's name." He recounted the
story of a nun who brought a prisoner's daughter to visit the facility. The prisoner
was, in his words, "pretty" and she had rejected an officer who had solicited her.
The day the nun visited, that officer was at the desk and denied the visit.
        In one prison we visited, it appears that, over a period of years, a male
corrections officer, Officer T, has repeatedly retaliated against women who resisted
his sexual advances or attempted to report his sexual involvement to prison
officials. Officer T worked on the honor unit in the prison and holds substantial
power over incarcerated women living there.
        Kathy T. told us that Officer T retaliated against her after she spoke to the
inspector general during an investigation into the officer's alleged misconduct.[115]
The officer was removed from the unit for eight or nine months, Kathy T. believes
in 1992, while apparently under investigation. The findings were inconclusive, and
Officer T was reinstated to the unit. Kathy T. stated that she and a few other
women who had assisted the investigation subsequently received poor evaluations
from him and were taken off the honor unit. At the time of our interview, she was
appealing the transfer.
        Nadine P. told us she lived on the honor unit until 1990 but was removed
after she filed a grievance for sexual harassment against Officer T and, as she put

---

[113] Interview, New York, April 1994.

[114] Interview, New York, January 17, 1994.

[115] Interview, New York, April 1994.

it, "He in turn wrote me a ticket."[116] Nadine P. stated that she spoke with the inspector general's investigator regarding her experience, after a friend came forward and "described his [Officer T's] manhood [penis]." In October 1994 another prisoner at the same prison living on the honor unit contacted us regarding Officer T, who allegedly began harassing her because she reported problems with "one of his playmates."

Rhea Schaenman Mallet, formerly of the Correctional Association of New York, who monitored the conditions of incarcerated women, told us about two victims of reprisal. One was transferred and the other was threatened with transfer from Bayview because they spoke about problems in the prison. Both also lost their work release status.[117] In Pam M.'s case, mentioned above, other officers retaliated against her after she reported Officer B's misconduct; she had to be placed in protective custody and was later transferred to another facility.

Impunity

Impunity for sexually abusive staff in the DOCS system has been an ongoing problem for at least a decade. While there have been a few dismissals over the years, officers have rarely been terminated for sexual misconduct. In Ruth Cassell's experience, officers were generally transferred off the living units or moved to other prison facilities. While, as noted above, several officers were terminated and others transferred from Bayview in the early 1980s, they were disciplined on grounds other than sexual misconduct.[118]

---

[116] Interview, New York, April 1994.

[117] Interview, Rhea Schaenman Mallet, Correctional Association of New York, August 12, 1994. One woman spoke at a conference; the other worked for the Correctional Association's AIDS Project.

[118] Interview, Ruth Cassell, Prisoners Legal Services, New York, April 19, 1994. According to another attorney with whom we spoke, an officer at Taconic was fired in the late 1980s for sexually assaulting a female prisoner. Her suit for damages was still pending. Although her attorney had heard that the officer had assaulted other female prisoners, he was unable to see the file because state law allows the presiding judge to decide if it contains any relevant information, and in this case the judge determined that it did not. Telephone interviews, Loren Glassman, attorney, June 16, 1994; February 12, 1996.

We were unable to locate any provision in DOCS policy indicating the appropriate sanction for sexual contact with a prisoner,[119] but our interviews with DOCS indicate that the appropriate sanctions would be dismissal. Anthony Annucci, DOCS counsel and deputy commissioner, told us that sexual relations with prisoners will not be tolerated and that the department has terminated employees for "mere letter writing."[120]

Contrary to Annucci's statement, it appears that even when reports are filed, not enough is done to pursue the allegations and to punish the officer responsible. According to a former DOCS employee,[121] he and a colleague filed an incident report on a corrections officer after they were approached by two female prisoners who told them that the officer was making passes at them and that, during count, while everyone else was locked in their rooms, he took two other prisoners into the closet for sexual activity. The former employee pursued the allegation by interviewing the two prisoners alleged to have been in the closet. Both, he said, denied the incident because, he believed, they were getting favorable treatment. Then he spoke to the corrections officer. In his words, "Once I talked to him and the women, I knew [it was true.]" He reported the incident to a captain and filed an incident report. But when he left the prison several months later, the officer was still at his job and nothing had happened. According to the former employee, the corrections officer had been investigated before for similar conduct and "had been doing it for years." As a result, he told us, nonsecurity staff had grown disillusioned with the procedure. They had ceased to file reports because of inaction on previous reports. When he himself saw nothing was done, the former employee said he, too, resisted pursuing other allegations. The prisoner impregnated by a guard at Bayview in mid-1995 provides another example. Although fifteen prisoners filed reports alleging that she was involved with a guard

---

[119] The DOCS employee manual merely provides that employees shall not engage in overfamiliar conduct with prisoners, but contains no table of disciplinary actions to correspond to a violation of this provision. Article 8 of the collective bargaining agreement between the corrections officers' union and the DOCS sets forth a range of disciplinary remedies available, but likewise has no table. Article 8.2 lists the following disciplinary sanctions "loss of leave credits or other privilege, written reprimand, fine, suspension without pay, reduction in grade, or dismissal from service."

[120] Telephone interview, Anthony Annucci, counsel, New York Department of Correctional Services, February 9, 1995.

[121] Interview, New York, January 17, 1994.

and that guard later admitted to impregnating her, an earlier DOCS investigation found no evidence of wrongdoing.[122]

According to DOCS, they sought dismissals for thirteen guards for sexual misconduct in 1994 and 1995.[123] Under the contract with the guards' union, all dismissals must be approved by independent arbitrators. The arbitrators dismissed four officers, suspended two, and placed one guard on six months probation.[124] The remaining five officers resigned in lieu of discipline. In the one case in which DOCS requested a fine for a guard for sexual misconduct instead of dismissal, the arbitrators issued a warning.[125]

As described above, in late 1995, DOCS referred an alleged rape of a women prisoner by a guard, Shelbourne Reid, to the local district attorney, but in that case there was physical evidence in addition to the prisoner's testimony.[126] The prisoner had preserved Reid's semen in a cooler and then presented it to a lieutenant. The prison authorities did not contact the district attorney for approximately three weeks, but once notified, the district attorney's office spoke to the woman several times and took pictures. Reid, who had just completed his post-hire probation, admitted the sexual contact and was fired. According to Cassell, Reid had allegedly raped another female prisoner, around the same time. However, there was no physical evidence of this rape and the district attorney decided not to prosecute. On December 13, 1995, Reid entered a plea for sex abuse of the first degree with a sentence of five years' probation and designation as a sex offender. In addition, he must participate in sex offender treatment. Both women received protection orders from Reid.[127]

Despite the Reid case, DOCS told Human Rights Watch, that they had not referred any cases of sexual misconduct to local law enforcement for prosecution.

---

[122] Interview, Ruth Cassell, Prisoners Legal Services, New York, February 16, 1996.

[123] Three officers at Albion, three at Bayview, five at Bedford Hills, and two officers at Taconic. Letter from James B. Flateau, public information director, New York Department of Correctional Services, to Human Rights Watch, September 25, 1996.

[124] Ibid.

[125] Ibid.

[126] Interview, Ruth Cassell, Prisoners Legal Services, New York, February 16, 1996.

[127] Telephone interview, Ruth Cassell, Prisoners Legal Services, April 9, 1996.

According to DOCS, it was determined by department staff that no criminal wrongdoing had occurred in any of the cases, including the cases of the twelve guards that DOCS sought to dismiss.[128] Significantly, DOCS noted that as a result of the 1996 law prohibiting all sexual contact between guards and prisoners, all such "incidents now will be referred to law enforcement authorities for criminal prosecution."[129]

Even officers accused of impregnating prisoners are seldom investigated and punished, despite the possibility of using paternity tests to establish their guilt or innocence. Cassell told us that in the cases of three pregnant women she has represented, DOCS declined to take any disciplinary action against the officer.[130] In each case, she was told by the inspector general's office that "they could not fire the guard unless they had proof" that the officer fathered the child. According to Cassell, the inspector general's staff stated that a prisoner's word was insufficient to uphold disciplinary action against an officer; they need to conduct "tissue testing" on the child. Yet, DOCS has repeatedly failed to conduct the necessary testing. In two of the three cases, the women miscarried or did not carry to term and, according to Cassell, "When the time came to do the test, they just didn't do it."[131] Iris R. told us that she sought an autopsy on the fetus but was told the fetus was lost. The officer whom she alleged impregnated her was transferred to a men's facility.

DOCS itself seems to be uncertain that it has the authority to obtain the necessary physical evidence to conduct a paternity test. Superintendent Elaine Lord told us that she did not believe she could require any employee to provide a blood sample. She stated that only one of her officers had been dismissed based on a paternity test and, in that case, he had voluntarily submitted a blood sample.[132]

The general failure to discipline officers is rooted, in large part, in the bias against prisoner testimony. Our interviews with Lord and Annucci indicate that

---

[128] Ibid.

[129] Ibid.

[130] In two of the six cases, tissue testing was conducted and the correctional officers were terminated. Disciplinary action is still pending in the latest case.

[131] Interview, Ruth Cassell, Prisoners Legal Services, New York, April 19, 1994.

[132] Interview, Elaine Lord, superintendent, Bedford Hills Correctional Facility, June 22, 1994.

another reason lies in a problem with the DOCS Department of Labor Relations, which appears to favor heavily corrections officers in appeals and arbitrations. Lord referred to a sexual assault that occurred at Bedford in the early 1980s, shortly after she started at that facility. She told us that the officer was suspended from DOCS and tried for allegedly raping a female prisoner. The officer asserted at his trial that the liaison with the prisoner was consensual. He was convicted of a misdemeanor offense. According to Lord, it then took two years of arbitration to dismiss the officer from DOCS.[133]

She also referred to another officer who was seen by a sergeant and other colleagues to be sexually harassing prisoners. The officer denied any misconduct, and the case went to binding arbitration. He was suspended for approximately eight months and found guilty of a minor offense. He lost one month's salary but retained his bid for the shift and unit he wanted. We believe, based on the time frame provided, that this may be the same officer who harassed Nadine P. and Kathy T. We received a letter in October 1994 from another prisoner on the unit indicating that after the officer returned, his misconduct continued.

DOCS's problems with removing abusive employees may be partially of its own making. Union contracts with correctional officers do not proscribe sexual harassment, a catchall term that would cover sexual contact with prisoners and the use of degrading and sexualized language. A 1992 Governor's Task Force on Sexual Harassment recommended that all union contracts contain language specifically prohibiting sexual harassment by employees, and make clear that acts of sexual harassment constitute violations of the contract and grounds for discipline.[134] DOCS has not acted on these recommendations.

RECOMMENDATIONS

I.   Prohibiting Sex in Custody
A.   The New York State district attorney should strictly enforce Section 130.05(3)(e) of the New York Penal Code prohibiting sexual contact with a person in custody. The consent of the victim, which is not a legal defense to a prosecution under this section, should not be a *de facto* bar to prosecution. Human Rights Watch would emphasize, however, that the

---

[133] Ibid.

[134] Governor's Task Force on Sexual Harassment, "Interim Progress Report: December 1992," Recommendation 31 (Albany: State of New York - Division for Women, 1992).

offense of prison sexual abuse is predicated on the abuse of custodial authority, not on distinctions between oral, anal, and vaginal sex that are entirely irrelevant to this key issue. For that reason, we recommend against prosecution under the New York sodomy law.

B.   DOCS should develop a specific sexual misconduct policy for its guards, along with specific disciplinary sanctions for violations of such a policy, including immediate dismissal for sexual contact with a prisoner.

C.   DOCS should amend Rule 101 of the prisoner rulebook to ensure that it does not punish women prisoners for sexual relations with corrections employees under any circumstances. Even in those instances where the evidence overcomes the presumption of some form of coercive influence on the prisoner, prison authorities should refrain from punishing her. Whatever penological interests might be served by such sanctions are outweighed by the deterrent effect that such punishments would have on prisoners' willingness to report custodial sexual abuse.

D.   DOCS should include in its employee manual a requirement that prisoners be treated humanely and be free from torture and cruel, inhuman or degrading treatment, to comply with U.S. obligations under international law, particularly the International Covenant on Civil and Political Rights and the Torture Convention.

E.   DOCS should integrate into the union contract a provision barring sexually abusive, profane or degrading language, sexual harassment, or sexual misconduct toward prisoners. Violations of this provision should constitute grounds for discipline.

II.   Safeguarding Prisoners Impregnated by Guards
A.   DOCS should refrain from administratively segregating pregnant prisoners, unless they expressly request it.

B.   DOCS should ensure that no women prisoners impregnated as a result of sexual misconduct are pressured in any way to undergo an abortion.

C.   DOCS should ensure that pregnant prisoners receive timely and adequate medical care, and that medical treatment recommended by physicians is provided as prescribed. Medical care should include professional psychiatric counseling for prisoners who are impregnated as a consequence of rape or sexual abuse or to others who request such assistance. Prisoners also should receive neutral counseling on the options available to them. Administrative segregation should not preclude the provision of adequate medical and hygienic requirements for a safe pregnancy.

D.   DOCS should reexamine its guidelines and practices for accepting women into the nursery program to ensure that the identity of a child's father is not grounds for exclusion.

III.   Prohibiting Abusive and Degrading Language
DOCS should vigorously enforce the prohibition in the DOCS employee manual against indecent, profane or abusive language or gestures. Any violation of this provision by corrections employees should constitute a disciplinary offense.

IV.   Protecting Privacy: The Need for a Policy
A.   DOCS should establish a policy to protect the privacy of women prisoners consistent with several federal court decisions recognizing that prisoners have a constitutionally protected right to privacy. Such a policy should include, among other things:
  1.   a requirement that male officers announce their presence before entering a women's housing unit;
  2.   permission for prisoners to cover their cell windows for limited intervals while changing or using the toilet in their cells; and
  3.   a restriction that showers and toilets be searched by female officers only.

B.   DOCS should enforce its policy that strip searches and strip frisks must be conducted by corrections employees of the same sex as the prisoner, except in emergency conditions. Even in emergencies, DOCS should use female officers as much as possible. For this policy to be meaningful, DOCS should ensure that male corrections officials are not present during strip searches or strip frisks, and also not in a position to witness or observe the search. In the event that a strip search is videotaped, the tapes should be reviewed solely by female officers.

C.   DOCS should stipulate in its policy and procedure for conducting pat-frisks that they be conducted by female officers, whenever possible. All officers should be trained in the appropriate conduct of such frisks and in the disciplinary sanctions associated with noncompliance. Prisoners who either pull away during offensive pat-searches, or who request that searches be administered by female officers, should not automatically be subject to disciplinary action.

V.   Ensuring an Effective Remedy
Grievances

A.   DOCS should investigate fully all grievances that allege violations of DOCS policies to ensure that these policies are properly implemented, and that prisoners' rights secured by the policies are safeguarded.

B.   DOCS should ensure that all prisoners are fully informed of their right to file grievances and the method for doing so.

C.   DOCS should also introduce protections to ensure prompt and impartial investigations into complaints of sexual misconduct by corrections employees. The grievance procedure should, among other things, protect the confidentiality of the complainant and witnesses while the implicated officer is still in a contact position over them; ensure that prisoner testimony is give due weight; and prohibit the implicated officer from conducting the investigation.

Investigative Procedures

A.   DOCS should promulgate a written, public procedure for conducting investigations into sexual misconduct. The investigative procedure should, at a minimum:

1.   specify the circumstances necessary to initiate an investigation;
2.   provide a special investigator trained to handle complaints with the necessary human and material resources to do so;
3.   set forth a clear structure and time frame for conducting investigations;
4.   ensure to the fullest extent possible the confidentiality for the complainant and witness;
5.   protect complainants and witnesses from retaliation and harassment; and
6.   guarantee accountability to outside monitors. The complainant's legal counsel should be provided a written record, upon request,

of the investigation, including all statements made by the complainant and witnesses.

B.   DOCS should require all corrections employees to report allegations promptly, including rumors, of sexual misconduct or other overfamiliar conduct by corrections employees to the prison warden or investigator. Failure to do so should be a punishable offense.

C.   DOCS should develop clear, published guidelines to govern the status of accused corrections employees during an investigation. Officers alleged to have committed rape, sexual assault or criminal sexual contact should be assigned to a noncontact position or suspended until the circumstances are clarified and the investigation is complete. Violations of restrictions on their movements should be additional grounds for discipline.

D.   DOCS should not, under any circumstances, assign implicated officers to investigate allegations of their own misconduct. While Human Rights Watch does not oppose the use of former corrections officers as investigators *per se*, the DOCS and the inspector general should ensure that those hired are not assigned to investigate former colleagues or prisoners formerly under their supervision.

VI.   Preventing Retaliation Against Complainants
A.   DOCS should authorize the use of administrative segregation during an investigation only at the prisoner's explicit request. Since a prisoner placed in administrative segregation for her own protection has not committed a disciplinary offense, she should retain the rights of the general population (e.g., telephone calls, visits, access to recreation, etc.). She should be returned to the general population when she wishes to do so. DOCS should train employees assigned to segregated housing units regarding such provisions.

B.   DOCS should investigate promptly and thoroughly all reports of harassment or retaliation against complainants, and discipline guilty corrections employees appropriately. DOCS should make every effort to ensure the confidentiality of complainants and witnesses. Their names should not be given to an accused officer while he or she remains in a contact position with the prisoner or is assigned to a facility where the complainant resides. DOCS should also prevent the prisoner's name from being revealed generally within the facility.

C.   DOCS should ensure that transfers to other facilities are not used punitively to relocate prisoners who raise complaints about ill-treatment or conditions of incarceration.

VII.   Ensuring Discipline

A.   DOCS should create clear guidelines on disciplinary action against abusive corrections employees. These guidelines should state explicitly that an employee found to be guilty of rape, sexual assault, or criminal sexual contact will be dismissed. The findings of the inspector general should be binding on Labor Relations and should obligate Labor Relations to take the disciplinary action appropriate to the employee's misconduct.

B.   DOCS should publish, at least quarterly, a report on disciplinary actions taken against corrections employees responsible for misconduct or abuse. If necessary, the reports can omit the names of employees, but should include dates, locations, and other relevant details about the reported incidents and the types of punishment applied.

C.   DOCS should refer any allegations of sexual contact between guards and prisoners to the local police.

VIII.   Hiring and Training Corrections Employees

A.   DOCS should review its screening procedures for applicants for corrections positions. Background checks should be completed before new employees are sent into correctional facilities. In no case should DOCS rehire an employee who has been convicted of an offense related to sexual misconduct in custody or who resigned in order to avoid such a charge.

B.   DOCS should implement, as soon as possible, comprehensive and mandatory training for all corrections employees on particular aspects of working with incarcerated women before they start their assignments in women's prisons. Corrections employees currently working in the women's prisons should receive the same training. Such training should include, among other things:

1.   a general profile of female prisoners and their potential vulnerability to sexual misconduct.

2.   DOCS policies on privacy and the prohibition on sexual relations, degrading language, and other sexualized or degrading behavior toward incarcerated women and the disciplinary or criminal sanctions associated with these policies.

3.   appropriate methods for conducting pat-searches, strip searches and searches of women's cells. DOCS should collaborate with local nongovernmental organizations experienced in issues such as rape and sexual assault.

IX.   Educating Prisoners

A.   DOCS should advise incarcerated women, as part of their orientation to the corrections system, as well as prisoners already serving their sentences, of protections regarding sexual misconduct, including a clear definition of sexual misconduct, including that corrections officers are strictly prohibited from having any sexual contact with prisoners. The orientation should also include a thorough review of departmental policies regarding privacy and humane treatment; the procedures for reporting and investigating sexual misconduct and the departmental and criminal law sanctions associated with it.

B.   DOCS should further clarify to prisoners that grievances regarding sexual misconduct may be filed directly and confidentially with the prison superintendent or prison investigator.

1.   Prisoners should be informed about the issues that may be dealt with through the grievance procedure, with particular emphasis on instances of sexual misconduct; the location of grievance forms in the prison library or other neutral place; bypass mechanisms available for reporting sexual misconduct; and the recourse available when corrections officers fail to respond.

2.   Prisoners should be made aware that complaints may also be resolved through the investigation procedure and/or the independent review board.

3.   DOCS should acquaint prisoners with their rights under international human rights treaties ratified by the U.S. and under U.S. law.

C.   The above information should be included in the prisoner handbook.

X.   Allocating Supplies

A.   DOCS should reexamine its allocation of basic personal hygiene items, including sanitary napkins, to prisoners to ensure that incarcerated women receive sufficient and appropriate supplies. These items should be available at a neutral location.

B.   The New York legislature should enact the proposed bill permitting incarcerated women to have access to sanitary napkins on an as needed basis.

XI.   Ensuring Accountability to Outside Monitors

DOCS should provide timely and full written information about an investigation to the prisoner and the people she designates, such as her attorney and her family, upon their request.

Creating an Independent Review Board

A.   The New York Legislature should create a fully empowered and independent review board to investigate, among other things, complaints of sexual misconduct that are not satisfactorily resolved by the grievance or investigative mechanisms. The review board should have the authority to turn over evidence of wrongdoing for criminal investigation and prosecution. The board should also be able to recommend remedial action—including temporary reassignment or suspension of the accused—to end abuses or other problems uncovered during an investigation.

B.   The review board should develop a system whereby the records of corrections employees who have been the subject of repeated complaints are reviewed by the appropriate authorities.

C.   The review board should provide a toll-free telephone number that prisoners can use to contact investigators or to file anonymous complaints of employee misconduct, including retaliation against complainants.

APPENDIX

STANDARD MINIMUM RULES FOR THE TREATMENT OF PRISONERS

Adopted Aug. 30, 1955 by the First United Nations Congress on the Prevention of Crime and the Treatment of Offenders, U.N. Doc. A/CONF/611, annex I, E.S.C. res. 663C, 24 U.N. ESCOR Supp. (No. 1) at 11, U.N. Doc. E/3048 (1957), amended E.S.C. res. 2076, 62 U.N. ESCOR Supp. (No. 1) at 35, U.N. Doc. E/5988 (1977).

1. The following rules are not intended to describe in detail a model system of penal institutions. They seek only, on the basis of the general consensus of contemporary thought and the essential elements of the most adequate systems of today, to set out what is generally accepted as being good principle and practice in the treatment of prisoners and the management of institutions.

2. In view of the great variety of legal, social, economic and geographical conditions of the world, it is evident that not all of the rules are capable of application in all places and at all times. They should, however, serve to stimulate a constant endeavor to overcome practical difficulties in the way of their application, in the knowledge that they represent, as a whole, the minimum conditions which are accepted as suitable by the United Nations.

3. On the other hand, the rules cover a field in which thought is constantly developing. They are not intended to preclude experiment and practices, provided these are in harmony with the principles and seek to further the purposes which derive from the text of the rules as a whole. It will always be justifiable for the central prison administration to authorize departures from the rules in this spirit.

4. (1) Part I of the rules covers the general management of institutions, and is applicable to all categories of prisoners, criminal or civil, untried or convicted, including prisoners subject to "security measures" or corrective measures ordered by the judge.

(2) Part II contains rules applicable only to the special categories dealt with in each section. Nevertheless, the rules under section A, applicable to prisoners under sentence, shall be equally applicable to categories of prisoners dealt with in sections B, C and D, provided they do not conflict with the rules governing those categories and are for their benefit.

5. (1) The rules do not seek to regulate the management of institutions set aside for young persons such as Borstal institutions or correctional schools, but in general part I would be equally applicable in such institutions.

(2) The category of young prisoners should include at least all young persons who come within the jurisdiction of juvenile courts. As a rule, such young persons should not be sentenced to imprisonment.

PART I: RULES OF GENERAL APPLICATION

Basic principle
6. (1) The following rules shall be applied impartially. There shall be no discrimination on grounds of race, color, sex, language, religion, political or other opinion, national or social origin, property, birth or other status.

(2) On the other hand, it is necessary to respect the religious beliefs and moral precepts of the group to which a prisoner belongs.

Register
7. (1) In every place where persons are imprisoned there shall be kept a bound registration book with numbered pages in which shall be entered in respect of each prisoner received:
> (a) Information concerning his identity;
> (b) The reasons for his commitment and the authority therefor;
> (c) The day and hour of his admission and release.

(2) No person shall be received in an institution without a valid commitment order of which the details shall have been previously entered in the register. Separation of categories

8. The different categories of prisoners shall be kept in separate institutions or parts of institutions taking account of their sex, age, criminal record, the legal reason for their detention and the necessities of their treatment. Thus,
> (a) Men and women shall so far as possible be detained in separate institutions; in an institution which receives both men and women the whole of the premises allocated to women shall be entirely separate;
> (b) Untried prisoners shall be kept separate from convicted prisoners;

(c) Persons imprisoned for debt and other civil prisoners shall be kept separate from persons imprisoned by reason of a criminal offense;

(d) Young prisoners shall be kept separate from adults.

Accommodation

9. (1) Where sleeping accommodation is in individual cells or rooms, each prisoner shall occupy by night a cell or room by himself. If for special reasons, such as temporary overcrowding, it becomes necessary for the central prison administration to make an exception to this rule, it is not desirable to have two prisoners in a cell or room.

(2) Where dormitories are used, they shall be occupied by prisoners carefully selected as being suitable to associate with one another in those conditions. There shall be regular supervision by night, in keeping with the nature of the institution.

10. All accommodation provided for the use of prisoners and in particular all sleeping accommodation shall meet all requirements of health, due regard being paid to climatic conditions and particularly to cubic content of air, minimum floor space, lighting, heating and ventilation.

11. In all places where prisoners are required to live or work,

(a) The windows shall be large enough to enable the prisoners to read or work by natural light, and shall be so constructed that they can allow the entrance of fresh air whether or not there is artificial ventilation;

(b) Artificial light shall be provided sufficient for the prisoners to read or work without injury to eyesight.

12. The sanitary installations shall be adequate to enable every prisoner to comply with the needs of nature when necessary and in a clean and decent manner.

13. Adequate bathing and shower installations shall be provided so that every prisoner may be enabled and required to have a bath or shower, at a temperature suitable to the climate, as frequently as necessary for general hygiene according to season and geographical region, but at least once a week in a temperate climate.

14. All pans of an institution regularly used by prisoners shall be properly maintained and kept scrupulously clean at all times.

Personal hygiene

15. Prisoners shall be required to keep their persons clean, and to this end they shall be provided with water and with such toilet articles as are necessary for health and cleanliness.

16. In order that prisoners may maintain a good appearance compatible with their self-respect, facilities shall be provided for the proper care of the hair and beard, and men shall be enabled to shave regularly.

Clothing and bedding

17. (1) Every prisoner who is not allowed to wear his own clothing shall be provided with an outfit of clothing suitable for the climate and adequate to keep him in good health. Such clothing shall in no manner be degrading or humiliating.

(2) All clothing shall be clean and kept in proper condition. Underclothing shall be changed and washed as often as necessary for the maintenance of hygiene.

(3) In exceptional circumstances, whenever a prisoner is removed outside the institution for an authorized purpose, he shall be allowed to wear his own clothing or other inconspicuous clothing.

18. If prisoners are allowed to wear their own clothing, arrangements shall be made on their admission to the institution to ensure that it shall be clean and fit for use.

19. Every prisoner shall, in accordance with local or national standards, be provided with a separate bed, and with separate and sufficient bedding which shall be clean when issued, kept in good order and changed often enough to ensure its cleanliness.

Food

20. (1) Every prisoner shall be provided by the administration at the usual hours with food of nutritional value adequate for health and strength, of wholesome quality and well prepared and served.

(2) Drinking water shall be available to every prisoner whenever he needs it.

Exercise and sport

21. (1) Every prisoner who is not employed in outdoor work shall have at least one hour of suitable exercise in the open air daily if the weather permits.

(2) Young prisoners, and others of suitable age and physique, shall receive physical and recreational training during the period of exercise. To this end space, installations and equipment should be provided.

Medical services

22. (1) At every institution there shall be available the services of at least one qualified medical officer who should have some knowledge of psychiatry. The medical services should be organized in close relationship to the general health administration of the community or nation. They shall include a psychiatric service for the diagnosis and, in proper cases, the treatment of states of mental abnormality.

(2) Sick prisoners who require specialist treatment shall be transferred to specialized institutions or to civil hospitals. Where hospital facilities are provided in an institution, their equipment, furnishings and pharmaceutical supplies shall be proper for the medical care and treatment of sick prisoners, and there shall be a staff of suitable trained officers.

(3) The services of a qualified dental officer shall be available to every prisoner.

23. (1) In women's institutions there shall be special accommodation for all necessary pre-natal and post-natal care and treatment. Arrangements shall be made wherever practicable for children to be torn in a hospital outside the institution. If a child is born in prison, this fact shall not be mentioned in the birth certificate.

(2) Where nursing infants are allowed to remain in the institution with their mothers, provision shall be made for a nursery staffed by qualified persons, where the infants shall be placed when they are not in the care of their mothers.

24. The medical officer shall see and examine every prisoner as soon as possible after his admission and thereafter as necessary, with a view particularly to the discovery of physical or mental illness and the taking of all necessary measures; the segregation of prisoners suspected of infectious or contagious conditions; the noting of physical or mental defects which might hamper rehabilitation, and the determination of the physical capacity of every prisoner for work.

25. (1) The medical officer shall have the care of the physical and mental health of the prisoners and should daily see all sick prisoners, all who complain of illness, and any prisoner to whom his attention is specially directed.

(2) The medical officer shall report to the director whenever he considers that a prisoner's physical or mental health has been or will be injuriously affected by continued imprisonment or by any condition of imprisonment.

26. (I) The medical officer shall regularly inspect and advise the director upon:
      (a) The quantity, quality, preparation and service of food;
      (b) The hygiene and cleanliness of the institution and the prisoners;
      (c) The sanitation, heating, lighting and ventilation of the institution;
      (d) The suitability and cleanliness of the prisoners' clothing and bedding;
      (e) The observance of the rules concerning physical education and sports, in cases where there is no technical personnel in charge of these activities.

(2) The director shall take into consideration the reports and advice that the medical officer submits according to rules 25 (2) and 26 and, in case he concurs with the recommendations made, shall take immediate steps to give effect to those recommendations; if they are not within his competence or if he does not concur with them, he shall immediately submit his own report and the advice of the medical officer to higher authority.

Discipline and punishment
27. Discipline and order shall be maintained with firmness, but with no more restriction than is necessary for safe custody and well-ordered community life.

28. (1) No prisoner shall be employed, in the service of the institution, in any disciplinary capacity.

(2) This rule shall not, however, impede the proper functioning of systems based on self-government, under which specified social, educational or sports activities or responsibilities are entrusted, under supervision, to prisoners who are formed into groups for the purposes of treatment.

29. The following shall always be determined by the law or by the regulation of the competent administrative authority:
      (a) Conduct constituting a disciplinary offense;
      (b) The types and duration of punishment which may be inflicted;
      (c) The authority competent to impose such punishment.

30. (1) No prisoner shall be punished except in accordance with the terms of such law or regulation, and never twice for the same offense.

(2) No prisoner shall be punished unless he has been informed of the offense alleged against him and given a proper opportunity of presenting his defense. The competent authority shall conduct a thorough examination of the case.

(3) Where necessary and practicable the prisoner shall be allowed to make his defense through an interpreter.

31. Corporal punishment, punishment by placing in a dark cell, and all cruel, inhuman or degrading punishments shall be completely prohibited as punishments for disciplinary offenses.

32. (1) Punishment by close confinement or reduction of diet shall never be inflicted unless the medical officer has examined the prisoner and certified in writing that he is fit to sustain it.

(2) The same shall apply to any other punishment that may be prejudicial to the physical or mental health of a prisoner. In no case may such punishment be contrary to or depart from the principle stated in rule 31.

(3) The medical officer shall visit daily prisoners undergoing such punishments and shall advise the director if he considers the termination or alteration of the punishment necessary on grounds of physical or mental health.

Instruments of restraint
33. Instruments of restraint, such as handcuffs, chains, irons and strait-jacket, shall never be applied as a punishment. Furthermore, chains or irons shall not be used as restraints. Other instruments of restraint shall not be used except in the following circumstances:

> (a) As a precaution against escape during a transfer, provided that they shall be removed when the prisoner appears before a judicial or administrative authority;
> (b) On medical grounds by direction of the medical officer;
> (c) By order of the director, if other methods of control fail, in order to prevent a prisoner from injuring himself or others or from damaging property; in such instances the director shall at once consult the medical officer and report to the higher administrative authority.

34. The patterns and manner of use of instruments of restraint shall be decided by the central prison administration. Such instruments must not be applied for any longer time than is strictly necessary.

Information to and complaints by prisoners

35. (1) Every prisoner on admission shall be provided with written information about the regulations governing the treatment of prisoners of his category, the disciplinary requirements of the institution, the authorized methods of seeking information and making complaints, and all such other matters as are necessary to enable him to understand both his rights and his obligations and to adapt himself to the life of the institution.

(2) If a prisoner is illiterate, the aforesaid information shall be conveyed to him orally.

36. (1) Every prisoner shall have the opportunity each week day of making requests or complaints to the director of the institution or the officer authorized to represent him.

(2) It shall be possible to make requests or complaints to the inspector of prisons during his inspection. The prisoner shall have the opportunity to talk to the inspector or to any other inspecting officer without the director or other members of the staff being present.

(3) Every prisoner shall be allowed to make a request or complaint, without censorship as to substance but in proper form, to the central prison administration, the judicial authority or other proper authorities through approved channels.

(4) Unless it is evidently frivolous or groundless, every request or complaint shall be promptly dealt with and replied to without undue delay.

Contact with the outside world

37. Prisoners shall be allowed under necessary supervision to communicate with their family and reputable friends at regular intervals, both by correspondence and by receiving visits.

38. (1) Prisoners who are foreign nationals shall be allowed reasonable facilities to communicate with the diplomatic and consular representatives of the State to which they belong. (2) Prisoners who are nationals of States without diplomatic or

consular representation in the country and refugees or stateless persons shall be allowed similar facilities to communicate with the diplomatic representative of the State which takes charge of their interests or any national or international authority whose task it is to protect such persons.

39. Prisoners shall be kept informed regularly of the more important items of news by the reading of newspapers, periodicals or special institutional publications, by hearing wireless transmissions, by lectures or by any similar means as authorized or controlled by the administration.

Books
40. Every institution shall have a library for the use of all categories of prisoners, adequately stocked with both recreational and instructional books, and prisoners shall be encouraged to make full use of it.

Religion
41. (1) If the institution contains a sufficient number of prisoners of the same religion, a qualified representative of that religion shall be appointed or approved. If the number of prisoners justifies it and conditions permit, the arrangement should be on a full-time basis.

(2) A qualified representative appointed or approved under paragraph (1) shall be allowed to hold regular services and to pay pastoral visits in private to prisoners of his religion at proper times.

(3) Access to a qualified representative of any religion shall not be refused to any prisoner. On the other hand, if any prisoner should object to a visit of any religious representative, his attitude shall be fully respected.

42. So far as practicable, every prisoner shall be allowed to satisfy the needs of his religious life by attending the services provided in the institution and having in his possession the books of religious observance and instruction of his denomination.

Retention of prisoners' property
43. (1) All money, valuables, clothing and other effects belonging to a prisoner which under the regulations of the institution he is not allowed to retain shall on his admission to the institution be placed in safe custody. An inventory thereof shall be signed by the prisoner. Steps shall be taken to keep them in good condition.

(2) On the release of the prisoner all such articles and money shall be returned to him except in so far as he has been authorized to spend money or send any such property out of the institution, or it has been found necessary on hygienic grounds to destroy any article of clothing. The prisoner shall sign a receipt for the articles and money returned to him.

(3) Any money or effects received for a prisoner from outside shall be treated in the same way.

(4) If a prisoner brings in any drugs or medicine, the medical officer shall decide what use shall be made of them.

Notification of death, illness, transfer, etc.
44. (1) Upon the death or serious illness of, or serious injury to a prisoner, or his removal to an institution for the treatment of mental affections, the director shall at once inform the spouse, if the prisoner is married, or the nearest relative and shall in any event inform any other person previously designated by the prisoner.

(2) A prisoner shall be informed at once of the death or serious illness of any near relative. In case of the critical illness of a near relative, the prisoner should be authorized, whenever circumstances allow, to go to his bedside either under escort or alone.

(3) Every prisoner shall have the right to inform at once his family of his imprisonment or his transfer to another institution.

Removal of prisoners
45. (1) When the prisoners are being removed to or from an institution, they shall be exposed to public view as little as possible, and proper safeguards shall be adopted to protect them from insult, curiosity and publicity in any form.

(2) The transport of prisoners in conveyances with inadequate ventilation or light, or in any way which would subject them to unnecessary physical hardship, shall be prohibited.

(3) The transport of prisoners shall be carried out at the expense of the administration and equal conditions shall obtain for all of them.

Institutional personnel

46. (1) The prison administration, shall provide for the careful selection of every grade of the personnel, since it is on their integrity, humanity, professional capacity and personal suitability for the work that the proper administration of the institutions depends.

(2) The prison administration shall constantly seek to awaken and maintain in the minds both of the personnel and of the public the conviction that this work is a social service of great importance, and to this end all appropriate means of informing the public should be used.

(3) To secure the foregoing ends, personnel shall be appointed on a full-time basis as professional prison officers and have civil service status with security of tenure subject only to good conduct, efficiency and physical fitness. Salaries shall be adequate to attract and retain suitable men and women; employment benefits and conditions of service shall be favorable in view of the exacting nature of the work.

47. (1) The personnel shall possess an adequate standard of education and intelligence.

(2) Before entering on duty, the personnel shall be given a course of training in their general and specific duties and be required to pass theoretical and practical tests.

(3) After entering on duty and during their career, the personnel shall maintain and improve their knowledge and professional capacity by attending courses of in-service training to be organized at suitable intervals.

48. All members of the personnel shall at all times so conduct themselves and perform their duties as to influence the prisoners for good by their example and to command their respect.

49. (1) So far as possible, the personnel shall include a sufficient number of specialists such as psychiatrists, psychologists, social workers, teachers and trade instructors.

(2) The services of social workers, teachers and trade instructors shall be secured on a permanent basis, without thereby excluding part-time or voluntary workers.

50. (1) The director of an institution should be adequately qualified for his task by character, administrative ability, suitable training and experience.

(2) He shall devote his entire time to his official duties and shall not be appointed on a part-time basis.

(3) He shall reside on the premises of the institution or in its immediate vicinity. (4) When two or more institutions are under the authority of one director, he shall visit each of them at frequent intervals. A responsible resident official shall be in charge of each of these institutions.

51. (1) The director, his deputy, and the majority of the other personnel of the institution shall be able to speak the language of the greatest number of prisoners, or a language understood by the greatest number of them.

(2) Whenever necessary, the services of an interpreter shall be used.

52. (1) In institutions which are large enough to require the services of one or more full-time medical officers, at least one of them shall reside on the premises of the institution or in its immediate vicinity.

(2) In other institutions the medical officer shall visit daily and shall reside near enough to be able to attend without delay in cases of urgency.

53. (1) In an institution for both men and women, the part of the institution set aside for women shall be under the authority of a responsible woman officer who shall have the custody of the keys of all that part of the institution.

(2) No male member of the staff shall enter the part of the institution set aside for women unless accompanied by a woman officer.

(3) Women prisoners shall be attended and supervised only by women officers. This does not, however, preclude male members of the staff, particularly doctors and teachers, from carrying out their professional duties in institutions or parts of institutions set aside for women.

54. (1) Officers of the institutions shall not, in their relations with the prisoners, use force except in self-defense or in cases of attempted escape, or active or passive physical resistance to an order based on law or regulations. Officers who have

recourse to force must use no more than is strictly necessary and must report the incident immediately to the director of the institution.

(2) Prison officers shall be given special physical training to enable them to restrain aggressive prisoners.

(3) Except in special circumstances, staff performing duties which bring them into direct contact with prisoners should not be armed. Furthermore, staff should in no circumstances be provided with arms unless they have been trained in their use.

Inspection
55. There shall be a regular inspection of penal institutions and services by qualified and experienced inspectors appointed by a competent authority. Their task shall be in particular to ensure that these institutions are administered in accordance with existing laws and regulations and with a view to bringing about the objectives of penal and correctional services.

PART II: RULES APPLICABLE TO SPECIAL CATEGORIES

A. Prisoners under Sentence
Guiding principles
56. The guiding principles hereafter are intended to show the spirit in which penal institutions should be administered and the purposes at which they should aim, in accordance with the declaration made under Preliminary Observation I of the present text.

57. Imprisonment and other measures which result in cutting off an offender from the outside world are afflictive by the very fact of taking from the person the right of self-determination by depriving him of his liberty. Therefore the prison system shall not, except as incidental to justifiable segregation or the maintenance of discipline, aggravate the suffering inherent in such a situation.

58. The purpose and justification of a sentence of imprisonment or a similar measure deprivative of liberty is ultimately to protect society against crime. This end can only be achieved if the period of imprisonment is used to ensure, so far as possible, that upon his return to society the offender is not only willing but able to lead a law-abiding and self-supporting life.

59. To this end, the institution should utilize all the remedial, educational, moral, spiritual and other forces and forms of assistance which are appropriate and available, and should seek to apply them according to the individual treatment needs of the prisoners.

60. (1) The regime of the institution should seek to minimize any differences between prison life and life at liberty which tend to lessen the responsibility of the prisoners or the respect due to their dignity as human beings.

(2) Before the completion of the sentence, it is desirable that the necessary steps be taken to ensure for the prisoner a gradual return to life in society. This aim may be achieved, depending on the case, by a pre-release regime organized in the same institution or in another appropriate institution, or by release on trial under some kind of supervision which must not be entrusted to the police but should be combined with effective social aid. 61. The treatment of prisoners should emphasize not their exclusion from the community, but their continuing part in it. Community agencies should, therefore, be enlisted wherever possible to assist the staff of the institution in the task of social rehabilitation of the prisoners. There should be in connection with every institution social workers charged with the duty of maintaining and improving all desirable relations of a prisoner with his family and with valuable social agencies. Steps should be taken to safeguard, to the maximum extent compatible with the law and the sentence, the rights relating to civil interests, social security rights and other social benefits of prisoners.

62. The medical services of the institution shall seek to detect and shall treat any physical or mental illnesses or defects which may hamper a prisoner's rehabilitation. All necessary medical, surgical and psychiatric services shall be provided to that end.

63. (1) The fulfilment of these principles requires individualization of treatment and for this purpose a flexible system of classifying prisoners in groups; it is therefore desirable that such groups should be distributed in separate institutions suitable for the treatment of each group.

(2) These institutions need not provide the same degree of security for every group. It is desirable to provide varying degrees of security according to the needs of different groups. Open institutions, by the very fact that they provide no physical security against escape but rely on the self-discipline of the inmates, provide the conditions most favorable to rehabilitation for carefully selected prisoners.

(3) It is desirable that the number of prisoners in closed institutions should not be so large that the individualization of treatment is hindered. In some countries it is considered that the population of such institutions should not exceed five hundred. In open institutions the population should be as small as possible.

(4) On the other hand, it is undesirable to maintain prisons which are so small that proper facilities cannot be provided.

64. The duty of society does not end with a prisoner's release. There should, therefore, be governmental or private agencies capable of lending the released prisoner efficient after-care directed towards the lessening of prejudice against him and towards his social rehabilitation.

Treatment
65. The treatment of persons sentenced to imprisonment or a similar measure shall have as its purpose, so far as the length of the sentence permits, to establish in them the will to lead law-abiding and self-supporting lives after their release and to fit them to do so. The treatment shall be such as will encourage their self-respect and develop their sense of responsibility.

66. (1) To these ends, all appropriate means shall be used, including religious care in the countries where this is possible, education, vocational guidance and training, social casework, employment counseling, physical development and strengthening of moral character, in accordance with the individual needs of each prisoner, taking account of his social and criminal history, his physical and mental capacities and aptitudes, his personal temperament, the length of his sentence and his prospects after release.

(2) For every prisoner with a sentence of suitable length, the director shall receive, as soon as possible after his admission, full reports on all the matters referred to in the foregoing paragraph. Such reports shall always include a report by a medical officer, wherever possible qualified in psychiatry, on the physical and mental condition of the prisoner.

(3) The reports and other relevant documents shall be placed in an individual file. This file shall be kept up to date and classified in such a way that it can be consulted by the responsible personnel whenever the need arises.

Classification and individualization

67. The purposes of classification shall be:
> (a) To separate from others those prisoners who, by reason of their criminal records or bad characters, are likely to exercise a bad influence;
> (b) To divide the prisoners into classes in order to facilitate their treatment with a view to their social rehabilitation.

68. So far as possible separate institutions or separate sections of an institution shall be used for the treatment of the different classes of prisoners.

69. As soon as possible after admission and after a study of the personality of each prisoner with a sentence of suitable length, a programme of treatment shall be prepared for him in the light of the knowledge obtained about his individual needs, his capacities and dispositions.

Privileges

70. Systems of privileges appropriate for the different classes of prisoners and the different methods of treatment shall be established at every institution, in order to encourage good conduct, develop a sense of responsibility and secure the interest and co-operation of the prisoners in their treatment.

Work

71. (1) Prison labor must not be of an afflictive nature.

(2) All prisoners under sentence shall be required to work, subject to their physical and mental fitness as determined by the medical officer.

(3) Sufficient work of a useful nature shall be provided to keep prisoners actively employed for a normal working day.

(4) So far as possible the work provided shall be such as will maintain or increase the prisoners, ability to earn an honest living after release.

(5) Vocational training in useful trades shall be provided for prisoners able to profit thereby and especially for young prisoners.

(6) Within the limits compatible with proper vocational selection and with the requirements of institutional administration and discipline, the prisoners shall be able to choose the type of work they wish to perform.

72. (1) The organization and methods of work in the institutions shall resemble as closely as possible those of similar work outside institutions, so as to prepare prisoners for the conditions of normal occupational life.

(2) The interests of the prisoners and of their vocational training, however, must not be subordinated to the purpose of making a financial profit from an industry in the institution.

73. (1) Preferably institutional industries and farms should be operated directly by the administration and not by private contractors.

(2) Where prisoners are employed in work not controlled by the administration, they shall always be under the supervision of the institution's personnel. Unless the work is for other departments of the government the full normal wages for such work shall be paid to the administration by the persons to whom the labor is supplied, account being taken of the output of the prisoners.

74. (1) The precautions laid down to protect the safety and health of free workmen shall be equally observed in institutions.

(2) Provision shall be made to indemnify prisoners against industrial injury, including occupational disease, on terms not less favorable than those extended by law to free workmen.

75. (1) The maximum daily and weekly working hours of the prisoners shall be fixed by law or by administrative regulation, taking into account local rules or custom in regard to the employment of free workmen.

(2) The hours so fixed shall leave one rest day a week and sufficient time for education and other activities required as part of the treatment and rehabilitation of the prisoners.

76. (1) There shall be a system of equitable remuneration of the work of prisoners.

(2) Under the system prisoners shall be allowed to spend at least a part of their earnings on approved articles for their own use and to send a part of their earnings to their family.

(3) The system should also provide that a part of the earnings should be set aside by the administration so as to constitute a savings fund to be handed over to the prisoner on his release.

Education and recreation

77. (1) Provision shall be made for the further education of all prisoners capable of profiting thereby, including religious instruction in the countries where this is possible. The education of illiterates and young prisoners shall be compulsory and special attention shall be paid to it by the administration.

(2) So far as practicable, the education of prisoners shall be integrated with the educational system of the country so that after their release they may continue their education without difficulty.

78. Recreational and cultural activities shall be provided in all institutions for the benefit of the mental and physical health of prisoners.

Social relations and after-care

79. Special attention shall be paid to the maintenance and improvement of such relations between a prisoner and his family as are desirable in the best interests of both.

80. From the beginning of a prisoner's sentence consideration shall be given to his future after release and he shall be encouraged and assisted to maintain or establish such relations with persons or agencies outside the institution as may promote the best interests of his family and his own social rehabilitation.

81. (1) Services and agencies, governmental or otherwise, which assist released prisoners to re-establish themselves in society shall ensure, so far as is possible and necessary, that released prisoners be provided with appropriate documents and identification papers, have suitable homes and work to go to, are suitably and adequately clothed having regard to the climate and season, and have sufficient means to reach their destination and maintain themselves in the period immediately following their release.

(2) The approved representatives of such agencies shall have all necessary access to the institution and to prisoners and shall be taken into consultation as to the future of a prisoner from the beginning of his sentence.

(3) It is desirable that the activities of such agencies shall be centralized or coordinated as far as possible in order to secure the best use of their efforts.

B. Insane and Mentally Abnormal Prisoners

82. (1) Persons who are found to be insane shall not be detained in prisons and arrangements shall be made to remove them to mental institutions as soon as possible.

(2) Prisoners who suffer from other mental diseases or abnormalities shall be observed and treated in specialized institutions under medical management.

(3) During their stay in a prison, such prisoners shall be placed under the special supervision of a medical officer.

(4) The medical or psychiatric service of the penal institutions shall provide for the psychiatric treatment of all other prisoners who are in need of such treatment.

83. It is desirable that steps should be taken, by arrangement with the appropriate agencies, to ensure if necessary the continuation of psychiatric treatment after release and the provision of social-psychiatric after-care.

C. Prisoners under Arrest or Awaiting Trial

84. (1) Persons arrested or imprisoned by reason of a criminal charge against them, who are detained either in police custody or in prison custody (jail) but have not yet been tried and sentenced, will be referred to as "untried prisoners,' hereinafter in these rules.

(2) Unconvicted prisoners are presumed to be innocent and shall be treated as such.

(3) Without prejudice to legal rules for the protection of individual liberty or prescribing the procedure to be observed in respect of untried prisoners, these prisoners shall benefit by a special regime which is described in the following rules in its essential requirements only.

85. (1) Untried prisoners shall be kept separate from convicted prisoners.

(2) Young untried prisoners shall be kept separate from adults and shall in principle be detained in separate institutions.

86. Untried prisoners shall sleep singly in separate rooms, with the reservation of different local custom in respect of the climate.

87. Within the limits compatible with the good order of the institution, untried prisoners may, if they so desire, have their food procured at their own expense from the outside, either through the administration or through their family or friends. Otherwise, the administration shall provide their food.

88. (I) An untried prisoner shall be allowed to wear his own clothing if it is clean and suitable.

(2) If he wears prison dress, it shall be different from that supplied to convicted prisoners.

89. An untried prisoner shall always be offered opportunity to work, but shall not be required to work. If he chooses to work, he shall be paid for it.

90. An untried prisoner shall be allowed to procure at his own expense or at the expense of a third party such books, newspapers, writing materials and other means of occupation as are compatible with the interests of the administration of justice and the security and good order of the institution.

91. An untried prisoner shall be allowed to be visited and treated by his own doctor or dentist if there is reasonable ground for his application and he is able to pay any expenses incurred.

92. An untried prisoner shall be allowed to inform immediately his family of his detention and shall be given all reasonable facilities for communicating with his family and friends, and for receiving visits from them, subject only to restrictions and supervision as are necessary in the interests of the administration of justice and of the security and good order of the institution.

93. For the purposes of his defense, an untried prisoner shall be allowed to apply for free legal aid where such aid is available, and to receive visits from his legal adviser with a view to his defense and to prepare and hand to him confidential instructions. For these purposes, he shall if he so desires be supplied with writing material. Interviews between the prisoner and his legal adviser may be within sight but not within the hearing of a police or institution official.

D. Civil Prisoners

94. In countries where the law perm its imprisonment for debt, or by order of a court under any other non-criminal process, persons so imprisoned shall not be subjected to any greater restriction or severity than is necessary to ensure safe custody and good order. Their treatment shall be not less favorable than that of untried prisoners, with the reservation, however, that they may possibly be required to work.

E. Persons Arrested or Detained Without Charge

95 Without prejudice to the provisions of article 9 of the International Covenant on Civil and Political Rights, persons arrested or imprisoned without charge shall be accorded the same protection as that accorded under part I and part II, section C. Relevant provisions of part II, section A, shall likewise be applicable where their application may be conducive to the benefit of this special group of persons in custody, provided that no measures shall be taken implying that re-education or rehabilitation is in any way appropriate to persons not convicted of any criminal offense.